Williams' Hebrew Syntax

Williams' Hebrew Syntax

Third edition

Ronald J. Williams

Revised and expanded by John C. Beckman

University of Toronto Press
Toronto Buffalo London

First edition
© University of Toronto Press Incorporated 1967

Second edition
© University of Toronto Press Incorporated 1976

Third edition
© University of Toronto Press Incorporated 2007

Toronto Buffalo London

Printed in Canada

ISBN 978-0-8020-9429-2

∞ Printed on acid-free paper

Library and Archives Canada Cataloguing in Publication

Williams, Ronald J. (Ronald James), 1917–1993
  Williams' Hebrew syntax / by Ronald J. Williams ; revised and
  expanded by John C. Beckman. – 3rd ed.

  Previous eds. published under title: Hebrew syntax.
  Includes bibliographical references and index.
  ISBN 978-0-8020-9429-2

  1. Hebrew language – Syntax. I. Beckman, John C. II. Williams,
  Ronald J. (Ronald James), 1917–1993. Hebrew syntax. III. Title.

  PJ4701.W5 2007   492.4'5   C2007–900781-3

University of Toronto Press acknowledges the financial assistance to its
publishing program of the Canada Council for the Arts and the Ontario
Arts Council.

University of Toronto Press acknowledges the financial support for its
publishing activities of the Government of Canada through the Book
Publishing Industry Development Program (BPIDP)

Contents

Preface to the Third Edition

Changes in the Third Edition

This third edition changes *Williams' Hebrew Syntax* by clarifying it, by directing readers to other literature, and by updating the analysis.

The main goal of this edition is to **clarify** the text by expanding definitions, explaining examples, and subdividing sections. Because members of the target audience for this edition (students in a third-semester Hebrew class) often have modest vocabulary knowledge and parsing skills, most examples have been supplied with an interlinear translation as well as a smoother translation. In both translations, the words that illustrate the grammatical point are *italicised* or put in SMALL CAPS. Where deemed helpful, additional examples have been provided, and potentially confusing examples have been removed.

In this third edition, readers are also **directed to additional literature** and informed about **alternate terminology**. Wherever a point is covered in any of five other Hebrew intermediate or reference grammars (BHRG, GBHS, GKC, IBHS, and JM), footnotes point the reader to the appropriate section(s) in those grammars. Footnotes also point the reader to other relevant literature. Because the literature often differs greatly in its terminology and analysis, a cross-reference to another publication indicates that it discusses the same grammatical phenomena, but does not imply that it uses the same terminology or analyses it similarly. To reduce the size of the footnotes, the author-date citation method is used.

The grammatical analysis has also been **updated**. Most changes are made through footnotes that point the readers to alternate analyses. Occasionally, however, changes are made in the main body and noted in the footnotes.

These changes have lengthened the text, making it no longer 'an outline' (as prior editions were subtitled). For ease of reference, a separate outline is provided for free download at www.hebrewsyntax.org.

Continuity with the Second Edition

This third edition is committed to preserving Williams' grammatical analysis of the first two editions. As a result, this remains a traditional, sentence-level syntax that concentrates on the meanings of morphological categories. Although discourse-level analysis has much to offer to an understanding of issues such as verb conjugations and word order, the dust has not yet settled. Furthermore, thoroughly incorporating discourse-level analysis would likely require fundamental changes to the approach and organization of this grammar. Literature that is based on discourse-level analysis is, however, referenced regularly in the footnotes.

The outline and section numbers are unchanged, although sometimes they have been subdivided (e.g., §28a and 28b cover what was §28 in previous editions). Existing category labels have been retained, although sometimes only as alternate terminology. A table that cross-references page numbers from the second to the third edition is available for free download at www.hebrewsyntax.org.

Acknowledgements

Heartfelt thanks are due to many. Sue Cheng, Chad Hard, Jonathan Kline, Rob Morris, Jeane Noh, and the fall 2006 intermediate Hebrew class at Gordon-Conwell found errors and suggested improvements. Joel Baden and Robert Holmstedt provided pre-publication manuscripts of their work. Ani Deyirmenjian, Siobhan McMenemy, and Richard Ratzlaff of the University of Toronto Press brought this to publication. Douglas Stuart supported this project from its inception, spent hours discussing syntax with me, proofread the manuscript, and tested it in his class. My wife Olivia took our family on vacation without me twice so that I could work. Thank you! Responsibility for changes made in this edition rests with me. Please report errors or suggestions at www.hebrewsyntax.org. לֹא לָנוּ יְהוָה לֹא לָנוּ כִּי־לְשִׁמְךָ תֵּן כָּבוֹד.

The first two editions of this textbook were dedicated to Theophile James Meek; this third edition is dedicated also to Ronald J. Williams (1917–1993). אַשְׁרֵי אָדָם מָצָא חָכְמָה וְאָדָם יָפִיק תְּבוּנָה (Prov 3:13).

John C. Beckman
Natick, MA, USA
3 March 2007

Preface to the Second Edition

The wide use being made of this manual has encouraged me to take the opportunity of a fourth printing to revise and slightly expand the text. In response to the request of a number of users, all the Hebrew examples which are quoted have been provided with translations. It is hoped that this will assist in clarifying the syntactic features which they illustrate.

Both in the bibliography and the text some account has been taken of recent studies. Outstanding among these is the work of Professor F.I. Andersen, whose thorough analysis of non-verbal clauses in the Pentateuch is a model of what such a study should be.

The lack of a subject index in the first edition led Professor Douglas Knight of Vanderbilt University, assisted by four of his graduate students, to prepare one for their own use. For their kind permission to incorporate this valuable compilation into the new edition of this volume I am most grateful.

A special word of thanks is owed to Miss Lorraine Ourom and her colleagues at the University of Toronto Press for their kindly interest and helpful advice in the preparation of the typescript for offset reproduction.

If this revision proves of greater service in making students aware of the subtleties and richness of expression of the language of the Old Testament, the author will be amply rewarded.

R.J.W.
4 September 1975

Preface to the First Edition

In offering this modest contribution to Hebrew studies, I am acutely aware of my indebtedness to a host of scholars. The brief bibliography at the end of this book is but a partial indication of this debt. To all, especially those who graciously read the manuscript in its earlier stages, I would express my obligation and gratitude.

The greatest debt of all, however, I owe to the late Professor T.J. Meek whose memory I revere as teacher, colleague and friend. His profound understanding of the principles of Hebrew syntax was the stimulation which aroused my special interest in the subject, and which resulted in this volume.

For many years he taught a course in Hebrew syntax which greatly enhanced Hebrew studies in the University of Toronto. When this duty passed to me on his retirement, it was his inspiration and never-failing help that afforded me courage to assume the task. We had hoped that during his retirement he would provide us with the long-awaited fruits of his lifetime studies. Ill health, alas, prevented this, and the present work must serve as a poor substitute. That I have dedicated it to him is a small token of my esteem and gratitude.

From the many students who have attended my classes all through the years I have learned much. As one of the sages observed long ago: הרבה למדתי מרבותי ומחברי יותר מרבותי ומתלמידי יותר מכלם. To them all I offer my heartfelt thanks.

R.J. Williams
University of Toronto
20 April 1967

Introduction

Intended Uses

Williams' Hebrew Syntax is designed to serve as the textbook for a one-semester course in Biblical Hebrew syntax at the intermediate level. It is also designed to serve as a grammatical reference.

This is an **intermediate** textbook; students are expected to have already completed a two-semester introductory Biblical Hebrew course. In comparison with other intermediate Hebrew grammars, this textbook is distinguished by doing much more 'hand holding' for students, as described in the preface to the third edition.

As a textbook on **syntax**, it does not teach how to parse words. Instead, this book is designed to help readers to figure out what a particular inflected form or combination of words means – after readers have first parsed the words and looked them up in a lexicon as needed. As such, this grammar provides a list of possible answers to questions like 'What is the significance of the fact that this noun is plural instead of singular?' and 'This clause begins with אֲשֶׁר, but a relative clause does not make sense here. How does this clause relate to the clauses around it?' As a traditional syntax, it concentrates on sentences and their constituents.

As a **one-semester** textbook, it is designed to be completely covered in a one-semester course. Although it is longer than the previous two editions, the interlinear translations and additional explanation are designed to reduce the time required to actually learn the material.

William's Hebrew Syntax also functions as a **grammatical reference**. Since it was first published in 1967, many commentaries, books, and articles have explained the meaning of particular grammatical features in Hebrew texts by referring to specific grammatical categories that are defined here. For readers who wish to study a topic further, footnotes point them to additional literature. Due to space constraints and the target audience, only publications in English are cited.

Organization

The first chapter of this book ('Syntax of Nominals') discusses nouns, pronouns, adjectives, and participles (with respect to their nominal features). The second chapter ('Syntax of Verbs') discusses the meaning of the inflected forms of verbs (e.g., 'What is the significance of the fact that this verb is a Qal imperfect?'). It also discusses how verbs relate to their subjects and to other verbs. The third chapter ('Syntax of Particles') is like a lexicon; it explains the possible meanings and syntactical functions of prepositions, adverbs, negatives, conjunctions, relative particles, the accusative particle אֵת, and the particle of existence יֵשׁ. The final chapter ('Syntax of Clauses') discusses how clauses relate to one another, the significance of word order within clauses, and the elision of words. At the end of the book, indexes allow readers to locate contents based on Biblical (or other) passage, subject, or Hebrew word.

A detailed outline is available for download at www.hebrewsyntax.org; it can be used as a preview or review of the material, as a summary to be memorized, and as a quick reference for figuring out the appropriate syntactical category for a particular feature of a Hebrew text.

Terminology

In order to help students, an attempt has been made to use the most common terminology for the major categories, even when that terminology is potentially misleading. Thus, for example, the prefix conjugation (yiqtol) is referred to as the 'imperfect,' even though verbs in that form do not necessarily have imperfect aspect.

To make it easier to relate the material to discussions elsewhere, an attempt has been made to note alternate terminology used for the same phenomena. Thus, for example, the labels 'yiqtol' and 'prefix conjugation' are listed as alternate names under the category 'imperfect conjugation.' Conflicting terminology is noted in the footnotes (see, for example, the footnotes to 'plural of composition' in §9–10).

Abbreviations

2fp	Second person, feminine plural
2mp	Second person, masculine plural
2ms	Second person, masculine singular
3fp	Third person, feminine plural
3fs	Third person, feminine singular
3mp	Third person, masculine plural
3ms	Third person, masculine singular
AJSL	*American Journal of Semitic Languages and Literature*
BDB	F. Brown, S.R. Driver, and C.A. Briggs. 1907. *A Hebrew and English lexicon of the Old Testament.* Oxford: Clarendon. Repr., Peabody: Hendrickson, 2005.
BHRG	C.H.J. van der Merwe, J.A. Naudé, and J.H. Kroeze. 2002. *A biblical Hebrew reference grammar.* Sheffield: Sheffield Academic.
Bib	*Biblica*
BSOAS	*Bulletin of the School of Oriental and African Studies*
BT	*Bible Translator*
CBQ	*Catholic Biblical Quarterly*
GBHS	B.T. Arnold and J.H. Choi. 2003. *A guide to biblical Hebrew syntax.* New York: Cambridge University Press.
GKC	W. Gesenius and E. Kautzsch. 1910. *Gesenius' Hebrew grammar.* Translated by A.E. Cowley. 2nd English ed. New York: Oxford University Press. Repr., Mineola: Dover, 2006.
HALOT	L. Koehler and W. Baumgartner. 1994–9. *The Hebrew and Aramaic lexicon of the Old Testament.* Translated and edited under the supervision of M.E.J. Richardson. 4 vols. Leiden: Brill.
HAR	*Hebrew Annual Review*
HS	*Hebrew Studies*
HUCA	*Hebrew Union College Annual*

IBHS	B.K. Waltke and M. O'Connor. 1990. *An introduction to biblical Hebrew syntax*. Winona Lake, IN: Eisenbrauns.
IOS	*Israel Oriental Studies*
JANES	*Journal of the Ancient Near Eastern Society*
JAOS	*Journal of the American Oriental Society*
JBL	*Journal of Biblical Literature*
JM	P. Joüon and T. Muraoka. 2006. *A grammar of biblical Hebrew*, revised edition. Subsidia biblica 27. Rome: Editrice Pontificio Istituto Biblico.
JM93	P. Joüon and T. Muraoka. 1993. *A grammar of biblical Hebrew*. 2 vols. Subsidia biblica 14/1–2. Rome: Editrice Pontificio Istituto Biblico. This edition is cited in the footnotes only where it differs from the 2006 edition.
JNES	*Journal of Near Eastern Studies*
JNSL	*Journal of Northwest Semitic Languages*
JQR	*Jewish Quarterly Review*
JSBLE	*Journal of the Society of Biblical Literature and Exegesis*
JSOT	*Journal for the Study of the Old Testament*
JSS	*Journal of Semitic Studies*
JTS	*Journal of Theological Studies*
Lambdin	T.O. Lambdin. 1971. *Introduction to biblical Hebrew*. New York: Scribner's.
Or	*Orientalia*
OrSu	*Orientalia Suecana*
OtSt	*Oudtestamentische Studiën*
RB	*Revue biblique*
TynBul	*Tyndale Bulletin*
VT	*Vetus Testamentum*
ZAH	*Zeitschrift für Althebräistik*
ZAW	*Zeitschrift für die alttestamentliche Wissenschaft*

1 Syntax of Nominals [1]

A Number [2]

Singular [3]

1 **Singular for a single item.** [4] A singular word may refer to a single person (e.g., מֶלֶךְ 'a king') or a single thing (e.g., מִזְבֵּחַ 'an altar').

2 **Singular for a collective.** [5] A singular word may refer to a group of people (e.g., עַם 'people') or a group of things (e.g., בָּקָר 'cattle').
   - Most collectives are feminine (§26), but some are masculine.
   - Some singular words may indicate either a single item or a collective, depending on the context (e.g., עֵץ 'a tree' or 'a group of trees').
   - A singular collective subject often takes a plural verb (§229).

Dual [6]

3 **The dual is used only with nouns.** [7] In earlier stages of the language, the dual may have been used for other parts of speech, but in Biblical Hebrew only nouns have a dual form.
   - Dual nouns are used with plural adjectives (§73), pronouns, and verbs (§231).

---

[1] Cf. BHRG §23–37; GBHS §2; GKC §32–113, 79–98, 122–39; IBHS §5–10, 12–19; JM §35–9, 86–101, 125–31, 134–49, 152. 'Nominals' refers to nouns, pronouns, adjectives, and participles (with respect to their adjective-like features).

[2] Cf. BHRG §24.3; GKC §123–4; IBHS §7; JM §135–6; Rosén 1984–6.

[3] Cf. BHRG §24.3.2; IBHS §7.2; JM §135, 136l.

[4] Cf. BHRG §24.3.2(i); IBHS §7.2.1a.

[5] Cf. BHRG §24.3.2(ii); GKC §123a–b; IBHS §7.2.1b–d; JM §135a–c; Young 1999; Young 2001. JM §135c distinguishes collective nouns from **nouns of species**.

[6] Cf. BHRG §24.3.4; GKC §87o, 88; IBHS §7.3; JM §91. Be aware that some nouns that appear to be dual in form are actually plural (e.g., שָׁמַיִם 'heavens' and מַיִם 'waters'); see BHRG §24.3.4(iii); GKC §88c–d; IBHS §7.3d; JM §91f–h.

[7] Cf. GKC §88a; IBHS §7.3a note 9; JM §91a. For a contrary view, see Rendsburg 1982.

4 Dual for two or more of something that comes in pairs.[8] A dual noun may refer to two or more of an object that usually exists in pairs. Examples include יָדַיִם 'hands,' אָזְנַיִם 'ears,' and נַעֲלַיִם 'sandals.'

- When a number is used with the dual form of a noun, the number indicates the total number of the object, not the number of pairs. For example, שֵׁשׁ כְּנָפַיִם (Isa 6:2) means 'six wings,' not 'six pairs of wings,' and אַרְבַּע רַגְלַיִם (Lev 11:23) means 'four feet' not 'four pairs of feet.'
- Not all objects that occur naturally in pairs use the dual. For example, to refer to two or more arms, the plural זְרוֹעוֹת is almost always used.

5 Dual for two of something.[9] A dual noun may refer to two of something that does not naturally come just in pairs. Examples include מָאתַיִם 'two hundred,' שְׁנָתַיִם 'two years,' אַמָּתַיִם 'two cubits,' and יוֹמַיִם 'two days.'

Plural [10]

6 Plural for two or more.[11] A plural word may refer to two or more of something. Examples include מְלָכִים 'kings,' and מִזְבְּחוֹת 'altars.'

7 Abstract plural.[12] A plural word may refer to a quality, a characteristic, a state, or the concept of an action. Examples include בְּתוּלִים 'virginity,' זְקֻנִים 'old age,' נְעוּרִים 'youth,' סַנְוֵרִים 'blindness,' חַיִּים 'life,' and שִׁלּוּמִים 'retribution.'

- Abstract plurals are usually masculine (§19).

8 Plural of respect.[13] A plural word may refer to a single honourable or fearful object or person (e.g., קְבֻרֹתֶיךָ 'your grave' in 2 Kgs 22:20, אֲדֹנִים 'master' in Isa 19:4, אֱלֹהִים 'God' in Gen 1:1 and elsewhere). This is also called the **honorific plural**, the **plural of majesty** (*pluralis majestatis*), the **plural of excellence** (*pluralis excellentiae*), **plural of intensity** (*pluralis intensivus*), or the **royal plural**.

- As discussed in §73, adjectives that modify a word that is in the plural of respect are usually singular; for example, אֱלֹהִים חַי 'the living God' (2 Kgs 19:4), אֲדֹנִים קָשֶׁה

---

[8] Cf. BHRG §24.3.4(i); GKC §88e–f; IBHS §7.3b; JM §91a, c, e–ea.

[9] Cf. BHRG §24.3.4(ii); GKC §88e–f, IBHS §7.3c; JM §91c, ea.

[10] Cf. BHRG §24.3.3; GKC §124; IBHS §7.4; JM §90, 136.

[11] Cf. BHRG §24.3.3(i); IBHS §7.4.1a; JM §136a.

[12] Cf. BHRG §24.3.3(v)–(vi); GKC §124d–f; IBHS §7.4.2; JM §136g–i.

[13] Cf. BHRG §24.3.3(vii); GKC §124g–k; IBHS §7.4.3; JM §136d–f; Walker 1957; Ember 1905. Walker argues that such nouns should be regarded as singular nouns with ם as a suffix.

'a harsh master' (Isa 19:4), but sometimes they are plural; for example, אֱלֹהִים חַיִּים 'the living God' (1 Sam 17:26).

- A subject in the plural of respect usually takes a singular verb (§232).

9 Plural of composition.[14] A plural word may refer to numerous items of the same material which form or constitute something.

- רֹאשׁ עַפְרוֹת תֵּבֵל   the first *dust of* the world
  world   *dusts of*   first   Prov 8:26

- Other possible examples include עַפְרֹת 'dust' (Job 28:6), עֵצִים 'timber' (2 Kgs 12:13), and כַּסְפֵּיהֶם 'their silver pieces' (Gen 42:25, 35).

10 Plural of a natural product in an unnatural condition.[15] A plural word may indicate that an object is not in its normal condition. For example, the plural חִטִּים is used for grains of wheat that have been harvested, whereas the singular חִטָּה is used for wheat that is still on the stalk. The plural and singular of spelt (כֻּסְּמִים vs כֻּסֶּמֶת) and barley (שְׂעֹרִים vs שְׂעֹרָה) are used in the same way. Similarly, blood that is in the blood vessels of a living person is referred to by the singular דָּם, whereas the plural דָּמִים refers to shed blood (e.g., Gen 4:10). This use of the plural is also referred to as the **plural of result** or the **plural of composition**.

11 Plural of extension.[16] A plural word may refer to a single object that consists of several parts; for example, פָּנִים 'face,' צַוָּארִים 'neck,' and שָׁמַיִם 'heaven' or 'sky.'[17] This is also called the **compounding plural**, the **complex plural**, or the **plural of a compound object**.

Pluralizing compound nouns

Some Hebrew nouns consist of two Hebrew words in a construct chain (§28). Sections §12–14 explain how to spell the plural of such terms.

---

[14] Cf. GKC §124l; IBHS §7.4.1c; JM §136b. Some scholars group the plural of composition (§9) with the plural of a natural product in an unnatural condition (§10). JM §136b points out that the dual is also used to indicate composition.

[15] Cf. BHRG §24.3.3(iii); GKC §124l–n; IBHS §7.4.1c, e; JM §136b. BHRG and IBHS describe this use of the plural as a collective that has been broken up or processed.

[16] Cf. BHRG §24.3.3(iv); GKC §124b–c; IBHS §7.4.1c, e; JM §136c.

[17] As explained in GKC §88c–d; IBHS §7.3d; JM §91f, שָׁמַיִם looks like it is dual, but it is actually the plural of שָׁמִי. Similarly, מַיִם is the plural of מִי.

12 **Compound plural formed by pluralizing the first word.**[18] Examples
include גִּבּוֹרֵי חַיִל 'soldiers' (1 Chr 7:2), כָּתְנוֹת עוֹר 'garments of skin' (Gen
3:21), and בְּנֵי יְמִינִי 'Benjaminites' (1 Sam 22:7).

13 **Compound plural formed by pluralizing both words.**[19] Examples
include גִּבּוֹרֵי חֲיָלִים 'valiant warriors' (1 Chr 7:5), שָׂרֵי הַחֲיָלִים 'the army
commanders' (1 Kgs 15:20), and בָּתֵּי כְלָאִים 'prisons' (Isa 42:22).

14 **Compound plural formed by pluralizing the second word.**[20] Examples
include בֵּית אָבוֹת 'families' (2 Chr 25:5) and בֵּית בָּמוֹת 'high-place
sanctuaries' (1 Kgs 12:31).

Repetition

15 **Distributive repetition.**[21] Repetition may give the sense of each, every,
all, one after another, etc. Examples include יוֹם יוֹם 'day *after* day' (Gen
39:10), אִישׁ אִישׁ '*any* man' (Lev 17:10), and יוֹם לַשָּׁנָה יוֹם לַשָּׁנָה 'a day for
each year' (Num 14:34). Section §100 gives additional examples.

16a **Emphatic repetition.**[22] Repetition may indicate an extreme quantity or
quality, for example, זָהָב זָהָב 'pure gold' (2 Kgs 25:15), גֵּבִים גֵּבִים 'full of
trenches' (2 Kgs 3:16), מְעַט מְעַט 'very gradually' (Exod 23:30), קָדוֹשׁ קָדוֹשׁ
קָדוֹשׁ 'holy, holy, holy' (Isa 6:3), and שָׁלוֹם שָׁלוֹם 'complete peace' (Isa
26:3). Other examples include Gen 14:10; Num 3:9; Deut 16:20.

16b **Repetition of endearment.** The name (or other term of address) of the
person spoken to may be repeated as a sign of emotion or intimate
relationship. Examples include בְּנִי בְּנִי 'my son, my son!' (2 Sam 19:1) and
אָבִי אָבִי 'my father, my father!' (2 Kgs 2:12, 13:14).

---

[18] Cf. GKC §124p; JM §136m.
[19] Cf. GKC §124q; JM §136o.
[20] Cf. GKC §124r; JM §136n.
[21] Cf. BHRG §24.3.2(iv), 29.3(viii), 37.2.3(v)a; GKC §123c–d, 134q; IBHS §7.2.3b,
12.5a, 15.6a–b; JM §135d, 142p.
[22] Cf. BHRG §24.3.2(vi), 24.3.3(ii); GKC §123e; IBHS §7.2.3c, 7.4.1a, 12.5; JM §135e.

B   Gender [23]

Masculine

17   **Masculine natural gender.**[24] A masculine word may refer to a male person or animal (e.g., אָב 'father,' מֶלֶךְ 'king').

18   **Masculine grammatical gender.**[25] Many words that are parsed as masculine refer to inanimate objects, for example, בַּיִת 'house,' דָּבָר 'word' or 'thing,' and לֵבָב 'heart' or 'mind.' The fact that the word is masculine does not imply that the object is male or is thought to have male characteristics. Grammatical gender is also referred to as **lexical gender**.

19   **Masculine plural abstract.** As discussed in §7, a masculine plural word may refer to an abstract idea (e.g., חַיִּים 'life,' זְקֻנִים 'old age').

Feminine

20   **Feminine natural gender.**[26] A feminine word may refer to a female person or animal, for example, אֵם 'mother' and מַלְכָּה 'queen.'

21   **Feminine grammatical gender.**[27] Just as is the case for many masculine words (§18), many feminine words refer to inanimate objects. Examples include חֶרֶב 'sword,' כּוֹס 'cup,' and אֵשׁ 'fire.'

22   **Feminine names of body parts.**[28] Many words for body parts are feminine, including many frequently used ones that occur in pairs. Examples include רֶגֶל 'foot,' אֹזֶן 'ear,' and קֶרֶן 'horn.'

23   **Feminine names of countries and cities.**[29] The proper names of countries and cities are usually feminine. Examples include מִצְרַיִם 'Egypt,' מוֹאָב 'Moab,' and צֹר 'Tyre.'

---

[23] Cf. BHRG §24.2; GKC §122; IBHS §6; JM §134; Ben-Asher 1978.

[24] Cf. JM §134b, d.

[25] Cf. IBHS §6.2–6.4a; JM §134e–g, m; Zehnder 2004. GKC erroneously correlates grammatical gender with perceived qualities of objects in §122e, h note 3, m, and u.

[26] Cf. GKC §122a; JM §134b, d.

[27] Cf. JM §134e, g–m; Zehnder 2004.

[28] Cf. BHRG §24.2.2(i)d; GKC §122m; IBHS §6.4.1b; JM §134j. Note, however, that many other words for body parts that occur in pairs are masculine, including שְׁכֶם 'shoulder,' נָחִיר 'nostril,' אַף 'nostril,' דַּד 'breast,' חָזֶה 'breast,' שַׁד 'breast,' עָקֵב 'heel,' אֶשֶׁךְ 'testicle,' מָתְנַיִם 'loins,' אִישׁוֹן 'pupil,' and עַפְעַף 'eyelid.'

[29] Cf. BHRG §24.2.2(i)e; GKC §122h–i ; IBHS §6.4.1c–d; JM §134g.

- When such names are treated as masculine, they usually refer to the inhabitants; for example, אֲרָם 'Arameans' is the subject of a masculine verb in 2 Sam 10:14. A reference to the inhabitants is sometimes treated as feminine, however; for example, אֲרַם דַּמֶּשֶׂק 'the Arameans of Damascus' is the subject of a feminine verb in 2 Sam 8:5.

24 **Feminine for an abstract idea.**[30] A feminine word may refer to an abstract idea, for example, אֱמוּנָה 'faithfulness,' אַהֲבָה 'love,' גְּבוּרָה 'strength,' and טוֹבָה 'welfare' or 'benefit.'

25 **Feminine for a neuter concept.**[31] A feminine pronoun or noun may refer to an event, situation, or concept for which there is no clear gender, or even a single word to describe it.

- For example, the feminine pronoun זֹאת 'this' in 2 Kgs 3:18 refers to YHWH filling trenches with water. Similarly, the feminine participle נִפְלָאֹת 'wonderful things' in Exod 34:10 refers to miracles that YHWH promises to do.

26 **Feminine singular for a collective.**[32] As discussed in §2, a feminine singular word may refer to a group, for example, יֹשֶׁבֶת 'inhabitants,' אֹיֶבֶת 'enemies,' and אֹרְחָה 'caravan.'

- Most collectives are feminine, but a few are masculine, for example, עַם 'people' and בָּקָר 'cattle.'

27 **Feminine singular for a singulative.**[33] A single component of a collective (e.g., one ship of a fleet) is called a **singulative** or a **noun of unit** (*nomen unitatis*), and is often referred to in Hebrew by means of a feminine singular word.

- For example, in 1 Kgs 10:22, the masculine singular אֳנִי is a collective (§2) that refers to a fleet of ships, whereas in Prov 30:19, the feminine singular אֳנִיָּה is a singulative that refers to a single ship.
- Similarly, שְׂעַר־רֹאשׁוֹ 'the hair of his head' (Judg 16:22) refers collectively to all of the hair on a person's head, so it uses the masculine singular collective, whereas מִשַּׂעֲרַת רֹאשׁוֹ 'a single hair of his head' (1 Sam 14:45) refers to a single hair, so it uses the feminine singular.

---

[30] Cf. BHRG §24.2.2(ii)a; GKC §122q; IBHS §6.4.2b; JM §134n.
[31] Cf. GKC §122q; IBHS §6.6d, 16.3.5c, 17.4.3b; JM §134n, 152a–b.
[32] Cf. BHRG §24.2.2(ii)b; GKC §122s; IBHS §6.4.2c; JM §134o, 135b.
[33] Cf. BHRG §24.2.2(ii)c; GKC §122t; IBHS §6.4.2d; JM §134p.

C   Construct Chain [34]

28a   A **construct chain** (also called a **bound structure** or a **genitive construction**) is a set of two (or more) nominals (nouns, participles, or adjectives) with the following features.

- Except for the last word, every word in the chain is in the **construct state** and is said to be the **construct noun**, the **construct term**, the **bound form**, the **head noun**, the **governing noun**, or the *nomen regens* of the word that follows it in the chain.

- Except for the first word, every word in the chain is said to be the **genitive**, the **governed noun**, the *postconstructus* or the *nomen rectum* of the word that precedes it in the chain. It modifies or clarifies the preceding word as described in §36–48.

- The last word in the chain is in the **absolute state** (or *status absolutus*). It is called the **free form**, the **absolute noun**, or the **absolute term**.

- With very few exceptions, no morphemes (e.g., words, suffixes, prefixes, etc.) may come between the construct term and the absolute term.

28b   **Construct chains may be longer than two words.** [35] A construct chain that is longer than two words can be thought of as several two-word construct chains linked together, where the genitive of one construct chain is the construct term for the following term. In such structures, the last word is in the absolute state, and all the other words are in the construct state. Each word (except the first) in such a structure is in a genitive relationship with the word immediately preceding it, limiting its meaning.

- כָּל־שְׁאֵרִית שָׂרֵי מֶלֶךְ בָּבֶל
  of Babylon   king of   princes of   rest of   all of   Jer 39:3
  all of the rest of the princes of the king of Babylon

  o   These five Hebrew words form a construct chain. The first four words are each in the construct state. The last word is in the absolute state.

  o   Each of the last four words is in a genitive relationship with the immediately preceding word, limiting the meaning of the preceding word. All of what? All of the rest. The rest of what? The rest of the princes. Which princes? The princes of the king. Which king? The king of Babylon.

---

[34] Cf. BHRG §25.1–25.4; GKC §89, 128, 130; IBHS §9; JM §92, 129; Kroeze 1997a.
[35] Cf. BHRG §25.1.2; GKC §128a; IBHS §9.3b–c; JM §129c.

29a **A word in the construct state very rarely has the article.**[36] Normally, the only word in a construct chain that can have the article is the last word in the chain.[37] Nevertheless, a few construct chains in the Bible break this rule by putting the article on a word in the construct state.

- וְאֵת כָּל־הַמַּמְלְכוֹת הָאָרֶץ   and all *the* kingdoms of the earth
  the earth *the* kingdoms of   all of   and   Jer 25:26

  o The word מַמְלְכוֹת 'kingdoms of' is in the construct state, so it is expected to lack the article. The fact that it has the article (⊙הַ 'the') is very unusual.

- Words in the construct state that have the article occur in Gen 31:13; Exod 9:18; Judg 8:11; Josh 3:14; 1 Kgs 14:24; 2 Kgs 23:17 (twice), 25:19; Isa 36:16; Ezek 46:19.

29b **A genitive phrase may modify a construct term.**[38] A construct term normally has only one genitive, the word that immediately follows it. If two genitives are closely related, however, they may form a **genitive phrase** that modifies the construct term.

- אֵם יַעֲקֹב וְעֵשָׂו   the mother of *Jacob and Esau*
  and Esau   Jacob   mother of   Gen 28:5

  o אֵם יַעֲקֹב וְעֵשָׂו 'the mother of Jacob and Esau' is a construct chain. The construct noun אֵם 'mother of' is modified by the genitive phrase יַעֲקֹב וְעֵשָׂו 'Jacob and Esau.' Both יַעֲקֹב and עֵשָׂו are in the absolute state.

- Other examples of genitive phrases include Gen 14:19 and Deut 10:18.

29c **Construct override.**[39] The word that immediately precedes a genitive is normally the only construct term that a genitive modifies. Occasionally, however, two or more words in the construct state can be modified by the same genitive. This is sometimes referred to as a **construct override**. It occurs more often in late texts than in early texts.

- סֵפֶר וּלְשׁוֹן כַּשְׂדִּים   *the literature and language* of the Chaldeans
  Chaldeans   *and language of*   writing of   Dan 1:4

---

[36] Cf. BHRG §25.3.1(ii); GKC §127f–h; IBHS §9.7a, 13.6b; JM §140c.

[37] If the last word in a construct chain is indefinite, then the entire chain is indefinite (e.g., 'a throne of a king'). If the last word is definite, then the entire chain is definite (e.g., 'the throne of David'). The last word in a construct chain is definite if it is a proper noun (e.g., 'David'), has the article ('the book'), or has a pronominal suffix ('his book'). See BHRG §24.4; GKC §127a. See GKC §127e; JM §139b–c, 140a for exceptions.

[38] Cf. BHRG §25.3.1(iv)b; IBHS §9.3b; JM §129a–b; Denio 1885; Verheij 1989.

[39] Cf. BHRG §25.3.1(iv)a; IBHS §9.3b; JM §129a.

- ○ Both סֵפֶר 'writing of' and לְשׁוֹן 'language of' are in the construct state. Both are modified by the genitive כַּשְׂדִּים 'Chaldeans.' Normally the genitive would be written twice, once after each construct noun (i.e., סֵפֶר כַּשְׂדִּים וּלְשׁוֹן כַּשְׂדִּים 'the writing of the Chaldeans and the language of the Chaldeans'), but in Dan 1:4 the genitive כַּשְׂדִּים 'Chaldeans' is written only once.
- Another example of a construct override is Ezek 31:16.

30a **A construct term may have the directive suffix הָ 'toward,'** even though this separates the construct term from its genitive.[40]

- בֵּיתָה יוֹסֵף   *into* Joseph's house
  Joseph *toward* house of   Gen 43:17

- מִדְבַּרָה דַמֶּשֶׂק   *toward* the wilderness of Damascus
  Damascus *toward* wilderness of   1 Kgs 19:15

  - ○ בֵּיתָה יוֹסֵף 'into Joseph's house' and מִדְבַּרָה דַמֶּשֶׂק 'towards the wilderness of Damascus' are both construct chains. בֵּיתָה 'toward house of' and מִדְבַּרָה 'toward wilderness of' are both in the construct state, yet they both have the directive suffix הָ, which indicates the direction of movement.

30b **Broken construct chain.**[41] On rare occasions, a word separates a construct noun from its genitive.

- כָּל־עוֹד נַפְשִׁי בִי   all of my life is *still* in me
  in me   my life   *still*   all of   2 Sam 1:9

  - ○ The word עוֹד 'still' separates the construct term כָּל 'all of' from its genitive נַפְשִׁי 'my life.' Normal word order would be כָּל־נַפְשִׁי עוֹד בִי 'all of *my life* is *still* in me.' Perhaps the unusual word order emphasizes עוֹד 'still,' drawing attention to the fact that the speaker had expected himself to have already died.
- Other examples include Job 27:3; Isa 19:8; Hos 14:3.

30c **Construct chain with a genitive prepositional phrase.**[42] Although the genitive in a construct chain is typically a noun or pronoun, a prepositional phrase can act as the genitive.

- מַשְׁכִּימֵי בַבֹּקֶר   early morning risers
  in the morning   early risers of   Isa 5:11

---

[40] Cf. BHRG §25.3.1(iii)a; IBHS §9.3d; JM §129a note 3; JM93 §129a note 4.

[41] Cf. Freedman 1972; Blommerde 1974; Frendo 1981. Prior editions of this textbook referred to this switch in word order as **hypallage**. GKC §128e states that the construct terms in these examples should be understood to be adverbs rather than construct terms.

[42] Cf. BHRG §25.3.1(iii)b, 25.3.1(iv)c; GKC §130a; IBHS §9.6b; JM §129l–o; Grossberg 1979–80.

    o   The prefixed preposition בְּ 'in' on the word בֹּקֶר 'morning' makes בַּבֹּקֶר a prepositional phrase. Because the prepositional phrase immediately follows the construct term מַשְׁכִּימֵי, it is a genitive prepositional phrase.

- Construct chains with genitive prepositional phrases are also found in 1 Sam 9:3; 1 Kgs 22:13; 2 Sam 1:21; Judg 5:10.

30d Construct chain with a genitive substantival clause.[43] Although the genitive in a construct chain is typically a noun or a participle, an entire clause (verb, subject, and modifiers) can act as the genitive in a construct chain (§489).

•	אִתָּם	הִתְהַלַּכְנוּ	יְמֵי	the time *we went about with them*
	with them	*we went about*	days of	1 Sam 25:15

    o   יְמֵי 'days of' is in the construct state. The genitive that modifies יְמֵי is the genitive substantival phrase הִתְהַלַּכְנוּ אִתָּם 'we walked with them.'

- Other examples include Lev 14:46 and Hos 1:2.

30e Construct chain with a genitive adjective.[44] Although the genitive in a construct chain is typically a noun or a participle, on rare occasions an adjective is used as the genitive.

•	הַקָּטָן	כְּלֵי	*the small* vessels
	the small	vessels of	Isa 22:24
•	הַטּוֹב	כְּיֵין	like *the best* wine
	the good	like wine of	Song 7:10

D Case [45]

31 Biblical Hebrew does not have cases.

- Some Semitic languages put different case endings on nominals (e.g., nouns, pronouns, etc.) depending on their function within their clause. Biblical Hebrew does not use case endings, but there is a general consensus that an earlier stage of Hebrew also used case endings.[46]
- This textbook groups functions of nominals using case names: nominative (§32–5), genitive (§36–49), and accusative (§50–60).[47]

---

[43] Cf. GKC §130d; IBHS §9.6c–e; JM §129p–q; Grossberg 1979–80; Grossberg 1980.
[44] Cf. GKC §128w; IBHS §14.3.3a–b.
[45] Cf. BHRG §25.1; GBHS §2; GKC §89a, 90; IBHS §8–10; JM §125–31.
[46] Cf. BHRG §25.1.1; GBHS pages 4–5; IBHS §8.1–8.2; JM §93b; JM page 410; JM93 page 440. For possible remnants of case endings in biblical Hebrew see IBHS §8.2.
[47] For arguments that cases should not be used in analysing Biblical Hebrew see Kroeze 1997b; Kroeze 2001; Hoftijzer 1965, 1–9.

Nominative case [48]

32   Nominative subject of a clause.[49]

- הַנָּחָשׁ   הִשִּׁיאַנִי   *The serpent* deceived me.
  deceived me   *the serpent*   Gen 3:13

- זֶה   הַיּוֹם   *This* is the day.
  the day   *this*   Judg 4:14

  o   The pronoun זֶה 'this' is the subject of a verbless equational clause (§561).

33a Predicate nominative.[50] A predicate nominative is a word that is equated with the subject in an equational clause (§561–5).[51]

- גֵרִים   הֱיִיתֶם   בְּאֶרֶץ   מִצְרָיִם   You were *sojourners* in the land of Egypt.
  Egypt   in land of   you were   *sojourners*   Deut 10:19

  o   גֵרִים הֱיִיתֶם בְּאֶרֶץ מִצְרָיִם 'sojourners you were in land of Egypt' is an equational clause, as indicated by the copulative verb הֱיִיתֶם 'you were' (§561). The subject is the 'you' that is implied by the verb הֱיִיתֶם 'you were.' The noun גֵרִים 'sojourners' is the predicate nominative.

- זֶה   הַיּוֹם   This is *the day*.
  the day   this   Judg 4:14

  o   זֶה הַיּוֹם 'this is the day' is a verbless equational clause (§561). The subject (§32) is זֶה 'this.' The noun הַיּוֹם 'the day' is the predicate nominative.

33b A predicate nominative normally lacks the article.[52] When a predicate nominative has the article, it is usually either superlative (§93) or distinctive (§88).

- אַתֶּם הַמְעַט מִכָּל־ הָעַמִּים   You were *the smallest* of all of the peoples.
  the peoples   than all of   *the small*   you   Deut 7:7 (superlative)

---

[48] Cf. GBHS §2.1; IBHS §8; Kroeze 2001.

[49] Cf. BHRG §34.1, 34.2; GBHS §2.1.1; IBHS §4.4, 8.3.

[50] Cf. BHRG §34.3; GBHS §2.1.2; IBHS §4.5c, 8.3–8.4. When Hebrew had case endings, it might have used the accusative for the predicate 'nominative'; see Barr 1969.

[51] Deciding which word is the subject and which is the predicate nominative can be difficult. Buth 1999, 100–1 suggests that the subject is normally the most definite (in the order first-, second-, then third-person independent pronoun, proper name, noun with the article, noun with a pronominal suffix) and normally the most presupposed in the context. In otherwise ambiguous cases, the subject precedes the predicate nominative. More detailed rules are supplied by Dyk and Talstra 1999; Lowery 1999. Cf. IBHS §8.3–8.4.

[52] Cf. JM §137l.

- יְהוָה הַצַּדִּיק וַאֲנִי וְעַמִּי הָרְשָׁעִים
  the wicked and my people and I *the righteous* YHWH   Exod 9:27 (distinctive)
  YHWH is *the righteous one*, whereas I and my people are *the wicked ones*.

34 Vocative use of the nominative.[53] When the name (e.g., 'O David'), title (e.g., 'O king'), or description (e.g., 'O wicked nation') of a person is used in direct address to that person, it is referred to as a 'vocative.'

- הוֹשִׁעָה הַמֶּלֶךְ
  the king help!   Help, *O king*!
                                                                2 Sam 14:4

  o The words הוֹשִׁעָה הַמֶּלֶךְ are spoken directly to the king, so הַמֶּלֶךְ is a vocative. As vocatives often do (§89), the vocative הַמֶּלֶךְ has the article (הַ⊙). With a vocative, the article is generally translated 'O' rather than 'the.'

35 Nominative absolute.[54] This is also called a **pendent nominative, rhetorical absolute,** *casus pendens*, **rhetorical exposure, topic–comment construction, focus marker, focus construction,** or **left dislocation.** A nominative absolute is a word or phrase at the beginning of a sentence that does not play a grammatical role in the rest of the sentence.

- A nominative absolute is typically used to clarify the sentence by stating the focus or topic of the sentence. It does not necessarily indicate emphasis.
- There is often a pronoun in the sentence that has the same referent as the nominative absolute, indicating the conceptual relationship between the nominative absolute and the main sentence. Such a pronoun is called a **resumptive pronoun.**

- שָׂרַי אִשְׁתְּךָ לֹא־תִקְרָא אֶת־שְׁמָהּ שָׂרָי
  Sarai HER name (you) call not *your wife* Sarai   Gen 17:15
                       Regarding your wife Sarai, do not call HER name Sarai.

  o The main clause is לֹא־תִקְרָא אֶת־שְׁמָהּ שָׂרָי 'do not call her name Sarai.' שָׂרַי אִשְׁתְּךָ 'your wife Sarai' is a nominative absolute. The resumptive pronominal suffix ה⊙ in שְׁמָהּ 'her name' refers to the nominative absolute.

- הַמָּקוֹם אֲשֶׁר־יִבְחַר יְהוָה ... שָׁמָּה תָּבִיאוּ
  you will bring THERE ... YHWH will choose which *the place*   Deut 12:11
                       the place which YHWH will choose ... you will bring THERE

  o The main clause is שָׁמָּה תָּבִיאוּ 'you will bring there ...' הַמָּקוֹם 'the place' is a nominative absolute that explains the referent of שָׁמָּה 'there' in the main clause.

---

[53] Cf. BHRG §34.4; GBHS §2.1.3; IBHS §4.7d, 8.3d. When Hebrew had cases, it might have used the accusative case for the vocative function; see Barr 1969.

[54] Cf. BHRG §34.5, 46.1.2(i)(3); GBHS §2.1.4; GKC §143; IBHS §4.7b–c, 8.3a; JM §156a, e–f, j; Muraoka 1985, 93–9; Driver 1892, 264–74; Naudé 1990.

Genitive case [55]

36 **A word is in the genitive case** if it follows a preposition or a word in the construct state. A genitive that follows a word in the construct state is also called a **postconstructus**. The following sections (§37–48) categorize the various ways in which a genitive can clarify the meaning or restrict the reference of the immediately preceding construct term.

37 **Subjective genitive.**[56] Also called the **genitive of agency** or **genitive of authorship**, a subjective genitive specifies the agent who performs or is characterized by the concept that is implied by the construct term.

- אַהֲבַת יְהוָה אֶתְכֶם   *YHWH* loved you.
  you   *YHWH*   love of   Deut 7:8

  o The construct noun אַהֲבַת 'love of' implies that someone loves someone else. יְהוָה is a subjective genitive, meaning that it describes the love as one that YHWH did – YHWH loved you.

- שִׂנְאַת יְהוָה אֹתָנוּ   *YHWH* hated us.
  us   *YHWH*   hate of   Deut 1:27

- If the construct term is a passive participle, then the genitive is a genitive of agent (§45a) rather than a subjective genitive.

38 **Objective genitive.**[57] Also called a **genitive of a mediated object**, an objective genitive receives the action implied by the construct term.

- חֲמַס אָחִיךָ   the violence done *to your brother*
  your brother   violence of   Obad 10

  o The construct noun חֲמַס 'violence of' implies the concept of doing a violent act. The objective genitive אָחִיךָ 'your brother' receives the action implied by the construct noun – a violent act is done to him.

  o If אָחִיךָ were a subjective genitive (§37), then חֲמַס אָחִיךָ would mean 'the violence done *by your brother*.'

---

[55] Cf. BHRG §25.4; GBHS §2.2; GKC §89, 127–30; IBHS §9; JM §129; Denio 1900; Avishur 1971–2.

[56] Cf. BHRG §25.4.1–25.4.2, 25.4.6(ii); GBHS §2.2.3; GKC §128g; IBHS §9.5.1a–c; JM §129d; Denio 1900, 108. GKC, IBHS, and JM all use the term 'subjective genitive' in a broader way than is used in this textbook.

[57] Cf. BHRG §25.4.2(iii); GBHS §2.2.4; GKC §128h; IBHS §9.5.2d–e; JM §129e; Denio 1900, 110. JM uses the term 'objective genitive' more broadly than this textbook.

39   **Possessive genitive.**[58] A possessive genitive owns ('my house') or is in relationship with ('my brother') the construct term. The latter use is sometimes termed the **genitive of relationship**.

- בֵּית   הַמֶּלֶךְ   *the king's* house
  the king   house of   1 Kgs 9:10

- הֵיכַל   יְהוָה   *YHWH's* temple
  YHWH   temple of   Jer 7:4

40a   **Material genitive.**[59] A material genitive is the substance out of which the construct term is constructed. This is a subcategory of the attributive genitive (§41).

- כְּלֵי   כֶסֶף   *silver* vessels
  silver   vessels of   1 Kgs 10:25

- אֲרוֹן   עֵץ   a *wooden* ark
  wood   ark of   Deut 10:1

40b   **Enumerated genitive.**[60] An enumerated genitive occurs when the construct term is a number or unit of measure, and the genitive specifies what is counted or measured by the construct noun.

- If the the number or unit of measure comes second, then it is a genitive of measure (§48a) or a genitive of number (§48b).

- שְׁלֹשֶׁת יָמִים   three *days*
  days   three of   Gen 30:36

41   **Attributive genitive.**[61] Also referred to as a **genitive of quality**, an attributive genitive describes the construct term in a way that is best translated into English with an attributive adjective.

- The material genitive (§40a) is a subcategory of attributive genitive.

- מֹאזְנֵי   צֶדֶק   *honest* scales
  justness   scales of   Lev 19:36

- הַר־   קָדְשִׁי   *my holy* mountain
  my holy   mountain of   Ps 2:6

---

[58] Cf. BHRG §25.4.1; GBHS §2.2.1, 2.2.2; IBHS §9.5.1g–h; JM 129d; Denio 1900, 109. JM treats this as a subcategory of subjective genitive.

[59] Cf. BHRG §25.4.6(i); GBHS §2.2.10; GKC §128o; IBHS §9.5.3d; JM §129f; Denio 1900, 111–12.

[60] Cf. GBHS §2.2.11; IBHS §9.5.3f; JM §129f. For more examples, see §95a–b. GBHS, IBHS, and JM all refer to this as a **genitive of measure**, whereas this textbook uses that term to refer to something else (§48).

[61] Cf. BHRG §25.3.1(iv)d, 25.4.4(v); GBHS §2.2.5; GKC §128p, 135n; IBHS §9.5.3b; JM §129f; Weingreen 1954; Denio 1900, 111–12.

      ○   A pronominal suffix on an attributive genitive modifies the construct noun, not the word to which it is attached ('*my* mountain of holiness,' not 'the mountain of *my* holiness'). This rule does not necessarily apply to other types of genitives.

42a   **Appositional genitive.**[62] Also called a **genitive of proper noun**, **genitive of apposition**, or **genitive of association**, an appositional genitive is an individual member of the class given by the construct term. The construction has the sense of, for example 'the river, that is, I mean specifically the Euphrates.' This is sometimes grouped with the **explicative genitive** (§43).

- נְהַר־פְּרָת
  Euphrates   river of   the river *Euphrates* / Gen 15:18

- אֶרֶץ מִצְרַיִם
  Egypt   land of   the land *Egypt* / Exod 7:19

- בַּת צִיּוֹן
  Zion   daughter of   the daughter *Zion* / 2 Kgs 19:21

42b   **Appositional genitive adjective.**[63] An adjective can be used substantively as an appositional genitive. This is common with ordinal numbers (§98a–9).

- בִּשְׁנַת הַתְּשִׁיעִית
  the ninth   in year of   in *the ninth* year / 2 Kgs 17:6

- עֹלַת הַתָּמִיד
  the regular   burnt offering of   *the regular* burnt offering / Num 28:31

43   **Explicative genitive.**[64] Also called a **genitive of species**, an explicative genitive specifies a subtype or genus within the broader category of the construct noun. An explicative genitive is usually translated into English by putting the genitive directly before the construct noun.

- עֲצֵי שִׁטִּים
  acacia   wood of   *acacia* wood / Exod 37:10

- אַבְנֵי־שַׁיִשׁ
  marble   stones of   *marble* stones / 1 Chr 29:2

---

[62] Cf. BHRG §25.4.4(iv); GBHS §2.2.12; IBHS §9.5.3h; JM §129f; Denio 1900, 112.

[63] Cf. GBHS §2.5.3; GKC §128w. Regarding Num 28:31, BDB says that תָּמִיד is a noun, in which case it would be an attributive genitive (§41). HALOT, however, describes it as a 'substantivized adj. in constr. expressions as nomen rectum,' which fits §42b.

[64] Cf. BHRG §25.4.4(iii); GBHS §2.2.12; GKC §128m; IBHS §9.5.3g. An explicative genitive has a meaning similar to a genus-species apposition (§65), not an explicative apposition (§70).

- o   'Marble' is an explicative genitive because marble is a type of stone.
- o   If 'marble' were a material genitive (§40a), it would mean that the stone was constructed out of marble.
- o   If 'marble' were an attributive genitive (§41), 'marble' would describe the stone without placing it in a standardized category (e.g., 'big stone,' since stones come in a continuous range of sizes, and what might be a big stone in one context may be considered small in another context). Marble, however, is a standardized category of stone, meaning that it is one of a limited number of types of stones (e.g., marble, granite, pumice), so it is an explicative genitive.
- o   If 'marble' were an appositional genitive (§42a), it would point to the stone by giving another name for the particular stone, just as 'Nile' in 'the river Nile' points to the particular river by giving its name. But 'marble' in 'stone of marble' points to or names a type of stone rather than an individual stone, so it is not an appositional genitive.

44a   Genitive of result.[65] A genitive of result specifies the outcome of the preceding construct term.

- • צֹאן   טִבְחָה   sheep *that are slaughtered*
      slaughtering   sheep of   Ps 44:23

- • מוּסַר   שְׁלוֹמֵנוּ   chastisement *that brings us peace*
      our peace   chastisement of   Isa 53:5

44b   Genitive of purpose.[66] A genitive of purpose specifies the purpose of the preceding construct term. A genitive of purpose differs from a genitive of result as follows. In a genitive of purpose, the purpose (perhaps fulfilled, perhaps unfulfilled) is the focus, whereas in a genitive of result, the result (perhaps intended, perhaps unintended) is the focus.

- • The examples in §44a (genitive of result) could also be classified as genitives of purpose and translated as 'sheep *for slaughter*' and 'chastisement *to bring us peace.*'

45a   Genitive of agent.[67] A genitive of agent states the person who performs the action implied by the construct term, which is a passive participle.

- • If the construct term is not a passive participle, then the genitive is not a genitive of agent. In such a case, the genitive might be a subjective genitive (§37).

- • מֻכֵּה   אֱלֹהִים   beaten *by God*
      God   beaten of   Isa 53:4

---

[65] Cf. BHRG §25.4.5(i); GBHS §2.2.8; Denio 1900, 111.

[66] Cf. BHRG §25.4.5(i); GBHS §2.2.8; GKC §128q; JM §129f (not in JM93).

[67] Cf. BHRG §25.4.2(ii); GBHS §2.2.9; IBHS §9.5.1b; JM §121p. Note that IBHS classifies genitive of agent with the subjective genitive.

45b **Genitive of means.**[68] Also called a **genitive of instrument**, a genitive of means states the mechanism by which the action implied by the construct term is performed. The construct term is a passive participle.

- If the genitive were animate (i.e., a person or an animal), it would be a genitive of agent (§45a) rather than a genitive of means.

- שְׂרֻפוֹת אֵשׁ   burned *by fire*
  fire   burned of   Isa 1:7

46 **Epexegetical genitive.**[69] Also called a **genitive of specification**, an epexegetical genitive occurs after the construct form of an adjective and is the thing that the adjective describes. The adjective in the construct state and the epexegetical genitive function together as a single adjective.

- עַם־ קְשֵׁה־ עֹרֶף   a stiff-*necked* people
  neck   hard of   people   Exod 32:9

- וַיְהִי יוֹסֵף יְפֵה־ תֹאַר   Joseph was *handsome*.
  form   fair of   Joseph   was   Gen 39:6

  o The construct terms קְשֵׁה 'hard of' and יְפֵה 'fair of' are adjectives. The epexegetical genitives עֹרֶף 'neck' and תֹאַר 'form' state the things to which the adjectives apply. The construct chain קְשֵׁה־עֹרֶף 'hard of neck' modifies עַם 'people' as an attributive adjective, and יְפֵה־תֹאַר 'fair of form' modifies יוֹסֵף 'Joseph' as a predicate adjective, meaning 'Joseph was handsome.'

47 **Superlative genitive.**[70] A superlative genitive (§80) combines with the construct term to mean the greatest of something. A superlative genitive is always plural and often articular. The construct term is often of the same root as the genitive.

- שִׁיר הַשִּׁירִים   *the best* song
  the songs   song of   Song 1:1

- אֱלֹהֵי הָאֱלֹהִים   *the supreme* God
  the gods   god of   Deut 10:17

48a **Genitive of measure.**[71] A genitive of measure indicates the quantity of the construct term in terms of a measurement.

---

[68] Cf. BHRG §25.4.5(iv); GBHS §2.2.9; IBHS §9.5.1d; JM §121p; Denio 1900, 108.

[69] Cf. BHRG §25.4.6(iii); GBHS §2.2.6; IBHS §9.5.3c; JM §129i–ia; Denio 1900, 110.

[70] Cf. BHRG §25.4.3(ii), 30.5.2(ii)d; GBHS §2.2.13; GKC §133i; IBHS §9.5.3j, 14.5b, d; JM §141l–m; Denio 1900, 113.

[71] Cf. GKC §128n; Denio 1900, 111–12. Be aware that the 'genitive of measure' in IBHS §9.5.3f; JM §129f is what this textbook refers to as an enumerated genitive (§40b).

- מֵי מָתְנַיִם   water *that was waist deep*

  hips water of   Ezek 47:4

  o   If the construct term were counted as discrete units (e.g., five people), it would
      be a genitive of number (§48b).

  o   To distinguish a genitive of number (§48b) from a genitive of measure (§48a),
      note that a genitive of measure requires some unit of measurement (e.g., cubits),
      whereas a genitive of number needs only a number.

  o   If מֵי 'water of' were in the absolute state rather than the construct state (מַיִם
      rather than מֵי), then מָתְנַיִם 'hips' would be an apposition of measurent (§69a)
      rather than a genitive of measure (§48a).

48b   Genitive of number.[72] A genitive of number indicates how many there
   are of the construct term. It is often, but not always, a number.

- בִּשְׁנַת שְׁתַּיִם   in *the second* year

  two   in year of   1 Kgs 15:25

- מְתֵי מִסְפָּר   *a few* men

  few   men of   Gen 34:30

  o   If the first word ('year' or 'men') were in the absolute state rather than the
      construct state, the second word ('two' and 'few') would be an apposition of
      number (§69b) rather than a genitive of number (§48b).

49   Genitive object of a preposition. The object of a preposition (sometimes
   called a **dependent genitive**) can be classified under the genitive case.
   The meaning of an object of a preposition may be found in a lexicon, as
   well as in §238–376.

Accusative case [73]

- Words in the accusative case modify a verb. Pragmatically, the
  accusative case tends to function as a catch-all; if the use of a noun
  does not fit under one of the categories of the nominative case (§32–
  5), does not follow a construct term or preposition (§36), and is not in
  apposition (§65–71), then it is considered to be accusative.

- אֵת (also spelled אֶת־), called the **definite direct-object marker**, the
  nota accusativi, or the **accusative particle**, is discussed in §475.

---

[72] Cf. GKC §128n; Denio 1900, 111–12.
[73] Cf. GBHS §2.3; GKC §117–18; IBHS §10; JM §125–8.

- All words preceded by the definite direct-object marker אֵת (אֶת־) are classified under the accusative case, but not all words classified under the accusative case are preceded by אֵת or אֶת־.

50 **Direct object accusative.**[74] The direct object of a verb is considered to be in the accusative case. To distinguish it from an object that is created by the verbal action (§52) or that has the same root as the verb (§51), a direct object accusative is also called the **affected-object accusative**.

- If the direct object is definite, it will often be preceded by the particle אֵת.

אֶת־הָֽאָדָם	אֱלֹהִים	וַיִּבְרָא	God created *mankind*.
the mankind	God	created	Gen 1:27

51 **Cognate accusative.**[75] When the accusative has the same root as the verb, it is called a cognate accusative. When a cognate accusative is not created by the verbal action (§52), it is also called an **internal-object accusative**. A cognate accusative has been traditionally understood to amplify the verb (e.g., 'sheer terror' instead of 'dread'). Nevertheless, many cognate accusatives are unlikely to be emphatic, as illustrated by Gen 8:20 below, and some scholars deny that a cognate accusative ever indicates emphasis.

פָּ֫חַד	פָּֽחֲדוּ	They were in *sheer* terror. Or They were in terror.
dread	they were in dread	Ps 14:5
חֵטְא	חָֽטְאָה יְרוּשָׁלַ֫͏ִם	Jerusalem sinned *greatly*. Or Jerusalem sinned.
Jerusalem sinned sin		Lam 1:8
עֹלֹת	וַיַּ֫עַל	He offered *burnt offerings*.
burnt offerings he offered		Gen 8:20

52 **Accusative of product.**[76] Also called an **accusative of result** or an **effected-object accusative**, an accusative of product is the result of the action of the verb.

- A cognate accusative (§51) may also be an accusative of product.

מִזְבֵּחַ אֶת־הָֽאֲבָנִים	וַיִּבְנֶה	He built the stones *into an altar*.
altar the stones	he built	1 Kgs 18:32
נֶ֫דֶר	כִּֽי־ תִדֹּר	if you vow *a vow*
a vow you vow if		Deut 23:22

---

[74] Cf. BHRG §33.2.1; GBHS §2.3.1(a); GKC §117a; IBHS §10.2.1c; JM §125a–b.

[75] Cf. BHRG §33.2.1(i)c, 33.3(v); GBHS §2.3.1(c); GKC §117p–r; IBHS §10.2.1f–g; JM §125q–r.

[76] Cf. BHRG §33.2.1(i)b; GBHS §2.3.1(b), 2.3.2(g); GKC §117ii; IBHS §10.2.1f; JM §125p, w. Some instances of an accusative of product may be classified as a double accusative; for examples, see GBHS §2.3.1(e.2).

o   In Deut 23:22, נֶדֶר 'a vow' is an accusative of product because the action of vowing creates a vow. נֶדֶר is also a cognate accusative (§51) because it is the accusative of product of the verb תִדֹּר 'you will vow,' which comes from the same root נדר (the initial nun has assimilated to the dalet; תִדֹּר ← תנדר).

53   **Accusative of material.**[77] An accusative of material states the substance with which the action of the verb is performed. If the accusative is thought of as a tool rather than as a material, it can be referred to as an **accusative of means**.

- וַיִּרְגְּמוּ אֹתוֹ כָל־ יִשְׂרָאֵל אֶבֶן   All Israel stoned him *with stones*.
  stone   Israel   all of   him   stoned   Josh 7:25

- וַיִּיצֶר יְהוָה אֱלֹהִים אֶת־הָאָדָם עָפָר   YHWH God formed the man *of dust*.
  dust   the man   God   YHWH   formed   Gen 2:7

54a   **Directive accusative.**[78] Also called a **terminative accusative**, **local accusative**, **accusative of motion toward a place**, **accusative of direction towards a goal**, or a subcategory of **accusative of place**, a directive accusative is used with a verb of motion to state the direction of motion or the place that is reached through the motion.

- צֵא הַשָּׂדֶה   Go out *to the field*.
  the field   go out   Gen 27:3

- The directive הָ◌ is often on the end of a directive accusative. See §62.

54b   **Accusative of place.**[79] An accusative of place gives the reference location for a verb – typically the location where the action of the verb occurs. This category is controversial.

- לָשֶׁבֶת בָּיִת   so that it may dwell *in a temple*
  temple   to dwell   Isa 44:13

- וַיַּעֲמֹד פֶּתַח־ הַבַּיִת   He stopped *at the door* of the house.
  the house   *door of*   and he stopped   2 Kgs 5:9

---

[77] Cf. BHRG §33.3(iv); GBHS §2.3.2(f); GKC §117hh; IBHS §10.2.3c–e; JM §125v.

[78] Cf. BHRG §33.2.3(ii); GBHS §2.3.2(a); GKC §118d, f; IBHS §10.2.2b; JM §125n; Meek 1940.

[79] Cf. BHRG §33.2.3(i); GBHS §2.3.2(a); GKC §118g; IBHS §10.2.2b; JM §133c; Meek 1940. In prior editions of this textbook, the accusative of place was not a recognized category. Instead, פֶּתַח in 2 Kgs 5:9 and בֵּית in 2 Kgs 19:37 were explained as prepositions derived from construct nouns. Nevertheless, as IBHS §10.2.2b argues, this explanation does not fit examples such as בָּיִת in Isa 44:13, where the 'preposition' is not a construct term, and where there is no following noun to be the object of the putative preposition.

- וַיְהִי הוּא מִשְׁתַּחֲוֶה בֵּית נִסְרֹךְ
  Nisroch *house of* worshipping he was   2 Kgs 19:37
  while he was worshipping *at the temple* of Nisroch

55 **Separative accusative.**[80] An accusative may be used with the verb יָצָא to indicate from whom or what the subject of the verb יָצָא departed. Such a word can be called a separative accusative. It could also be considered to belong to a subcategory of **accusative of place**, because it indicates the reference location for a verb, and because the separation is indicated by the verb יָצָא rather than by the accusative itself.

- בָּנַי יְצָאֻנִי וְאֵינָם   My sons have gone *from me* and are no more.
  and are not   left *me* my sons   Jer 10:20

  o In Jer 10:20, the subject (בָּנַי 'my sons') went out from the separative accusative (the pronominal suffix נִי 'me' in יְצָאֻנִי 'left me').

- הֵם יָצְאוּ אֶת־הָעִיר   They left *the city.*
  the city   left they   Gen 44:4

56a **Temporal-duration accusative.**[81] A temporal-duration accusative answers the question 'for how long?' It expresses the length of time throughout which the verb occurs.

- עָפָר תֹּאכַל כָּל־יְמֵי חַיֶּיךָ   You will eat dust *all the days of your life.*
  your life days of all of you will eat dust   Gen 3:14

- וּשְׁתַּיִם שָׁנִים מָלָךְ   And he reigned *for two years.*
  he reigned *years   and two*   2 Sam 2:10

56b **Temporal-point accusative.**[82] A temporal-point accusative answers the question 'when?' It states the time at which the verb occurs. This category is controversial; some scholars argue that an accusative only expresses duration of time (§56a) and never a point in time.

- וַיְדַבֵּר אֶל־קֹרַח ... לֵאמֹר בֹּקֶר וְיֹדַע יְהוָה
  YHWH will make known *morning* saying Korah to he said   Num 16:5
  He spoke to Korah … saying, '*In the morning* YHWH will make known …'

- The broader category **temporal accusative**, **accusative of time**, or **accusative of temporal determination** subsumes both the temporal-duration accusative and the temporal-point accusative.

---

[80] Cf. BHRG §33.2.3(ii); IBHS §10.2.2b; JM §125n; Pardee 1979.

[81] Cf. BHRG §33.3(i)b; GBHS §2.3.2(b); GKC §118k; IBHS §10.2.2c; JM §126i; Meek 1940.

[82] Cf. BHRG §33.3(i)a; GBHS §2.3.2(b); GKC §118i; IBHS §10.2.2c; JM §126i; Meek 1940.

57a **Accusative of specification.**[83] Also called an **accusative of limitation**, an accusative of specification states the sphere in which the verb applies or the extent to which the verb occurs.

- As described in §492, an entire clause may function as an accusative of specification.

- אֶת־רַגְלָיו   חָלָה   He was diseased *in his feet.*
  his feet   he was sick   1 Kgs 15:23

- נֶפֶשׁ   נַכֶּנּוּ   לֹא   Let us not wound him *with respect to life.*
  life we will wound him not   Gen 37:21

- קָרוּעַ   כֻּתָּנְתּוֹ   with *his tunic* torn
  his tunic   torn   2 Sam 15:32

57b **Predicate accusative.**[84] A predicate accusative is like a predicate nominative (§33a); the difference is that a predicate accusative asserts something about another accusative rather than about the subject of the clause. Thus a predicate accusative follows another accusative, and there is an implied copulative verb between the two accusatives, equating them. A predicate accusative lacks the article (⊙הַ) and is often an adjective or a participle. The main verb of the clause is often a verb of perception, knowledge, or naming.

- אֹתְךָ   רָאִיתִי   צַדִּיק   I have seen you *to be righteous.*
  righteous I have seen you   Gen 7:1

  o   צַדִּיק 'righteous' can be classified as a predicate accusative because it lacks the article, it follows the accusative אֹתְךָ 'you,' and the two accusatives 'you' and 'righteous' are equated by an implied copulative verb (you *are* righteous).[85]

- בֹּכֶה   אֶת־הָעָם   מֹשֶׁה   וַיִּשְׁמַע   Moses heard the people *weeping.*
  weeping the people Moses heard   Num 11:10

58 **Emphatic accusative of specification.**[86] A word is an emphatic accusative of specification if it precedes the verb, is the logical subject of

---

[83] Cf. BHRG §33.3(iii); GBHS §2.3.2(e); GKC §117ll; IBHS §10.2.2e; JM §125j, 126g, 127b. Be aware that IBHS uses the term 'accusative of specification' in §10.2.2e differently from the way it is used here, although there is significant overlap.

[84] Cf. GKC §117h; IBHS §10.2.3c; JM §126a–c. JM says that a predicate accusative can refer to the subject. Many or all predicate accusatives could be classified as the second object of a verb that takes two objects; see GKC §117h.

[85] Alternately, the verb רָאִיתִי could be described as taking two objects, where צַדִּיק is the second object (and not a predicate accusative).

[86] Cf. BHRG §33.4.2(vii); GKC §117h–i; IBHS §10.3.2; MacDonald 1964, 266–9; Walker 1955; Saydon 1964, 195–205; Muraoka 1985, 146–58; Hoftijzer 1965; Zewi 1997; Rooker 1990, 88–90.

the verb, and is preceded by the accusative particle אֵת / אֶת־. Despite the name, such a construction does not necessarily indicate emphasis.

- If it were not preceded by the particle אֵת, an emphatic accusative of specification would be classed as the nominative subject of a clause (§32) instead.

- This is a controversial topic, and there are other explanations for these texts. For example, some scholars argue that the word following אֵת can be the subject of a clause (§32). Examples with a verb of perception (e.g., Gen 12:14) or cognition (e.g., 2 Sam 3:25) can often be explained as having a verb that takes two objects.

- וְאֶת־הַבַּרְזֶל נָפַל אֶל־ הַמָּיִם   *The iron* fell into the water.
  the water to   fell *the iron*   2 Kgs 6:5

  o הַבַּרְזֶל 'the iron' can be classified as an emphatic accusative of specification because it precedes the verb נָפַל 'it fell,' is the logical subject of the verb, and is preceded by אֶת־.[87]

- יָדַעְתָּ אֶת־אַבְנֵר בֶּן־ נֵר כִּי לְפַתֹּתְךָ בָּא
  he came to deceive you that *Ner ben Abner* you know   2 Sam 3:25

  You know that *Abner ben Ner* came to deceive you.

  o אַבְנֵר בֶּן־נֵר 'Abner ben Ner' can be classified as an emphatic accusative of specification because it precedes the verb בָּא 'he came,' is the logical subject of the verb, and is preceded by אֶת־.[88]

- וַיִּרְאוּ הַמִּצְרִים אֶת־הָאִשָּׁה כִּי־ יָפָה הִוא מְאֹד
  very she beautiful that *the woman* the Egyptians saw   Gen 12:14

  The Egyptians saw that *the woman* was very beautiful.

- וַיִּשְׁאַל אֶת־נַפְשׁוֹ לָמוּת   He requested that *his life* might die.
  to die *his life* he asked   1 Kgs 19:4

  o נַפְשׁוֹ 'his life' is preceded by אֶת־, precedes the verb לָמוּת 'to die,' and is the logical subject of that verb, so it can be classified as an emphatic accusative of specification.

- וְאִישׁ אֶת־קֳדָשָׁיו לוֹ יִהְיוּ   As for anyone, *his holy things* will be his.
  will be to him *his holy things* and a man   Num 5:10

  o וְאִישׁ 'and a man' is a nominative absolute (§35). קֳדָשָׁיו 'his holy things' is an emphatic accusative of specification.

---

[87] In 2 Kgs 6:5, some scholars would classify הַבַּרְזֶל 'the iron' as the nominative subject of the verb (despite the אֵת־), as a nominative absolute (§35), or as an accusative absolute.

[88] In 2 Sam 3:25, instead of 'Abner' being an emphatic accusative of specification, one could understand the verb יָדַעְתָּ to take two objects, 'Abner ben Ner' and 'that he came to deceive you.' Or one could understand 'Abner ben Ner' as the only direct object of יָדַעְתָּ and understand 'that he came to deceive you' as a predicate accusative (§57b).

- Other possible examples include Gen 1:4; Num 11:22; Judg 6:28; 2 Sam 21:22; 1 Kgs 5:17.

59 **Determinative accusative.**[89] A word is a determinative accusative if it follows a verb, is the logical subject of the verb, and is preceded by the accusative particle אֵת / אֶת־. The verb is often, but not always, passive.

- A determinative accusative usually lacks concord with the verb.
- If it lacked the particle אֵת, it would be classed as the subject of a clause (§32).
- If it preceded the verb, it could be classified as an emphatic accusative of specification (§58).
- This is a controversial topic, and there are other explanations for these texts.
- וַיֻּגַּד לְרִבְקָה אֶת־דִּבְרֵי עֵשָׂו   *Esau's words* were told to Rebekah.
  Esau words of to Rebekah was told   Gen 27:42

  o דִּבְרֵי עֵשָׂו 'words of Esau' is a determinative accusative because it is preceded by the accusative particle אֶת־ and is the logical subject of the preceding verb וַיֻּגַּד 'it was told.'

- בְּהִוָּלֶד לוֹ אֵת יִצְחָק בְּנוֹ   when *his son Isaac* was born to him
  his son Isaac to him when born   Gen 21:5

- הֻגֵּד הֻגַּד לַעֲבָדֶיךָ אֵת אֲשֶׁר צִוָּה יְהוָה   Josh 9:24
  YHWH commanded what to your servants was told to be told

                       What YHWH had commanded ... was certainly told to your servants.

- הַמְעַט־לָנוּ אֶת־עֲוֹן פְּעוֹר   Was the *sin at Peor* too small for us?
  of Peor sin to us small?   Josh 22:17

- Other possible examples of a determinative accusative include Gen 17:5, 21:8, 29:27; Num 17:2; Deut 12:22; 1 Sam 20:13; 2 Sam 11:25; 1 Kgs 2:21; 2 Kgs 18:30; Neh 9:32; Amos 4:2.

60 **Accusative of manner.**[90] Also called the **adverbial accusative**, an accusative of manner describes the way in which the action of the verb takes place. An accusative of manner lacks the article. A clause can be an accusative of manner (§491), as can an infinitive absolute (§204).

- וָאוֹלֵךְ אֶתְכֶם קוֹמְמִיּוּת   I made you walk *uprightly*.
  uprightness you I made walk   Lev 26:13

  o קוֹמְמִיּוּת is a noun that means 'uprightness.' It is used as an accusative of manner, meaning that it is used adverbially.

---

[89] Cf. BHRG §33.4.2(vii); GKC §117i–m; IBHS §10.3.2, 23.2.2e; JM §128b; MacDonald 1964, 272; Walker 1955; Saydon 1964, 195–205; Muraoka 1985, 146–58; Hoftijzer 1965; Zewi 1997.

[90] Cf. GKC §118m–q; GBHS §2.3.2(c); IBHS §10.2.2e; JM §126d.

- וַתֵּשְׁבוּ בֶּטַח   You lived *securely*.

  security you lived   1 Sam 12:11

- מְאֹד 'very' is a noun that is predominantly used as an accusative of manner, so it is often parsed as an adverb.

E Directive הָ [91]

61 **The directive suffix** הָ was once thought (e.g., GKC §90a, c) to be the old accusative case ending that had dropped off elsewhere (§31). This view has been discarded now that materials written in Ugaritic have been discovered and deciphered; Ugaritic is very close to Hebrew and has both the case endings (which Hebrew dropped) and a separate directive suffix (spelled 'h' in Ugaritic transcription). [92]

62 **Directive** הָ.[93] Also called the **terminative** ה or the **directional** ה, the directive הָ is used as a suffix on a noun to indicate a direction towards the thing named by the noun, often in reference to motion that ceases upon arrival. This category is often combined with §64b, 'locative הָ.'

- הַשָּׁמַיְמָה   הַבֶּט־נָא   Look *at* the heavens!

  the direction of the heavens   look!   Gen 15:5

- הַבָּיְתָה   הָבֵא אֶת־הָאֲנָשִׁים   Bring the men *into* the house.

  the direction of the house the men   bring!   Gen 43:16

63 **Temporal** הָ.[94] In the phrase מִיָּמִים יָמִימָה (Exod 13:10; Judg 11:40, 21:19; 1 Sam 1:3, 2:19), the suffix הָ indicates 'motion' through time. Literally, the phrase is 'from days toward days,' but it means 'from year to year' or 'yearly.'

64a **Separative** הָ.[95] The directive suffix הָ on a noun that is prefixed with the preposition מִן 'from' can indicate the direction away from the noun (whereas it normally refers to the direction towards the noun, §62).

- מִבָּבֶלָה   מוּשָׁבִים

  from *the direction of* Babylon   they will be brought back   Jer 27:16

  They will be brought back from Babylon.

---

[91] Cf. JM §93c–f; Hoftijzer 1981.

[92] Cf. IBHS §10.5a; JM §93c. But see Wernberg-Møller 1988.

[93] Cf. BHRG §28; GKC §90c; IBHS §10.5b; JM §93c–d; Meek 1940, 228–9.

[94] Cf. IBHS §10.5c; JM §93d.

[95] Cf. GKC §90e; IBHS §10.5b; JM §93f.

- מִצָּפוֹנָה   from the north
  from *the direction of* the north   Josh 15:10

64b **Locative** הָ.[96] Also called the **local** ה or the *He locale*, the directive suffix הָ on a noun that is a place name which is prefixed with the preposition בְּ 'at' or preceded by the preposition אֵצֶל 'near' may be redundant with the preposition and indicate a location rather than a direction. This category is often combined with §62, 'directive הָ.'

- וַיֵּשֶׁב דָּוִד בַּחֹרְשָׁה   David remained at Horesh.
  in Horesh David remained   1 Sam 23:18

- אֲשֶׁר אֵצֶל צָרְתָנָה   which is near Zarethan
  Zarethan near which   1 Kgs 4:12

- Other examples of this include 1 Sam 23:15, 19, 31:13; 2 Sam 20:15.

F Apposition [97]

- Two substantives in the same clause with the same referent and the same syntactical function are in apposition.[98] Because they have the same referent, they almost always match in definiteness (i.e., both are definite or both are indefinite). Most examples of apposition consist of two nouns side by side.

65 **Genus-species apposition.**[99] In genus-species apposition, a general term is followed by a more specific term that is a subset of the first.

- אִשָּׁה אַלְמָנָה   a *widow*
  widow woman   1 Kgs 7:14

- נַעֲרָה בְתוּלָה   a young *virgin*
  virgin young woman   1 Kgs 1:2

- אִישׁ כֹּהֵן   a *priest*
  priest man   Lev 21:9

66 **Attributive apposition.**[100] In attributive apposition, the second term describes the first term and is translated into English as an attributive adjective.

---

[96] Cf. GKC §90d; IBHS §10.5b; JM §93e; Meek 1940, 228–9.

[97] Cf. BHRG §29; GBHS §2.4; GKC §131; IBHS §12; JM §131; Driver 1892, 246–63; Avishur 1971–2.

[98] Cf. GBHS §2.4; GKC §131a; IBHS §12.1–12.2; JM §131a.

[99] Cf. BHRG §29.3(ii); GBHS §2.4.1; GKC §131b; IBHS §12.3b, 13.8b; JM §131b.

[100] Cf. BHRG §29.3(iii); GBHS §2.4.2; GKC §131c; IBHS §12.3c; JM §131c.

● This has the same meaning as an attributive genitive (§41). The difference is that for an attributive genitive (§41) the first word is in the construct state, whereas for attributive apposition the two words are in apposition.

● אֲמָרִים אֱמֶת
   truth   words

true words
Prov 22:21

● יַיִן תַּרְעֵלָה
  staggering   wine

intoxicating wine
Ps 60:5

● לְשׁוֹן רְמִיָּה
  deceit   tongue

a *deceitful* tongue
Ps 120:3

67 **Predicate apposition**. In predicate apposition, the first term acts as a predicate adjective (§75).

● הֲשָׁלוֹם אֲבִיכֶם הַזָּקֵן
  the old   your father   *wellness*?

Is your old father *well*?
Gen 43:27

● אֱמֶת הָיָה הַדָּבָר
  the word   was   *truth*

The report was *true*.
1 Kgs 10:6

68 **Apposition of material**.[101] In apposition of material, the second term states the type of substance of which the first term consists.

● הַבָּקָר הַנְּחֹשֶׁת
  the bronze   the oxen

the bronze oxen
2 Kgs 16:17

● סֹלֶת סְאָה־
  finely milled flour   seah

a seah *of finely milled flour*
2 Kgs 7:1

  ○ The seah is made up of סֹלֶת 'finely milled flour.' If the word order were switched, it would be an apposition of measure (§69).

● שָׁנָתַיִם יָמִים
  days   two years

two *full* years
Gen 41:1

● שְׁלֹשָׁה בָנִים
  sons   three

three *sons*
Gen 6:10

  ○ In Gen 6:10, בָנִים 'sons' is in apposition of material to שְׁלֹשָׁה 'three' because בָנִים follows שְׁלֹשָׁה, is in apposition to it, and is the material out of which the 'three' is composed. If the word order were switched, it would be an apposition of number (§69b). If the first word שְׁלֹשָׁה 'three' were in the construct state (i.e., שְׁלֹשֶׁת), then בָנִים 'sons' would be an enumerated genitive (§40b).

---

[101] Cf. BHRG §29.3(iv); GBHS §2.4.3, 2.4.4; GKC §131d; IBHS §12.3c–d; JM §131d–e, g. Note that this definition of apposition of material is broader than that used in IBHS and JM. If the first term is a number or measuring unit, some scholars (e.g., GBHS §2.4.4; JM §131e) classify it as apposition of measure (§69b).

- מַיִם הַמַּבּוּל   the flood *waters*
  waters   the flood   Gen 6:17

  o   Words in apposition usually agree in definiteness, but in Gen 6:17, הַמַּבּוּל 'the
      flood' is definite, whereas מַיִם 'waters' is indefinite. This might indicate that the
      author was thinking of the two words as a compound term.

69a   Apposition of measurement.[102] In apposition of measurement (or
apposition of measure), the second term states how much there is of the
first term as a measurement (e.g., waist-high water).

- מַיִם בִּרְכָּיִם   *knee-deep* water
  two knees   waters   Ezek 47:4

- If the second term counts (e.g., five, few, many) rather than measures (e.g., knee-
  deep), then it is an apposition of number (§69b).
- If the first term is in the construct state, then the second term is not in apposition.
  Instead, the second term is a genitive of measure (§48a).
- If the first term (instead of the second term) is the measurement, then it is an
  apposition of material (§68), not an apposition of measurement, since the second
  term is the one that is used to classify this type of apposition.[103]

69b   Apposition of number.[104] In apposition of number, the second term
counts how many there are of the first term.

- יָמִים מִסְפָּר   a *few* days
  few   days   Num 9:20

  o   If יָמִים 'days' were in the construct state, then מִסְפָּר would be a genitive of
      number (§48a).

70   Explicative apposition.[105] In explicative apposition, one term gives the
name of the other, just like an appositional genitive (§42a).

- The two terms can come in either order. If the name is second, a preposition or אֵת
  that precedes the first term is usually repeated before the second term (e.g., Gen 4:2,
  24:4. Exceptions include Gen 24:12; 1 Sam 25:19; Job 1:8). But if the name is first,
  a preposition or אֵת that precedes it is not usually repeated before the second term
  (e.g., Gen 4:8, 16:3; 1 Kgs 2:17).

- הָאָרֶץ כְּנַעַן   the land *of Canaan* (or '*Canaan*-land')
  Canaan   the land   Num 34:2

---

[102] Cf. BHRG §29.3(v); GBHS §2.4.4; GKC §131e; IBHS §12.3d.
[103] Be aware that if the first term is the measurement, some grammars classify it as an
apposition of measurement (e.g., GBHS §2.4.4).
[104] Cf. BHRG §29.3(v); GBHS §2.4.4; GKC §131e; IBHS §12.3d; JM §131f.
[105] Cf. BHRG §29.3(i); GKC §131f–g; IBHS §12.3e; JM §131h–k.

   o If the first word (e.g., הָאָרֶץ in Num 34:2) were in the construct state, then the second word (e.g., כְּנַעַן in Num 34:2) would be an appositional genitive (§42a) rather than a word in explicative apposition (§70).

●   לִשְׁלֹמֹה הַמֶּלֶךְ   to *King* Solomon
      the king to Solomon   1 Kgs 2:17

●   וְלָקַחְתָּ אִשָּׁה לִבְנִי לְיִצְחָק   You will take a wife for my son *Isaac.*
      to Isaac for my son a wife you will take   Gen 24:4

71   **Anticipative apposition.**[106] In anticipative apposition, a pronominal suffix is in apposition to and precedes its referent. The pronominal suffix is usually omitted in English translation.

●   וַתִּרְאֵהוּ אֶת־הַיֶּלֶד   She saw *the child.*
      the child she saw *him*   Exod 2:6

●   בְּבֹאוֹ הָאִישׁ   when *the man* entered
      the man when *he* to enter   Ezek 10:3

●   Other examples include 1 Kgs 21:13 and 2 Sam 24:17.

G   Hendiadys

72   **Hendiadys.**[107] The English word 'hendiadys' comes from the Greek phrase ἓν διὰ δυοῖν 'one through two,' meaning that one meaning is expressed by means of two words. English examples of hendiadys include 'assault and battery' and 'kith and kin.' In Hebrew, whenever two substantives are joined by the conjunction וְ 'and' (§430b), they are a hendiadys if the combination expresses a single concept. To translate a hendiadys from Hebrew to English, the second substantive can often be translated as an adjective that modifies the first substantive.

●   This is sometimes referred to as **nominal hendiadys** because it joins two words that are functioning as nouns, as opposed to **verbal hendiadys**, which is referred to as verbal coordination (§224) in this grammar.

●   הַרְבָּה אַרְבֶּה עִצְּבוֹנֵךְ וְהֵרֹנֵךְ
      and your pregnancy *your pain* I will multiply to multiply   Gen 3:16
                                I will greatly multiply your *labour pain.*

   o Gen 3:16 states that her labour pain will increase, not that her pain will increase and that she will also become pregnant more often!

---

[106] Cf. BHRG §29.3(vii); GKC §131k–o; IBHS §12.4; JM §146d; Rooker 1990, 91–3.

[107] Cf. GBHS §4.3.3(g); IBHS §4.4.1b, 4.6.1, 32.3b, 39.2.5; Avishur 1971–2; Van der Westhuizen 1978.

- חָמָס   וָשֹׁד   *devastating violence*
  and devastation   violence   Jer 6:7, 20:8; Ezek 45:9; Amos 3:10

- חֹשֶׁךְ   וְצַלְמָוֶת   *blackest darkness*
  and deep shadow   darkness   Job 10:21

- תֹּהוּ   וָבֹהוּ   *a formless void*
  and emptiness   formlessness   Gen 1:2

- Other possible examples include חֶסֶד וֶאֱמֶת 'loyalty and truth' ('true loyalty'?) in
  Exod 34:6; Josh 2:14; 2 Sam 2:6, 15:20; Prov 16:6; נִין וָנֶכֶד 'offspring and progeny'
  in Gen 21:23; Isa 14:22; Job 18:19; הַבְּרִית וְהַחֶסֶד 'covenant and loyalty'
  ('covenant loyalty'?) in Deut 7:9, 12; 1 Kgs 8:23; Neh 9:32; הוֹד וְהָדָר 'majesty and
  splendour' ('majestic splendour'?) in Job 40:10; and דְּמָמָה וָקוֹל 'whisper and
  voice' ('a whispering voice'?) in Job 4:16.

H   Adjectives [108]

73   **Attributive adjective.**[109] An attributive adjective modifies a substantive,
for example, 'big' in 'a big book'). In Hebrew, an attributive adjective
follows the substantive that it modifies and has the same gender, number,
and definiteness as the substantive. There are some exceptions to this rule
of concord, as discussed in the examples below.

- In Hebrew, a participle can function as an attributive adjective, for example, Job 4:4.

- אֱלֹהִים   אֲחֵרִים   *other* gods
  other   gods   Deut 8:19

- בִּתִּי   הַגְּדוֹלָה   my *older* daughter
  the older   my daughter   1 Sam 18:17

- בִּרְכַּיִם   כֹּרְעוֹת   *tottering* knees
  tottering   two knees   Job 4:4

  o   The noun בִּרְכַּיִם 'two knees' is dual, but כֹּרְעוֹת 'tottering' (a participle that is
      functioning as an attributive adjective) is plural because participles (like
      adjectives) lack a dual form; they use the plural form when modifying a dual
      noun.[110]

- אֱלֹהִים   חַי   the *living* God
  living   God   2 Kgs 19:4

  o   In 2 Kgs 19:4, the noun אֱלֹהִים is a plural of respect (§8), so it is plural in form
      but singular in meaning. The adjective חַי 'living' is singular. This is an example

---

[108] Cf. BHRG §30; GBHS §2.5; GKC §132–3; IBHS §14, 17; JM §141, 148.
[109] Cf. BHRG §30.2; GBHS §2.5.1; GKC §132a; IBHS §14.3.1; JM §141b, 148a, c, d.
[110] Cf. BHRG §30.1.1; GKC §132f; IBHS §14.2b; JM §148a.

of *constructio ad sensum*, meaning that the sentence is written according to its logic (אֱלֹהִים refers to an individual) rather than according to its form (אֱלֹהִים is grammatically plural). A similar example is Isa 19:4 (אֲדֹנִים קָשֶׁה 'a harsh master'). Contrast this, however, with אֱלֹהִים חַיִּים 'the living God' in 1 Sam 17:26, where a plural adjective is used; thus *constructio ad sensum* is not always followed.[111]

- גַּל־אֲבָנִים גָּדוֹל   a *great* heap of stones
  great stones heap of   Josh 7:26

  o Because an adjective cannot break up a construct chain by coming between a word in the construct state and its genitive (§30), an adjective that modifies a word in the construct state must follow the entire construct chain.[112]

- קְנֵה הַטּוֹב   the *sweet* cane
  the good reed   Jer 6:20

  o In Jer 6:20, a definite attributive adjective modifies an indefinite substantive. Other examples include 1 Sam 12:23; 1 Kgs 7:12; Ezek 40:28.[113]

74a   Demonstrative adjective.[114] A demonstrative adjective (for example, זֹאת 'this' or הוּא 'that;' §117a) comes after both the substantive that it modifies and any attributive adjectives that modify the substantive.[115] A demonstrative adjective exhibits concord of gender, number, and definiteness.

- הַמִּשְׁפָּחָה הָרָעָה הַזֹּאת   *this* wicked clan
  the this the wicked   the clan   Jer 8:3

- בַּיָּמִים הָרַבִּים הָהֵם   within *those* many days
  the those the many   in the days   Exod 2:23

- בַּלַּיְלָה הוּא   on *that* night
  that   in the night   Gen 19:33, 30:16, 32:23; 1 Sam 19:10

  o In the phrase בַּלַּיְלָה הוּא, one might expect the demonstrative הוּא to also have the article (and be spelled הַהוּא) because the noun is definite.

74b   Demonstrative pronoun in attributive apposition.[116] When a demonstrative modifies a substantive that has a pronominal suffix, the

---

[111] Cf. BHRG §30.2.2(iv); GKC §132g–h; IBHS §14.2c; JM §148a; Revell 2002.
[112] Cf. BHRG §30.2.3(iii); GKC §132a; JM §139a.
[113] Cf. IBHS §14.3.1d; JM §138c.
[114] Cf. BHRG §36.2.2(ii), 36.2.3; IBHS §17.4.1; JM §143h–i, 149d.
[115] Exceptions to this include Jer 13:10 and 2 Chr 1:10, where a demonstrative adjective precedes the attributive adjective.
[116] Cf. IBHS §17.4.1; JM §138f.

demonstrative usually lacks the article.[117] Because of the lack of concord,
the demonstrative is a demonstrative pronoun in attributive apposition
(§66, 117b) rather than a demonstrative adjective (§74a).

- An alternate analysis that removes the need for this category is to consider a
  demonstrative to be intrinsically definite and thus still in concord with the noun.

- זֶה   בְּכֹחֲךָ   לֵךְ   Go in *this* strength of yours.
  this in your strength go!   Judg 6:14

  o In Judg 6:14, the demonstrative זֶה 'this' lacks the article. It modifies the noun
     כֹחֲךָ 'your strength,' which is definite because of the pronominal suffix.

- Other examples of this include Gen 24:8; Deut 5:29; Josh 2:20; 2 Kgs 1:13.

75 Predicate adjective.[118] Whereas an attributive adjective (§73) modifies a
substantive, a predicate adjective asserts something about it (§563).
Furthermore, a predicate adjective asserts something about the subject of
the clause, whereas an attributive adjective can modify any substantive.[119]

- A predicate adjective usually has the same gender and number as the subject, but it
  normally lacks the article.
- A predicate adjective may be used with a copulative verb (e.g., הָיָה 'he was'). A
  predicate adjective may also occur in a verbless clause (§561, 563).
- In a verbless clause, a predicate adjective normally precedes the subject (§579). In a
  concomitant circumstantial clause (§494) or a subordinate clause, however, a
  predicate adjective normally follows the subject.

- הָאָדָם   רָעַת   רַבָּה   The wickedness of mankind was *great*.
  the mankind wickedness of *great*   Gen 6:5

  o As expected, the predicate adjective רַבָּה has the same gender and number as
     the subject רָעַת הָאָדָם, it precedes the subject, and it lacks the article.

- רַחֲמָיו   רַבִּים   His mercy is *great*.
  his mercy   *great*   1 Chr 21:13

- כִּי   הַמָּקוֹם   קָדֹשׁ   because the place is *holy*
  holy   the place   because   Ezek 42:13

  o The conjunction כִּי in Ezek 42:13 makes the clause that follows it a subordinate
     clause. As a result, the predicate adjective follows the subject.

---

[117] On rare occasions (e.g., Josh 2:17 and 2 Chr 1:10), a noun with a pronominal suffix is
followed by a demonstrative with the article. In such cases, the demonstrative is
considered to be a demonstrative adjective (§74a) rather than a demonstrative pronoun in
attributive apposition (§74b).
[118] Cf. BHRG §30.3; GBHS §2.5.2, 5.1.1(b); IBHS §4.5c, 13.8c, 14.3.2; JM §148b.
[119] If an adjective asserts something about a word other than the subject of the clause, it is
categorized as a predicate accusative (§57b) rather than as a predicate adjective.

- יָשָׁר   מִשְׁפָּטֶיךָ   Your judgments are *upright*.

  your judgments *upright*   Ps 119:137

  - o The subject מִשְׁפָּטֶיךָ 'your judgments' is plural, whereas the predicate adjective יָשָׁר 'upright' is singular. This lack of concord is unusual and suggests the judgments are being considered as a set rather than as multiple individuals.

Comparative

76 Comparative adjectives.[120] To indicate comparison, English often uses a comparative form of an adjective (e.g., 'greater' instead of 'great') or puts 'more' before the adjective (e.g., 'more excellent'). Hebrew, however, has no comparative forms of adjectives. Instead, Hebrew expresses comparison by using a normal form of an adjective (e.g., רַב 'great') and the preposition מִן 'than' (or its prefix form מִ) before the thing to which comparison is made. The comparison can be relative (e.g., 'taller than …' §317) or absolute ('too tall to …' §318).

- גָּבֹהַּ   מִכָּל־   הָעָם   He was *taller than* all the people.

  the people *than* all of *tall*   1 Sam 9:2

- כִּי־   הָיָה   רְכוּשָׁם   רַב   מִשֶּׁבֶת   יַחְדָּו   •

  together *than* to dwell *great* their property it was because   Gen 36:7

                Their possessions were *too great for* [them] to live together.

Superlative

- To indicate a superlative, English often uses the superlative form of an adjective (e.g., 'greatest' instead of 'great') or puts 'most' before the adjective (e.g., 'most excellent'). Hebrew, however, has no superlative forms of adjectives. Instead, Hebrew expresses the superlative in a variety of ways as discussed in §77–81.[121]

77a Attributive adjective with the article as superlative.[122] An attributive adjective that has the article may be superlative (§93). Recall, however, that an attributive adjective will have an article if it modifies a definite noun (§73), so whether a particular adjective with the article is superlative or not must be decided based on context.

---

[120] Cf. BHRG §30.5.1, 39.14.8; GBHS §2.5.4(a), 4.1.13(h); GKC §119w, 131a–f, 133c; IBHS §11.2.11e, 14.4, 24.2h; JM §141g–i; Blake 1915, 200.

[121] Cf. BHRG §30.5.2; GBHS §2.5.4(b); GKC §133g–l; IBHS §14.5; JM §141j–n.

[122] Cf. BHRG §24.4.3(iii), 30.5.2(ii)a; GBHS §2.5.4(b); GKC §133g; IBHS §14.5c; JM §141j; Blake 1915, 200–1.

- בְּנוֹ הַקָּטָן   his *youngest* son
  the young his son   Gen 9:24

77b **Predicate adjective with the article as superlative.**[123] A predicate adjective normally lacks the article (§75), so if it has the article it is likely to be superlative (§93).

- אַתֶּם הַמְעַט מִכָּל־הָעַמִּים   You are *the least* of all the peoples.
  the peoples from all of *the little* you   Deut 7:7

78 **Adjective in construct as superlative.**[124] An adjective in construct to a substantive that is definite may be superlative.

- קְטֹן בָּנָיו   *the youngest* of his sons
  his sons *young of*   2 Chr 21:17

79 **Adjective with a pronominal suffix as superlative.**[125] An adjective with a pronominal suffix may be superlative.

- טוֹבָם כְּחֵדֶק   *The best of them* is like a briar.
  like briar *good of them*   Mic 7:4

- מִקְּטַנָּם וְעַד־גְּדוֹלָם   from *the least of them* to *the greatest of them*
  great of them and unto from small of them   Jer 6:13

80 **Superlative genitive.** As discussed in §47, a superlative genitive combines with its construct term to mean the greatest of something. A superlative genitive is always plural. The construct term is usually singular and often of the same root as the genitive.

- עֶבֶד עֲבָדִים   an *abject* slave
  servants servant of   Gen 9:25

- הֲבֵל הֲבָלִים   *utter* futility
  futilities futility of   Eccl 1:2

81 **Divine epithet as a superlative.**[126] When a name or title for God is used to describe an item, it may function as a superlative. Examples include אַרְזֵי־אֵל '*highest* cedars' (Ps 80:11), חֶרְדַּת אֱלֹהִים 'a *terrible* panic' (1 Sam 14:15), and חִתַּת אֱלֹהִים 'a *great* terror' (Gen 35:5).

---

[123] Cf. BHRG §24.4.3(iii), 30.5.2(ii)a; IBHS §13.5.2d; JM §137l, 141j; Blake 1915, 200–1, 203. In Deut 7:7, the superlative is also suggested by מִכָּל; cf. BHRG §30.5.2(ii)e.

[124] Cf. BHRG §30.5.2(ii)b, d; GBHS §2.5.4(b); GKC §133g–i; IBHS §14.3.3b, 14.5c; JM §141e.

[125] Cf. BHRG §30.5.2(ii)b; GBHS §2.5.4(b); IBHS §14.5c, e; JM §141j.

[126] Cf. BHRG §30.5.2(i)d; GBHS §2.2.13 note 19; IBHS §9.5.3j note 33, 14.5b; JM §141n; Brin 1992; Thomas 1953; Thomas 1968; Smith 1929; Kelso 1903.

I The Article[127]

82a **The article**

- English has two articles, the definite article ('the') and the indefinite article ('a' or 'an'). Hebrew has only one, which corresponds roughly to the English definite article. Because Hebrew has only one article, it is referred to as 'the article' rather than as 'the definite article.'
- A word that has the article is **articular** (e.g., הָעִיר 'the city').
- A word without the article is **anarthrous** (e.g., עִיר 'a city').
- A word that refers to a particular thing is **definite**. In general, a word is definite if it is a proper noun (e.g., יְרוּשָׁלַם 'Jerusalem'), has a pronominal suffix (e.g., עִירוֹ 'his city'), has the article (e.g., הָעִיר 'the city'), or is in a construct chain where the last word in the chain is definite (e.g., עִיר דָּוִד 'the city of David').[128]
- A word that does not refer to a particular thing is **indefinite**. A word is indefinite if it is not a proper noun, does not have a pronominal suffix, and does not have the article (e.g., עִיר 'a city').

82b **A word in the construct state normally lacks the article**. See §29a.

82c **A word with a pronominal suffix normally lacks the article**.[129] The reason for this is that a pronominal suffix makes a word definite, so an article is not needed. For example, הָעִיר ('the city') and עִירוֹ ('his city') both occur, but הָעִירוֹ ('the his city') does not.

- On rare occasions (e.g., Lev 27:23; Num 32:6; Josh 7:21, 8:33; 2 Kgs 15:16; Mic 2:12) a word does have both a pronominal suffix and the article.
- This rule does not apply to a participle that begins a relative clause (§82d).

82d **A participle that begins a relative clause often has the article**, even if the participle has a pronominal suffix. See §90 for more information. This is an exception to the rule in §82c.

- מָן   הַמַּאֲכִלְךָ   who fed you manna
  manna *the* one feeding you   Deut 8:16
  - הַמַּאֲכִלְךָ 'the one feeding you' is a participle with both the article (הַ 'the') and a pronominal suffix, ךָ 'you.' The presence of both the article and a

---

[127] Cf. BHRG §24.4; GBHS §2.6; GKC §126; IBHS §13.2–13.3, 13.5–13.7; JM §35, 137; Barr 1989.

[128] This is a simplification. Cf. BHRG §24.4; GKC §125–7; IBHS §13.4; JM §137–40.

[129] Cf. GKC §127i; IBHS §13.6b; JM §140c.

pronominal suffix would be atypical on a noun or adjective, but both often occur together on a participle that begins a relative clause, as in Deut 8:16.

82e   **The article is rare in poetry**[130] because poetry tends to be somewhat archaic in its language and therefore reflects the language of the period before the development of the article.

- קֹנֵה שָׁמַיִם וָאָרֶץ   the creator of sky and earth
  and earth heavens creator of   Gen 14:19

  o   'Heavens and earth' is normally written with the article before each noun (e.g., הַשָּׁמַיִם וְהָאָרֶץ 'the heavens and the earth' in Gen 2:1). But the articles are missing in Gen 14:19 because the passage is in archaic poetic style.

83   **Anaphoric article.**[131] An article may be used to indicate that the word to which it is attached is the one mentioned previously. This 'pointing back' use is sometimes subsumed under a broader category of the **referential use of the article**.

- וַיֹּאמֶר הַמֶּלֶךְ קְחוּ לִי־ חָרֶב וַיָּבִאוּ הַחֶרֶב לִפְנֵי הַמֶּלֶךְ
  the king before the sword they brought sword to me bring! the king said
      The king said, 'Fetch me a sword,' so they brought a sword to the king. 1 Kgs 3:24

  o   The first time that חֶרֶב 'sword' is mentioned in 1 Kgs 3:24, it is anarthrous because the king is requesting any sword, not a particular one. The second time that חֶרֶב 'sword' is mentioned, it is articular (הַחֶרֶב 'the sword') because it has been previously mentioned. In English, however, we typically translate it as 'a sword' both times.

- Another example is Gen 18:7–8 (בֶּן־בָּקָר in 18:7 and בֶּן־הַבָּקָר in 18:8).

84   **Article on something that is definite in the mind of the narrator.**[132] Sometimes the article is used on something that is definite in the mind of the narrator, but that might be considered indefinite in English and translated accordingly. This category is very subjective and debatable.

- בַּסֵּפֶר   on a scroll
  in the scroll   1 Sam 10:25

- וַיְהִי הַיּוֹם   one day
  the day happened   2 Kgs 4:8

---

[130] Cf. GBHS §2.6; GKC §2s, 126h; IBHS §13.7; JM §137f note 4; JM93 §137f note 1; Andersen and Forbes 1983; Barr 1989, 310–12.

[131] Cf. BHRG §24.4.4(ii)b; GBHS §2.6.1; IBHS §13.5.1d; JM §137f.

[132] Cf. GKC §126q–t; IBHS §13.5.1e; Ehrensvärd 1999, 68–76. The discussion in JM §137m–o is relevant, but analyses the phenomenon differently. Barr 1989, 312–16, questions the consistency of this category.

- וַיֵּשֶׁב עַל־הַבְּאֵר

  the well by he sat down

  He sat down by *a* well.

  Exod 2:15

85 **Article on a well-known substantive.**[133] If a person or thing was expected to be a well known or recognized fact, it might have the article. This is sometimes subsumed under a category of the **referential use of the article**. Applying this category to an example can be very debatable.

- וְדָוִד יוֹשֵׁב בֵּין־ שְׁנֵי הַשְּׁעָרִים

  the gates two of between sitting and David

  David was sitting between *the* two gates

  2 Sam 18:24

  - Three other possible examples are found in Gen 22:6, where the original readers might expect a sacrifice to require wood, fire, and a knife.

86 **Possessive article.**[134] Sometimes the article is used instead of a possessive pronominal suffix (§111) and is best translated into English as a personal possessive pronoun (e.g., 'his').

- וַתִּקַּח הַצָּעִיף

  the veil she took

  She took *her* veil.

  Gen 24:65

- וְלָקַח דָּוִד אֶת־הַכִּנּוֹר וְנִגֵּן

  and play *the* lyre David would take

  David would take *his* lyre and play [it].

  1 Sam 16:23

87 **Demonstrative article.**[135] Sometimes the article points to a particular item as a demonstrative pronoun does (§113). Examples include הַיּוֹם 'the day' ('this day' or 'today' in 1 Sam 24:19 and elsewhere) and הַפַּעַם 'the time' ('this time' in Gen 2:23 and elsewhere).

88 **Distinctive article.**[136] Sometimes the article points to an item that is unique in its class, such that with an article, the class noun becomes a name or title that can only apply to one individual. This is also called the **naming use of the article** or the **solitary use of the article**. Determining that a given example of the article fits in this category can be quite debatable.

- הַנָּהָר

  the river

  the Euphrates

  Gen 31:21

  - There are many rivers, but in the Hebrew Bible, הַנָּהָר 'the river' usually denotes the Euphrates.

---

[133] Cf. BHRG §24.4.4(ii)a, e; GBHS §2.6.1; GKC §126d; IBHS §13.5.1c.

[134] Cf. GBHS §2.6.7; IBHS §13.5.1e; JM §137f.

[135] Cf. BHRG §24.4.4(i); GBHS §2.6.6; GKC §126a–b; IBHS §13.5.2b; JM §137f.

[136] Cf. BHRG §24.4.4(ii)e; GBHS §2.6.3, 2.6.4; GKC §126d; IBHS §13.6a; JM §137h.

- יְהוָה הוּא הָאֱלֹהִים   YHWH is God!
  the God   he   YHWH   1 Kgs 18:39

  o The word אֱלֹהִים occurs more than 2600 times in the Hebrew Bible. It has the
     article approximately 370 times. The reason for the article is often unclear. But
     in 1 Kgs 18:39 (at the end of the contest on Mount Carmel, when Baal did not
     answer but YHWH answered with fire), it is possible that the article presents the
     people as exclaiming that YHWH is THE God, the only God who matters, in
     contrast with Baal, who is not.

89 Vocative article.[137] Sometimes the article is prefixed to a person's name
or title in direct speech to that person, and can often be translated 'O.'

- הוֹשִׁיעָה אֲדֹנִי הַמֶּלֶךְ   Help, my lord, *O* king!
  the king my lord Help!   2 Kgs 6:26

90 Article on a participle that begins a relative clause.[138] The article is
usually prefixed to a participle that begins (or can be translated as) a
relative clause (§218, 539a).

- יְהוָה הַנִּרְאֶה אֵלָיו   YHWH, *who* had appeared to him
  to him the appearing YHWH   Gen 12:7

- וְאֶל־ מֶלֶךְ יְהוּדָה הַשֹּׁלֵחַ אֶתְכֶם   but to the king of Judah *who* sent you
  you the sending of Judah king but to   2 Kgs 22:18

91 Article on a perfect verb that begins a relative clause.[139] Sometimes the
article is prefixed to a verb with perfect aspect (i.e., the suffixed
conjugation; §161–6) and can be translated as a relative pronoun.

- וְכֹל הַהִקְדִּישׁ שְׁמוּאֵל   and all *that* Samuel had dedicated
  Samuel *the* (he) dedicated and all   1 Chr 26:28

- הֶהָלְכוּא אִתּוֹ   *who* had accompanied him
  with him *the* (they) went   Josh 10:24

---

[137] Cf. BHRG §24.4.3(i); GBHS §2.6.2; GKC §126d–f; IBHS §13.5.2c; JM §137g; Barr
1989, 319–22.
[138] Cf. BHRG §24.4.3(ii)b, 36.3.4; GBHS §5.2.13a; GKC §138i–k; IBHS §13.5.2d,
19.7b, 37.5; JM §145d, e; Barr 1989, 322–5; Holmstedt 2002, 83–90. IBHS §19.7b
argues that 'it is misleading to consider the article as a dependent relative marker with a
participle' because a participle can function as a relative clause even without the article.
[139] Cf. BHRG §24.4.3(ii)a, 36.3.4; GKC §138i–k; IBHS §19.7c–d; JM §145d–e;
Holmstedt 2002, 83–90. IBHS §19.7d and JM §145e state that it is unlikely that the
article was used on perfect verbs in early texts and suggest that examples in early books
should be repointed as participles.

92 **Generic article.**[140] Sometimes the article is used on a word that refers to a class rather than to an individual. This use of the article is particularly common in comparisons.

- הַכְּנַעֲנִי

  the Canaanite

  the Canaanites

  Judg 1:1

- אֶת־הַצַּדִּיק וְאֶת־הָרָשָׁע יִשְׁפֹּט הָאֱלֹהִים

  God will judge and *the* wicked *the* righteous

  God will judge *the* righteous and *the* wicked.

  Eccl 3:17

- כַּאֲשֶׁר יָלֹק הַכֶּלֶב

  the dog laps as

  as *a* dog laps (or 'as dogs lap')

  Judg 7:5

- אֲדֻמִּים כַּדָּם

  as (*the*) blood red

  red as blood

  2 Kgs 3:22

- The generic article is also used in 2 Kgs 5:27; 1 Sam 9:9, 17:34; Amos 5:19.

93 **Article on an adjective to indicate the superlative.** See §77a–b.

- כִּי־ אַתֶּם הַמְעַט מִכָּל־ הָעַמִּים

  the peoples from all of *the* little you because

  For you are *the least* of all the nations.

  Deut 7:7

- וּרְאִיתֶם הַטּוֹב וְהַיָּשָׁר מִבְּנֵי אֲדֹנֵיכֶם

  your masters from sons of and *the* upright *the* good (you) pick!

  Pick *the best* and *the most upright* of your master's sons.

  2 Kgs 10:3

J Numerals [141]

Cardinal numerals [142]

94 **One.**[143] The number אֶחָד 'one' is an attributive adjective. As an attributive adjective, it agrees in gender, number, and definiteness with the noun that it modifies (§73). Occasionally, however, אֶחָד 'one' lacks the article even when its substantive is determined (e.g., 1 Sam 13:17, below).

- אִישׁ אֶחָד

  one man

  one man

  Judg 18:19

- אִשָּׁה אַחַת

  one woman

  a *certain* woman

  2 Kgs 4:1

---

[140] Cf. BHRG §24.4.4(ii)d; GBHS §2.6.5; GKC §126l–p; IBHS §13.5.1f; JM §137c, i; Barr 1989, 316–19.

[141] Cf. BHRG §37; GBHS §2.7; GKC §97–8, 134; IBHS §15; JM §100–1, 142.

[142] Cf. BHRG §37.2; GBHS §2.7.1; GKC §97, 134; IBHS §15.2; JM §100, 142a–n.

[143] Cf. BHRG §37.2.2(i); GKC §97a; IBHS §13.8a, 15.2.1a–g, 15.2.6; JM §100b, 137u–v, 142b–ba, m.

- הַמַּחֲנֶה הָאַחַת
  the *one*   the camp

  the *one* camp
  Gen 32:9

- הָרֹאשׁ   אֶחָד
  one   the military unit (lit. 'head')

  the *one* military unit
  1 Sam 13:17

95a   Two.[144]

- Whereas 'one' is an adjective (§94), 'two' is a noun. Despite being a noun, the number two has separate masculine and feminine forms, and agrees in gender with whatever it counts.
- As expected, 'two' is dual. The object counted is either dual or plural, so 'two' agrees in number with whatever it counts.
- 'Two' can be used in the construct state, followed by an enumerated genitive (§40b).
- 'Two' can be in the absolute state, used in apposition. If 'two' comes first, then the thing counted is an apposition of material (§68), whereas if 'two' comes second, then it is an apposition of number (§69b).

- שְׁנֵי אֲנָשִׁים
  men   *two of*

  two men
  2 Sam 4:2 (enumerated genitive)

- שְׁתֵּי נָשִׁים
  women   *two of*

  two women
  1 Chr 4:5 (enumerated genitive)

95b   Three through ten.[145]

- The numbers 'three' through 'ten' are nouns with masculine and feminine forms. They are spelled in such a way that they look like they are of the opposite gender of what they count. In other words, when counting a masculine noun, the number is spelled with a 'feminine' suffix (הָ◌ or תָ◌), whereas when counting a feminine noun, the number is spelled without a suffix (as is typical for the spelling of masculine words). This is sometimes called **chiastic concord.**[146]

---

[144] Cf. BHRG §37.2.2(ii); GKC §134a e; IBHS §15.2.1h–j; JM §100c, 142c, l; Weitzman 1996.

[145] Cf. BHRG §37.2.2(iii); GKC §97a–b, 134a–e; IBHS §15.2.2, 15.2.6; JM §100d, 142d, l; Weitzman 1996.

[146] Be aware that this phenomenon can be described in two ways. If numbers with feminine endings are parsed as feminine, then the numbers have the opposite gender of what they count. Alternately, if numbers with feminine endings are parsed as masculine, then the numbers have the same gender as what they count. JM §100d takes the former approach, whereas the Groves-Wheeler Westminster Morphology and Lemma Database (commonly used in Bible software) takes the latter approach.

- The numbers 'three' through 'ten' are singular because the masculine plural forms of numbers 'three' through 'nine' are used for the numbers 'thirty' through 'ninety,' and the masculine plural of 'ten' is used for the number 'twenty.'
- Like 'two,' the numbers 'three' through 'ten' can be used in the construct state, followed by an enumerated genitive (§40b), or they can be in the absolute state, used in apposition (§68 or §69b).

חֲמֵשֶׁת מַלְכֵי מִדְיָן Midian kings of *five of*	the *five* kings of Midian Num 31:8 (enumerated genitive)

  o Notice that מַלְכֵי 'kings' is masculine, whereas (because of chiastic concord) the number חֲמֵשֶׁת 'five' is spelled with a feminine ending (תֹ).

וַחֲמִשָּׁה אֲנָשִׁים men and *five*	and *five* men 2 Kgs 25:19 (apposition of material)

וַחֲמֵשׁ מֵאוֹת hundreds and *five of*	and *five* hundred Job 1:3 (enumerated genitive)

וְחָמֵשׁ נַעֲרֹתֶיהָ her young women and *five*	and her *five* female servants 1 Sam 25:42 (apposition of material)

אַמּוֹת חָמֵשׁ *five* cubits	*five* cubits 2 Chr 3:11 (apposition of number)

שִׁבְעָה בָנִים וְשָׁלוֹשׁ בָּנוֹת daughters and *three* sons *seven*	*seven* sons and *three* daughters Job 1:2 (apposition of material)

- Exceptions to chiastic concord include Gen 7:13; 1 Sam 10:3; Job 1:4.

6a   Eleven through nineteen.[147]
- The cardinal numbers 'eleven' through 'nineteen' are nouns.
- These numbers normally are in the absolute state and precede what they count as an apposition of material (§68). Occasionally, however, the number follows what it counts (with both words in the absolute state), in which case the number is an apposition of number (§69b).
- The numbers 'eleven' through 'nineteen' are constructed with the number עֶשֶׂר 'ten' and a number between 'one' and 'nine' for the units digit. The number עֶשֶׂר 'ten' is singular and agrees in gender with what it counts. The units digit is also singular, except for 'two,' which is dual. For the numbers 'eleven' and 'twelve,' the units digit ('one' and 'two') has the same gender as what it counts, as expected (§94–5). And, as expected, for the numbers 'thirteen' through 'nineteen,' the

---

[147] Cf. BHRG §37.2.2(iv); GKC §97d–e, 134f; IBHS §15.2.3, 15.2.6; JM §100e–h, 142e, l; Weitzman 1996, 177–85.

units digit ('three' through 'nine') follows the rule of **chiastic concord** that is discussed in §95a.

- The item counted is usually plural. A few common words, however, are generally in the singular when they follow the number, although they too are plural when they precede the number. The words that are singular when they follow the number include אִישׁ 'man,' נֶפֶשׁ 'soul,' שֶׁקֶל 'shekel,' שָׁנָה 'year,' and יוֹם 'day.' The words כֹּר 'kor' and אֶלֶף 'military unit' are also often used in the singular.
- When the article is used, it may be attached either to the number or to the thing counted.

שְׁנֵים־עָשָׂר נְשִׂיאִם	*twelve* princes
princes *ten two*	Gen 17:20 (apposition of material)
חֲמִשָּׁה עָשָׂר בָּנִים	*fifteen* sons
sons *ten five*	2 Sam 9:10 (apposition of material)
שְׁנֵים הֶעָשָׂר אִישׁ	the *twelve* men
man the *ten two*	Josh 4:4 (apposition of material)

96b Multiples of ten.[148]

- Multiples of ten (e.g., twenty, fifty, eighty) are nouns.
- The gender and number of these words are invariant; they do not exhibit concord with the thing counted.
- The number עֶשְׂרִים 'twenty' is the masculine plural form of 'ten' עֶשֶׂר.
- Multiples of ten between שְׁלֹשִׁים 'thirty' and תִּשְׁעִים 'ninety' are the masculine plural forms of the numbers שָׁלֹשׁ 'three' through תֵּשַׁע 'nine.'
- The number מֵאָה 'one hundred' is feminine singular.
- The number אֶלֶף 'one thousand' is masculine singular.
- The item counted is usually plural except for a few common words that are used in the singular when they follow the number (§96a).
- When the article is used, it may be attached either to the number or to the thing counted.

אַרְבָּעִים בָּנִים	*forty* sons
sons *forty*	Judg 12:14 (apposition of material)
חֲמִשִּׁים שֶׁקֶל כֶּסֶף	*fifty* shekels of silver
silver shekels *fifty*	Lev 27:3 (apposition of material)

---

[148] Cf. BHRG §37.2.2(v); GKC §97f–g, 134g; IBHS §15.2.4–15.2.6; JM §100i, k–l, 142f–g, i–j.

- כֶּסֶף־שְׁקָלִים אַרְבָּעִים
  forty   shekels silver

  forty shekels of silver
  Neh 5:15 (apposition of number)

- אֶלֶף וּמֵאָה הַכֶּסֶף
  the silver and *hundred thousand*

  the *eleven hundred* (shekels of) silver
  Judg 17:2 (apposition of material)

97 Multiples of ten plus units.[149]
- Cardinal numbers that are a multiple of ten plus units (e.g., thirty-two, eighty-five, twenty-one) may have the enumerated object (in the singular) after the number in the apposition of material (§68). Alternately, they may have the number after the enumerated object (in the plural) in the apposition of number (§69b).
- The article may be prefixed to the number or to the enumerated object.

- שְׁתַּיִם וְשִׁשִּׁים שָׁנָה
  year and *sixty two*

  sixty-two years
  Gen 5:20 (apposition of material)

- וְאַחֲרֵי הַשָּׁבֻעִים שִׁשִּׁים וּשְׁנַיִם
  and *two   sixty*   the weeks   and after

  after the *sixty-two* weeks
  Dan 9:26 (apposition of number)

- חָמֵשׁ שָׁנִים וְשִׁבְעִים שָׁנָה
  year and *seventy* years *five*

  seventy-five years
  Gen 12:4 (apposition of material)

  o In Gen 12:4, the thing enumerated is repeated after each digit of the number, so the syntax of the number 'five' follows the rules in §95, and the syntax for the number 'seventy' follows the rules specified in §96.

- הַשְּׁלֹשָׁה וְהַשִּׁבְעִים וְהַמָּאתָיִם
  and the *two hundred*   and the *seventy*   the *three*

  the *two hundred and seventy-three*
  Num 3:46

Ordinal numerals [150]

8a First through tenth.[151] The ordinal numbers 'first' through 'tenth' are adjectives. They are normally used as attributive adjectives, so they follow the numbered item and match it in gender, number, and definiteness (§73). Occasionally, however, they occur as appositional genitive adjectives (§42b) after the construct state of the numbered item.

- בַּשָּׁנָה הַשֵּׁנִית
  the *second* in the year

  in the *second* year
  Gen 47:18

- יוֹם הַשְּׁבִיעִי
  the *seventh* day of

  the *seventh* day
  Deut 5:14

---

[149] Cf. BHRG §37.2.2(v); GKC §97f, 134h–i; IBHS §15.2.4, 15.2.6; JM §100j, m, 142h, k–l.

[150] Cf. BHRG §37.3; GBHS §2.7.2; GKC §98, 134o–p; IBHS §15.3; JM §101, 142o.

[151] Cf. BHRG §37.3.2; GKC §98, 134p; IBHS §15.3; JM §101, 142o.

98b **First through tenth using cardinal numbers.**[152] Although the Hebrew ordinal numbers (§98a) are normally used for 'first' through 'tenth,' the Hebrew cardinal numbers (§94–5) are occasionally used for that purpose.

- בִּשְׁנַת שְׁתַּיִם   in the *second* year
  two   in year of   2 Kgs 15:32

- שֵׁם הָאֶחָד בַּעֲנָה   The name of the *first* was Baanah.
  Baanah the *one* name of   2 Sam 4:2

99 **Eleventh and higher.**[153] Unlike for 'first' through 'tenth,' Hebrew does not have any distinct words for higher ordinal numbers. Instead, it uses the cardinal numbers (§96–7) for the ordinal numbers 'eleventh' and higher.

- The enumerated object typically lacks the article. When the expression is definite, the article is usually attached to the highest digit of the number, although it is occasionally attached to the lowest digit instead or omitted altogether.

- וְהוּא בִּשְׁנַיִם הֶעָשָׂר   he being with the *twelfth*
  the *ten* with *two* and he   1 Kgs 19:19 (article with the highest digit)

- הַשְּׁנַיִם עָשָׂר   the *twelfth*
  ten the *two*   1 Chr 25:19 (article with the lowest digit)

- בְּשִׁבְעָה עָשָׂר יוֹם   on the *seventeenth* day
  day *ten* in *seven*   Gen 7:11 (no article)

- בִּשְׁנַת עֶשְׂרִים וָשֶׁבַע   in the *twenty-seventh* year
  and *seven* *twenty* in year of   1 Kgs 16:10 (no article)

K Distribution [154]

- The concept of distribution is expressed in English by such words as 'every,' 'each,' and 'by' (as in 'room by room' or 'by hundreds'). Hebrew expresses the same concepts through a variety of means described in §100–5.

100 **Distributive repetition.** See §15.

- שְׁנַיִם שְׁנַיִם   two *by* two
  two   two   Gen 7:9, 15

- בַּבֹּקֶר בַּבֹּקֶר   *every* morning
  in the morning   in the morning   Exod 30:7

---

[152] Cf. GBHS §2.7.1(e); GKC §134p; JM §142o.
[153] Cf. GKC §123c, 134o; IBHS §15.3; JM §101, 142o.
[154] Cf. GKC §123c–d, 134q; IBHS §7.2.3b, 11.2.5f, 11.2.10c, 12.5a, 15.6, 23.4b; JM §135d, 142p.

101 **Distributive repetition with** וְ.[155] Distribution can be expressed by repeating the word over which something is distributed and putting the conjunction וְ 'and' before the second occurrence (§442).

• וָדוֹר	דּוֹר	*every* generation
and generation	generation	Deut 32:7
• שֵׁשׁ וָשֵׁשׁ		six *each*
and six six		2 Sam 21:20

102 **Distributive repetition with** בְּ.[156] Distribution can be expressed by repeating the word over which something is distributed and putting the preposition בְּ 'by' before the second occurrence (§254).

• חֶדֶר בְּחָדֶר		room *by* room
by room room		1 Kgs 20:30
• כְּשָׁנָה בְּשָׁנָה		as *every* year
by year as year		2 Kgs 17:4

• Other examples of distributive repetition with בְּ include 1 Sam 1:7 and 1 Chr 12:23.

103 **Distribution with** לְ.[157] Distribution can be expressed by prefixing the preposition לְ to the word over which something is distributed (§281).

• וְלַאֲלָפִים	לְמֵאוֹת	*by* hundreds and thousands
and *according to* thousands	*according to* hundreds	1 Sam 29:2
• זִבְחֵיכֶם לַבֹּקֶר וְהָבִיאוּ		Bring in your sacrifices *every* morning!
your sacrifices *according to* morning bring in!		Amos 4:4

104 **Distribution with plural subject and singular predicate.**[158] Distribution can be expressed by using a plural subject (usually a participle) and a singular predicate, giving the meaning 'everyone who.' A plural subject with a singular predicate can have other meanings (e.g., §228, 230, 232, 233), so one must check the context to see if it indicates distribution.

• מְאֻשָּׁר וְתֹמְכֶיהָ		*Everyone who* holds to her is fortunate.
fortunate and *ones* grasping her		Prov 3:18
• מְחַלְלֶיהָ מוֹת יוּמָת		
(he) will be killed to die *ones* profaning it		Exod 31:14
	Everyone who profanes it will certainly be put to death.	

• Other examples include Gen 27:29 and Lev 17:14.

---

[155] Cf. BHRG §24.3.2(iv), 37.2.3(v)b; GKC §123c; IBHS §7.2.3b; JM §135d, 142p.
[156] Cf. BHRG §24.3.2(iv); GKC §123c; IBHS §7.2.3b, 11.2.5f, 15.6a.
[157] Cf. BHRG §37.2.3(v)c, 39.11.I.4; GBHS §4.1.10(i); GKC §123c, 134q; IBHS §7.2.3b, 11.2.10c, 15.6a–b; JM §142p.
[158] Cf. IBHS §15.6c.

105 **Distribution with כֹּל followed by an indefinite substantive.**[159] The noun כֹּל 'all' followed by an indefinite substantive has a distributive sense in some contexts.

- מָבוֹא   כָּל־בַּיִת   סֻגַּר   *Every house* is barred from entry.
  from to come in *house all of* is shut up   Isa 24:10

- Other examples include Gen 2:9 and Ruth 4:7.

L   Pronouns[160]

Independent personal pronouns[161]

106 **Independent personal pronoun as the subject of a finite verb.**[162] Because the form of a finite verb in Hebrew indicates the person, number, and gender of the subject – albeit sometimes ambiguously – the use of an independent personal pronoun to indicate the subject is often unnecessary and therefore such a pronoun is usually omitted. When an independent personal pronoun is included as the subject of a finite verb, the pronoun may serve to clarify the subject, to contrast the subject with someone else, to indicate emotion, or to focus attention on the subject.

- בּוֹ   תִּמְשָׁל־   וְאַתָּה   But *you* are the one who must master it.
  in it *(you)* must rule but *you*   Gen 4:7

  o In Gen 4:7, the finite verb תִּמְשָׁל 'you must rule' is Qal imperfect 2ms. The subject of the verb is the personal pronoun אַתָּה 'you,' which is 2ms. Strictly speaking, if the subject אַתָּה 'you' were omitted, the sentence could have the same translation into English and might seem to have the same meaning. But in this context, where YHWH has just warned Cain that sin desires to dominate him, the use of the personal pronoun serves to contrast the subject (Cain) with sin (personified as a predator). So the sense is 'Sin desires [to master] you, Cain, but *you*, you are the one who must master it.'

- A similar example is Deut 5:31.

107a **Independent personal pronoun in apposition to a pronominal suffix in genitive or accusative functions.**[163] As discussed in §36 and 50, a

---

[159] Cf. IBHS §15.6c; JM §147e.
[160] Cf. BHRG §36; GKC §32–7, 135–8; IBHS §16–19; JM §36–9, 143–7.
[161] Cf. BHRG §36.1.I; GKC §32, 135; IBHS §16; JM §39, 146.
[162] Cf. BHRG §36.1.I.2; GKC §32b, 135a–c; IBHS §16.3.1–16.3.2; JM §146a; Muraoka 1985, 47–66.
[163] Cf. GKC §135d–h; IBHS §4.4.1a, 16.3.4; JM §146d.

pronominal suffix may function as a genitive or as an accusative. An independent personal pronoun may be added in apposition to such a pronominal suffix to focus attention on the person to whom it refers.

- בָּרֲכֵנִי גַם־ אָנִי   Bless *me, even me* also!
      I   also bless *me*!   Gen 27:34

  o The independent personal pronoun אָנִי 'I' is in apposition to the accusative pronominal suffix נִי◌ 'me' on the imperative verb בָּרֲכֵנִי 'bless me!' because it is in the same clause and has the same referent (Esau) and syntactical function (direct object of the verb). It focuses attention on Esau in his plea that *he* would receive a blessing.

- מִי־ יִתֵּן מוּתִי אָנִי   If only *I myself* had died!
    I *my* to die will give who?   2 Sam 19:1

  o The phrase מִי־יִתֵּן 'who will give?' is an idiom that means 'if only' (§122). In 2 Sam 19:1, the independent personal pronoun אָנִי 'I' is in apposition to the genitive pronominal suffix י◌ 'my' on the infinitive construct מוּתִי 'my to die' (i.e., 'my dying'). It is in apposition because it is in the same clause and has the same referent (David) and syntactical function (genitive that possesses 'to die'). It focuses attention on David in his wish that *he* would have died.

- Another possible example is the words אִתָּנוּ אֲנַחְנוּ in Deut 5:3.

7b Independent personal pronoun as a nominative absolute.[164] An independent personal pronoun may function as a nominative absolute (§35). There is often a pronominal suffix in the sentence that has the same referent as the nominative absolute.

- גַם אָנֹכִי חָלִילָה לִי   Moreover, *as for me*, far be it from *me*!
  to *me* far be it from *I* moreover   1 Sam 12:23

8a Independent personal pronoun as the subject of a participle.[165] An independent personal pronoun can function as the subject of a participle. For an active participle, the subject is the one performing the action of the participle. For a passive participle, the subject is the one receiving the action of the participle. In this role, the pronoun usually functions for clarity rather than for emphasis.

- אָנֹכִי מְצַוְּךָ הַיּוֹם   *I* am commanding you today.
  the day commanding you *I*   Deut 8:1

---

[164] Cf. IBHS §4.7c; JM §146e.
[165] Cf. BHRG §36.1.I.2(i).

108b **Independent personal pronoun as the subject of a verbless clause.**[166]
An independent personal pronoun can be the subject of a clause that does
not have a verb. In this role, the pronoun usually functions for clarity
rather than for emphasis.

- אַתֶּם עַם־ קְשֵׁה־ עֹרֶף   *You* are a stiff-necked people.
  neck   hard of people *you*   Exod 33:5

Suffixed personal pronouns [167]

109 **Suffixed personal pronoun as subject.**[168] A suffixed personal pronoun
on an infinitive construct may be the subject of the infinitive.

- אֲכָלְכֶם   *your* eating
  your to eat   Gen 3:5

- בְּהִבָּרְאָם   when *they* were created
  in *their* to be created   Gen 2:4

- לְבִלְתִּי עָבְרִי   that *I* should not cross
  my to cross   not   Deut 4:21

110 **Suffixed personal pronoun as object.**[169] A suffixed personal pronoun
may be the direct object of the word to which it is attached.

- וַיַּנִּחֵהוּ ... לְעָבְדָהּ וּלְשָׁמְרָהּ   He put *him* … to cultivate *it* and to guard *it*
  and to guard *it* to serve *it*   he put *him*   Gen 2:15

- In addition to being used on a finite verb, a suffixed personal pronoun can also be
  used on an infinitive construct (e.g., לְדָרְשֵׁנִי 'to consult *me*' in Jer 37:7). It can even
  be used on a noun as the object of the verbal idea that is implied by the noun (e.g.,
  חֲמָסִי 'my wrong,' meaning 'the wrong done to me' in Gen 16:5).

111 **Suffixed personal pronoun as possessive.**[170] A suffixed personal
pronoun on a substantive may indicate the one who owns the substantive
(e.g., 'my sandal') or is in relationship with it (e.g., 'my sister'). Examples
include בְּרִיתִי ('*my* covenant' in Gen 6:18) and מַלְכֵּנוּ ('*our* king' in Ps
89:19).

---

[166] Cf. BHRG §36.1.I.2(i).
[167] Cf. BHRG §26, 36.1.II–VIII; GKC §33, 58–61, 91, 100o–p, 103, 135d–r; IBHS
§16.4; JM §39d, 61–6. 94; Slonim 1941. Rooker 1990, 78–81, argues that 3mp
pronominal suffixes are increasingly used with 3fp antecedents in late biblical Hebrew.
[168] Cf. BHRG §36.1.III.2(i); IBHS §16.4d; JM §65a.
[169] Cf. BHRG §36.1.III.2(ii); GKC §33b, 61a; IBHS §16.4f; JM §61a, 65a.
[170] Cf. BHRG §36.1.III.2(iv); GKC §33c,135m; IBHS §16.4d–e.

12 **Suffixed personal pronoun as the object of a preposition.**[171] When the object of a preposition is a pronoun, a pronominal suffix is appended to the preposition (rather than an independent personal pronoun being used).

- Pronominal suffixes that are used on nouns come in two types: 'type 1' suffixes, which are used on singular nouns (e.g., ךָ 'your'), and 'type 2' suffixes, which are used on plural nouns (e.g., ךָֽיׁ 'your'). Most prepositions use type 2 suffixes, but some use type 1; which type of suffix a preposition takes makes no difference to the meaning.

Demonstrative pronouns [172]

Demonstrative pronouns are also called **deictic pronouns**.

13 **Forward vs backward reference of a demonstrative.**[173]
- The demonstratives זֶה (ms), זֹאת (fs), and אֵלֶּה (cp) can refer to something that has already been mentioned (**anaphoric use**) or that is about to be mentioned (**cataphoric use**).
- The third-person independent personal pronouns הוּא (ms), הִיא (fs), הֵם (mp), הֵמָּה (mp), הֵן (fp), and הֵנָּה (fp), when used as demonstratives, refer only to something that has already been already mentioned (**anaphoric use**).

- אֲשֶׁר אֹמַר אֵלֶיךָ זֶה יֵלֵךְ אִתָּךְ הוּא יֵלֵךְ אִתָּךְ
   with you he will go *that* with you he will go *this* to you I say whom   Judg 7:4
   The one of whom I say to you, '*This one* shall go with you,' *that one* will go with you.

   o In Judg 7:4, זֶה 'this' and הוּא 'that' refer to the same person; זֶה 'this' is used before the person is mentioned (unless אֲשֶׁר constitutes a mention), and הוּא 'that' is used after he was already mentioned.

14 **Demonstrative as the subject of a verbless clause.**[174] This use of the demonstrative is also called **explicative**.

- זֶה הַיּוֹם   *This* is the day.
   the day *this*   Judg 4:14

- אֵלֶּה שְׁמוֹת בְּנֵי־עֵשָׂו   *These* are the names of Esau's sons.
   these names of sons of Esau   Gen 36:10

- הוּא יָם הַמֶּלַח   *That* is the Salt Sea.
   that sea the salt   Gen 14:3

---

[171] Cf. BHRG §39.1.1; GKC §33d–e, 103, 135i; IBHS §11; JM §103e–n
[172] Cf. BHRG §36.2; GKC §34, 136; IBHS §17; JM §36, 143; Allegro 1955.
[173] Cf. GKC §126a–b; IBHS §17.3d, 17.4.2e; JM §143b.
[174] Cf. BHRG §36.2.2(ii)c; IBHS §17.3b.

115 **Demonstrative as copula (is, am, are).**[175] A demonstrative (or the third-person independent personal pronoun) can function as the copulative verb 'to be.' Such a clause is sometimes called a **tripartite nominal clause**. A copulative demonstrative always comes after the subject, so it is sometimes referred to as **anaphoric**.

- אֶרֶץ מִצְרַיִם לְפָנֶיךָ הִיא
  it before you of Egypt land

  The land of Egypt *is* before you.
  Gen 47:6

- אֲנִי־הוּא הַמְדַבֵּר
  the one speaking *he* I

  I *am* the one speaking.
  Isa 52:6

- אַתָּה־הוּא הָאֱלֹהִים
  God *he* you

  You *are* God!
  2 Sam 7:28

116 **Contrastive use of a repeated demonstrative.**[176] A demonstrative can be repeated in order to contrast two persons or things. This is also called the **antithetical use of a repeated demonstrative**.

- וְקָרָא זֶה אֶל־זֶה
  this to *this* and called out

  And *the one* called out to *the other*.
  Isa 6:3

- אֵלֶּה מִזֶּה וְאֵלֶּה מִזֶּה
  from *this* and *these* from *this* these

  some on *this side* and *others* on *that side*
  Josh 8:22

117a **Demonstrative adjective.** As discussed in §74a, a demonstrative can be used as an attributive adjective, coming after both the substantive that it modifies and any attributive adjectives that modify the substantive, and exhibiting concord of gender, number, and definiteness.

- הַדְּבָרִים הָאֵלֶּה
  the *these* the words

  these words
  1 Sam 18:23

117b **Demonstrative pronoun in attributive apposition.** As discussed in §74b, when a demonstrative without the article modifies a substantive that is definite, the demonstrative is considered to be a demonstrative pronoun in attributive apposition (§66) rather than a demonstrative adjective, due to the lack of concord.

- דְּבָרֵנוּ זֶה
  this   our matter

  this matter of ours
  Josh 2:20

---

[175] Cf. BHRG §36.1.2(iii); IBHS §8.4.1b, 16.3.3; JM §154i–ja; JM93 §154i–j; Muraoka 1985, 67–77; Muraoka 1999; Zewi 2000; Joosten 1991; Khan 2006. Some scholars argue that the demonstrative (or third-person personal) pronoun never acts as a copula.

[176] Cf. IBHS §17.3c, 17.4.2d.

118 Demonstrative as an emphatic particle (really, indeed).[177] A demonstrative can be used for emphasis, rather than to point to something.

- Because it does not refer to anything, a demonstrative that is used as an emphatic particle is undeclined, meaning that it does not change form to indicate a particular gender and number. The verb עָשָׂה 'to do, to make' uses the demonstrative זֹאת. Other types of expressions (e.g., Gen 31:38, below) use the demonstrative זֶה.

- Because the demonstrative often loses its accent when used this way, this use is sometimes called the **enclitic use of the demonstrative**.

- וַאֲמֻשְׁךָ בְּנִי הַאַתָּה זֶה בְּנִי עֵשָׂו אִם־לֹא
  not or Esau my son *really* you? my son I will feel you   Gen 27:21

      I will feel whether you are *really* my son Esau or not.

  ○ In Gen 27:21, זֶה 'this' does not actually point to anything, so it is not functioning as a demonstrative. Instead, it focuses attention on the fact that blind Isaac wants verification before accepting the claim that Esau is talking with him.

- עַתָּה זֶה יָדַעְתִּי כִּי אִישׁ אֱלֹהִים אָתָּה
  you God man of that I know *really* now   1 Kgs 17:24

      Now I *really* know that you are a man of God.

- עַתָּה שַׁבְנוּ זֶה פַעֲמָיִם By now *indeed* we could have returned twice.
  two times *indeed* we returned now   Gen 43:10

- Other possible examples include Gen 27:36, 31:38; 1 Sam 10:11, 17:28; 1 Kgs 19:5.

Interrogative pronouns [178]

119 The interrogative pronouns מִי 'who?' **and** מָה 'what?' do not have gender, number, or person.

120 מִי **as an interrogative pronoun (who?).**[179] The word מִי can be used as an interrogative personal pronoun 'who?' in the sense of 'what person?'

- מִי הִגִּיד לְךָ   *Who* told you?
  to you told *who?*   Gen 3:11

- מִי־הֱבִיאֲךָ הֲלֹם   *Who* brought you here?
  here brought you *who?*   Judg 18:3

121 מִי **as an indefinite pronoun (whoever).**[180] The word מִי can be used as an indefinite pronoun meaning 'whoever.' As an indefinite pronoun, it does

---

[177] Cf. BHRG §36.2.2(vi); GKC §136c–d; IBHS §17.4.3c; JM §143f.
[178] Cf. BHRG §43.3; GBHS §5.3.1(c); GKC §137; IBHS §18; JM §144.
[179] Cf. BHRG §43.3.1(i)–(iii); GBHS §5.3.1(c); GKC §137a–b; IBHS §18.2b–d, g; JM §144a–b.
[180] Cf. BHRG §43.3.1(vi); GKC §137c; IBHS §18.2e; JM §144f–fa.

not indicate a question. Instead, it refers to one or more unspecified
people.

- מִי לַיהוָה אֵלָי   *Whoever* is for YHWH, come to me!
  to me   for YHWH   who?   Exod 32:26

- מִי־ יָרֵא וְחָרֵד   *whoever* is afraid and trembling
  and trembling   afraid   who?   Judg 7:3

122 **Desiderative or optative use of מִי (if only).**[181] As discussed in §547, the
word מִי followed by an imperfect verb (usually יִתֵּן 'he will give') can
begin a statement of a wish or desire.

- מִי יְשִׂמֵנִי שֹׁפֵט בָּאָרֶץ   *If only* I were appointed judge in the land!
  in the land   judging   will put me   who?   2 Sam 15:4

- מִי־ יִתֵּן מוּתֵנוּ   *Would that* we had died!
  we to die   will give   who?   Exod 16:3

123 **מִי as an interrogative adverb (how?).**[182] In Amos 7:2 and 7:5 (and
nowhere else), מִי is traditionally understood to mean 'how?'

- מִי יָקוּם יַעֲקֹב   *How* can Jacob stand?
  Jacob   he will stand   how?   Amos 7:2, 5

124 **מָה as an interrogative pronoun (what?).**[183] The word מָה can be used as
an interrogative impersonal pronoun that asks 'what?' in the sense of
'what thing?'

- מֶה עָשִׂיתָ   *What* did you do?
  you did   what?   Gen 4:10

- מַה־ בֶּצַע כִּי נַהֲרֹג אֶת־אָחִינוּ   *What* profit is there if we kill our brother?
  our brother   we kill   if   profit   what?   Gen 37:26

125 **מָה as an indefinite pronoun (whatever).**[184] The word מָה can be used as
an indefinite pronoun meaning 'whatever.' As an indefinite pronoun, it
does not ask a question. Instead, it refers to one or more unspecified
things.

- וּדְבַר מַה־ יַרְאֵנִי   and *whatever* thing he shows me
  he will show me   whatever   and thing   Num 23:3

- וְרָאִיתִי מָה וְהִגַּדְתִּי לָךְ   And *whatever* I see, I will tell you.
  to you   and I will tell   whatever   and I will see   1 Sam 19:3

---

[181] Cf. BHRG §43.3.1(iv); GBHS §5.3.3(b); IBHS §18.2f; JM §163d.
[182] Cf. IBHS §18.2d, which suggests that Amos 7:2, 5 might mean 'Who is Jacob that he
can stand?' If so, then מִי in Amos 7:2, 5 is an interrogative personal pronoun (§120).
[183] Cf. BHRG §43.3.2(i); GBHS §5.3.1(c); IBHS §18.3b, g; JM §144c–d.
[184] Cf. BHRG §43.3.2(v); GKC §137c; IBHS §18.3e; JM §144f–fa.

126 מָה as an interrogative adverb (how? why?).[185] The word מָה can be used as an interrogative adverb meaning 'how?' or 'why?'

- מָה אֶתֵּן זֶה לִפְנֵי מֵאָה אִישׁ   *How* can I set this before a hundred men?
  man hundred before this I will set *how?*   2 Kgs 4:43

- מָה־ אוֹחִיל לַיהוָה עוֹד   *Why* should I wait for YHWH any longer?
  still to YHWH I will wait *why?*   2 Kgs 6:33

- Other examples include Gen 44:16; Exod 14:15; Num 23:8; 2 Kgs 7:3.

127 מָה as an exclamation (how!).[186] The word מָה can be used as an exclamation, translated 'how!'

- מַה־ נּוֹרָא הַמָּקוֹם הַזֶּה   *How* awesome this place is!
  the this the place being feared *how!*   Gen 28:17

- מַה־ טֹּבוּ אֹהָלֶיךָ   *How* beautiful are your tents!
  your tents good *how!*   Num 24:5

128 מָה in rhetorical questions that expect a negative answer.[187] The word מָה can be used in rhetorical questions that expect a negative answer. Depending on the idiom and the translation style, they can either be translated 'what?' leaving the rhetorical question intact, or the rhetorical question can be translated as a negative statement such as 'there is not.'

- מַה־ לָּנוּ חֵלֶק בְּדָוִד וְלֹא־ נַחֲלָה בְּבֶן־ יִשַׁי
  of Jesse in son inheritance and no in David portion to us *what?*   1 Kgs 12:16

  What portion have we in David? We have no inheritance in Jesse's son!

  Or   We have *no* portion in David! We have no inheritance in Jesse's son!

  o In 1 Kgs 12:16, מַה is used in a rhetorical question. The context indicates that a negative answer is expected. Many English translations (KJV, NRSV, NIV, NASB, ESV) leave the rhetorical question intact by translating מָה as 'what?' A few translations (NJPS, NET), however, translate the rhetorical question as a negative statement such as 'we have no ...' thereby translating מַה as 'no.'

- אִם־ אֲדַבְּרָה לֹא־ יֵחָשֵׂךְ כְּאֵבִי וְאַחְדְּלָה מַה־ מִנִּי יַהֲלֹךְ
  it will go from me *what?* I will be silent my pain it will be spared not I will speak if
                                                                   Job 16:6

  If I speak, my pain is not spared, and if I am silent, *what* will leave me?

  Or   If I speak, my pain is not spared, and if I am silent, it will *not* leave me.

- Another example is Song 8:4.

---

[185] Cf. BHRG §43.3.2(ii); IBHS §18.3b–c; JM §144e. Although מָה means 'why?' in some contexts, 'why?' is more commonly expressed with לָמָה.

[186] Cf. BHRG §43.3.2(iv); IBHS §18.3f; JM §144e, 162a.

[187] Cf. BHRG §43.3.2(iii); GKC §137b note 1; IBHS §18.3g; JM §144h; Dahood 1975b.

Relative pronouns

129a **The relative pronoun זוּ (who, which, that).**[188] The relative pronoun זוּ (also spelled זֹו and זֶה) is rare and occurs only in poetry.

- גָּאָלְתָּ   זוּ   עַם־   the people *whom* you redeemed
  you redeemed *whom* people   Exod 15:13

- אֲלַמְּדֵם   זוֹ   וְעֵדֹתִי   my testimonies *which* I will teach them
  I will teach them *which* my testimonies   Ps 132:12

- יָצַרְתָּ   זֶה־   לִוְיָתָן   Leviathan *whom* you formed
  you formed *whom* Leviathan   Ps 104:26

- Other examples include Exod 15:16; Ps 9:16, 10:2; Job 19:19.

129b **The relative particle שֶׁ◌ (who, which, that).** See §470–4.

- הַיָּם   שְׂפַת־   שֶׁעַל־   כַּחוֹל   as the sand *that* is on the seashore
  of the sea the edge *that* on as the sand   Judg 7:12

- שֶׁנַּעֲשׂוּ   הַמַּעֲשִׂים   כָּל־   all the works *that* have been done
  that were done the works all of   Eccl 1:14

129c **The relative particle אֲשֶׁר (who, which, that).** See §462–9.

- מְלַאכְתּוֹ אֲשֶׁר עָשָׂה   his work, *which* he had done
  he did *which* his work   Gen 2:2

Other pronouns

130 **Reflexive pronoun (-self).**[189] Hebrew lacks a dedicated reflexive pronoun (e.g., 'myself,' 'himself'), but the reflexive idea may be expressed with a verb in the Niphal stem (§135), a verb in the Hithpael stem (§152, 154, 155), a pronominal suffix (particularly on לְ, §272), or with נֶפֶשׁ 'soul.'

- בָּךְ   לָהֶם   נִשְׁבַּעְתָּ   You swore to them by *yourself.*
  by *yourself* to them you swore   Exod 32:13

- אֹתָם   הֲלוֹא ... מַכְעִסִים   הֵם   הַאֹתִי
  themselves not? provoking they me?   Jer 7:19
  Is it me that they provoke? … Is it not *themselves*?

- בְּנַפְשׁוֹ   יְהוָה   אֲדֹנָי   נִשְׁבַּע   The Lord YHWH has sworn by *himself.*
  by *his soul* YHWH Lord swore   Amos 6:8

---

[188] Cf. BHRG §36.2.2(iii), 36.3.3; GBHS §5.2.13a; GKC §138g–h; IBHS §19.2d, 19.5; JM §38, 145c; Holmstedt 2002, 81–2.

[189] Cf. GKC §119s, 135i–l; IBHS §16.4g; JM §146k; Blake 1915, 123–8.

131 **Distributive pronoun (each).**[190] Hebrew lacks a distributive pronoun, but the distributive idea may be expressed with the noun אִישׁ, by the repetition of a word (§15, 100–2, 254), with the preposition לְ (§103), by using a plural subject with a singular predicate (§104), or by using כֹּל followed by an indefinite substantive (§105).

- חֲלֹמוֹ   כְּפִתְרוֹן   אִישׁ ... חֲלֹמוֹ אִישׁ שְׁנֵיהֶם חֲלוֹם וַיַּחַלְמוּ
  of his dream as interpretation *man* his dream *man* two of them dream dreamed

  Gen 40:5

  They both had a dream, *each* his own dream … *each* dream with its own meaning.

- אֱלֹהָיו   בְּשֵׁם   אִישׁ יֵלְכוּ הָעַמִּים   כָּל־
  his god in name of *man* walk the peoples all of   Mic 4:5

  All the peoples walk, *each* in the name of his god.

- Other examples include Exod 12:3; Job 42:11; Mic 4:4.

132 **Reciprocal pronoun (each other).**[191] Hebrew lacks a reciprocal pronoun (e.g., 'each other'), but the reciprocal idea of mutual action may be expressed with a verb in the Niphal stem (§137), a verb in the Hithpael stem (§153), a verb in the Poel stem (§156), or with appropriately paired words (see the examples below).

- רֵעֵהוּ   אֶל־ אִישׁ וַיֹּאמְרוּ   and they said *to one another*
  his companion to *man* said   Gen 11:3

- רֵעֵהוּ   שְׂפַת אִישׁ יִשְׁמְעוּ לֹא   his companion speech of *man* will hear not   Gen 11:7

  They will not understand *one another's* speech.

- זֶה אֶל־ זֶה וְקָרָא   And they called out to *each other*.
  this to *this* and called   Isa 6:3; cf. §116

---

[190] Cf. GKC §123c–d, 134q; IBHS §7.2.3b, 11.2.5f, 11.2.10c, 12.5a, 15.6; JM §135d, 142p. When אִישׁ is used as a distributive or indefinite pronoun, it often precedes the verb. See JM §155nf; Muraoka 1985, 34–5; Shimasaki 2002, 209–15; Blake 1915, 148–61.

[191] Cf. BHRG §36.2.2(iv).

2 Syntax of Verbs

A Stem (Theme)

- **Stem.**[192] By 'stem' or 'theme' we refer to such things as the Qal, Niphal, and Piel. Some grammars use the term **binyan** (בִּנְיָן; plural **binyanim** בִּנְיָנִים) or the term **conjugation**. The latter term, however, is often used to refer to such things as the perfect (§161–6) and imperfect (§167–75), so it is avoided here.

Qal [193]

- The Qal stem is also called the **G stem** (from the German *Grundstamm* 'basic stem') or the **B stem** (for 'basic stem').[194]

133 **Stative Qal.**[195] A verb in the Qal stem can express a state or a condition; such meanings are called **stative** or **dynamic**. For example, כָּבֵד 'he is heavy,' קָטֹן 'he is small,' and בּוֹשׁ 'he is ashamed.'

---

[192] For a discussion of the terminology, see GKC §39c; IBHS §21.1; JM §40a. What this grammar calls 'stems' (e.g., Qal, Niphal, Piel, etc.), GKC and JM call 'conjugations,' IBHS calls 'stems,' and earlier editions of this grammar called 'themes.' Be aware that GKC (§30a–c) uses the term 'stem' to refer to the Qal perfect 3ms form of a word (e.g., קָטַל, קָדַשׁ, הָלַךְ, etc.). For a discussion of the concept of stems (e.g., Qal, Niphal, Piel, etc.) and how the various stems relate to each other, see GKC §39; IBHS §21; JM §40a.

[193] Cf. BHRG §16.2; GBHS §3.1.1; GKC §43; IBHS §22; JM §41.

[194] Cf. GKC §39e; IBHS §22.1a; JM §40a. The name 'Qal' comes from קַל 'light' (in the sense of weight, not in the sense of illumination), because the Qal stem is not 'weighed down' with the prefixes or dagesh that are used in other stems.

[195] Cf. BHRG §16.2.2(ii); GBHS §3.1.1b; IBHS §20.2k, 22.2, 22.4b–e, 22.5; JM §40b, 41b–d, f; Blake 1903. Be aware that §133 discusses the meaning of verbs, not their spelling. Many, but not all, stative verbs are spelled with a tsere or holem as the second vowel of the Qal perfect 3ms.

134   Fientive Qal.[196] A verb in the Qal stem can express an action; such verbs are called **fientive verbs** or **verbs of action**. Examples include הָלַךְ 'he goes,' נָתַן 'he gives,' and שִׂים 'he puts.'

- Stative and fientive are an exhaustive, mutually exclusive set of categories; a particular usage of a verb is either fientive or else it is stative.[197] Some verbs, however, are stative in some contexts and fientive in other contexts.
- Fientive is not the same thing as transitive. A transitive verb takes a direct object (e.g. 'to thank' takes a direct object, namely the person who is thanked). A fientive verb expresses an action (e.g., 'to thank' or 'to fall'). Most transitive verbs are fientive, but not all fientive verbs are transitive (e.g., 'to fall' is a fientive verb that does not take a direct object, so it is not transitive).
- Stative is not the same thing as intransitive. An intransitive verb is one that takes no direct object. Stative verbs are usually intransitive, but many intransitive verbs are not stative. For example, 'to hop' is intransitive, but it is fientive rather than stative.

Niphal [198]

- The Niphal (or **Nifal**) stem is also called the **N stem**, in reference to the letter נ that is prefixed to many verb forms in this stem.

135   Reflexive Niphal.[199] The subject of a reflexive Niphal verb acts upon itself, so the subject is also the direct object (hence the name **double status Niphal**). For example, נִשְׁמַר 'he guards himself,' נִסְתַּר 'he hides himself,' and נֶהְפַּךְ 'he turns himself over.'

136   Middle Niphal.[200] Also called a **benefactive construction**, a verb in the Niphal stem can express an action where the subject acts for its own

---

[196] Cf. BHRG §16.2.2(i); GBHS §3.1.1a; IBHS §20.2k, 22.2.1, 22.2.3, 22.4a, 22.5; JM §40b, 41a.

[197] This is a simplification; there are some exceptions. See IBHS §22.3b.

[198] Cf. BHRG §16.3; GBHS §3.1.2; GKC §51; IBHS §23; JM §51; Siebsma 1991.

[199] Cf. BHRG §16.3.2(ii); GKC §51c; IBHS §23.4b, h; JM §51c. Note that what GBHS §3.1.2c calls 'reflexive' is what this grammar calls 'middle' (§136).

[200] Cf. BHRG §16.3.2(ii); GBHS §3.1.2c; GKC §51e; IBHS §23.4d; JM §51c. Note that what IBHS §23.2.1 refers to as the 'Niphal middle' is a subcategory of what this grammar calls a 'Niphal Passive' (§139). What this grammar calls 'middle' is what

benefit. For example, נִשְׁאַל 'he asks for himself' (1 Sam 20:6, 28) and נִכְבַּד 'he achieves glory for himself' (Ezek 39:13).

137 Reciprocal Niphal.[201] A verb in the Niphal stem can express an action where multiple subjects act upon each other. For example, וַיִּנָּצוּ 'they fought with each other' (Lev 24:10). A reciprocal Niphal is usually plural, and is often followed by the word יָחַד 'together.' For example, נִשָּׁפְטָה יָחַד 'let us go to law with one another' (Isa 43:26), and נִלָּחֲמָה יָחַד 'let us fight with one another' (1 Sam 17:10).

138 Tolerative Niphal.[202] A verb in the Niphal stem can express an action where the subject allows itself to be acted upon. For example, נִדְרָשׁ 'he let himself be consulted' (Ezek 14:3) and לְהִזָּהֵר 'to let oneself be instructed' (Eccl 4:13). This is also called the **Niphal** *tolerativum*.

139 Passive Niphal.[203] A verb in the Niphal stem can express an action where the subject is acted upon.

- This passive meaning in the Niphal stem usually corresponds to an active meaning in the Qal stem. For example, the passive meaning נוֹלַד 'he is born' in the Niphal stem corresponds to the active meaning יָלְדָה 'she gave birth to' in the Qal stem.
- Sometimes, however, the passive meaning in the Niphal stem corresponds to an active meaning in the Piel stem or the Hiphil stem. For example, the Niphal נִכְבַּד 'he was honoured' corresponds to the Piel כִּבֵּד 'he honours'; it does not correspond to the Qal כָּבֵד 'he is dull' or 'he is weighty.' Similarly, the verb שׁמד only occurs in the Niphal and Hiphil stems; the Niphal נִשְׁמַד 'he was exterminated' corresponds to the Hiphil הִשְׁמִיד 'he exterminated.'

Piel and Pual [204]

- The Piel stem is also called the **D stem**, in reference to the doubling (with a Dagesh Forte) of the second consonant of the root.[205]
- The Pual stem is also called the **Dp stem**, meaning 'D passive.' The Pual typically has the passive meaning of the corresponding Piel.

GBHS §3.1.2c calls 'reflexive,' and what GBHS §3.1.2b calls 'middle' is analysed as 'passive' (§139) in this grammar.

[201] Cf. BHRG §16.3.2(ii); GBHS §3.1.2c; GKC §51d; IBHS §23.4e; JM §51c.

[202] Cf. GBHS §3.1.2c; GKC §51c; IBHS §23.4f–g; JM §51c.

[203] Cf. BHRG §16.3.2(i), 16.5.2(ii); GBHS §3.1.2a; GKC §51f–h; IBHS §23.2; JM §51c.

[204] Cf. BHRG §16.4–16.5; GBHS §3.1.3–3.1.4; GKC §52; IBHS §24; JM §52, 56.

[205] Cf. IBHS §24.1a.

140 Piel and Pual not necessarily intensive.[206] The Piel and Pual are often described as 'intensive,' but this is inaccurate. It is difficult to find any fundamental meaning that unites all of their varied meanings (§140–6).

141 Factitive Piel and Pual.[207]

- If a verb has a factitive meaning in the Piel, then the subject of the verb in the Piel causes its direct object to enter a state that can be described by the same verb in the Qal.[208]
  - o For example, the subject of the Piel כִּבֵּד 'he glorified' causes the direct object to enter the state described by that verb in the Qal (כָּבֵד 'he was glorious'). Similarly, the Piel מִלֵּא 'he filled' corresponds to the Qal מָלֵא 'he was full.'

- If a verb has a factitive meaning in the Pual, then the subject of the verb in the Pual is caused to enter a state that can be described by the same verb in the Qal.[208]
  - o For example, the subject of the Pual כֻּבַּד 'he was glorified' is caused to enter the state described by the Qal כָּבֵד 'he was glorious.'

142 Causative Piel and Pual.[209]

- Whereas 'factitive' refers to causing a state (§141), 'causative' refers to causing an action. Causative verbs are rare in the Piel and Pual.

- The subject of a causative verb causes the direct object to do some action.[210] For example, in 'They made him sing,' the subject 'they' causes the direct object 'him' to do the action 'to sing,' so the verb 'to make' has a causative meaning in that sentence.

---

[206] Cf. GBHS §3.1.3; IBHS §21.2.2, 24.1; JM §52d; Goetze 1942. For an opposing view, see Weingreen 1983; Joosten 1998.

[207] Cf. BHRG §16.4.2(i), 16.7.2(iii)(1–2); GBHS §3.1.3a, 3.1.4a; GKC §52g; IBHS §20.2m, 24.2, 25.2; JM §52d, 56c. Note that this is a slightly different definition of 'factitive' than that used in IBHS and JM, which define 'factitive' in terms of the Qal being *intransitive*. This grammar, on the other hand, defines 'factitive' in terms of the Qal being *stative*. Because most stative verbs are intransitive (see IBHS §22.3b for exceptions), most verbal meanings that this textbook classifies as factitive would also be classified as factitive by IBHS and JM. But because some intransitive verbs are fientive, some verbal meanings that IBHS and JM would classify as factitive would be classified as causative (§142) by this textbook.

[208] In principle, it is possible to have a verb that is factitive in the Piel and Pual stems that does not occur in the Qal stem in the Hebrew Bible.

[209] Cf. GKC §52g; IBHS §20.2m.

[210] Note that this textbook restricts the term 'causative' to refer to causing an action. Some scholars include in the category 'causative' verbs that cause a state, but this book refers to such verbs as factitive.

- Some verbs permit rather than cause the direct object to do something. Such verbs can be referred to as **permissive** or **tolerative**. For example, in 'She permitted him to walk,' the subject 'she' allows the direct object 'him' to perform the action 'to walk,' so the verb 'to permit' is **tolerative**. In this grammar, tolerative verbs are included in the category of causative verbs.
- If a verb has a causative meaning in the Piel, then the subject of the verb in the Piel causes its direct object to do an action that can be described by the same verb in the Qal.[211]
  - For example, the Piel לִמֵּד 'he taught' corresponds to the Qal לָמַד 'he learned.' Similarly, the Piel בְּיַלֶּדְכֶן 'when you help <someone> to give birth' (Exod 1:16) corresponds to the Qal יָלְדָה 'she gave birth.'
- If a verb has a causative meaning in the Pual, then the subject of the verb in the Pual is caused to perform an action that can be described by the same verb in the Qal.[211]
  - For example, the subject of the Pual לֻמַּד 'he was taught' is caused to undergo the action described by the Qal לָמַד 'he learned.'

143 Iterative Piel and Pual.[212] Also called **plurative**, **frequentative**, or **repetitive**, a verb in the Piel or Pual stems may refer to an activity that is done multiple times or to multiple objects. Although the concepts of **habitual**, **customary**, and **characteristic** action can be distinguished from iterative action, those senses are subsumed under 'iterative' here.
  - Examples include: שִׁבֵּר 'he smashed repeatedly,' בִּקֵּשׁ 'he searched repeatedly,' הִלֵּךְ 'he walked around,' קִבֵּר 'he buried many things,' וְשָׁאֵלוּ 'let them beg habitually [as their livelihood]' (Ps 109:10).

144 Denominative Piel and Pual.[213] When a verb is derived (etymologically) from a noun, the verb form is called denominative. For example, the nouns 'fax' and 'email' came to be used as verbs, as in 'Fax the letter to her' or 'Email me.' Because the verbs 'fax' and 'email' were created from the previously existing nouns 'fax' and 'email,' the verbs 'to fax' and 'to email' are denominative verbs.

---

[211] In principle, it is possible to have a verb that is causative in the Piel and Pual stems that does not occur in the Qal stem in the Hebrew Bible.

[212] Cf. GBHS §3.1.3c, 3.1.4c; GKC §52f; IBHS §24.3.3, 24.5, 25.3c, 25.5a; JM §52d, 56c.

[213] Cf. BHRG §16.4.2(iii); GBHS §3.1.3b, 3.1.4b; GKC §52h; IBHS §24.4, 25.4; JM §52d, 56c.

- Examples include Piel שֵׁרֵשׁ 'he uprooted' and Pual שׁוֹרַשׁ 'he was uprooted' from the noun שֹׁרֶשׁ 'a root (of a plant),' Piel כִּהֵן 'he acted as a priest' from the noun כֹּהֵן 'a priest,' and Piel שִׁלֵּשׁ 'he did three times' and Pual שֻׁלַּשׁ 'it was threefold' from the noun שָׁלֹשׁ 'three.'

145 **Delocutive Piel and Pual.**[214] Also called **declarative**, 'delocutive verbs can be defined as verbs derived from a base X which mean "by saying or uttering 'X' (to someone) to perform an act which is culturally associated with the meaning or force of X."'[215] For example, the English verb 'to shush' means 'to say "shush" to someone.' Similarly, the expression 'attaboy' led to the colloquial delocutive verb 'to attaboy' as in 'He attaboy'ed him when he heard the news.'

- The Piel verb אִשֵּׁר 'he pronounced someone to be happy' is delocutive because it means that he said to someone, 'you are אַשְׁרֵי (happy).'
- The Pual verb אֻשַּׁר 'he was pronounced happy' is delocutive because it means that someone said to him, 'you are אַשְׁרֵי (happy).'
- Similarly, the Piel verbs נִקָּה 'he pronounced someone to be innocent,' saying 'you are נָקִי (innocent),' and צִדֵּק 'he pronounced someone to be in the right,' saying 'you are צַדִּיק (in the right),' are also delocutive.

146 **Privative Piel and Pual.**[216] A privative verb is a verb that refers to removing something. In English, the verbs 'to peel,' 'to skin,' and 'to husk' are privative because they refer to removing the peel, the skin, and the husk (respectively). Hebrew examples include סִקֵּל 'he cleared of stones' and חִטֵּא 'he purified from sin.'

Hiphil and Hophal [217]

- The Hiphil (or **Hifil**) stem is also called the **H stem**, in reference to the letter ה that is prefixed to many verb forms in this stem. It is also sometimes called the **C stem**, in reference to its typical causative meaning.

---

[214] Cf. GBHS §3.1.3d, 3.1.4d; IBHS §20.2m, 24.2f, 25.2b; JM §52d, 56c; Hillers 1967; Claassen 1972; Tigay 1999. Note that the definition of delocutive in IBHS is broader than that used here. IBHS defines delocutive as 'a verb form referring to a speech act' (p. 690, cf. §24.2f–g). As defined here, the meaning of a delocutive verb is the speech act of saying the word from which the verb is derived.

[215] Plank 2005, 459.

[216] Cf. GKC §52h; IBHS §24.4f; JM §52d, 56c.

[217] Cf. BHRG §16.7–16.8; GBHS §3.1.6–3.1.7; GKC §53; IBHS §27–28; JM §54, 57.

- The Hophal (or **Hofal**) stem may be called the **Hp stem** or **Cp stem**, meaning 'H passive' and 'C passive.' The Hophal is typically the passive of the Hiphil.[218]

147 Causative Hiphil and Hophal.[219] It is common for a Hiphil or Hophal verb to be causative (§142).

- The subject of the Hiphil הוֹצִיא 'he brought out' causes its direct object to do the action described by that verb in the Qal (יָצָא 'he went out'). The Hiphil וַיַּאֲכִלְךָ 'he fed you' (e.g., Deut 8:3) corresponds to the Qal אָכַל 'he ate.' The Hiphil הֶרְאָה 'he showed' corresponds to the Qal רָאָה 'he saw.'

- The subject of the Hophal מוּצֵאת 'she was brought out' (e.g., Gen 38:25) is caused to do the action described by that verb in the Qal (יָצָא 'he went out'). The Hophal וְהָרְאָה 'it will be shown' (e.g., Lev 13:49) corresponds to the Qal רָאָה 'he saw.'

148 Delocutive Hiphil.[220] A Hiphil verb can be delocutive (§145).

- For example, if it is delocutive, the Hiphil verb הִצְדִּיק 'he justified' means 'he caused someone to say to someone, "you are צַדִּיק (in the right)."'

- Similarly, if it is delocutive, the Hiphil verb הִרְשִׁיעַ 'he condemned' means 'he caused someone to say to someone, "you are רָשָׁע (guilty)."'

149 Factitive Hiphil and Hophal.[221] Hiphil and Hophal verbs can be factitive (§141), but this is uncommon.

- For example, the subject of the Hiphil verb הֶלְאָה 'he caused someone to become weary' causes the direct object to enter the state described by that same verb in the Qal לָאָה 'he was weary.' Other examples include the Hiphil הֶעְמִיק 'he caused something to be deep' which corresponds to the Qal עָמֹק 'it was deep,' וַיַּגְבִּיהֶהָ 'he caused it to be high' in 2 Chr 33:14 corresponds to the Qal גָּבַהּ 'he was high,' תַּקְרִיב 'you will cause <them> to be near' in Exod 29:4 corresponds to the Qal קָרַב 'he was near,' and הֶחֱיִתָנוּ 'you have saved our lives' in Gen 47:25 corresponds to the Qal חָיָה 'he lived.'

- There are no unambiguous examples of a Hophal factitive verb. One possibility is הָשַׁמָּה in Lev 26:35 'the fact of her having been caused to enter the state of being

---

[218] The various uses of the Hophal and its relationships to other stems are described in detail in Kroeze 2002.

[219] Cf. BHRG §16.7.2, 16.8.2; GBHS §3.1.6a, 3.1.7a; GKC §53c, g, h; IBHS §27–8; JM §54d, 57c.

[220] Cf. GBHS §3.1.6c; GKC §53c; IBHS §27.2e.

[221] Cf. GBHS §3.1.6b, 3.1.7b; IBHS §27.2.

desolated' (from the Qal שָׁמֵם 'it was desolate'). It might be causative, however, meaning 'the fact that she underwent the process of being desolated.'[222]

150   **Intransitive Hiphil.**[223] A Hiphil intransitive verb does not take a direct object. Instead, it describes its subject as exhibiting a state or quality or as entering into and remaining in a state or condition. Verbs that have an intransitive meaning in the Hiphil typically have a corresponding stative meaning in the Qal.

- For example, the subject of the Hiphil intransitive verb יַזְקִין 'it grows old' (Job 14:8) enters into the state that is indicated by the Qal stative verb זָקֵן 'it was old.' Other examples include הוֹבִישׁ 'it dried up' (e.g., Joel 1:10) from the Qal יָבֵשׁ 'it was dry,' יַעֲרִימוּ 'they act craftily' (e.g., Ps 83:4) from the Qal עָרֹם 'he was crafty,' and הִרְשִׁיעַ 'he acted wickedly' (e.g., 2 Chr 20:35) from the Qal רָשַׁע 'he was wicked.'

- A Hiphil intransitive differs from a Hiphil factitive (§149) as follows: The subject of a Hiphil factitive verb causes someone or something to be in a state, whereas the subject of a Hiphil intransitive verb is in a state.

151   **Denominative Hiphil and Hophal.**[224] As discussed in §144, a denominative verb is derived (etymologically) from a noun.

- The Hiphil verb יַשְׁרֵשׁ 'he will take root' (e.g., Isa 27:6) was created from the previously existing noun שֶׁרֶשׁ 'a root (of a plant),' so it is denominative. Other examples include מַקְרִן 'having horns' (e.g., Ps 69:32) from קֶרֶן 'horn,' תַּלְשֵׁן 'you will slander' (e.g., Prov 30:10) from לָשׁוֹן 'tongue,' and אֵימִנָה 'I shall go to the right' (e.g., Gen 13:9) from יָמִין 'right side.'

Hithpael [225]

- The Hithpael (or **Hitpael**) stem is also called the **tD stem** or the **HtD stem**, in reference to the prefix הת and the doubling (with a dagesh forte) of the second root consonant in certain verb forms.[226]
- The Hithpael is typically the reflexive or reciprocal of the Piel.[227]

---

[222] Cf. IBHS §28.2c.

[223] Cf. GBHS §3.1.6b; IBHS §27.2f–g; JM §54d.

[224] Cf. GBHS §3.1.6d, 3.1.7c; GKC §53g; IBHS §27.4a–b, 28.4a; JM §54d.

[225] Cf. BHRG §16.6; GBHS §3.1.5; GBHS §3.1.5; GKC §54; IBHS §26; JM §53; Speiser 1955.

[226] Cf. GBHS §3.1.5; IBHS §26.1.1a.

[227] Cf. GBHS §3.1.5; GKC §54d; IBHS §26.2a; JM §53i.

152 **Reflexive-iterative Hithpael**.[228] The subject of a reflexive-iterative verb acts on itself repeatedly (cf. §135 and §143).

- Examples include הִתְחַבְּאוּ 'they have been hiding themselves' (1 Sam 14:11), הִתְהַלַּכְנוּ 'we walked about' (1 Sam 25:15), and יִתְקַדָּשׁוּ 'let them consecrate themselves' (Exod 19:22).

153 **Reciprocal-iterative Hithpael**.[229] The subjects of a reciprocal-iterative verb act upon one another repeatedly (cf. §137 and §143).

- For example, the Hithpael תִּתְרָאוּ 'you are looking at one another' in Gen 42:1 refers to how Jacob's sons keep looking at one another. Be aware that some reciprocal verbs in the Hithpael may not be iterative; for example, נִתְרָאֶה 'let us face each other' (2 Chr 25:17).

154 **Reflexive-factitive Hithpael**.[230] The subject of a reflexive-factitive verb causes itself to enter a state (cf. §135 and §141).

- The Hithpael verb יִתְגַּדֵּל 'he will magnify/aggrandize himself' (Dan 11:36) corresponds to the Qal גָּדַל 'he is great.'

155 **Reflexive-estimative Hithpael**.[231] The subject of a reflexive-estimative verb regards or presents itself as being in a state.

- Examples include תִּשְׂתָּרֵר 'you will regard yourself as a prince' (Num 16:13), corresponding to Qal שָׂרַר 'he was a prince,' and וַיִּתְחָל 'he pretended to be sick' (2 Sam 13:6), corresponding to the Qal חָלָה 'he was sick.'
- The Hithpael וַיִּתְנַבֵּא 'he acted as a prophet' (i.e., 'he prophesied,' e.g., 1 Sam 10:10) has a reflexive-estimative meaning, but the verb does not occur in the Qal.
- Many reflexive-estimative Hithpael verbs are denominative (§144). תִּשְׂתָּרֵר 'you will regard yourself as prince' is derived from the noun שַׂר 'a prince.' וַיִּתְנַבֵּא 'he acted as a prophet' is derived from the noun נָבִיא 'a prophet.'

Poel [232]

- The Poel is a minor stem that is similar in meaning to the Piel. When it occurs with non-geminate verbs, it is sometimes referred to as the **Polel stem**.

---

[228] Cf. GBHS §3.1.5a, c; GKC §54d, l; IBHS §26.1.2b–d; JM §53i.
[229] Cf. GBHS §3.1.5b–c; GKC §54f; IBHS §26.2g.
[230] Cf. GBHS §3.1.5a; GKC §54d, l; IBHS §26.2b–d; JM §53i.
[231] Cf. GBHS §3.1.5a; GKC §54d; IBHS §26.2f, 26.4a; JM §53i.
[232] Cf. BHRG §18.9.3(iii); GKC §55b–c; IBHS §21.2.3a; JM §59a.

156 **Reciprocal Poel**. The subjects of a reciprocal verb act upon one another (cf. §135). In Job 9:15, the Poel participle מְשֹׁפְטִי may be reciprocal, meaning 'my opponent at law.'

B Voice

Active voice

157 **Active Qal, Piel, or Hiphil**. The subject of an active-voice verb performs the action of the verb or is in the state described by the verb. The active voice is typically expressed with a verb in the Qal, Piel, or Hiphil stem.

Middle voice

158 **Middle Niphal**. The subject of a middle-voice verb performs the action of the verb for its own benefit.[233] The middle voice is often expressed with a verb in the Niphal stem (§136).

Passive voice

The subject of a passive-voice verb receives the action of the verb; the subject is acted upon by the agent of the verbal action.

159a **Passive stems**. In Hebrew, the passive voice may be expressed by using a verb in a passive stem such as the Pual and the Hophal, a Qal passive participle, or a Niphal verb (§138–9).

- Be aware that although in English it is common to specify the agent of a passive verb (e.g., 'the window was broken *by the ball*'), this is rarely done in Hebrew.[234]

159b **Qal passive**.[235] In our Hebrew Bible (with Masoretic pointing) there is no distinctly spelled Qal passive stem (other than the Qal passive participle, which is typically treated as being in the Qal stem). Several other Semitic languages, however, have a passive stem that corresponds to a Qal passive, just as the Pual is the passive of the Piel and the Hophal is the

---

[233] Be aware that many authors use the term 'middle voice' to refer to the subject acting upon itself, which is what this grammar refers to as 'reflexive' (§135). Landes (2001, 8) defines the middle voice as the subject acting 'with an inferred agent.'

[234] Cf. GBHS §3.1.2a; GKC §121f; Lambdin §128. IBHS §23.2.2e–f calls a passive construction with the agent unspecified an 'incomplete passive' and a passive construction with the agent specified a 'complete passive.'

[235] Cf. GKC §52e, 53u; IBHS §22.6; JM §58; Ginsberg 1929; Fassberg 2001, 252–5.

passive of the Hiphil in Hebrew, and it seems likely that some verb forms
that are pointed as Pual perfects or Hophal imperfects are actually Qal
passives.

- For example, the context of Num 32:5 suggests that the verb יֻתַּן has a passive
  meaning: 'let it be given.' It is pointed as a Hophal imperfect (or jussive) 3ms from
  the root נתן. But because the Hiphil of the verb נתן does not exist, יֻתַּן may be the
  Qal passive stem, jussive 3ms of נתן.

- Similarly, the verb form יֻקַּח 'let it be taken' in Gen 18:4 may be a Qal passive.

160 **Impersonal third person as passive.**[236] For a third-person verb in an
active stem (e.g., Qal, Piel, or Hiphil) the subject is sometimes left
unstated and refers to no one in particular. A similar construction is used
with the word 'they' in English (e.g., 'They call her Miriam'). Such a
construction is sometimes best translated into English with a passive verb
(e.g., 'She is called Miriam').

- עַל־כֵּן   קָרָא   שְׁמָהּ   בָּבֶל   Therefore, its name *is called* Babel.
  Babel   its name   *(he) called*   therefore   Gen 11:9

  o The verb קָרָא is the Qal perfect 3ms of קרא 'he called.' But in the context of
     Gen 11:9, it is not specified who called it Babel, so the verb is impersonal (but
     active). It can be translated into English with a passive verb, 'its name is called.'

- וְיִתְּנוּ־   לָנוּ   שְׁנַיִם פָּרִים   Let two oxen *be given* to us.
  oxen   two   to us   *let (them) give*   1 Kgs 18:23

C Conjugation (Aspect) [237]

The **conjugation** of a verb refers to such things as the perfect (qatal) and
imperfect (yiqtol). The conjugation of a verb is also referred to as its
aspect, **tense**, or **form**. Be aware that some grammarians use the term
'conjugation' to refer to what this book calls 'stem' (e.g., Qal).

Perfect conjugation [238]

The **perfect conjugation** is also referred to as the **qatal**, the **qtl**, the **suffix**

---

[236] Cf. GKC §144b–i; Williams 1964.
[237] Cf. BHRG §14–15, 19; GBHS §3.2; GKC §106–7, 111–12; IBHS §29–33; JM §112–
13, 115, 117–19; Driver 1892; Blake 1951; Gentry 1998; Talstra 1997a; Andersen 2000;
Gropp 1991; Revell 1989a; Junger 1989; Niccacci 1990; Niccacci 1994a; Niccacci 1997;
Niccacci 2006; McFall 1982; Joosten 1997; Longacre 1992.
[238] Cf. BHRG §19.2; GBHS §3.2.1; GKC §106; IBHS §30; JM §112; Driver 1892, 13–
26.

conjugation, the **suffixed conjugation**, or the **perfective conjugation**.

161 **Stative perfect.**[239] A perfect verb may express a state or a condition. This is often translated with the English present tense in dialogue (e.g., 'I am old'), but other contexts suggest a past tense translation (e.g., 'He was old').

- וַאֲנִי זָקַנְתִּי וְשַׂבְתִּי
  and was gray   was old   and I

  I *am old* and *gray*.
  1 Sam 12:2

- וְהַמֶּלֶךְ דָּוִד זָקֵן
  was old   David   and the king

  King David *was old*.
  1 Kgs 1:1

162 **Complete-action perfect.**[240] A perfect verb with the meaning of complete action describes the event as a complete whole, with its beginning, middle, and end all in view. (This is in contrast to the imperfect, §167, which does not have the end in view.)[241] The action may be already finished, or it may simply be described that way. (This is sometimes referred to as being completed 'in the mind of the speaker.')

(1) Past

- בְּרֵאשִׁית בָּרָא אֱלֹהִים
  God   created   in the beginning

  In the beginning, God *created* …
  Gen 1:1

(2) Perfect (a present state resulting from a previously completed action)

- שָׁכַח אֵל הִסְתִּיר פָּנָיו
  his face   hid   God   forgot

  God *has forgotten*, he *has hidden* his face.
  Ps 10:11

- Other examples include the last three verbs in Isa 1:4.

(3) Pluperfect (a past state resulting from a previously completed action):

- The subject usually precedes the verb (cf. §573d) and often has a prefixed waw.

- רָחֵל גְּנָבָתַם
  stole them   Rachel

  Rachel *had stolen* them.
  Gen 31:32

- Other examples include 1 Sam 9:15 and 2 Kgs 7:17.

(4) Future perfect (a future state resulting from an action that will have been completed by that time)

- הָאָרֶץ … אֲשֶׁר נָתַן־לָךְ
  to you   he gave   which   the land

  the land … which *he will have given* you
  Deut 8:10

---

[239] Cf. BHRG §19.2.2; GBHS §3.2.1b; GKC §106g; IBHS §30.2.3, 30.5.3; JM §112a–b.

[240] Cf. BHRG §19.2.1; GBHS §3.2.1a; GKC §106; IBHS §29.6, 30.1b, d, 30.3–30.5.2; JM §112c–i.

[241] Be aware that this 'aspectual' approach to the perfect and imperfect is controversial; some scholars argue against it. Cf. JM §111f; Zevit 1988; Zevit 1998, 39–48; Joosten 2002; Hughes 1970.

- כָּל־ הַמְּקֹמוֹת ... אֲשֶׁר הִדַּחְתִּים   all the places ... where *I will have driven* them
  I drove them which   the places all of   Jer 8:3

163 **Experience perfect.**[242] A perfect verb that is fientive (i.e., not stative; cf.
§133 and §134) can express a state of mind. Such verbs are sometimes
described as **quasi-stative**.

- וַיֹּאמֶר לֹא יָדַעְתִּי   He said, '*I do* not *know*.'
  I knew not he said   Gen 4:9

- מָאַסְתִּי חַגֵּיכֶם   *I despise* your festivals.
  your festivals *I hate*   Amos 5:21

- זָכַרְנוּ אֶת־הַדָּגָה   *We remember* the fish.
  the fish   *we remember*   Num 11:5

164 **Instantaneous perfect.**[243] Also called the **performative perfect**, an
instantaneous perfect verb indicates a speech act, meaning that the action
denoted by the verb occurs by means of speaking the sentence (or other
linguistic unit) in which the verb occurs.

- הַעִדֹתִי בָכֶם הַיּוֹם   *I testify* against you today.
  the day   against you *I testify*   Deut 8:19

- This category can also be applied to other actions that accompany the
  act of speaking, as shown in the next example.

- הֲרִימֹתִי יָדִי אֶל־ יְהוָה   *I raise* my hand [in an oath] to YHWH.
  YHWH   to   my hand *I raised*   Gen 14:22

- Other examples include 2 Sam 19:30 and Jer 22:5.

165 **Perfect of certitude.**[244] Also called the **prophetic perfect**, **rhetorical
future**, **accidental perfective**, or **perfect of confidence**, such a verb
describes a future event as if it had already happened.

- This can be difficult to distinguish from a future perfect, §162(4).

- גָּוַעְנוּ אָבַדְנוּ כֻּלָּנוּ אָבָדְנוּ
  we perished all of us *we perished* we died   Num 17:27
       We will die! *We will perish*! *We will* all *perish*! [i.e., 'We are as good as dead!']

- גָּלָה עַמִּי   My people *will go into exile*.
  my people *went into exile*   Isa 5:13

---

[242] Cf. GBHS §3.2.1c; JM §112a.
[243] Cf. BHRG §19.2.3; GBHS §3.2.1f; IBHS §30.5.1d; JM §112f; Rogland 2003, 115–26;
Klein 1990.
[244] Cf. BHRG §19.2.5(ii) and page 364; GBHS §3.2.1d; GKC §106m–n; IBHS §30.5.1e;
JM §112h; Rogland 2003, 53–114.

- This sometimes is used to describe the future as something that a prophet has seen or visited. For example, רָאִיתִי אֶת־כָּל־יִשְׂרָאֵל נְפֹצִים '*I saw* all Israel scattered' (1 Kgs 22:17).

166 Conditional perfect.[245] A perfect verb may be used in the protasis (the 'if' part) of an unreal conditional sentence (§516a–17) or in an unfulfilled desire clause (§547–8).

- אֶתְכֶם הָרַגְתִּי לֹא אוֹתָם הַחֲיִתֶם לוּ

  you   I killed   not   them   *you left alive*   if only   Judg 8:19

                              If *you had* only *left* them *alive*, then I would not kill you.

- מִצְרַיִם בְּאֶרֶץ מַתְנוּ לוּ־   If only *we had died* in the land of Egypt!

  of Egypt   in land   *we died*   if only   Num 14:2

Imperfect conjugation [246]

The **imperfect conjugation** is also referred to as the **yiqtol**, the **yqtl**, the **prefix conjugation**, the **prefixed conjugation**, the **imperfective conjugation**, the **non-perfective conjugation**, or the **future**.

167 Incomplete-action imperfect.[247] An imperfect verb with an incomplete-action meaning describes the event without having the end of the event in view. This is in contrast to the perfect (§162), which has the event's beginning, middle, and end all in view.[248] The action may not have been finished, or it may simply be described that way (this is sometimes referred to as being incomplete 'in the mind of the speaker').

(1) The situation or event may be present from the speaker's perspective.

- תְּבַקֵּשׁ מַה־ לֵאמֹר הָאִישׁ וַיִּשְׁאָלֵהוּ

  you are seeking   what?   saying   the man   asked him   Gen 37:15

                                      The man asked him, 'What *are you seeking*?'

- Another example is 1 Sam 1:8.

(2) The situation or event may be in the past from the speaker's perspective, particularly when preceded by טֶרֶם or בְּטֶרֶם, meaning 'before' or 'not yet,' or עַד 'until' (§311). Although this is often translated

---

[245] Cf. BHRG §19.2.1(iii); GKC §106p; IBHS §30.5.4; JM §167g–i.

[246] Cf. BHRG §19.3; GBHS §3.2.2; GKC §107; IBHS §31; JM §113; Driver 1892, 27–49.

[247] Cf. BHRG §19.3.1–3; GBHS §3.2.2a, c; GKC §107a–d, f, h–l; IBHS §31.1, 31.2c, 31.3b–d, 31.6.3c; JM §113a, b, d, f, j, k; Joosten 1999a, 17–19.

[248] This description of the imperfect is controversial. See footnote 241.

with the English past tense, this is not the preterite (§176–7c) because the incomplete-action imperfect is describing the event as incomplete.

- יִשְׁכָּבוּ   טֶרֶם   before *they lay down*
  they lying down   before   Gen 19:4

(3) The situation or event may be future from the point of view of the speaker. This often occurs with both stative verbs and fientive verbs.

- בְּקֹלִי   יִשְׁמְעוּ   וְלֹא   לִי   יַאֲמִינוּ   לֹא־
  to my voice   *they will listen*   and not   to me   *they will believe*   not   Exod 4:1

  They will not believe me or *listen* to my voice.

- Another example is Exod 6:1.

(4) The situation or event may be future from a past point of view.

- לָחֶם   יֹאכְלוּ   שָׁם   כִּי־   שָׁמְעוּ
  bread   *they will eat*   there   that   they heard   Gen 43:25

  They had heard that *they would eat* a meal there.

- Another example is Gen 43:7.

168 **Iterative imperfect.**[249] Also called the **frequentive imperfect**, **customary imperfect**, or **habitual imperfect**, the iterative imperfect describes an action as one that is done repeatedly, customarily, habitually, or characteristically. Because this is particularly common in proverbial sayings, the iterative imperfect is sometimes called the **proverbial imperfect**. Although the concepts of **habitual**, **customary**, and **characteristic** action can be distinguished from iterative action, those senses are subsumed under 'iterative' here.

- הַיָּמִים   כָּל־   אִיּוֹב   יַעֲשֶׂה   כָּכָה   Thus Job *did* continually.
  the days   all of   Job   *he does*   thus   Job 1:5

- הַדְּבֹרִים   תַּעֲשֶׂינָה   כַּאֲשֶׁר   אֶתְכֶם   וַיִּרְדְּפוּ   They chased you as bees *do*.
  the bees   *do*   as   you   they chased   Deut 1:44

- אָב   יְשַׂמַּח־   חָכָם   בֵּן   A wise son *makes* a father *glad*.
  father   *makes glad*   wise   son   Prov 15:20

- Other examples include Gen 6:21, 43:32; 1 Kgs 5:25.

169 **Potential imperfect (can).**[250] Also called the **non-perfective of capability**, this expresses (or denies) the ability to do or be something. This is similar to יָכֹל followed by the infinitive but perhaps less forceful.

---

[249] Cf. BHRG §19.3.4; GBHS §3.2.2b; GKC §107e, g; IBHS §31.2b, 31.3b, e, c; JM §113c, e; Fokkelman 1991; Joosten 1999a, 21–3.

[250] Cf. BHRG §19.3.5(i); GKC §107r, w; IBHS §31.4b–c; JM §113l; Joosten 1999a, 19–21.

- Where ability is an issue and customary or characteristic activity also fits the context, the categories of potential imperfect and habitual imperfect (§168) may merge. If the verb יָכֹל is used, classify it as a habitual imperfect because the sense of ability is carried primarily by the lexeme rather than the conjugation.

- אֵיכָה אֶשָּׂא לְבַדִּי טָרְחֲכֶם   How *can I bear* the burden of you alone?
  load of you alone *I can bear* how?   Deut 1:12

- לֹא־יֹאמְרוּ זֹאת אִיזָבֶל   *They will* not *be able to say*, 'This is Jezebel.'
  Jezebel this *they can say* not   2 Kgs 9:37

- Another example is Job 4:17.

170 Permissive imperfect (may).[251] Also called the **non-perfective of permission**, this authorizes the subject to perform the action of the verb.

- אֶת־שְׁנֵי בָנַי תָּמִית   *You may kill* my two sons.
  you may kill my sons two of   Gen 42:37

- וְאַחַר דַּבְּרִי תַּלְעִיג   After I have spoken, *you may mock*.
  you may mock I spoke and after   Job 21:3

- Another example is Gen 2:16.

171 Desiderative imperfect (want to).[252] A desiderative imperfect verb discusses whether or not the subject of the verb desires to do the action of the verb. It is typically translated into English using 'want,' 'wish,' or 'desire.' In contexts where it is clear that the subject will do the action of the verb if she desires to do so, it may be translated using 'will.'

- הֲתֵלְכִי עִם־הָאִישׁ הַזֶּה   *Do you want to go* with this man?
  the this the man with *you want to go?*   Gen 24:58

- אִם־אֹתָהּ תִּקַּח־ לְךָ קָח   If *you want to take* it for yourself, take it!
  take! to you *you want to take* her if   1 Sam 21:10

- Another example is Judges 4:8.

172 Obligative imperfect (ought to, should).[253] Also called the **non-perfective of obligation**, this indicates that the subject of the verb should (or should not) do the action of the verb.

- מַעֲשִׂים אֲשֶׁר לֹא־ יֵעָשׂוּ עָשִׂיתָ עִמָּדִי
  with me you did *they should be done* not which doings   Gen 20:9
  You did to me things which *ought* not *to be done*.

---

[251] Cf. GBHS §3.2.2d2; GKC §107s; IBHS §31.4d; JM §113l; Joosten 1999a, 19–21.
[252] Cf. BHRG §19.3.5(ii); IBHS §31.4h; JM §113n.
[253] Cf. BHRG §19.3.5(ii); GBHS §3.2.2d3; GKC §107n, w; IBHS §31.4f–g.

- וְכֵן לֹא יֵעָשֶׂה
  it should be done not and thus
  Such a thing *ought* not *to be done*.
  Gen 34:7

- Other possible examples include Lev 4:13 and 2 Sam 13:12.

173a Injunctive imperfect (must).[254] Also called the **non-perfective of injunction**, this requests or commands that the subject of the verb perform the action of the verb. It is often a very forceful command, typically translated with 'must,' 'shall,' 'are to,' or 'will.' In some contexts (e.g., prayer), however, it can be a request.

- וְאֶת־ חֻקֹּתַי תִּשְׁמֹרוּ
  you must keep my statutes and
  You must keep my statutes.
  Lev 18:4

- עַל־ גְּחֹנְךָ תֵלֵךְ וְעָפָר תֹּאכַל
  you must eat and dust *you must go* your belly on
  Gen 3:14
  On your belly *you shall go*, and dust *you shall eat*.

- Another example is Exod 21:12.
- The injunctive imperfect is typically much stronger in force than the jussive and cohortative (§185). In some contexts it is stronger than the imperative (§188).

173b Prohibitive imperfect (shall not). Also called the **non-perfective of prohibition**, an imperfect verb preceded by לֹא 'not' (§396) may request or command that the subject of the verb not perform the action of the verb. It is often a permanent prohibition of a general nature, typically translated with 'never,' 'must not,' 'shall not,' 'are not to,' or 'will not.' In some contexts (e.g., prayer), however, it can be a request, albeit a forceful one.

- לֹא תִּנְאָף
  you will commit adultery not
  You shall not commit adultery.
  Exod 20:14

- לֹא תֹאכַל מִמֶּנּוּ
  from it *you will eat* not
  You shall not eat from it.
  Gen 3:17

- Other examples include most of the Decalogue (Exod 20:3–5, 7, 10, 13–17).

174 Conditional imperfect.[255] A verb in the imperfect may be used to express a condition in the future, that is, the protasis (the 'if' part) of a real conditional sentence (§512–15). The imperfect is also used with לוּ to express unfulfilled wishes, as is the conditional perfect (§166).

- In the protasis of a conditional clause, the imperfect generally indicates a real condition, whereas the perfect generally indicates an unreal condition (§166).

---

[254] Cf. BHRG §19.3.5(iii); GBHS §3.2.2d4; GKC §107n–o; IBHS §31.4; JM §113m; Shulman 2001.
[255] Cf. GBHS §3.2.2d1; GKC §107x; IBHS §31.6.1b; JM §167g–i.

- גַּם כִּי־ אֵלֵךְ בְּגֵיא צַלְמָוֶת   even though *I walk* in a very dark valley

  darkness   in valley of   *I walk*   even though   Ps 23:4

- לוּ שָׁקוֹל יִשָׁקֵל כַּעְשִׂי

  my vexation   *it could be weighed out*   to weigh out   if only   Job 6:2

  If only my vexation *might be weighed out*!

  o לוּ indicates that the condition is unreal (§459a) or optative (§460).

175   **Imperfect after a telic particle.**[256] Imperfect verbs are commonly used after telic particles. **Telic particles**, also called **final conjunctions**, indicate a purpose or goal. Telic particles include פֶּן 'lest' (§461), לְמַעַן or לְמַעַן אֲשֶׁר 'in order that' (§367, 521, 524), לְבִלְתִּי 'in order that not' (§424, 524), בַּעֲבוּר 'in order that' (§522a–b), and occasionally אֲשֶׁר 'so that' (§466). The imperfect is also used with a simple waw to indicate purpose (§180).

- לֹא תִגְּעוּ בּוֹ פֶּן־ תְּמֻתוּן   You shall not touch it LEST *you die.*

  you will die   LEST   in it   you shall touch   not   Gen 3:3

- לְמַעַן יִיטַב־ לִי   IN ORDER THAT *it go well* with me

  to me   *it will go well*   IN ORDER THAT   Gen 12:13; cf. Jer 42:6

- Other examples include Gen 27:4; Exod 20:20; Deut 4:40.

Preterite conjugation

176   **The preterite conjugation**[257] refers to an action or state in past time (past from the point of view of the speaker). Unlike the Perfect, it refers strictly to past time, and says nothing about whether or not the action of the verb is complete. The preterite in Biblical Hebrew is controversial; everything in §176–7c is disputed.

- The preterite conjugation has the same spelling as the jussive conjugation, so it is spelled the same as the imperfect, except in the Hiphil and for some weak Qal verbs.

77a   **Preterite in waw consecutive**. The 'converted imperfect' (the *wayyiqtol*) might be a preterite with a waw prefixed to it. This is discussed in §178. The 'converted perfect' (§179) may have been formed by analogy.

---

[256] Cf. GKC §107q; IBHS §31.6.1c.

[257] Cf. BHRG §15.5; GBHS §3.2.2; GKC §48f–g; IBHS §29, 31.1, 34.2.1; JM §113g–k, 117c; Muraoka and Rogland 1998; Zevit 1998, 49–65; Gianto 1996, 505–8; Greenstein 1988; Rainey 1986; Zevit 1988. For a discussion of the preterite (*iprus*) in Akkadian, see Huehnergard 2000, 18–19, 157. The debate about the origin and meaning of the conjugations in Biblical Hebrew (of which the debate over the preterite is a part) is surveyed and evaluated in IBHS §29 and 31.1.

177b **Preterite in poetry.**[258] In poetry, particularly old poetry (or poetry that imitates an old style), some verb forms that look like the imperfect or jussive refer to the past, so they may be preterite.

- יֹאבַד יוֹם אִוָּלֶד בּוֹ   May the day perish on which *I was born.*
  in it *I was born* day it will perish   Job 3:3

- יִמְצָאֵהוּ בְּאֶרֶץ מִדְבָּר   *He found him* in a desert land.
  of desert in land *he found him*   Deut 32:10

- Other examples include Exod 15:12, 14–15; Job 3:11.

177c **Preterite in prose after אָז.**[259] The particle אָז is often followed by a verb that is spelled like the imperfect but appears to have a past-time meaning. Such verbs might be preterite rather than imperfect.

- One difficulty with this view is that the verb following אָז is usually spelled as an imperfect rather than as a jussive; it is not shortened as the preterite is thought to be.

- אָז יָשִׁיר־מֹשֶׁה   Then Moses *sang.*
  Moses *sang* then   Exod 15:1 (spelling not shortened)

- אָז יַקְהֵל שְׁלֹמֹה אֶת־זִקְנֵי יִשְׂרָאֵל
  of Israel elders Solomon *he assembled* then   1 Kgs 8:1 (spelling shortened)
       Then Solomon *assembled* the elders of Israel.

- Other examples include Deut 4:41; Num 21:17; Josh 8:30, 10:12.

- The perfect conjugation is also used after אָז. Examples include Gen 4:26; Josh 10:33; 2 Kgs 14:8.

Consecution (verbs with a waw prefix) [260]

178 **Imperfect waw consecutive.** This is known by a wide variety of other names, including the **imperfect waw conversive**, the **relative waw with a prefix form**, the **wayyqtl**, the **wayyiqtol form**, the **waw consecutive + imperfect**, the **relative waw + suffix form**, the **inverted future**, the **converted imperfect**, and the **consecutive preterite**. It is typically formed by prefixing וַ to the imperfect (which is shortened in the Hiphil

---

[258] This point (§177a) is particularly controversial. Cf. BHRG §19.3.6; GBHS §3.2.2e; IBHS §29, 31.1; JM §113h; Revell 1989a, 12–13, 15; Muraoka and Rogland 1998. IBHS §31.1.1g states, 'Whether or not the prefix conjugation … can serve as a preterite, especially in its unbound form in Hebrew poetry, cannot be decided beyond reasonable doubt at present.'

[259] Cf. GBHS §3.2.2e; GKC §107c; IBHS §31.6.3; JM §113i; Muraoka and Rogland 1998; Rabinowitz 1984; Joosten 1999a, 24–5.

[260] Cf. Van der Merwe 1994; Longacre 1994; Andersen 1994; Niccacci 1990; Niccacci 1994a; Niccacci 1994b; Buth 1994; Wolde 1997; Rooker 1990, 100–2.

and for some weak verbs). The waw prefix is referred to by a variety of names, including **waw consecutive**, **waw conversive**, **waw relative**, **waw inversive**, and **waw of succession**.

- As the variety of terminology suggests, the imperfect waw consecutive is a controversial topic, and the literature about it is voluminous.[261]
- The imperfect waw consecutive typically refers to a complete action, like the perfect conjunction (§162). It typically is part of a temporal sequence in past-time narrative (§496), although sometimes an imperfect waw consecutive is still used when the narrative takes a jump back in time to replay the events from another perspective. It sometimes has other nuances as well, such as expressing the result of a previous clause (§525).

- הֶהָרִים   כָּל־   וַיְכֻסּוּ   הָאָרֶץ   עַל־   מְאֹד   מְאֹד   גָּבְרוּ   וְהַמַּיִם

  the mountains all of *were covered* the earth on very very swelled the waters

  > The waters swelled greatly on the earth *so that* all the mountains *were covered*.

  > Gen 7:19

- בָּקָר   בֶּן־   וַיִּקַּח   אַבְרָהָם   רָץ   הַבָּקָר   וְאֶל־

  cattle son of *took* Abraham ran the cattle and to   Gen 18:7

  > Abraham ran to the herd *and took* a calf.

- The origin of this form is disputed. It may be the preterite conjugation (§176–7c) with an old spelling of the conjunction waw.

179   Perfect waw consecutive.[262] By analogy with the imperfect waw consecutive (§178), the consecutive waw occurs with the perfect. Because this was a later historical development than the imperfect waw consecutive, the conjunction waw is spelled in the normal fashion in the perfect waw consecutive (typically וְ), unlike in the imperfect waw consecutive (typically וַ; §178).

---

[261] Cf. BHRG §21.1–21.2; GBHS §3.5–3.5.1; GKC §49, 111; IBHS §33; JM §47, 117–18, 166b, 169c; Driver 1892, 70–99; Revell 1988; Revell 1991; Sasson 1997; Muraoka and Rogland 2003; Blake 1944; Saydon 1954; Buth 1994; Niccacci 1990; Niccacci 1994a; Zevit 1998, 49–65; Washburn 1994; Revell 1984; Cook 2004; Gosling 1998; Smith 1991; Collins 1995; Gibson 1995.

[262] Cf. BHRG §21.1, 21.3; GBHS §3.5, 3.5.2; GKC §49, 112; IBHS §32; JM §43, 117, 119, 166b, 169c; Driver 1892, 114–57; Berry 1904; Sheehan 1975; Blau 1971; Revell 1984; Revell 1985; Blake 1944; Longacre 1994; Niccacci 1990; Niccacci 1994a; Zevit 1998, 49–65; Moomo 2005; Cook 2004, 264–9; Fassberg 2006; Joosten 2006; Smith 1991; Gibson 1995; Revell 1985.

- The perfect waw consecutive is also called the **waw consecutive + perfect**, the **inverted perfect**, the **waw conversive**, the **relative waw + suffix conjugation**, the **weqatal**, the **w-qataltí**, and the **wəqataltí** (the accent on the last two names is critical).
- The perfect waw consecutive is a subject of ongoing research and dispute. The perfect waw consecutive is traditionally said to refer to an action without having the completion of the action in view, just like the incomplete-action imperfect (§167), and to often form a temporal sequence in a future-time narrative (§496). It sometimes has other nuances, such as being the result of a previous clause (§525), or continuing the imperatival sense of a preceding imperative or infinitive absolute. Recent studies have focused attention on its use as the normal, unmarked verb form in texts that discuss future events, discuss procedures, or give instructions.

- פֶּן־יֶחְדַּל אָבִי מִן־הָאֲתֹנוֹת וְדָאַג לָנוּ

  about us *and be worried* the donkeys from my father cease lest   1 Sam 9:5

  lest my father cease to be concerned about the donkeys and *become worried* about us

- תֵּלֵךְ וְלָקַחְתָּ אִשָּׁה לִבְנִי לְיִצְחָק   Go *and take* a wife for my son Isaac.

  to Isaac to my son woman *and take* (you) go   Gen 24:4

- This verb form is common in contexts that discuss future events, discuss procedures, or give instructions. For examples, see Deut 4:15, 16, 19, 22, 23, 25.

180 Imperfect with simple waw.[263]

- By 'simple waw' we mean a waw other than the 'consecutive waw' (§178–9). This simple waw is often called a **conjunctive waw** or a **copulative waw**, and is typically spelled וְ (not וַ) (§178).
- An imperfect with a simple waw is also called the **wəyqtl** or **wəyiqtol**. It has the exact same spelling as a jussive with waw (§181a–b) for almost all verbs, and for a few verbs is spelled just like a cohortative.
- The meaning of an imperfect with simple waw is disputed. Forms that might be (based on spelling alone) imperfect, jussive, or cohortative can have the same meaning as an imperfect, jussive, or cohortative without waw (§167–173a, 184a, 185, 187). Such ambiguous forms usually indicate purpose or result when the preceding verb is a jussive,

---

[263] Cf. BHRG §21.4, 21.5.1(iv), 40.8.2(ii); GBHS §3.5.1(b), 3.5.3; GKC §165a, 166a; IBHS §33.4, 39.2.1c; JM §117a, 168a; Lambdin §107c; Driver 1892, 64–9, 158–64; Kelly 1920; Zevit 1998, 49–65; Qimron 1986–7; Gibson 1995.

cohortative, or imperative. It has recently[264] been argued that forms with a simple waw that are unambiguously imperfect (rather than jussive or cohortative) always indicate purpose or result, regardless of the preceding verb.

• אַף־ עַל־ יָתוֹם   תַּפִּילוּ   וְתִכְרוּ   עַל־ רֵיעֲכֶם

your friend over *and you would bargain* you would cast lots orphan on even

Job 6:27 (ambiguous form)

You would even cast lots over an orphan and *you would bargain* over your friend.

• וְכָל־ יִשְׂרָאֵל יִשְׁמְעוּ וְיִרָאוּן   All Israel will hear, and (*as a result*) *will be afraid.*

will fear will hear Israel all of   Deut 13:12 (unambiguous form)

• Examples with unambiguous forms include Exod 2:7; 2 Sam 19:38; 1 Kgs 15:19.

• Examples with ambiguous forms include Gen 22:17 and 49:7.

81a **Jussive, cohortative, or imperative with simple waw for purpose or result.**[265] Prefixing a simple waw (**conjunctive waw** or **copulative waw**) to a jussive, cohortative, or imperative verb can indicate purpose or result, particularly when the preceding verb is jussive, cohortative, or imperative (§187, 189, 518). This use is also called the **indirect jussive**, **indirect cohortative**, **indirect volitive**, or **indirect imperative**.

• קַח מִמֶּנִּי   וְאֶקְבְּרָה   אֶת־מֵתִי שָׁמָּה

there my dead *and let me bury* from me take!   Gen 23:13

Accept it from me *so that I may bury* my dead there.

• וְאֶעֱשֶׂה   עִמּוֹ   חֶסֶד   *so that I may show* loyalty to him

loyalty with him *and let me do*   2 Sam 9:1

81b **Jussive, cohortative, or imperative with simple waw for command or request.**[266] A jussive or cohortative may indicate a command or a request with (or without) a simple waw (§185).

• וִיהִי־נָא   פִּי־   שְׁנַיִם בְּרוּחֲךָ אֵלָי

to me your spirit two portion *and may it be*   2 Kgs 2:9

Let there be a double portion of your spirit on me.

182 **Perfect with simple waw.**[267] Sometimes called the **waw-conjunctive plus qatal** form, a perfect verb with a simple waw is primarily used when the perfect is part of a series of closely related verbs.

---

[264] Baden, forthcoming.

[265] Cf. BHRG §21.5.1, 21.5.2, 40.8.2(ii); GBHS §3.5.3b, 5.2.3a; GKC §108d–f, 110f–i, 165a, 166a; IBHS §33.4, 34.5.2, 34.6; JM §116, 168b, 169b, i; Lambdin §107c; Driver 1892, 64–9; Gibson 1995; Niccacci 1990. For a contrary opinion, see Muraoka 1997.

[266] Cf. BHRG §19.4, 21.5.3; JM §114a; Niccacci 1990.

- הוּא הֵסִיר אֶת־הַבָּמוֹת וְשִׁבַּר אֶת־הַמַּצֵּבֹת

  the pillars   *and shattered*   the high places   removed   he   2 Kgs 18:4

  וְכָרַת אֶת־הָאֲשֵׁרָה וְכִתַּת נְחַשׁ הַנְּחֹשֶׁת

  the bronze   snake of   *and beat into pieces*   the Asherah   *and cut down*   (cont.)

  He removed the high places, *shattered* the pillars,

  cut down the Asherah, and *beat* the bronze snake *into pieces*.

- Other examples of a perfect verb that is closely linked to a preceding verb with a simple waw include 2 Sam 7:9–13; 2 Kgs 21:6, 23:4–5. In 2 Kgs 8:10 there is a perfect with a simple waw (וְהִרְאַנִי) that is not in series with the preceding verb.

- Sometimes a perfect verb with a simple waw is used where we expect an imperfect waw consecutive (§178). Examples include Eccl 1:12–13 and 2:12–13.

D Volitive Moods [268]

The volitive moods (also called **volitives**, **volitional forms**, **modals**, or **projectives**) are the imperative, jussive, and cohortative. **Volitives** usually deal with the will: commands, requests, desires, purposes, etc.

Jussive and cohortative [269]

The jussive and cohortative can together be called the **precative**, although that term is often used to include the imperative as well.

183 **Origin and form of the jussive and cohortative.**[270] The jussive is identical in form with the preterite, but may have had a different origin historically (§176). The cohortative likely had a different origin from both.

- This is a controversial topic; some scholars argue that the jussive and cohortative are distinguished from the imperfect by the fact that they occur first in a clause rather than by their spelling. So a jussive might not be shortened (even, e.g., for a 3-ה verb), and a cohortative might not have the הָ suffix.[271]

---

[267] Cf. IBHS §32.3; JM §117a; Driver 1892, 158–64; Huesman 1956b; Rubinstein 1963; Longacre 1994, 68–71; Zevit 1998, 49–65; Gibson 1995; Niccacci 1990, §158(ii).

[268] Cf. BHRG §19.4; GBHS §3.3; GKC §46, 48, 108–110; IBHS §34; JM §45–6, 48, 114; Gentry 1998, 21–39; Niccacci 1990.

[269] Cf. BHRG §19.4.3–19.4.4; GBHS §3.3.1, 3.3.3; GKC §48, 108–109; IBHS §34.1–34.3, 34.5; JM §45–6, 114; Driver 1892, 50–63, 212–18.

[270] Cf. IBHS §34.1–34.2; JM §45–6; Gentry 1998, 31–3.

[271] See Gentry 1998, 31–5. Qimron (1986–7) argues that short forms with a prefixed simple waw are often imperfect rather than jussive.

184a **Jussive and cohortative for a desire.**[272] Often called the **optative use** or the **desiderative** use, the jussive and cohortative can be used to express a strong desire or wish (§546).

- יְחִי הַמֶּלֶךְ   *May* the king *live!* (i.e., *Long live* the king!)
  the king *may live*   1 Sam 10:24

- אַךְ יָקֵם יְהוָה אֶת־דְּבָרוֹ   *May* YHWH *establish* his word!
  only *may establish* YHWH his word   1 Sam 1:23

- Other examples include Deut 12:20 and 17:14.

184b **Jussive and cohortative for a negative desire.**[273] The jussive and cohortative can be used with אַל 'not' to express a strong desire or wish that something not happen.

- אַל־אֶרְאֶה בְּמוֹת הַיָּלֶד   *I do not want to see* the boy's death!
  not *let me look* upon death of the boy   Gen 21:16

185 **Jussive and cohortative for a command or request.**[274] See §181b.

- נֵלְכָה וְנַעַבְדָה אֱלֹהִים אֲחֵרִים   *Let us go* and *serve* other gods!
  let us go! let us serve! and gods other   Deut 13:7

- וִיהִי־נָא פִּי־ שְׁנַיִם בְּרוּחֲךָ אֵלָי   *and may it be*   2 Kgs 2:9
  and may it be portion two your spirit to me
  Let there be a double portion of your spirit on me!

- Other examples include Judg 15:2 and 1 Kgs 18:23.

186 **Jussive with אַל for negative command.**[275] Also called the **vetitive**, אַל 'not' followed by a jussive gives a negative command. The prohibition often applies to a specific situation rather than being a general prohibition (in contrast with לֹא with the imperfect, §173b). אַל with a second-person jussive is the negative of the imperative (§188).

- זְכֹר אַל־תִּשְׁכַּח   Remember! *Do not forget!*
  remember! not *may (you) forget*   Deut 9:7

- אַל־תֹּאכַל לֶחֶם וְאַל־ תֵּשְׁתְּ מָיִם   *Do not eat* bread or *drink* water!
  not *(you) eat* bread and *not* *(you) drink* water   1 Kgs 13:22

---

[272] Cf. BHRG §19.4.3(ii), 19.4.4(ii); GBHS §3.3.1(b–c), 3.3.3(b), 5.3.3(a); GKC §108c, 109b–c, 151a; IBHS §34.3, 34.5.1; JM §114b–c, g–h, 163a.

[273] Cf. BHRG §19.4.3(ii), 19.4.4(ii); GBHS §3.3.1(d), 3.3.3b; GKC §108c, 109c; IBHS §34.3, 34.5.1; JM §114c, i, 163a.

[274] Cf. BHRG §19.4.3(i), 19.4.4(i); GBHS §3.3.1(a), 3.3.3(c); GKC §108b–c, 109b; IBHS §34.3, 34.5.1; JM §114b–h.

[275] Cf. BHRG §19.4.2(1), 19.4.4(i); GBHS §3.3.1d; GKC §109c–e; IBHS §34.3, 34.4a; JM §114i.

187 **Jussive or cohortative with waw for purpose or result**. See §181a.

- וְאֹכֵלָה   לִי   וְהָבִיאָה   Bring it to me *so that I may eat.*
  and let me eat to me and (you) bring!   Gen 27:4

- Another example is 1 Kgs 21:2. More examples are noted in §181a, 518.

Imperative [276]

188 **Imperative for command or request**.[277] The imperative is used for positive commands or requests in the second person.

- For negative commands or requests in the second person, אַל is used with the jussive (§186) or לֹא is used with the imperfect (§173b). For commands or requests in the first and third person, the cohortative and jussive are used, respectively (§185).

- וֶאֱמָץ   חֲזַק   *Be courageous* and *strong!*
  and *be strong!* *be courageous!*   Deut 31:23

- הַיַּרְדֵּן   מִן־   עֲלוּ   *Come up* from the Jordan!
  the Jordan from *come up!*   Josh 4:17

189 **Imperative with waw for purpose or result**. See §181a.

- וּמַלְּטִי אֶת־נַפְשֵׁךְ   עֵצָה   נָא   אִיעָצֵךְ   לְכִי
  your life *and save!* advice let me advise you come!   1 Kgs 1:12
                                  Come and let me advise you *so that you may save* your life.

- יְהוָה   אֶת־נַחֲלַת   וּבָרְכוּ   אֲכַפֵּר   וּבַמָּה
  of YHWH inheritance *and bless!* I can atone and in how?   2 Sam 21:3
                                  How can I atone *so that you will bless* the inheritance of YHWH?

- Another example is 2 Kgs 5:10. More examples are noted in §519.

190 **Imperatives joined by waw for conditional**.[278] Two imperatives, the second of which has a waw, may indicate a conditional sentence (i.e., if … then). The sense of a command is still present.

- This category may be difficult to distinguish from an imperative with waw for purpose or result (§189). For a conditional, the sense of uncertainty predominates.

- גַּפְנוֹ   אִישׁ־   וְאִכְלוּ   אֵלַי   וּצְאוּ   בְרָכָה   אִתִּי   עֲשׂוּ־
  his vine man *and eat!* to me *and come out!* blessing me *make!*   Isa 36:16
                                  Give me a blessing *and come out* to me; *if you do, then* each *may eat* from his vine.

---

[276] Cf. BHRG §19.4.2; GBHS §3.3.2; GKC §46, 110; IBHS §34.1, 34.2.2, 34.4; JM §114m–p; Fassberg 1999; Gentry 1998, 30–1; Joosten 1999b; Fassberg 2006.

[277] Cf. BHRG §19.4.2(i); GBHS §3.3.2(a); GKC §110a, d; IBHS §34.4a–b; JM §114m–o; Shulman 2001.

[278] Cf. GKC §110f.

- זֹאת עֲשׂוּ וִחְיוּ   *If you do* this (*and I command you to do so*), *then you will live.*
  and live! do! this   Gen 42:18

191 Imperative as interjection.[279] A singular imperative may serve as an interjection; it is often used to get someone's attention before a command that follows. In some translation styles, this may be left untranslated, or a colloquial expression (e.g., 'hey!' or 'come on!') may be used. This phenomenon only occurs with certain verbs, such as קוּם 'get up!' הָבָה 'come on!' and לְכָה 'come on!'

- קוּם עֲשֵׂה־לָנוּ אֱלֹהִים   *Get up!* Make gods for us!
  gods   for us make! get up!   Exod 32:1

- הָבָה נִלְבְּנָה לְבֵנִים   *Come on!* Let us make bricks!
  bricks let us make bricks come on!   Gen 11:3; see Gen 11:7

- לְכָה נַשְׁקֶה אֶת־אָבִינוּ   *Come on!* Let us make our father drink!
  our father let us cause to drink come on!   Gen 19:32

E Verbal Nouns

Infinitive construct [280]

192 Infinitive construct as subject.[281] An infinitive construct may be the subject of a clause. The preposition לְ is sometimes prefixed to it (§276).

- לֹא־טוֹב הֱיוֹת הָאָדָם לְבַדּוֹ   For the man *to be* alone is not good.
  to solitude the man to be good not   Gen 2:18

- אִם רַע בְּעֵינֵיכֶם לַעֲבֹד אֶת־יְהוָה   if *serving* YHWH is evil in your sight
  YHWH to serve in your eyes it is evil if   Josh 24:15

- Another example is 1 Sam 18:23.

193 Infinitive construct as object.[282] An infinitive construct may be the direct object of a verb. It may be preceded by the accusative particle אֵת (§50) or the preposition לְ (§276).

- לֹא אֵדַע צֵאת וָבֹא   I do not know how *to go out* or *come in.*
  or to come in to go out I know not   1 Kgs 3:7; see Deut 10:10

---

[279] Cf. GKC §110h; JM §177f.
[280] Cf. BHRG §20.1; GBHS §3.4.1; GKC §45, 62, 114–15; IBHS §35.1, 36; JM §49, 124; Miller 1970.
[281] Cf. BHRG §20.1.2; GBHS §3.4.1a(1); GKC §114a; IBHS §36.2.1b, 36.2.3b; JM §124b, m.
[282] Cf. GBHS §3.4.1a(3); GKC §114c, m; IBHS §36.2.1d; JM §124c, m.

- לֹא־ נְתַתִּיךָ לִנְגֹּעַ אֵלֶיהָ
  to her   to touch   I gave you   not

  I did not allow you *to touch* her.

  Gen 20:6

- אֵלָי   הִתְרַגֶּזְךָ   אֵת ... יָדַעְתִּי
  to me   *your being enraged*   I know

  I know ... *your raging* against me.

  2 Kgs 19:27 = Isa 37:28

194   Infinitive construct after a word in the construct state.[283] See §36–49.

- תָּמוּת   מוֹת   מִמֶּנּוּ   אֲכָלְךָ   בְּיוֹם
  you will die   to die   from it   *of your eating*   in day

  Gen 2:17

  On the day *that you eat* from it, you will surely die.

- הַמִּקְנֶה   הֵאָסֵף   עֵת   לֹא־
  the livestock   *being gathered*   time of   not

  Gen 29:7

  It is not the time *that* the livestock *is gathered.*

195   Explanatory use of the infinitive construct (by …ing).[284] The infinitive construct, with prefixed לְ (לְ of manner §274a) or preceded by לְבִלְתִּי for negative uses, can follow a verb, spelling out in more detail what it means. This can be considered to be a subcategory of the **adverbial accusative** or the **accusative of manner** (§60). This use of the infinitive construct is also called **epexegetical**, **specification**, **gerundive**, or **complementary**.

- הַדָּם   עַל־   לֶאֱכֹל   לַיהוָה   חֹטִאים   הָעָם
  the blood   on   *by eating*   against YHWH   sinning   the people

  1 Sam 14:33

  The people are sinning against YHWH *by eating* [meat] with the blood.

  ○   The infinitive construct לֶאֱכֹל 'by eating' explains the verb חֹטִאים 'sinning.'

- אֶרְדֹּף   לֵאמֹר   בַּיהוָה   דָּוִד   וַיִּשְׁאַל
  I will pursue   *saying*   in YHWH   David   he asked

  1 Sam 30:8

  David asked YHWH, *saying,* 'Should I pursue?'

- Other examples include Exod 5:19, 31:16; Deut 8:11; 1 Sam 12:17.

196   Infinitive construct of obligation (should be …ed).[285] An infinitive construct, with prefixed לְ (לְ of product §278) can indicate something that should or must be done. Things that should or must not be done can be indicated by לֹא 'not' (§397) or אֵין 'there is not' (§410a–b; typically in late texts). This meaning is sometimes called **gerundive**.

---

[283] Cf. GBHS §3.4.1a(2); GKC §114b; IBHS §36.2.1c; JM §124d.

[284] Cf. BHRG §20.1.3(v); GBHS §3.4.1(g); GKC §114o–p; IBHS §36.2.3e; JM §124o; Miller 1994, 206–9. Miller argues that לֵאמֹר to introduce direct speech (e.g., the example from 1 Sam 30:8) is not the explanatory use; instead, it 'has become grammaticalized as a complementizer introducing the complement of direct speech' (p. 209).

[285] Cf. GBHS §3.4.1e; GKC §114h, k–l; IBHS §36.2.3f; JM §124l.

- מֶה לַעֲשׂוֹת לָךְ   What *should be done* for you?
  to you *to do* what?   2 Kgs 4:13

- הַס כִּי לֹא לְהַזְכִּיר בְּשֵׁם יְהוָה
  YHWH in name of *to mention* not because hush!   Amos 6:10

  Hush! For the name of YHWH *should not be mentioned*.

- Other examples include Josh 2:5; Esth 3:14, 4:2.

197   **Infinitive construct of purpose (in order to).**[286] The infinitive construct can indicate the reason why something is or should be done. When used this way, the infinitive construct is preceded by לְ (§277), לְמַעַן (§367), or בַּעֲבוּר (§522a–b). The infinitive construct can also be preceded by לְבִלְתִּי 'not' (§424) to express a negative purpose, meaning that the purpose is to avoid the action or state denoted by the infinitive construct.

198   **Infinitive construct of result (thus …ing).**[287] The infinitive construct can indicate the **consequence** or **result** of something. When used this way, it is typically preceded by לְ (§279), although לְמַעַן (§368) is also used.

- וַעֲשִׂיתֶם הָרַע בְּעֵינֵי יְהוָה־אֱלֹהֶיךָ לְהַכְעִיסוֹ
  angering him your God YHWH in eyes of the evil you will do   Deut 4:25

  You do what is evil in the eyes of YHWH your God, *thus angering him*.

- לְמַעַן חַלֵּל אֶת־שֵׁם קָדְשִׁי
  my holiness name of *polluting* with the result that   *thus polluting* my holy name
                                               Amos 2:7

- Other examples include Num 11:11; Lev 20:3; 1 Kgs 2:27; 2 Kgs 22:17; Ruth 2:10.

199   **Infinitive construct of degree (enough to …).** The infinitive construct can be used with לְ (לְ of degree §275) to indicate that something is sufficient to cause the infinitive construct to happen.

- חָלָה חִזְקִיָּהוּ לָמוּת   Hezekiah was sick *enough to die*.
  to die Hezekiah he was sick   2 Kgs 20:1

- וּבְאַהֲרֹן הִתְאַנַּף יְהוָה מְאֹד לְהַשְׁמִידוֹ
  to destroy him very YHWH he was angry and at Aaron   Deut 9:20

  And YHWH was very angry at Aaron – *angry enough to destroy him*.

- Another example is 2 Sam 13:2.

200   **Infinitive construct as object of a preposition.**[288] Frequently, an infinitive construct is the object of a preposition. The nuance of the

---

[286] Cf. BHRG §20.1.3(iv), 39.9.2(i); GBHS §3.4.1c; GKC §114f–h; IBHS §36.2.2b, 36.2.3d; JM §124l, 168c.

[287] Cf. BHRG §20.1.3(vi); GBHS §3.4.1d; IBHS §36.2.2b, 36.2.3d; JM §124l, 169d, g.

[288] Cf. GBHS §3.4.1b; GKC §114q; IBHS §36.2.2, 36.2.3; JM §124k–p.

infinitive construct is then a function of the preposition and the context. Some uses of an infinitive construct after a preposition include temporal (§503–8), causal (§535), and concessive (§532).

Infinitive absolute [289]

201   **The name 'infinitive absolute' can be misleading**, because the infinitive absolute is not the absolute state of 'the infinitive.' The infinitive construct is not in the construct state. The infinitive absolute and the infinitive construct have different origins historically; one is not derived from the other. The infinitive absolute does not take pronominal suffixes, and it takes prepositional prefixes only rarely.[290]

202   **Infinitive absolute as the subject of a clause.**[291] An infinitive absolute can function as the subject of a clause, particularly in poetry.

- הַכֵּר־ פָּנִים בְּמִשְׁפָּט בַּל־ טוֹב   *To show partiality* in judgment is not good.
  good   not   in judgment   faces   *to regard*   Prov 24:23

203   **Infinitive absolute as the object of a verb.**[292] An infinitive absolute can function as the direct object of a verb, particularly in poetry.

- לֹא־ יִתְּנֵנִי הָשֵׁב רוּחִי   He will not allow me *to draw my breath*.
  my breath   *to bring back*   he will give me   not   Job 9:18

- לִמְדוּ הֵיטֵב   Learn *to do good*!
  to do good   learn!   Isa 1:17

204   **Infinitive absolute as adverb of manner.**[293] An infinitive absolute can describe the style or manner with which the verb takes place. This is similar to the adverbial accusative of manner (§60).

- רִדְפוּ מַהֵר אַחֲרֵיהֶם   Pursue them *quickly*!
  after them   *to hurry*   pursue!   Josh 2:5

  o   מַהֵר is the Piel infinitive absolute of מהר 'to hurry.' It is used so often as an adverb of manner (meaning 'quickly') that it is given a separate entry as an adverb in the BDB lexicon.

- שָׁאַלְתָּ הֵיטֵב   You will inquire *thoroughly*.
  to cause to go well   you will ask   Deut 13:15

---

[289] Cf. BHRG §20.2; GBHS §3.4.2; IBHS §35; JM §49a–b, 123.
[290] Cf. BHRG §20.2; GBHS §3.4.2; GKC §113a; IBHS §35.1; JM §123c.
[291] Cf. GBHS §3.4.2a(1); GKC §113b; IBHS §35.3.3a; JM §123b.
[292] Cf. GBHS §3.4.2a(3); GKC §113c; IBHS §35.3.3b; JM §123b.
[293] Cf. BHRG §20.2.3; GBHS §3.4.2c; GKC §113h–k; IBHS §35.4; JM §123r.

- Other examples include Gen 21:16 and 1 Sam 3:12.

205 Infinitive absolute to emphasize a verb of the same root.[294] The combination of an infinitive absolute and a finite verb[295] of the same root can indicate emphasis of various types, such as affirming that the action of the verb is very certain to occur. The finite verb does not need to be in the same stem (e.g., Qal, Piel) as the infinitive absolute, but it must have the same root (e.g., both from נתן). This use of the infinitive absolute is also called the **internal object accusative**, the **absolute complement**, the **intensifying infinitive**, or the **tautological infinitive**.

- The infinitive absolute usually comes before the finite verb, but sometimes it follows it (e.g., 2 Kgs 5:11). When it used with an imperative verb, the infinitive always follows the imperative (e.g., Num 11:15).

- If the finite verb is negated (e.g., with לֹא 'not'), the typical word order is <infinitive absolute> + <negative> + <finite verb> (e.g., Judg 1:28), but the word order <negative> + <infinitive absolute> + <finite verb> also occurs (e.g., Gen 3:4).

- תָּמוּת מוֹת   You will *surely* die.
  you will die *to die*   Gen 2:17

- יָצוֹא   יֵצֵא   אֵלַי   He will *surely* come out to me.
  to come out he will come out to me   2 Kgs 5:11

- הָרְגֵנִי נָא הָרֹג   Kill me *immediately*!
  to kill kill me!   Num 11:15

- הוֹרִישׁוֹ   לֹא   וְהוֹרֵישׁ   But he did not dispossess him *completely*.
  he dispossessed him not and *to dispossess*   Judg 1:28

- תְּמֻתוּן   מוֹת   לֹא־   You *surely* will not die.
  you will die *to die* not   Gen 3:4

- Other examples include Exod 21:12; Judg 15:13; 1 Kgs 3:26; Isa 30:19; Amos 9:8; Ps 49:8; Job 6:2.

206 Infinitive absolute to express continuous action or repetition.[296] An infinite absolute that follows a finite verb[295] may indicate that the finite verb or the infinitive absolute occurs continually or repeatedly. The infinitive and finite verb are often of the same root (e.g., both from נתן).

---

[294] Cf. BHRG §20.2.1; GBHS §3.4.2b; GKC §113l–r; IBHS §35.3.1; JM §123d–q; Muraoka 1985, 83–92; Riekert 1979; Goldenberg 1971; Eskhult 2000.

[295] A 'finite verb' is a verb form that has 'person' (i.e., 1st, 2nd, or 3rd). Thus verbs in the perfect, imperfect, imperative, jussive, and cohortative are all finite verb forms, whereas participles and infinitives are not.

[296] Cf. GBHS §3.4.2b; GKC §113r–u; IBHS §35.3.2b–c; JM §123l, s; Riekert 1979.

- The finite verb that precedes the infinitive absolute is often modified by a word such as an infinitive absolute (e.g., 1 Sam 6:12), an adjective (e.g., 1 Sam 14:19), or a participle.

- This use of the infinitive absolute is particularly common for הָלוֹךְ 'to go.'

- וְגָעוֹ   הָלֹךְ   הָלְכוּ   They went *along*, lowing as they went.
  and to low *to walk* they went   1 Sam 6:12

- וָרָב   הָלוֹךְ   וַיֵּלֶךְ ... וְהֶהָמוֹן   The tumult went *on* and increased.
  and great *to go* it went   and the tumult   1 Sam 14:19

- וְקָרֵב   הָלוֹךְ   וַיֵּלֶךְ   And he *kept on* coming nearer.
  and near *to go* he went   2 Sam 18:25

- Other possible examples include Gen 8:3, 8:5, 31:15; Num 11:32; Judg 14:9.

207a **Infinitive absolute after a word in the construct state.**[297] An infinitive absolute may follow a term in the construct state, thereby acting as a genitive (§36–49). This is rare and disputed.

- הַשְׂכֵּל   מִדֶּרֶךְ   תּוֹעֶה   אָדָם
  to understand from way of one wandering off man   Prov 21:16

  a man who wanders off from the way of *understanding*

- הַשְׁמֵד   בְּמַטְאֲטֵא   וְטֵאטֵאתִיהָ
  to exterminate with broom of I will sweep it   Isa 14:23

  I will sweep it with the broom of *extermination*.

207b **Infinitive absolute after a preposition.**[298] This is very rare and disputed.

- לְהֵרָאֹה   יְהוָה   מַלְאַךְ   עוֹד   יָסַף   וְלֹא־
  to appear YHWH angel of again he added and not   Judg 13:21

  And the angel of YHWH did not *appear* again.

- שָׁתֹה   אַחֲרֵי ... חַנָּה   וַתָּקָם
  to drink after Hannah she rose   1 Sam 1:9

  Hannah rose ... *after drinking*.

- Other examples occur in 1 Sam 3:21; 2 Kgs 13:17, 19.

208 **Infinitive absolute as a finite verb.**[299] As discussed in §209–12, an infinitive absolute can function as a finite verb.

209 **Infinitive absolute as an imperfect verb.**[300] An infinitive absolute can function as an imperfect verb (§167–75).

---

[297] Cf. GBHS §3.4.2(a.2); GKC §113e; IBHS §35.3.3a; JM §123c.

[298] Cf. GBHS §3.4.2(a.2); GKC §113e; IBHS §35.3.3a; JM §123c, 124r.

[299] Cf. BHRG §20.2.4; GBHS §3.4.2d; GKC §113y–gg; IBHS §35.5; JM §123u–y; Rubinstein 1952; Huesman 1956a.

- רָגוֹם אֹתוֹ בָאֲבָנִים כָּל־ הָעֵדָה

  the congregation   all of   with stones   him   *to stone*   Num 15:35

  All the congregation *will stone* him with stones.

- וְהוֹתֵר אָכֹל

  and *to have left over*   *to eat*   *They will eat* and *they will have some left over.*
  2 Kgs 4:43

- Other examples include Gen 17:10; Exod 12:48; Num 30:3; Deut 15:2.

210 **Infinitive absolute as a perfect verb.**[301] An infinitive absolute can function as a perfect verb (§161–6). Sometimes the infinitive absolute is followed by an independent personal pronoun (e.g., Eccl 4:2).

- וְנָפוֹץ הַכַּדִּים

  the jars   *and to smash*   *They smashed* the jars.
  Judg 7:19

- בָּחֹר אֹתוֹ מִכָּל־ שִׁבְטֵי יִשְׂרָאֵל

  Israel   tribes of   from all of   him   *to choose*   *I chose* him from all of the tribes of Israel.
  1 Sam 2:28

- Other examples include Gen 41:43; Ps 17:5; Eccl 4:2; Esth 3:13, 9:1.

211 **Infinitive absolute as an imperative verb.**[302] An infinitive absolute can function as an imperative verb, giving a command in the second person (§188).

- הָלוֹךְ וְרָחַצְתָּ שֶׁבַע־פְּעָמִים

  times   seven   and he washed   *to go*   *Go* and wash seven times!
  2 Kgs 5:10

- זַעֲקִי־ עִיר נָמוֹג פְּלֶשֶׁת

  Philistia   *to melt*   city   cry out!   Cry out, O city! *Melt*, O Philistia!
  Isa 14:31

212 **Infinitive absolute as a jussive verb.**[303] An infinitive absolute can function as a jussive verb, giving a command in the third person (§185).

- הַקְרֵב אֹתָהּ בְּנֵי־ אַהֲרֹן

  Aaron   sons of   it   *to present*   The sons of Aaron *shall present* it.
  Lev 6:7

- פָּגוֹשׁ דֹּב שַׁכּוּל בְּאִישׁ וְאַל־ כְּסִיל בְּאִוַּלְתּוֹ

  in his folly   fool   and not   with man   bereaved of children   bear   *to meet*   Prov 17:12

  Let a bear robbed of her cubs *meet* a man rather than a fool in his folly [meet him].

---

[300] Cf. BHRG §20.2.4; GBHS §3.4.2d; GKC §113y–aa, ee–ff; IBHS §35.5.2; JM §123v–y; Rubinstein 1952.

[301] Cf. BHRG §20.2.4; GBHS §3.4.2d; GKC §113y–aa, ff; IBHS §35.5.2; JM §123w–y; Rubinstein 1952; Huesman 1956b.

[302] Cf. BHRG §20.2.4; GBHS §3.4.2d; GKC §113y–bb; IBHS §35.5.1; JM §123u–v, x–y; Rubinstein 1952; Hospers 1991; Watts 1962; Fassberg 2006. Hospers argues that the infinitive absolute should be understood as serving to focus attention rather than as being a substitute for an imperative verb.

[303] Cf. GBHS §3.4.2d; GKC §113y–aa, cc; IBHS §35.5.2; JM §123x–y; Rubinstein 1952.

Participle[304]

213 **Participle as a repeated or continuous predicate.**[305] A participle can act as the predicate of a verbless clause, indicating a repeated, continuous, or characteristic action.

- The action may be in the past, present, or future. To indicate past time, הָיָה in the perfect often precedes the participle (e.g., 1 Sam 2:11). To indicate future time, הָיָה in the imperfect often precedes the participle.

- אֶת־אַחַי אָנֹכִי מְבַקֵּשׁ   I am *seeking* my brothers.
  seeking   I   my brothers   Gen 37:16

- וְהַנַּעַר הָיָה מְשָׁרֵת אֶת־יְהוָה   And the boy was *serving* YHWH.
  YHWH   *serving*   was   and the boy   1 Sam 2:11

- Other examples include Gen 3:5; Judg 16:21; 1 Sam 23:1; 1 Kgs 3:3; 2 Kgs 7:9, 17:25; Job 1:14.

214 **Participle for an imminent action.**[306] A participle can indicate an action that is about to occur.

- וַאֲנִי הִנְנִי מֵבִיא אֶת־הַמַּבּוּל   I *am about to bring* the flood.
  the flood   *bringing*   (behold) me   and I   Gen 6:17

- הִנְּךָ מֵת   You *are about to die.*
  dying   (behold) you   Gen 20:3

- Another example is 1 Kgs 20:13.

215a **Participle as an attributive adjective.**[307] A participle can function as an attributive adjective, describing a substantive (§73). It follows the substantive that it describes and usually exhibits concord with it (i.e., the participle and the substantive that it modifies have the same gender, number, and definiteness).

- יְהוָה אֱלֹהֶיךָ אֵשׁ אֹכְלָה   YHWH your God is a *consuming* fire.
  consuming   fire   your God   YHWH   Deut 4:24

215b **Participle as a predicate adjective.**[308] A participle can function as a predicate adjective, asserting something about a substantive (§75), and

---

[304] Cf. BHRG §20.3; GBHS §3.4.3; GKC §50, 61, 116; IBHS §37; JM §50, 121; Driver 1892, 165–73; Smith 1999.

[305] Cf. BHRG §20.3.1(i); GBHS §3.4.3, 5.1.1(c); GKC §107d, 116a–c; IBHS §37.1d–e, 37.6d–f, 37.7.1b; JM §121a–h.

[306] Cf. BHRG §20.3.1(ii); GBHS §3.4.3b(3); GKC §116p; IBHS §37.6f; JM §121e.

[307] Cf. BHRG §20.3.3; GBHS §3.4.3a; GKC §116d–l; IBHS §37.4; JM §121i.

[308] Cf. GBHS §3.4.3b, 5.1.1(c); GKC §116d–l; IBHS §37.4.

thus acting like a verb (§213). A predicate adjective usually has the same gender and number as the subject, but lacks the article.

- וְאַבְרָהָם עוֹדֶנּוּ עֹמֵד לִפְנֵי יְהוָה

  YHWH   before   *standing*   still him   but Abraham   Gen 18:22

  But Abraham *was* still *standing* before YHWH.

216 Participle indicating what should or may be done.[309] A participle, usually in the Niphal or Pual stem, can indicate something that ought to be done (also called the **gerundive** sense) or that is allowed to be done (also called the **admissive** sense). Such a participle typically acts as an attributive adjective (§215a) or a predicate adjective (§215b).

- מִמִּזְרַח־שֶׁמֶשׁ עַד־מְבוֹאוֹ מְהֻלָּל שֵׁם יְהוָה

  YHWH   name of   *praised*   its setting   unto   sun   from rising of   Ps 113:3

  From the rising of the sun to its setting, the name of YHWH *is to be praised*.

- כִּי־יְהוָה עֶלְיוֹן נוֹרָא   because YHWH Most High *is to be feared*

  feared   Most High   YHWH   because   Ps 47:3

217 Substantival participle.[310] Participles are often used as nouns.

- Examples include אוֹיֵב 'enemy,' רֹעֶה 'shepherd,' יוֹשֵׁב 'inhabitant,' חֹזֶה 'seer,' and שֹׁמֵר 'watchman' or 'spy.'

218 Participle as a relative clause.[311] A participle is often best translated as a relative clause (§539a). Such a participle often has the article (§90).

- יְהוָה הַנִּרְאֶה אֵלָיו   YHWH, *who had appeared* to him

  to him   *the one appearing*   YHWH   Gen 12:7

- הֹעֲלָה עַל־הַמִּזְבֵּחַ הַבָּנוּי   It was sacrificed on the altar *which had been built.*

  the built   the altar   on   it was sacrificed   Judg 6:28

- Other examples include 2 Kgs 22:18 and Gen 26:11.

219 Participle in a circumstantial clause.[312] A participle can act as the verb of a circumstantial clause (§494).

---

[309] Cf. GKC §116c; IBHS §37.4d; JM §121i.

[310] Cf. BHRG §20.3.2; GBHS §3.4.3c; GKC §116g; IBHS §37.2; Wernberg-Møller 1959.

[311] Cf. BHRG §20.3.3; GBHS §3.4.3a; GKC §116x, 138i–k; IBHS §13.5.2d, 19.7b, 37.5; JM §121i, 145e; Barr 1989, 322–5. Some understand such a participle to be functioning as a relative clause in Hebrew. Others argue that such a participle is functioning as an attributive adjective in Hebrew (§215a), and that the use of a relative clause in translation is an issue of English style rather than Hebrew grammar.

[312] Cf. GBHS §5.2.11; IBHS §37.6d–f.

- אֹכֵל לָחֶם   וְאֵינְךָ   סָרָה   רוּחֲךָ

  FOOD   *eating*   AND THERE IS NOT TO YOU   sullen   your spirit   1 Kgs 21:5

  Your spirit is sullen SUCH THAT YOU ARE NOT *eating* FOOD.

- וַיָּבֹאוּ שְׁנֵי הַמַּלְאָכִים ... וְלוֹט יֹשֵׁב בְּשַׁעַר־סְדֹם

  SODOM   IN GATE OF   *sitting*   AND LOT   the angels   two of   they came   Gen 19:1

  The two angels came AS LOT WAS *sitting* IN THE GATE OF SODOM.

220 **Participle to indicate simultaneous action.** See §236–237.

- הֵם מַגִּשִׁים אֵלֶיהָ וְהִיא מוֹצָקֶת   They were *bringing* the vessels *as* she *poured.*

  pouring and she to her *bringing* they   2 Kgs 4:5

- הִיא רֹכֶבֶת עַל־הַחֲמוֹר וְיֹרֶדֶת בְּסֵתֶר הָהָר

  mountain   in hidden of   *and coming down*   the donkey   on   *riding*   she   1 Sam 25:20

  She was *riding* on her donkey *and coming down* in the hidden part of the mountain.

- Another example is 2 Kgs 2:12. More examples are noted in §236–7.

221 **Attributive participle for repeated or continuous action.**[313] Just as when it acts as a finite verb (§213), a participle that acts as an attributive adjective (§215a) may describe a repeated, continuous, or characteristic action.

- עֵשֶׂב מַזְרִיעַ זֶרַע לְמִינֵהוּ וְעֵץ עֹשֶׂה־פְּרִי

  fruit *making*   and tree   according to its kind   seed   *bearing seed*   plant   Gen 1:12

  a plant *bearing seed* according to its kind and a tree *bearing* fruit

- יְהוָה אֱלֹהֶיךָ אֵשׁ אֹכְלָה   YHWH your God is a *consuming* fire.

  consuming fire your God YHWH   Deut 4:24

222 **Participle to indicate an indefinite subject.**[314] A participle can be used to indicate an action or state of affairs that applies to anyone. Such a participle is often preceded by a finite verb[295] of the same root.

- כִּי־יִפֹּל הַנֹּפֵל מִמֶּנּוּ   if *anyone* falls from it

  from it *the falling one* he falls if   Deut 22:8

- וְשָׁמַע הַשֹּׁמֵעַ וְאָמַר   *anyone* who hears will say

  and he said *the hearing one* and he heard   2 Sam 17:9

- Other examples include Amos 9:1 and Jer 9:23.

F   Verbal Coordination

223 **Verbal coordination** is a combination of two verbs such that the first verb indicates the manner in which the second verb happens. The first verb can

---

[313] Compared to the second edition, §221 has been modified to distinguish it from §213.

[314] Cf. IBHS §37.5c.

typically be translated with an adverb. This is sometimes called **verbal hendiadys** (cf. §72).[315]

224   Coordination of two finite verbs connected by the conjunction waw.[316]

- Certain verbs are frequently used as the first verb in a verbal coordination. Examples include שׁוּב 'he returned' (meaning 'again'), יָסַף 'he added' (meaning 'again'), שָׁכַם 'to rise early' (meaning 'early' or 'eagerly'), מִהַר 'to hurry' (meaning 'quickly').

• וַיִּשְׁכָּב	וַיָּשָׁב	*He lay down again.*
and he lay down and he returned		1 Kgs 19:6

• כַּדָּהּ	וַתֹּרֶד	וַתְּמַהֵר	*She quickly lowered* her jar.
her jar *and she lowered and she hurried*			Gen 24:18

- Other examples include Gen 25:1; Josh 8:10, 14.

225   Coordination of two finite verbs without a waw to connect them.[317] Most examples of this are with imperatives or occur in poetry.

• מַעֲשָׂיו	שָׁכְחוּ	מִהֲרוּ	*They quickly forgot* his works.
his works *they forgot they hurried*			Ps 106:13

• שְׁכָב	שׁוּב	קָרָאתִי	לֹא־	וַיֹּאמֶר	He said, 'I did not call. *Lie down again*.'
lie down! return! I called not he said					1 Sam 3:5

- Other examples include Gen 30:31; 1 Sam 2:3, 3:6; Hos 1:6.

226   Coordination of a finite verb with an infinitive construct.[318] The finite verb usually comes first. The infinitive construct usually has the preposition לְ (§276).

• לִבְרֹחַ	נַחְבֵּאתָ	לָמָּה	Why did *you* RUN AWAY *secretly*?
TO RUN AWAY *you hid* why?			Gen 31:27

• לִשְׁאוֹל	הִקְשִׁיתָ	*You have* MADE A *difficult* REQUEST.
TO ASK *you were hard*		2 Kgs 2:10

• הַיּוֹם	בֹּא	מִהַרְתֶּן	מַדּוּעַ	Why *have you* COME *quickly* today?
the day TO COME *you hurried* why?				Exod 2:18

- Other examples include Num 22:15; 1 Sam 3:6, 8, 15:12; Ps 126:2, 3.

---

[315] Cf. GBHS §4.3.3(g); JM §102g, 177b–d; Eskhult 1998.
[316] Cf. GKC §120d–e; JM §177b–d.
[317] Cf. GKC §120g; JM §177g.
[318] Cf. BHRG §20.1.3(iii); GKC §114m–n.

G Concord of Subject and Verb[319]

Concord (also called **congruence** or **agreement**) refers to two words sharing certain grammatical characteristics, such as gender and number.

227 Concord when subject precedes verb.[320] When the subject precedes the verb, the verb usually has the same gender and number as its subject.

- וְתַרְדֵּמָה   נָפְלָה   עַל־אַבְרָם   A DEEP SLEEP *fell* on Abram.
  Abram on *it fell* and DEEP SLEEP   Gen 15:12

  o   The verb is 3fs because it follows a 3fs subject.

- Occasionally, however, the rule of concord is violated.

  o   יֵאָכֵל   מַצּוֹת   UNLEAVENED BREAD *will be eaten.*
     it will be eaten UNLEAVENED BREAD   Exod 13:7

  o   The verb is 3ms even though it follows a 3fp subject.

228 Third-person masculine singular verb before subject.[321] When the verb precedes the subject, the verb is often 3ms even when the subject is feminine and/or plural. This is particularly true when the subject is not a person (i.e., the subject is inanimate or an animal).

- לְאֹתֹת   וְהָיוּ   ... הַשָּׁמָיִם   בִּרְקִיעַ   מְאֹרֹת   יְהִי
  for signs and let them be the heavens in expanse of LIGHTS *let (it) be*   Gen 1:14
       Let there be LIGHTS in the expanse of the heavens ... and let them be for signs.

  o   The verb יְהִי 'let it be' is 3ms because it precedes the subject. The verb וְהָיוּ 'let
     them be' is 3mp because it follows the 3mp subject מְאֹרֹת 'lights' (§227).

- סֻכּוֹת   שָׂרֵי   וַיֹּאמֶר   THE LEADERS of Succoth *said*
  Succoth LEADERS of *and (he) said*   Judg 8:6

- Other examples include Gen 39:5; 2 Kgs 3:18, 26.

229 A collective singular subject often takes a plural verb.[322] When the subject of a verb is a singular collective (§2), the verb is often plural. This is sometimes called a type of **agreement** *ad sensum*, meaning that the verb agrees with the sense of the subject (i.e., plural) rather than with the morphology of the subject (i.e., singular) (cf. §232, 233).

---

[319] Cf. BHRG §35; GKC §145–6; IBHS §6.6, 7; JM §150; Slonim 1944.

[320] Cf. BHRG §35(i); GKC §145a, n.

[321] Cf. BHRG §35(vi); GKC §145a, o–q; IBHS §6.6c; JM §150j.

[322] Cf. BHRG §35(iii); GKC §145b–g; IBHS §6.6b, 7.2.1b; JM §150e; Revell 2002; Rooker 1990, 94–6.

- הַדָּבָר טוֹב וַיֹּאמְרוּ הָעָם כָּל־ הָעָם וַיַּעַן
  the word good (they) said THE PEOPLE ALL OF (he) answered   1 Kgs 18:24

  ALL OF THE PEOPLE *answered* and *said*, 'That is a good idea.'

  - o The subject כָּל־הָעָם 'all of the people' is a collective singular. Collective singular subjects sometimes use a singular verb (e.g., וַיַּעַן), and sometimes use a plural verb (e.g., וַיֹּאמְרוּ 'they said').

- אֲרָם וַיָּנֻסוּ   THE ARAMEANS *fled.*
  ARAM (they) fled   1 Kgs 20:20

- Other examples include Job 1:14 and 1 Sam 17:46.

230 **Singular verb before, and plural verb after a compound subject.**[323] A compound subject consists of two or more subjects, usually joined by וְ 'and.' A verb before a compound subject is usually singular, and a verb after a compound subject is usually plural.

- לוֹ וַתֹּאמַרְנָה וְלֵאָה רָחֵל וַתַּעַן
  to him (they) said AND LEAH RACHEL (she) answered   Gen 31:14

  RACHEL AND LEAH *answered* and *said* to him

- בְּנָיוֹת וַיֵּשְׁבוּ וּשְׁמוּאֵל הוּא וַיֵּלֶךְ
  in Naioth (they) dwelt AND SAMUEL HE (he) went   1 Sam 19:18

  HE AND SAMUEL *went* and *dwelt* in Naioth.

- Other examples include Num 12:1–2; 2 Kgs 3:9.

231 **A dual subject normally takes a plural verb.**[324] As discussed in §3, there is no dual form for verbs in Biblical Hebrew. Therefore, when the subject is dual (§4–5), the verb is usually plural.

- יָדֶיךָ תֶּחֱזַקְנָה   YOUR HANDS *will be strong.*
  YOUR TWO HANDS (they) will be strong   Judg 7:11

232 **A subject in the plural of respect normally takes a singular verb.**[325] When a subject is a plural of respect (§8), its verb is normally singular. This is another example of **agreement *ad sensum*** (§229).

- אִשָּׁה לוֹ יִתֶּן אֲדֹנָיו אִם־   if HIS MASTER *gives* him a wife
  woman to him (he) will give HIS MASTERS if   Exod 21:4

  - o In Exod 21:4, the subject אֲדֹנָיו [lit. 'his masters'] is plural, but it is a plural of respect (§8), referring to a single master, so the verb יִתֵּן is singular.

---

[323] Cf. BHRG §35(viii, ix); GKC §146d–h; JM §150q; Naudé 1999.
[324] Cf. BHRG §35(ii); GKC §145n; JM §150d.
[325] Cf. BHRG §35(v); GKC §145h–i; JM §150f.

- בָּרָא אֱלֹהִים   GOD *created.*
  GOD(S)   *created*   Gen 1:1

233   **An abstract plural subject may take a singular verb.**[326] When a subject is an abstract plural (§7, 19), its verb is often singular. This is another example of **agreement *ad sensum*** (§229).

- נְעוּרָיְכִי   כַּנֶּשֶׁר   תִּתְחַדֵּשׁ   YOUR YOUTH *will be renewed* like the eagle.
  YOUR YOUTH   like the eagle   *(it) will be renewed*   Ps 103:5

234a   **Second-person feminine plural subject with a masculine verb.**[327] 2fp verbs are rare. A 2fp subject usually takes a 2mp verb instead.

- כַּאֲשֶׁר עֲשִׂיתֶם   as *you have done*
  you have done   as   Ruth 1:8

  o   In Ruth 1:8, the verb עֲשִׂיתֶם 'you have done' is 2mp. But the subject of the verb is Naomi's daughters-in-law, so the subject is 2fp.

- שִׁמְעוּ הַדָּבָר הַזֶּה פָּרוֹת הַבָּשָׁן   *Hear* this, O COWS of Bashan!
  of the Bashan   COWS   the this   the word   *hear!*   Amos 4:1

- Another example is Joel 2:22.

234b   **Third-person feminine plural subject with a masculine imperfect verb.**[328] 3fp imperfect verbs are rare. For an imperfect verb, a 3fp subject often takes a 3mp verb, particularly when the verb precedes the subject.

- וְשֶׁבַע הַשִּׁבֳּלִים הָרֵקוֹת ... יִהְיוּ שֶׁבַע שְׁנֵי רָעָב
  famine   years of   seven   *will be*   the empty   THE EARS OF GRAIN   and seven

       THE seven empty EARS OF GRAIN ... *will be* seven years of famine. (Gen 41:27)

- אִם־יֵצְאוּ בְנוֹת־שִׁילוֹ   if THE DAUGHTERS of Shiloh *come out*
  of Shiloh   DAUGHTERS   *come out*   if   Judg 21:21

- Other examples of this include 2 Sam 4:1 and 1 Kgs 11:3.

H   Synchronism (Simultaneous Action)

- Synchronism describes two actions or states as occurring at the same time. It can often be translated with 'when,' 'as,' 'just as,' or 'no sooner.' Synchronism is likely to be present when any of the following three structures (§235–7) occurs.

- Synchronism is usually indicated when the following three conditions are all met: (1) the two verbs are perfect verbs or participles, (2) the

---

[326] Cf. BHRG §35(v); GKC §145k.

[327] Cf. GKC §110k, 144a, 145p, t; IBHS §6.6c; JM §150a, k.

[328] Cf. GKC §144a, 145p, t; IBHS §6.6c; JM §150b–c, k.

subject of each verb comes before its verb, and (3) the subject of the first verb lacks the conjunction וְ 'and.'

235 Synchronism of two perfect verbs.[329] The three conditions for synchronism (above) can be met with two perfect verbs.

- לְנַעֲרוֹ אָמַר וְשָׁאוּל צוּף בְּאֶרֶץ בָּאוּ הֵמָּה
  to his young man *said* and Saul Zuph in land of *came* they   1 Sam 9:5

  As they *entered* Zuph, Saul *said* to his servant

- לִקְרָאתוֹ הֵרִיעוּ וּפְלִשְׁתִּים לֶחִי עַד־ בָּא הוּא־
  to meet him *shouted* and Philistines Lehi unto *entered* he   Judg 15:14

  As he *entered* Lehi, the Philistines *came shouting* to meet him.

- אֵלָיו הָיָה יְהוָה וּדְבַר־ ... יָצָא לֹא יְשַׁעְיָהוּ וַיְהִי
  to him *was* YHWH and word of *went out* not Isaiah and was   2 Kgs 20:4

  Isaiah had not yet *gone out* ... when the word of YHWH *came* to him.

- Other examples include Gen 44:3, 4.

236 Synchronism of two participles.[330] The three conditions for synchronism (above) can be met with two participles.

- יֹצֵא שְׁמוּאֵל וְהִנֵּה הָעִיר בְּתוֹךְ בָּאִים הֵמָּה
  coming out Samuel and behold the city midst of *entering* they   1 Sam 9:14

  As they *were entering* the city, behold, Samuel *was coming out.*

- מְצַעֵק וְהוּא רֹאֶה וֶאֱלִישָׁע   As Elisha *saw* it, he *cried out.*
  crying out and he *seeing* and Elisha   2 Kgs 2:12

  o 2 Kgs 2:12 is unusual because the subject has the conjunction וְ.

- Other examples include 1 Sam 25:20 and 2 Kgs 8:5. See also §220.

237 Synchronism of a participle and a perfect verb.[331] The three conditions for synchronism (above) can be met with a participle and a perfect verb.

- נְעָרוֹת מָצְאוּ וְהֵמָּה הָעִיר בְּמַעֲלֵה עֹלִים הֵמָּה
  young women *found* and they the city in ascent of *going up* they   1 Sam 9:11

  As they were *going up* the ascent to the city, they *found* young women.

- אָמַר וּשְׁמוּאֵל הָעִיר בִּקְצֵה יוֹרְדִים הֵמָּה
  said and Samuel the city into end of *going down* they   1 Sam 9:27

  as they were *going down* to the edge of the city, Samuel *said*

---

[329] Cf. BHRG §36.1.I.3(iv), 47.2(iv); GKC §164a–b; JM §166c.
[330] Cf. BHRG §36.1.I.3(iv), 47.2(iv); GKC §116u–v, 164a–b; JM §166e.
[331] Cf. BHRG §36.1.I.3(iv), 47.2(iv); GKC §116u–v, 164a–b; JM §166f.

3 Syntax of Particles [332]

A Prepositions [333]

238 **A preposition is usually repeated before each object.**[334] When a preposition governs more than one object, the preposition is usually repeated before each object.

- אָבִֽיךָ   וּמִבֵּית   וּמִמּֽוֹלַדְתְּךָ   מֵאַרְצְךָ   לְךָ ־ לֶךְ
  your father   and *from* house of   and *from* your kin   *from* your land   you   go!

  Go *from* your land, *from* your kin, and *from* the house of your father! Gen 12:1

- Occasionally, however, a preposition is not repeated; this is called a **preposition override**.

- וּזְבָחִים   בְּעֹלוֹת   לַיהוָה   הַחֵפֶץ
  and sacrifices   *in* burnt offerings   has YHWH   pleasure?

  Has YHWH pleasure *in* burnt offerings and *in* sacrifices?   1 Sam 15:22

  o In 1 Sam 15:22, the preposition בְּ 'in' has two objects (עֹלוֹת 'burnt offerings' and זְבָחִים 'sacrifices'), so one would expect the preposition to be repeated before the second object (e.g., וּבִזְבָחִים 'and in sacrifices'). But in this text, the preposition is not repeated. This is an example of a preposition override.

The preposition בְּ [335]

- The preposition בְּ sometimes occurs in a biform, בְּמוֹ, as an independent preposition.[336]

---

[332] Cf. BHRG §38–44; GBHS §4; GKC §99–104, 119; IBHS §4.2.2, 4.6.2, 11.1.2, 38.1a, 39.3.1d, 39.3.4; JM §102–5, 132–3, 176–7; Van der Merwe 1993; Shereshevsky 1967. Additional information about each particle can be found in a lexicon.

[333] Cf. BHRG §39; GBHS §4.1; GKC §101–3, 119; IBHS §11; JM §103, 132–3; Glinert 1982.

[334] Cf. GKC §102, 103g, 119hh; IBHS §11.4.2; JM §132g. According to Rooker (1990, 115), this is accurate only for early biblical Hebrew.

[335] Cf. BHRG §39.6; GBHS §4.1.5; GKC §119h–q; IBHS §9.5.2f, 11.2.5; JM §103b–c, f, 133c.

239 בְּ often expresses rest or movement in place or time.[337]

240 **Locative בְּ (in, on, through).**[338] Also called the ***beth locale***, the preposition בְּ often indicates a location.

- Examples include בַּבַּיִת 'in the house,' בָּאָרֶץ 'in the land' or 'through the land,' and בָּהָר 'on the mountain.'

241 **Temporal-point בְּ (in, when).**[339] The preposition בְּ can indicate a point in time.

- The object of the preposition can be a noun (e.g., בַּבֹּקֶר 'in the morning').
- The object of the preposition can be an infinitive construct (e.g., בְּהִבָּרְאָם 'when they were created' in Gen 2:4). This is discussed in §504.
- The object of the preposition can be a clause, as in Amos 4:7 (below). Such a clause is a genitive substantival clause (§489), because it is the object of a preposition. It is also a type of temporal clause (§499).

- בְּעוֹד   שְׁלֹשָׁה   חֳדָשִׁים   לַקָּצִיר

  until the harvest   months   three   *when* still   Amos 4:7

  when there were still three months until the harvest

  ○ The object of the preposition בְּ is the clause עוֹד שְׁלֹשָׁה חֳדָשִׁים לַקָּצִיר 'there were still three months until the harvest.'

242 **Adversative בְּ (against, in spite of).**[340] The preposition בְּ can indicate that something opposes its object, works to the disadvantage of its object, or occurs in spite of its object.

- יָדוֹ   בַכֹּל   וְיַד   כֹּל   בּוֹ

  against him   all   and hand of   *against* the all   his hand   Gen 16:12

  His hand will be *against* everyone, and everyone's hand will be *against* him.

- עַד־   אָנָה   לֹא־   יַאֲמִינוּ   בִי   בְּכֹל   הָאֹתוֹת

  the signs   *in spite of* all   in me   they will believe   not   when?   until   Num 14:11

  Until when will they not believe in me *in spite of* all of the signs?

- Other examples include 1 Sam 18:17 and Isa 9:11.

---

[336] Cf. IBHS §11.1.2d; JM §103g note 5; JM93 §103g note 2.

[337] Cf. BHRG §39.6.1–2; GKC §119h; IBHS §11.2.5b–c; JM §133c.

[338] Cf. BHRG §39.6.1; GBHS §4.1.5(a); GKC §119h; IBHS §9.5.2f, 11.2.5b; JM §133c.

[339] Cf. BHRG §39.6.2; GBHS §4.1.5(b), 5.2.4; GKC §119h; IBHS §11.2.5c, 36.2.2b; JM §166l.

[340] Cf. GBHS §4.1.5(d); IBHS §11.2.5d; JM §133c.

243 **Instrumental בְּ (with, by).**[341] Also called the **beth instrumenti**, the preposition בְּ can indicate the means, instrument, or mechanism by which something happens.

- בְחָרֶב אוֹ בַדֶּבֶר יִפְגָעֵנוּ פֶּן־
  with the sword or *with* the plague he will attack us lest   Exod 5:3

  lest he attack us *with* plague or *with* the sword

- בָרָעָב הַזֶּה הַקָּהָל אֶת־כָּל־ לְהָמִית
  with (the) hunger the this the assembly all of to kill   Exod 16:3

  to kill this entire assembly *with* hunger

- Other examples include Mic 4:14.

244 **בְּ of transitivity (*untranslated*).**[342] Some verbs take a prepositional phrase beginning with בְּ where English would use a direct object.

- In many cases, it can be difficult to distinguish this from the instrumental בְּ (§243).

- וַיָּרֶם בַּמַּטֶּה   He lifted the staff.
  (בְּ) the staff he lifted   Exod 7:20

  o In the Hiphil, the verb רוּם 'to lift up' typically takes a direct object. For example, Num 20:11 states וַיָּרֶם מֹשֶׁה אֶת־יָדוֹ 'Moses lifted his hand,' with אֶת־ used to mark the direct object 'his hand.' In Exod 7:20, however, the preposition בְּ in בַּמַּטֶּה seems to mark the direct object 'the staff.'

- פָּעֲרוּ עָלַי בְּפִיהֶם   They opened their mouth at me.
  (בְּ) their mouth at me they opened   Job 16:10

  o In בְּפִיהֶם 'with their mouth,' בְּ might be instrumental (§243). But in the other three occurrences of the verb פער (Job 29:23; Ps 119:131; Isa 5:14), the thing that is opened is not preceded by any particle, so it seems to be a direct object.

- Other examples are Prov 6:13 (contrast Prov 10:10) and Ps 46:7 (contrast Joel 2:11).

245 **בְּ of agent (by).**[343] The object of the preposition בְּ is sometimes the agent who causes the action of a passive construction. This is rare (§159a).

- בָאָדָם דָּמוֹ יִשָּׁפֵךְ   *by* a human his blood will be shed
  will be shed his blood *by* (the) human   Gen 9:6

- וַאדֹנִי צֻוָּה בַיהֹוָה   my Lord was commanded *by* YHWH
  by YHWH was commanded and my Lord   Num 36:2

---

[341] Cf. BHRG §39.6.3(i)a; GBHS §4.1.5(c); GKC §119o; IBHS §11.2.5d; JM §132e.

[342] Cf. BHRG §39.1.3(ii)a; GKC §119k, q; IBHS §11.2.5f; JM §125m.

[343] Cf. BHRG §39.6.3(i)b; IBHS §23.2.2f; JM §132e. Be aware that JM §132e argues that this use of בְּ is doubtful, that the use of בְּ in Gen 9:6 is instrumental, and that the text of Num 36:2 may be corrupt.

246 בְּ **of price or exchange (for).**[344] Also called the ***beth pretii***, the preposition בְּ can indicate the price paid for something. The price can be metaphorical.

- בְּכֶסֶף אֶת־כַּרְמְךָ לִי תְּנָה־
  for silver   your vineyard   to me   give!

  Sell me your vineyard *for* money.

  1 Kgs 21:6

- בְּנַפְשׁוֹתָם הַהֹלְכִים הָאֲנָשִׁים הֲדַם
  for their lives   the ones going   the men   blood of?

  2 Sam 23:17

  [Shall I drink] the blood of the men who went *at the risk of* their lives?

- Other examples include 1 Kgs 2:23 and 10:29.

247 בְּ **of cause (because).**[345] Also called the ***beth causa***, the preposition בְּ (or the compound בַּאֲשֶׁר) can indicate the cause of something else. The object of the preposition can be a noun, an infinitive construct (§535), or a genitive substantival clause (§534).

- הָעִיר אֶת־כָּל־ בַּחֲמִשָּׁה הֲתַשְׁחִית
  the city   all of   *because of* five   you will destroy?

  Gen 18:28

  Will you destroy the whole city *because of* five?

- יְהוָה אֶת־מִצְוֹת בַּעֲזָבְכֶם
  YHWH   commandments of   *because* your to abandon

  1 Kgs 18:18

  because you abandoned the commandments of YHWH

- בַּאֲשֶׁר אַתְּ־ אִשְׁתּוֹ
  his wife   you   *because*

  because you are his wife

  Gen 39:9

- Another example is Gen 39:23.

248 בְּ **of accompaniment (with).**[346] Also called the ***beth comitantiae***, the preposition בְּ can indicate something that goes along with something else.

- בָשָׂר בְּנַפְשׁוֹ דָמוֹ לֹא תֹאכֵלוּ
  you will eat   not   its blood   *with* its life   flesh

  Gen 9:4

  You will not eat flesh *with* its life, that is, its blood.

- בְּבָנֵינוּ וּבִבְנוֹתֵנוּ בְּצֹאנֵנוּ וּבִבְקָרֵנוּ נֵלֵךְ Exod 10:9
  we will go   and *with* our herd   *with* our flock   and *with* our daughters   *with* our sons

  We will go *with* our sons and *with* our daughters, *with* our flocks and *with* our herds.

- Other examples include 1 Kgs 10:2 and 19:19.

---

[344] Cf. BHRG §39.6.3(ii); GBHS §4.1.5(j); GKC §119p; IBHS §11.2.5d; JM §133c; Gordon 1981.

[345] Cf. BHRG §39.6.3(iv); GBHS §4.1.5(f); IBHS §11.2.5e, 38.4a; JM §170j; Dahood 1971.

[346] Cf. BHRG §39.6.3(iii); GBHS §4.1.5(g); GKC §119m; IBHS §11.2.5d; JM §133c.

249 בְּ **of identity (is, as).**[347] The object of the preposition בְּ can act as a predicate nominative (§33), meaning that the subject is equated with it. This use of בְּ is also called the ***beth essentiae*, beth of essence, pleonastic beth,** or **beth of predication.**

- בְּעֶזְרִי   אָבִי   אֱלֹהֵי   The God of my father *was* my help.
  was my help of my father God   Exod 18:4

- שַׁדָּי   בְּאֵל ... אַבְרָהָם אֶל וָאֵרָא   I appeared to Abraham ... *as* God Almighty.
  Almighty *as* God Abraham to and I appeared   Exod 6:3

- Other examples include Deut 26:5 and 28:62.

250 בְּ **of specification (i.e., of,** *untranslated*).[348] When בְּ is repeated in a clause, the objects of בְּ can be the parts of which the whole consists.

- וּבַחַיָּה   וּבַבְּהֵמָה   בָּעוֹף ... בָּשָׂר כָל־ וַיִּגְוַע
  and *i.e.* animals and *i.e.* cattle *i.e.* birds flesh all of it died   Gen 7:21
  All flesh died: birds, cattle, and animals.

- וּבַבְּהֵמָה   בָּאָדָם ... בְּכוֹר כָל־ לִי קַדֶּשׁ־
  and *i.e.* beast *i.e.* man firstborn all of to me consecrate   Exod 13:2
  Consecrate to me every firstborn: ... human and animal.

- Another example is Exod 12:19.

251 Partitive בְּ (some of).[349] The object of the preposition בְּ can indicate the whole from which a part is taken. This is also called the **wholative beth,** because בְּ is attached to the word that refers to the whole.

- הָעָם   בְּמַשָּׂא   אִתְּךָ   וְנָשְׂאוּ
  the people *some of* burden of with you they will carry   Num 11:17
  They will bear with you *some of* the burden of the people.

- בְּמִשְׁמַנֵּיהֶם   וַיַּהֲרֹג   He killed *some of* their fat ones.
  some of their fat ones he killed   Ps 78:31

- Other examples include Deut 1:35 and 2 Kgs 17:25.

252 בְּ **of a state or condition (with, in).**[350] Also called **beth of the norm** or **beth of manner,** the preposition בְּ can indicate a state or a condition.

- Examples include בְּשָׁלוֹם 'in peace' (e.g., Gen 15:15), בְּתֻמּוֹ 'in his integrity' (e.g., Prov 19:1), and בְּצֶדֶק 'in righteousness' (e.g., Lev 19:15).

---

[347] Cf. GBHS §4.1.5(h); GKC §119i; IBHS §11.2.5e; JM §133c; Gordon 1981; Manross 1954.

[348] Cf. GBHS §4.1.5(e); IBHS §11.2.5e.

[349] Cf. BHRG §39.6.1(iii); GKC §119m; IBHS §11.2.5f.

[350] Cf. GBHS §4.1.5(i); IBHS §11.2.5e; JM §133c.

253 **Terminative בְּ (into).**[351] When used with a verb of motion, the object of the preposition בְּ can indicate a place toward which something moves and in or at which it then comes to rest. This is sometimes called **pregnant בְּ.**

- וְשִׁלַּח אֶת־הַשָּׂעִיר בַּמִּדְבָּר   He will send the goat *into* the wilderness.
  into the wilderness   the goat   he will send   Lev 16:22

- בָּאוּ בְּצֵל קֹרָתִי   They came *under* the shade of my roof.
  my roof   *into* shade of   they came   Gen 19:8

254 **Distributive בְּ (by, after, every).** As discussed in §102, distribution can be expressed in Hebrew by repeating the word over which something is distributed and by putting the preposition בְּ before the second occurrence.

- וּמְהַלְלִים לַיהוָה יוֹם בְּיוֹם   and praising YHWH day *after* day
  by day   day   (לְ) YHWH   and praising   2 Chr 30:21

- יַעֲשֶׂה שָׁנָה בְשָׁנָה   It happened year *after* year.
  by year   year   it happened   1 Sam 1:7

- Other examples include 1 Sam 18:10; Ezra 3:4; Neh 8:18; 1 Chr 27:1.

The preposition כְּ [352]

- The preposition כְּ also occurs in the biform כְּמוֹ as an independent preposition.[353]

255 **The preposition כְּ often expresses likeness**, which may be either similarity or identity.[354]

256 **Comparative כְּ (as, like, such as).**[355] The object of the preposition כְּ (or the compound כַּאֲשֶׁר) can be something to which something else is compared. When repeated, the meaning is often 'the same as.'

- וַיְשַׁסְּעֵהוּ כְּשַׁסַּע הַגְּדִי
  the young goat   *as* to tear to pieces   he tore it to pieces   Judg 14:6
  He tore it to pieces *as* one tears to pieces a young goat.

- כְּהָנִיף שֵׁבֶט וְאֶת־מְרִימָיו כְּהָרִים מַטֶּה לֹא־עֵץ
  wood   not   staff   *as* to lift   one lifting it   rod   *as* to wield   Isa 10:15
  as if a rod *were* to wield the one lifting it, or *as if* a staff *were* to lift what is not wood

---

[351] Cf. GBHS §4.1.5(a); IBHS §11.2.5b.

[352] Cf. BHRG §39.10; GBHS §4.1.9; GKC §118s–x; IBHS §11.2.9; JM §103b–c, g, 133g–ha (JM93 lacks §133ha).

[353] Cf. IBHS §11.1.2d; JM §103g.

[354] Cf. JM §133g.

[355] Cf. BHRG §39.10.1(i); GBHS §4.1.9(a)–(b), 5.2.6; GKC §118s–w; IBHS §11.2.9; JM §133g, 174c–d, i.

- ○ כְּ is translated 'as if' in Isa 10:15 because the situation is hypothetical.
- • אִישׁ   כָּזֶה   הֲנִמְצָא   Can we find a man *like* this?
  man   *like* this   can we find?   Gen 41:38
- • עָתָּה   וּכְכֹחִי   אָז   כְּכֹחִי
  now   and *like* my strength   then   *like* my strength   Josh 14:11
  My strength now and my strength then *are alike*.
- • Other examples include Gen 18:25, 34:12, 44:7; Deut 4:32; 2 Sam 3:34, 11:25; 1 Kgs 22:4; Jer 5:9.

257   כְּ of approximation (about, around, approximately).[356] When the object of the preposition כְּ is a numeral, כְּ may indicate approximation.

- • שָׁנִים   כְּעֶשֶׂר   שָׁם   וַיֵּשְׁבוּ   They lived there *about* ten years.
  years   *about* ten   there   they lived   Ruth 1:4
- • הַגְּבָרִים   רַגְלִי   אֶלֶף   מֵאוֹת   כְּשֵׁשׁ־
  the men   on foot   thousand   hundreds   *about* six of   Exod 12:37
  approximately six hundred thousand men on foot
- • Another example is 1 Sam 9:22.

258   Concessive כְּ (although). When the object of the preposition כְּ is an infinitive construct, it can indicate a concessive idea (§532).

- • יוֹם   יוֹם   יוֹסֵף   אֶל־   כְּדַבְּרָהּ   וַיְהִי
  day   day   Joseph   to   *although* her to speak   (was)   Gen 39:10
  although she spoke to Joseph day after day

259   כְּ of the norm (according to).[357] The object of the preposition כְּ can be a standard or a norm.

- • כַּמִּשְׁפָּט   הָעַמּוּד   עַל־   עֹמֵד   הַמֶּלֶךְ
  according to the custom   the pillar   by   standing   the king   2 Kgs 11:14
  The king was standing by the pillar, *according to* the custom.
- • כְּחַסְדֶּךָ   אֱלֹהִים   חָנֵּנִי
  according to your loyalty   God   be gracious to me   Ps 51:3
  Be gracious to me, O God, *according to* your loyalty.
- • Another example is 1 Sam 13:14.

260   Causal כַּאֲשֶׁר (because).[358] Rarely, a causal clause can begin with כַּאֲשֶׁר (§534).

---

[356] Cf. BHRG §39.10.1(iii); GBHS §4.1.9(a)–(b); IBHS §11.2.9b; JM §133g.
[357] Cf. BHRG §39.10.1(ii); IBHS §11.2.9b.
[358] Cf. JM §170k; Gaenssle 1915a, 141.

- כַּאֲשֶׁר לֹא־ שָׁמַעְתָּ בְּקוֹל יְהוָה

  YHWH   voice of   you listened   not   *because*   1 Sam 28:18

  because you have not listened to the voice of YHWH

- כַּאֲשֶׁר מְרִיתֶם פִּי   *because* you rebelled against my command

  my mouth   you rebelled   *because*   Num 27:14

- Other examples include Judg 6:27 and 2 Kgs 17:26.

261 Asseverative כְּ (such a, truly).[359] When someone earnestly asserts that something is (or will be) something else, the preposition כְּ may precede that 'something else.' This use of כְּ is sometimes called the **_kaph veritatis_**.

- שַׂמְתִּיךְ כְּרֹאִי   I will make you *such a* spectacle.

  such a spectacle   I will make you   Nah 3:6

- כִּי־ הוּא כְּאִישׁ אֱמֶת   because he is a *truly* honest man

  truth   *such a* man of   he   because   Neh 7:2

- Other possible examples include Num 11:1; 1 Sam 20:3; 2 Sam 9:8; Job 10:9.

262a Temporal כְּ (as soon as, at the very time).[360] The object of the preposition כְּ can be the precise time at which something happens. The object of the preposition כְּ can be an infinitive (§505) or a clause (§500a).

- כָּעֵת מָחָר אֶשְׁלַח אֵלֶיךָ אִישׁ

  man   to you   I will send   tomorrow   *as soon as* the time   1 Sam 9:16

  At this very time tomorrow, I will send you a man.

- וַיְהִי כְּבוֹא אַבְרָם מִצְרָיְמָה   *as soon as* Abram entered Egypt

  toward Egypt   Abram   *as soon as* to enter   (was)   Gen 12:14

- Other examples include Gen 18:10 and 18:14.

262b Temporal כַּאֲשֶׁר / ◉כְּשֶׁ (when).[361] The compounds כַּאֲשֶׁר and ◉כְּשֶׁ can indicate the time when something else occurs (§500b).

- כַּאֲשֶׁר אָמְרוּ תְּנָה־ לָּנוּ מֶלֶךְ   *when* they said, 'Give us a king!'

  king   to us   give!   they said   *when*   1 Sam 8:6

- כְּשֶׁתִּפּוֹל עֲלֵיהֶם פִּתְאֹם   *when* it falls on them suddenly

  suddenly   on them   *when* she will fall   Eccl 9:12

- On rare occasions, the biform כְּמוֹ (see page 101) may be used temporally.

  ○ וּכְמוֹ הַשַּׁחַר עָלָה   and *when* the dawn rose

  it went up   the dawn   and *when*   Gen 19:15

---

[359] Cf. GKC §118x; IBHS §11.2.9b, c; JM §133g; Gordis 1943.

[360] Cf. BHRG §39.10.3; GBHS §4.1.9(c), 5.2.4; GKC §118u; IBHS §11.2.9d, 36.2.2b; JM §166m.

[361] Cf. JM §166n; Gaenssle 1915a, 137–40.

263   **Pregnant** כְּ.[362] When the meaning of the text requires a second preposition to follow כְּ, the second preposition is sometimes omitted. This is a type of ellipsis (§583–98). It is sometimes said that the כְּ has **absorbed** the other preposition. In such cases, the preposition כְּ is called 'pregnant.' A pregnant כְּ is translated with 'as' (for the כְּ) and another word that depends on the second preposition that is omitted.

- כְּהַר־   פְּרָצִים   יָקוּם   יְהוָה   כְּעֵמֶק   בְּגִבְעוֹן   יִרְגָּז
  he will rage in Gibeon *as* valley YHWH he will rise Perazim *as* mountain of

  YHWH will arise *as on* the mountain of Perazim;
  he will rage *as in* the valley in Gibeon. Isa 28:21

  o In Isa 28:21, the preposition בְּ ('on' or 'in') is implied, so the preposition כְּ is pregnant and should be translated 'as on' or 'as in.'

- כָּכֶם   לַאֲחֵיכֶם   יְהוָה   יָנִיחַ
  as you to your brothers YHWH will give rest   Josh 1:15

  YHWH will give rest to your brothers *as to* you.

  o In Josh 1:15, the preposition לְ 'to' is omitted after כְּ.

- Sometimes a second preposition is specified instead of using a pregnant כְּ.

  o כְּבָרִאשֹׁנָה   לְפָנֵינוּ   הֵם   נִגָּפִים
     as IN the first before us they being struck down   Judg 20:32

     They are being struck down before us, *as* AT the first.

264   **כַּאֲשֶׁר for comparison (just as … so).**[363] The compound כַּאֲשֶׁר (often followed by כֵּן) can be used in a comparison.

- כַּאֲשֶׁר   צִוָּה   יְהוָה   אֹתָם   כֵּן   עָשׂוּ
  they did *so* them YHWH commanded *just as*   Exod 7:6

  Just as YHWH commanded them, *so* they did.

- וְכַאֲשֶׁר   יְעַנּוּ   אֹתוֹ   כֵּן   יִרְבֶּה   וְכֵן   יִפְרֹץ
  he spreads and *so* he increases *so* him they afflict and *just as*   Exod 1:12

  And *the more* they afflicted him, *the more* he increased and *the more* he spread out.

  o In Exod 1:12, כַּאֲשֶׁר… כֵּן is still a comparison, but in this context, it may be better to translate it as 'the more.' This has been called כַּאֲשֶׁר of **degree**.

---

[362] Cf. IBHS §11.2.9a; JM §133h.
[363] Cf. IBHS §38.5a; JM §174a.

The preposition לְ [364]

- The preposition לְ also occurs in the biforms לְמוֹ and לָמוֹ as independent prepositions.[365]

265 The preposition לְ typically expresses relation to something or motion towards a thing or person.[366]

266a **Spatially terminative לְ (to, up to).**[367] The object of the preposition לְ can be an ending location.

- בָּא לָעִיר   He came *to* the city.
  to the city   he came   1 Sam 9:12

266b **Temporally terminative לְ (to, up to).**[368] The object of the preposition לְ can be an ending time.

- לְאֶלֶף דּוֹר   *to* a thousand generations
  generation   *to* thousand of   Deut 7:9
- לְעוֹלָם   '*to* eternity' OR 'forever'
  to long time   2 Kgs 5:27

267 **לְ of direction (towards).**[369] The object of the preposition לְ can be a direction. This is also called a **directive לְ**.

- לְאָחוֹר וְלֹא לְפָנִים   *backwards* and not *forwards*
  towards faces   and not   *towards* back   Jer 7:24
- מָתְנָיו וּלְמַטָּה ... וּמִמָּתְנָיו וּלְמַעְלָה
  and *towards* above   and from his loins   and *towards* below   his loins   Ezek 8:2
  from his loins and *downward* ... and from his loins and *upward*

268a **Temporal point לְ (by).**[370] The object of the preposition לְ can be a point in time by which time something happens.

- וְהָיֵה נָכוֹן לַבֹּקֶר   Be ready *by* morning.
  by the morning   ready   be!   Exod 34:2
- לָעֶרֶב יְמוֹלֵל   *By* the evening it withers.
  it will wither   *by* the evening   Ps 90:6

---

[364] Cf. BHRG §39.11; GBHS §4.1.10; GKC §114f–s, 117n, 119r–u, 121f, 123d, 129, 143e; IBHS §10.4, 11.2.10; JM §103b–c, f, 130, 133d; Dahood 1966; Dahood 1981.

[365] Cf. IBHS §11.1.2d; JM §103f, g note 5; JM93 §103f, g note 2.

[366] Cf. BHRG §39.11; GKC §119r; IBHS §10.4a, 11.2.10b; JM §133d; Sutcliffe 1955.

[367] Cf. BHRG §39.11.I.1.a; GBHS §4.1.10(a); IBHS §11.2.10b.

[368] Cf. BHRG §39.11.I.1.f; GBHS §4.1.10(c); IBHS §11.2.10c.

[369] Cf. BHRG §39.11.I.1.a; GBHS §4.1.10(a); IBHS §11.2.10b; JM §133d.

[370] Cf. BHRG §39.11.I.1.f; GBHS §4.1.10(c); IBHS §11.2.10c, 36.2.3d.

- Other examples include Gen 17:21; Exod 19:11; 2 Kgs 4:16.

268b   **Temporal duration לְ (for).**[371] In late texts, the object of the preposition לְ may be a length of time during which something happens (like §56a).

- לְשָׁנִים שָׁלוֹשׁ

  three *for* years

  for three years

  2 Chr 11:17

- לְיָמִים שְׁמוֹנָה

  eight *for* days

  for eight days

  2 Chr 29:17

269   **Indirect object לְ (to, *untranslated*).**[372] The object of the preposition לְ can be the indirect object of the verb, meaning that it receives the action of the verb. An English example of an indirect object is the word 'her' in the sentence 'He gave *her* a ring.' When used this way, לְ is sometimes referred to as a ***nota dativi***.

- וַיִּתֶּן־לוֹ צֹאן וּבָקָר

  and herd   flock   *to* him   he gave

  He gave flocks and herds *to* him.

  Gen 24:35

  o   The preposition לְ can also be left untranslated: 'He gave him flocks and herds.'

270   **Possessive לְ (of, belonging to).**[373] The preposition לְ can indicate that its object is owned or possessed by someone. The idea of possession is not necessarily literal; it may indicate a relationship other than possession, as in 'my parents' or 'my God.' This is also called the **periphrastic לְ** or the **genitive לְ**. When the object of לְ is someone who wrote something, it is sometimes referred to as the **לְ of author** or the **לְ *auctoris***.

- הַצֹּפִים לְשָׁאוּל

  of Saul   the watchmen

  'Saul's watchmen'   OR   'the watchmen *of* Saul'

  1 Sam 14:16

- הַבַּיִת לֶאֱלִישָׁע

  of Elisha   the house

  'Elisha's house'   OR   'the house *of* Elisha'

  2 Kgs 5:9

- A construct chain can communicate the same meaning (§39), but only if both words are definite or both are indefinite. When the possessor is definite but the object possessed is indefinite (as in 'A son of Jesse'), a possessive לְ must be used.

- רָאִיתִי בֵּן לְיִשַׁי

  of Jesse   son   I saw

  I saw a son *of* Jesse.

  1 Sam 16:18

---

[371] Cf. BHRG §39.11.I.1.f; GBHS §4.1.10(c); IBHS §11.2.10c, 36.2.3d.

[372] Cf. BHRG §39.11.I.1.b; GBHS §4.1.10(e); IBHS §11.2.10d.

[373] Cf. BHRG §39.11.I.3; GBHS §4.1.10(f); GKC §129; IBHS §9.7a–c, 10.3.2b, 11.2.10d, f; JM §130.

- Other possible examples include Deut 5:9 and 1 Kgs 18:22. The לְ in the common superscription מִזְמוֹר לְדָוִד 'a psalm of David' (e.g., Ps 3:1, 4:1, 5:1, 6:1, 8:1, 9:1) is probably a possessive לְ, although this is disputed.

271a **לְ of advantage (for).**[374] The object of the preposition לְ can be a person or thing to whose advantage something is. This is sometimes said to have the meaning of a *dativus commodi*.

- אָרָה־ לִּי אֶת־הָעָם הַזֶּה   Curse this people *for* me!
  the this   the people   *for* me   curse!   Num 22:6

- בְּנֵה־ לִּי בָזֶה שִׁבְעָה מִזְבְּחֹת   Build seven altars *for* me here!
  altars   seven   in this   *for* me   build!   Num 23:1

- Another example is 1 Sam 9:20.

- The לְ of Advantage and the לְ of Disadvantage (§271b) are the two subsets of the broader category לְ **of Interest**.

271b **לְ of disadvantage (against).**[375] The object of the preposition לְ can be a person or thing to whose disadvantage something is. This is also referred to as an **adversative** לְ and as the equivalent of the *dativus incommodi*.

- מִתְאַנֶּה הוּא לִי   He is picking a fight *with* me.
  against me   he   seeking a quarrel   2 Kgs 5:7

- וַיִּלְכֹּד גִּלְעָד אֶת־מַעְבְּרוֹת הַיַּרְדֵּן לְאֶפְרָיִם
  against Ephraimites   the Jordan   fords of   Gilead   he captured   Judg 12:5
  The Gileadites captured the fords of the Jordan *against* the Ephraimites.

272 **Reflexive לְ** (*untranslated*).[376] When the object of the preposition לְ refers to the person who is the subject of the verb and the context indicates that the subject acts upon itself, the לְ is a reflexive לְ. A reflexive לְ and its object are often both left untranslated in English. This is sometimes referred to as the **ethical dative**, the *dativus ethicus*, or the **centripetal לְ**.

- לֶךְ־ לְךָ מֵאַרְצְךָ   Leave your country!
  from your country   (לְ) you   go!   Gen 12:1

- שׁוּבוּ לָכֶם לְאָהֳלֵיכֶם   Return to your tents!
  to your tents   (לְ) you   return!   Deut 5:30

- Other examples include Gen 21:16 and Num 22:34.

---

[374] Cf. GBHS §4.1.10(e.1); GKC §119s; IBHS §11.2.10d, 16.4d, 18.3b; JM §133d.
[375] Cf. GBHS §4.1.10(e.2); GKC §119s; IBHS §11.2.10d, 18.3b; JM §133d.
[376] Cf. BHRG §39.11.I.5(iii); GBHS §4.1.10(m); GKC §119s; IBHS §11.2.10d; JM §133d; Noss 1995; Muraoka 1978.

273a לְ **of specification (with respect to, for, *untranslated*).**[377] Like an accusative of specification (§57a), a לְ of specification indicates the sphere in which the verb applies or the extent to which the verb occurs.

- לֹא־רָאִיתִי כָהֵנָּה ... לָרֹעַ

  with respect to bad quality   like them   I saw   not   Gen 41:19

  I have not seen their like ... *for* ugliness.

- וְלָאֲתֹנוֹת   הָאֹבְדוֹת

  the lost ones   and *with respect to* the donkeys   and *as for* the donkeys which were lost

                                                                                1 Sam 9:20

- בַּמַּיִם מִתַּחַת לָאָרֶץ

  with respect to the earth   under   in the waters   Deut 5:8

  in the waters which are underneath the earth

- וְנִסְלַח   לוֹ

  with respect to him   and it will be forgiven   It will be forgiven him.

                                                                                Lev 4:26

273b לְ **for direct object (*untranslated*).**[378] Some verbs take a prepositional phrase beginning with לְ where English would use a direct object.

- בְּ is used similarly (§244). This use of לְ is very common in Aramaic.

- לְשַׁחֵת לָעִיר בַּעֲבוּרִי

  on account of me   (לְ) the city   to destroy   to destroy the city on account of me

                                                                                1 Sam 23:10

- זְכֹר לַעֲבָדֶיךָ לְאַבְרָהָם לְיִצְחָק וּלְיַעֲקֹב

  and (לְ) Jacob   (לְ) Isaac   (לְ) Abraham   (לְ) your servants   remember!   Deut 9:27

  Remember your servants, Abraham, Isaac, and Jacob!

- Other examples include Gen 1:5, 10; 2 Sam 3:30; Amos 8:9; Job 5:2.

273c לְ **for the subject of a passive verb (*untranslated*).**[379] The object of the preposition לְ may be the subject of a passive verb.

- יְבֻלַּע לַמֶּלֶךְ וּלְכָל־ הָעָם

  the people   and (לְ) all of   (לְ) the king   will be swallowed up   2 Sam 17:16

  The king and all of the people will be swallowed up.

- לְזֹאת יִקָּרֵא אִשָּׁה

  woman   will be called   (לְ) this   This one will be called 'woman.'

                                                                                Gen 2:23

273d לְ **in place of a repeated preposition (and, *untranslated*).**[380] Sometimes the preposition לְ is used instead of repeating another preposition.

---

[377] Cf. BHRG §39.11.1.2(i); GBHS §4.1.10(h); GKC §114o, 119u; IBHS §11.2.10d, g; JM §130g.

[378] Cf. BHRG §39.1.3(ii)a, 39.11.I.5(ii); GKC §117n; IBHS §10.4b, 11.2.10g, 11.4.1b; JM §125k; Rooker 1990, 97–9.

[379] Cf. IBHS §10.4c; IBHS §11.2.10g; JM §132f.

[380] Cf. JM §133d; Barr 1978; Rooker 1990, 117–19.

- בֵּין מַיִם לָמָיִם

  between waters waters between

  between waters *and* waters

  Gen 1:6

- בֵּין־ טוֹב לְרָע

  between evil good between

  between good *and* evil

  2 Sam 19:36

- Another example is Deut 17:8.

74a לְ **of manner (according to, in).**[381] Just like an accusative of manner (§60), the object of the preposition לְ can describe the style or mode with which the verb takes place or the standard which it follows. This is also called לְ **of the norm**. A subclass called the לְ **of class and type** is sometimes distinguished. Sometimes the object of the preposition can be translated as an adverb.

- עֹשֶׂה פְּרִי לְמִינוֹ

  according to its kind fruit bearing

  bearing fruit *according to* its kind

  Gen 1:11

- וַיֵּשֶׁב יְהוּדָה וְיִשְׂרָאֵל לָבֶטַח

  according to safety and Israel Judah dwelt

  Judah and Israel lived secure*ly*

  1 Kgs 5:5

- Other examples include Gen 13:17; Isa 8:6, 42:3.

74b לְ **of comparison (as).**[382] The object of the preposition לְ is sometimes a standard of comparison.

- עַד אֲשֶׁר־ דַּק לְעָפָר

  as dust it was crushed fine until

  until it was crushed as fine *as* dust

  Deut 9:21

75 לְ **with infinitive construct for degree (enough to).** See §199.

- חָלָה חִזְקִיָּהוּ לָמוּת

  enough to die Hezekiah was sick

  Hezekiah was sick *enough to* die.

  2 Kgs 20:1

- וּבְאַהֲרֹן הִתְאַנַּף יְהוָה מְאֹד לְהַשְׁמִידוֹ

  enough to destroy him very YHWH was angry and at Aaron

  Deut 9:20

  And YHWH was very angry at Aaron – *angry enough to* destroy him.

- Another example is 2 Sam 13:2.

76 לְ **before an infinitive construct that is a subject or direct object.** See §192 and §193. When used this way, לְ is usually left untranslated.

- Because the same meaning can be expressed without the preposition לְ, the preposition is pleonastic, meaning that it is a redundant word. To see this, compare 2 Chr 2:13, which has לְ, and Amos 3:10, which does not.

- יוֹדֵעַ לַעֲשׂוֹת בַּזָּהָב

  with the gold [לְ] *to* do knowing

  knowing how to work in gold

  2 Chr 2:13 (with לְ)

---

[381] Cf. BHRG §39.11.I.2(ii); GBHS §4.1.10(j); IBHS §11.2.10d; JM §124o.
[382] Cf. IBHS §11.2.10d; JM §133d.

- וְלֹא־ יָדְעוּ עֲשׂוֹת־ נְכֹחָה   They do not know how to do what is right.
  what is right to do they know and not   Amos 3:10 (without לְ)

277 לְ **of purpose (to, for).**[383] The object of the preposition לְ (frequently an infinitive construct, §197) can be the purpose for something.

- וַיַּעַשׂ אֱלֹהִים ... אֶת־הַמָּאוֹר הַגָּדֹל לְמֶמְשֶׁלֶת הַיּוֹם
  the day *for* dominion of the great the light   God   made   Gen 1:16

  God made ... the great light *to* govern the day.

- אַיֵּה הַשֶּׂה לְעֹלָה   Where is the lamb *for* the burnt offering?
  for burnt offering the lamb where?   Gen 22:7

- Another example is Judg 20:20.

278 לְ **of product (into, for).**[384] The object of the preposition לְ may be a state or condition that is the result of another action. When the verb הָיָה means 'become,' it is often followed by a לְ of product.

- וְאֶעֶשְׂךָ לְגוֹי גָּדוֹל   I will make you *into* a great nation.
  great *into* nation and I will make you   Gen 12:2

- וְהַמַּטֶּה אֲשֶׁר־ נֶהְפַּךְ לְנָחָשׁ   and the staff which was turned *into* a snake
  into snake was turned which and the staff   Exod 7:15

- Other examples include Exod 21:2 and 1 Sam 15:1.
- When an infinitive construct is used with a לְ of product, it has the sense of something that ought to be done ('gerundive,' §196).

279 לְ **of result (thus ...ing, for).** The object of the preposition לְ (usually an infinitive construct, §198) can be a result.

- הַתִּקֵם כְּצֹאן לְטִבְחָה   Drag them off like sheep *for* slaughter!
  for slaughter like sheep drag them off!   Jer 12:3

  o This could be a noun with לְ of result, but it could also be לְ of purpose (§277).

- For examples with an infinitive construct as the object of לְ, see §198.

280 לְ **of agent (by).**[385] The preposition לְ can indicate the agent who performs the action of a passive verb. This is rare.

- הֲלוֹא נָכְרִיּוֹת נֶחְשַׁבְנוּ לוֹ
  by him we are considered as foreigners not?   Gen 31:15

  Are we not reckoned as foreigners *by* him?

---

[383] Cf. BHRG §39.11.II; GBHS §4.1.10(d), 5.2.3; GKC §165a; IBHS §11.2.10d; JM §168c.
[384] Cf. BHRG §39.11.I.1.c; GBHS §4.1.10(e.2); GKC §119t; IBHS §11.2.10d.
[385] Cf. BHRG §39.11.I.5(i); GBHS §4.1.10(l); GKC §121f; IBHS §11.2.10g, 23.2.2f; JM §132f; Althann 1981.

- אֲשֶׁר יֵאָכֵל לְכָל־נֶפֶשׁ הוּא לְבַדּוֹ יֵעָשֶׂה לָכֶם
  by you will be made it alone it person by all of will be eaten which   Exod 12:16
  What will be eaten *by* every person, that alone may be prepared *by* you.

81 Distributive לְ (every, by). Distribution can be indicated with לְ (§103).

- וַתִּפְקְדֶנּוּ לִבְקָרִים לִרְגָעִים תִּבְחָנֶנּוּ
  you test him *by* moments *by* mornings you examine him   Job 7:18
  You examine him *every* morning and test him *every* moment.

- עֹבְרִים לְמֵאוֹת וְלַאֲלָפִים passing over *by* hundreds and *by* thousands
  and *by* thousands *by* hundreds passing over   1 Sam 29:2

- Other examples include 1 Kgs 10:22 and Amos 4:4.

82 לְ of partisanship (for, on the side of).[386] The object of the preposition לְ
can be the one whose side someone takes. This is also called the **לְ of
assistance** and is a subcategory of the לְ of advantage (§271a).

- הֲלָנוּ אַתָּה אִם־לְצָרֵינוּ   Are you *for* us or *for* our foes?
  for our foes or you for us?   Josh 5:13

83 Asseverative לְ (truly).[387] Also called a **לְ of emphasis**, on rare occasions,
it is possible that what appears to be the preposition לְ emphasizes the
certainty or truth of something. This is quite controversial.

- לַיהוָה מָגִנֵּנוּ וְלִקְדוֹשׁ יִשְׂרָאֵל מַלְכֵּנוּ
  our king Israel *truly* holy of our shield *truly* YHWH   Ps 89:19
  Truly YHWH is our shield; *Truly* the Holy One of Israel is our king.

- לְגַבֵּי־חֹמֶר גַּבֵּיכֶם   Your defences are *truly* defences of clay.
  your defences clay *truly* defences of   Job 13:12

84 לְ of obligated person (incumbent upon, had to, ought).[388] Also called
the **לְ of obligation**, the object of the preposition לְ can be a person who is
obligated to do something. This is rare; usually עַל is used instead (§294).

- הֲלוֹא לָכֶם לָדַעַת אֶת־הַמִּשְׁפָּט
  the justice to know *incumbent upon* you not?   Mic 3:1
  Is it not *incumbent upon* you to be familiar with justice?

- וְלָנוּ הַסְגִּירוֹ בְּיַד הַמֶּלֶךְ
  the king into hand of to hand him over and *incumbent upon* us   1 Sam 23:20
  And our *responsibility* will be to hand him over to the king.

---

[386] Cf. GBHS §4.1.10(e.1); IBHS §11.2.10d.

[387] Cf. GKC §143e; IBHS §11.2.10i; Muraoka 1985, 113–23; Dahood 1956; Dahood
1975a; Huehnergard 1983, 590–1.

[388] Cf. GKC §114l; IBHS §11.2.10d, 36.2.3f; JM §124l.

• Another example is 2 Chr 13:5.

The preposition עַל [389]

285   The preposition עַל frequently expresses motion or rest on or above something. It was originally a substantive meaning 'height' or 'high' (cf. Gen 49:25 and 2 Sam 23:1).[390]

286   **Locative עַל (on, over, above, at, beside).**[391]

•   וְעוֹף יְעוֹפֵף עַל־ הָאָרֶץ   Let birds fly *above* the earth.
    the earth *over* let fly and bird   Gen 1:20

•   וַיִּבֶן עַל־ קִיר הַבַּיִת יָצִיעַ   1 Kgs 6:5
    a structure the house wall of *beside* he built

                    He built a structure *beside* the wall of the house.

•   Other examples include Exod 20:12 and Deut 28:23.

287   **Terminative עַל (onto, down upon).**[392] The motion of a verb of motion can end on the object of the preposition עַל.

•   וַיֵּרֶד הָעַיִט עַל־ הַפְּגָרִים   the carcasses *onto* the birds of prey went down   Gen 15:11

                    The birds of prey swooped down *onto* the carcasses.

•   שָׂם עַל־ שִׁכְמָהּ   He put [them] *onto* her shoulder.
    her shoulder *onto* he put   Gen 21:14

•   Another example is Exod 20:26.

288a   **עַל of disadvantage (against).**[393] The object of the preposition עַל can be the one to whose disadvantage something happens. This use of עַל is also called the **adversative עַל** or is said to have the meaning of a *dativus incommodi*.

•   כִּי־ תִקְרַב אֶל־ עִיר לְהִלָּחֵם עָלֶיהָ   *against* it to fight city (to) you approach when   Deut 20:10

                    when you approach a city to fight *against* it

---

[389] Cf. BHRG §39.19; GBHS §4.1.16; GKC §119aa–dd; IBHS §11.2.13; JM §103m, 133f.
[390] Cf. GKC §101a; IBHS §11.2.13a; JM §103a; Reider 1940.
[391] Cf. BHRG §39.19.1; GBHS §4.1.16(a); GKC §119aa, cc; IBHS §11.2.13b; JM §133f; Sutcliffe 1955.
[392] Cf. BHRG §39.19.1; GBHS §4.1.16(a); IBHS §11.2.13b.
[393] Cf. GBHS §4.1.16(f); GKC §119dd; IBHS §11.2.13c; JM §133f.

- מֵתָה עָלַי רָחֵל   Rachel died, *to my sorrow*.
  Rachel *against* me died   Gen 48:7

- Other possible examples include 1 Sam 21:16 and Ps 142:4.

88b   Concessive עַל (although, in spite of).[394] The object of the preposition עַל can be a concessive clause (§531).

- עַל־דַּעְתְּךָ כִּי־ לֹא אֶרְשָׁע   *although* you know that I am not guilty
  I am guilty not that you to know *although*   Job 10:7

- עַל לֹא־ חָמָס עָשָׂה   *although* he had done no violence
  he did violence no *although*   Isa 53:9

289   עַל of specification (concerning, with regard to, for).[395] The object of an עַל of specification states the sphere in which the verb applies or the extent to which the verb occurs. This is like an accusative of specification (§57a) and a לְ of specification (§273a).

- וְעַל הִשָּׁנוֹת הַחֲלוֹם   and *concerning* the repetition of the dream
  the dream to repeat and *concerning*   Gen 41:32

- עַל־ כָּל־ דְּבַר־ פֶּשַׁע עַל־ שׁוֹר עַל־ חֲמוֹר   Exod 22:8
  donkey *concerning* ox *concerning* transgression thing of all of *concerning*
  concerning any type of transgression, *concerning* ox or *concerning* donkey

290   עַל of norm (in accordance with, *idiomatic*).[396] The object of the preposition עַל can be a standard or a norm to which something is compared and with which it is judged to be in accordance (or not in accordance). This is like the כְּ of the norm (§259) and is also called the עַל of manner.

- עַל כָּל־ הַדְּבָרִים הָאֵלֶּה   *in accordance with* all these words
  the these the words all of *in accordance with*   Exod 24:8

- הוֹצִיא יְהוָה אֶת־בְּנֵי יִשְׂרָאֵל ... עַל־ צִבְאֹתָם   Exod 12:51
  their armies *in accordance with* ... Israel sons of YHWH brought out
  YHWH brought out the Israelites ... *by* their armies.

- וּמְשַׁלֵּם עַל־ יֶתֶר עֹשֵׂה גַאֲוָה
  pride doing abundance *in accordance with* and repaying   Ps 31:24
  and abundant*ly* paying back the one who acts in pride

- Another example is Num 35:24.

---

[394] Cf. GBHS §4.1.16(f), 5.2.12; GKC §160c; IBHS §11.2.13f, 36.2.2b; JM §171a, e.
[395] Cf. BHRG §39.19.4(i).
[396] Cf. BHRG §39.19.4(ii); GBHS §4.1.16(e); IBHS §11.2.13e.

291   **Causal עַל (because, because of).**[397] The object of the preposition עַל can be the cause of something else. The object of the preposition can be a noun, an infinitive construct (§535), or a substantival clause (§534).

- הָאִשָּׁה   עַל־   מֵת   הִנְּךָ
  the woman   *because of*   dead   (behold) you   Gen 20:3 (noun)

  You are a dead man *because of* the woman.

- חָטָאתִי   לֹא   אָמְרֵךְ   עַל־   אוֹתָךְ   נִשְׁפָּט   הִנְנִי
  I sinned   not   you to say   *because*   you   judging   (behold) me   Jer 2:35 (infinitive)

  I will judge you *because* you say, 'I have not sinned.'

- תוֹרָתֶךָ   שָׁמְרוּ   לֹא־   עַל   *because* they do not keep your law
  your law   they kept   not   *because*   Ps 119:136 (clause)

- Other examples include Gen 31:20; Exod 17:7; Deut 9:18.

292   **עַל of addition (in addition to).**[398] The object of the preposition עַל can be something to which something else is added.

- הַתָּמִיד   עֹלַת   עַל־   *in addition to* the regular burnt offering
  the regular   burnt offering   *in addition to*   Num 28:10

- רָעָה   חַטֹּאתֵינוּ   כָּל־   עַל־   יָסַפְנוּ
  evil   our sins   all of   *in addition to*   we added   1 Sam 12:19

  We have added [this] evil *to* all of our sins.

- Other examples include Gen 28:9 and Num 31:8.

293   **עַל of accompaniment (with, accompanied by, together with).**[399] The object of the preposition עַל can be what accompanies something else.

- יֹאכְלֻהוּ   מְרֹרִים   עַל־   וּמַצּוֹת
  they will eat it   bitter things   *with*   and unleavened bread   Exod 12:8

  They will eat it with unleavened bread *accompanied by* bitter herbs.

- הַנָּשִׁים   עַל־   הָאֲנָשִׁים   וַיָּבֹאוּ   The men came, *together with* the women.
  the women   *with*   the men   they came   Exod 35:22

- Another example is 1 Kgs 15:20.

294   **עַל of obligated person (incumbent upon, had to, ought).**[400] The object of the preposition עַל can be a person who is obligated to do something (like לְ §284). This is also called the **עַל of obligation** or the **עַל of duty**.

---

[397] Cf. BHRG §39.19.5; GBHS §4.1.16(d), 5.2.5; GKC §158b–c; IBHS §11.2.13e, 38.4a; JM §170h.

[398] Cf. BHRG §39.19.3(ii); GBHS §4.1.16(g); GKC §119aa note 2; IBHS §11.2.13d; JM §133f.

[399] Cf. BHRG §39.19.3(i); GBHS §4.1.16(g); IBHS §11.2.13d.

[400] Cf. BHRG §39.19.1(iv); GBHS §4.1.16(b); GKC §119aa; IBHS §11.2.13c, 36.2.3f.

- זִבְחֵי שְׁלָמִים עָלָי הַיּוֹם שִׁלַּמְתִּי נְדָרָי
  my vows I paid the day *incumbent upon* me peace sacrifices of Prov 7:14
  I *had to* offer peace offerings; today I have paid my vows.

- חֹדֶשׁ בַּשָּׁנָה יִהְיֶה עַל־הָאֶחָד לְכַלְכֵּל
  to provide the one *had to* in the year month 1 Kgs 4:7
  Each one *had to* provide for one month in the year.

- Other examples include 2 Sam 18:11 and 2 Kgs 18:14.

295 עַל **of advantage (on behalf of, for the sake of, for).**[401] The object of the preposition עַל can be a person to whose advantage something is. This is the opposite in meaning to the עַל of disadvantage (§288a).

- נִלְחַם אָבִי עֲלֵיכֶם My father fought *for* you.
  for you my father fought Judg 9:17

- אֲדַבֵּר עָלֶיךָ אֶל־הַמֶּלֶךְ I will speak to the king *for* you.
  the king to *for* you I will speak 1 Kgs 2:18

- Other examples include Gen 19:17 and 2 Kgs 10:3.

296 עַל **with an indirect object (to,** *untranslated***).**[402] The object of the preposition עַל can be the indirect object of a verb. This is a late use; in earlier texts, אֶל is used for this purpose (§300).

- אִם־עַל־הַמֶּלֶךְ טוֹב if it pleases the king
  good the king (*to*) if Esth 1:19

- וְעָלַי הִטָּה־חֶסֶד He extended loyalty *to* me.
  loyalty he stretched out and *to* me Ezra 7:28

The preposition אֶל [403]

297 **The preposition** אֶל often expresses motion towards a person or thing. The object of the preposition אֶל is never an infinitive or a noun clause.[404]

298 **Spatially terminative** אֶל **(into, unto).**[405] The object of the preposition אֶל can be an ending location.

---

[401] Cf. GKC §119bb; IBHS §11.2.13c.
[402] Cf. IBHS §11.2.13g; JM §133f.
[403] Cf. BHRG §39.3; GBHS §4.1.2; GKC §119g; IBHS §11.2.2; JM §103m, 133b; Mitchell 1888. The article by Mitchell includes a concordance that categorizes (in terms of meaning) every occurrence of אֶל in the Hebrew Bible.
[404] Cf. JM §133b.
[405] Cf. BHRG §39.3.1; GBHS §4.1.2(a); GKC §119g; IBHS §11.2.2; JM §133b.

- וְלֹא־ תָבִיא תוֹעֵבָה אֶל־ בֵּיתֶךָ

  your house *into* abominable thing you will bring and not   Deut 7:26

  You will not bring an abominable thing *into* your house.

- וּבָאתָ אֶל־ הַתֵּבָה   You will enter *into* the ark.

  the ark *into* and you will enter   Gen 6:18

299 אֶל **of direction (towards, to).**[406] The object of the preposition אֶל can be a direction. This is also called the **directive** אֶל.

- יִתְפַּלְלוּ אֶל־ הַמָּקוֹם הַזֶּה   They will pray *towards* this place.

  the this the place *towards* they will pray   1 Kgs 8:30

- לִהְיוֹת עֵינֶךָ פְתֻחוֹת אֶל־ הַבַּיִת הַזֶּה

  the this the house *towards* opened your eyes to be   1 Kgs 8:29

  May your eyes be open *towards* this house.

- Other examples include Gen 32:31 and 39:7.

300 **Indirect object** אֶל **(to,** *untranslated*)**.**[407] The object of the preposition אֶל can be the indirect object of the verb.

- וַיִּקְרָא מֹשֶׁה אֶל־ כָּל־ יִשְׂרָאֵל וַיֹּאמֶר אֲלֵהֶם

  to them and he said Israel all of (*to*) Moses he called   Deut 5:1

  Moses called all Israel and said *to* them …

- וַיִּתְפַּלֵּל אַבְרָהָם אֶל־הָאֱלֹהִים   Abraham prayed *to* God.

  the God *to* Abraham he prayed   Gen 20:17

- Other examples include Gen 16:11 and 2 Kgs 6:11.

301 אֶל **of partisanship (for, on the side of).**[408] The object of the preposition אֶל can be the one whose side someone takes. Also called the אֶל **of assistance**, this is a subcategory of the אֶל of advantage (§302).

- הִנְנִי אֲלֵיכֶם   Behold, I *am on* your *side*!

  on the side of you behold me   Ezek 36:9

- אֵין נַפְשִׁי אֶל־ הָעָם הַזֶּה   My heart is not *with* this people.

  the this the people *on the side of* my soul there is not   Jer 15:1

- Another example is 2 Kgs 6:11.

302 אֶל **of advantage (for, for the sake of, on behalf of).**[409] The object of the preposition אֶל can be a person or thing to whose advantage something is.

---

[406] Cf. BHRG §39.3.1; GBHS §4.1.2(a); GKC §119g; IBHS §11.2.2; JM §133b.

[407] Cf. BHRG §39.3.1; GBHS §4.1.2(a), (c), (d); IBHS §11.2.2; JM §133b.

[408] Cf. BHRG §39.3.1; GBHS §4.1.2(b); IBHS §11.2.2.

[409] Cf. BHRG §39.3.1; GBHS §4.1.2(b); IBHS §11.2.2.

Advantage (§302) and disadvantage (§303) are together called the **estimative uses** of אֶל.

- וַיָּנֻסוּ אֶל־נַפְשָׁם   They fled *for* their lives.
  their life *for* they fled   2 Kgs 7:7

- וַיַּרְא וַיָּקָם וַיֵּלֶךְ אֶל־נַפְשׁוֹ   He was afraid, so he rose and ran *for* his life.
  his life *for* he went he rose he was afraid   1 Kgs 19:3

303   אֶל **of disadvantage (against).**[410] The object of the preposition אֶל can be the one to whose disadvantage or against whom something happens. This is also called the **adversative** אֶל.

- וַיָּקָם קַיִן אֶל־הֶבֶל אָחִיו וַיַּהַרְגֵהוּ
  killed him   his brother   Abel   *against*   Cain   rose up   Gen 4:8
                   Cain rose up *against* his brother Abel and killed him.

- חֲרוֹן אַף־יְהוָה אֶל־יִשְׂרָאֵל   the burning anger of YHWH *against* Israel
  Israel   *against*   YHWH   anger of   burning of   Num 32:14

- Another example is Jer 21:13.

304   אֶל **of accompaniment (accompanied by, together with, with).**[411] The object of the preposition אֶל can be something that accompanies something else. This is also called the **comitative** use of אֶל.

- וְלֹא־תֶחֶטְאוּ לַיהוָה לֶאֱכֹל אֶל־הַדָּם
  the blood   *with*   by eating   against YHWH   [you] sin   and not   1 Sam 14:34
               Do not sin against YHWH by eating [it] *with* the blood.

305   אֶל **of addition (in addition to).**[412] The object of the preposition אֶל can be something to which something else is added. This is also called the **comitative** use of אֶל.

- הוֹסַפְתָּ חָכְמָה וָטוֹב אֶל־הַשְּׁמוּעָה
  the report   *in addition to*   and prosperity   wisdom   you added   1 Kgs 10:7
         You have added wisdom and prosperity *in addition to* [what was in] the report.

306   אֶל **of specification (about, concerning, with respect to).**[413] אֶל can specify the sphere in which the verb applies or the extent to which the verb occurs.

- הִתְאַבֵּל שְׁמוּאֵל אֶל־שָׁאוּל   Samuel grieved *over* Saul.
  Saul   *about*   Samuel   mourned   1 Sam 15:35

---

[410] Cf. BHRG §39.3.1; GBHS §4.1.2(b); IBHS §11.2.2; JM §133b.
[411] Cf. BHRG §39.3.2(i); GBHS §4.1.2(e); IBHS §11.2.2.
[412] Cf. BHRG §39.3.2(ii); GBHS §4.1.2(e); IBHS §11.2.2.
[413] Cf. GBHS §4.1.2(g); IBHS §11.2.2.

- וַתִּשְׁמַע אֶת־הַשְּׁמֻעָה אֶל־ הִלָּקַח אֲרוֹן
  ark to take *about* the news she heard   1 Sam 4:19

  She heard the news *about* the capture of the ark.

- Another example is 2 Sam 24:16.

307 **אֶל of norm (according to, on the basis of).**[414] אֶל can state a standard or a norm to which something is compared.

- נָתַן חֵלֶק ... אֶל־ פִּי יְהוָה
  YHWH mouth of *according to* portion he gave   Josh 15:13

  He gave a portion ... *according to* YHWH's command.

- וַיֵּדַע כִּי־ בָא שָׁאוּל אֶל־ נָכוֹן
  dependability *according to* Saul came that he knew   1 Sam 26:4

  He knew *according to* dependable information that Saul had come.

308 **Locative אֶל (at, by, near).**[415] אֶל can indicate a location at, by, or near its object.

- וַיִּשְׁחָטוּהוּ אֶל־ מַעְבְּרוֹת הַיַּרְדֵּן
  the Jordan fords of *at* they slaughtered him   Judg 12:6

  They slaughtered him *at* the fords of the Jordan.

- Another example is 1 Kgs 13:20.

The preposition עַד [416]

309 **Spatially terminative עַד (to, as far as).**[417] The object of the preposition עַד can be an ending location.

- וַיָּבֹאוּ עַד־ חָרָן   They came *as far as* Haran.
  Haran *to* they came   Gen 11:31

- וְנֵלְכָה עַד־ הָרֹאֶה   Let us go *to* the seer.
  the seer *to* we will go   1 Sam 9:9

310 **Locative עַד (near, at, by).** The preposition עַד can be used to specify a location near, at, or by its object.

- וַיֶּאֱהַל עַד־ סְדֹם   He pitched his tents *near* Sodom.
  Sodom *near* he pitched his tent   Gen 13:12

- הַיֹּשְׁבִים בַּחֲצֵרִים עַד־ עַזָּה   the ones living in villages *near* Gaza
  Gaza *near* in villages the ones living   Deut 2:23

---

[414] Cf. IBHS §11.2.2.
[415] Cf. BHRG §39.3.3; GBHS §4.1.2(f); GKC §119g; IBHS §11.2.2; JM §133b.
[416] Cf. BHRG §39.18; GBHS §4.1.15; IBHS §11.2.12; JM §103m.
[417] Cf. BHRG §39.18.1; GBHS §4.1.15(a); IBHS §11.2.12b, 36.2.3d.

- Another possible example is Judg 4:11.

311   **Temporal עַד (to, until, by, during, while, as long as).**[418] The preposition עַד can indicate that something occurs up to the time indicated by its object or, rarely, during the time indicated by its object. The object of a temporal עַד can be a noun, an infinitive construct (§508; with לְ §276), or a clause that begins with אֲשֶׁר (§502) or כִּי (§497). The expression עַד־לֹא can mean 'before.'

- הַזֶּה הַיּוֹם עַד שֶׁבַע בְּאֵר הָעִיר שֵׁם־
  the this the day *until* Beersheba the city name of   Gen 26:33 (noun)

  The name of the city is Beersheba *until* this day.

- הָאֲדָמָה אֶל־ שׁוּבְךָ עַד לֶחֶם תֹּאכַל
  the ground to your to return *until* bread you will eat   Gen 3:19 (infinitive)

  You will eat bread *until* you return to the ground.

- בָּאתִי אֲשֶׁר־ עַד לַדְּבָרִים הֶאֱמַנְתִּי וְלֹא־
  I came [which] *until* (לְ) the words I believed and not   1 Kgs 10:7 (אֲשֶׁר clause)

  But I did not believe the report *until* I came.

- הַבֹּקֶר עַד־ יוּמַת לוֹ יָרִיב אֲשֶׁר
  the morning *by* he will be killed for him will contend whoever   Judg 6:31 (noun)

  Whoever will contend for him will be killed *by* morning.

- הָרַבִּים ... אִיזֶבֶל זְנוּנֵי עַד־ הַשָּׁלוֹם מָה
  the numerous Jezebel harlotries of *during* the peace what?   2 Kgs 9:22 (noun)

  What peace can there be, *as long as* the harlotries of Jezebel … are so many?

- עַד־לֹא עָשָׂה אֶרֶץ   *before* he made the earth
  land he made *not until*   Prov 8:26 (clause)

- Other examples include Gen 41:49; 1 Sam 25:22; 2 Sam 17:22; 1 Kgs 18:29.

312   **עַד for degree (up to, to the point that, to the level of).**[419] The preposition עַד can indicate a level or standard of comparison.

- אָב לֹא הַשְּׁלֹשָׁה וְעַד־   But he did not attain *to* the three.
  he came not the three but *to the level of*   2 Sam 23:19

---

[418] Cf. BHRG §39.18.2; GBHS §4.1.15(b), 5.2.4(b); GKC §107c; IBHS §11.2.12b, 30.5.2b, 36.2.2, 38.7a; JM §104b, 112i, 113k, 166i, k; Gaenssle 1915a, 153–7; Barr 1982; Hughes 1982.

[419] Cf. BHRG §39.18.3; IBHS §11.2.12c–d. What GBHS §4.1.15(c) calls 'עַד of degree' can be considered a subset of this category, restricted to the instances where מְאֹד 'very' is the object of the preposition.

- עַד־ הִשְׁלִכוֹ אֹתָם מֵעַל פָּנָיו

  his face   from on   them   he sent him   *to the level of*   2 Kgs 24:20

  to the point that he sent them out from his presence

313 **Inclusive עַד (as well as, and, from … to).** The object of the preposition עַד may be an additional item or part of a range of items that are included. When repeated or used with מִן (§327) it can give a range ('from … to').

- וַיִּתְּנֵהוּ לְדָוִד וּמַדָּיו וְעַד־ חַרְבּוֹ וְעַד־קַשְׁתּוֹ

  his bow *and* his sword *as well as* and his garment to David he gave it   1 Sam 18:4

  He gave it and his garment to David, *as well as* his sword *and* his bow.

- עַד־ יְרֵכָהּ עַד־ פִּרְחָהּ   *from* its base *to* its flowers

  its flower *to* its base *from*   Num 8:4

- Other examples include Gen 19:4; Exod 9:25; Lev 11:42; 1 Sam 5:9.

314 **Emphatic עַד (even).** The preposition עַד can draw attention to the fact that something extends as far as its object.

- לֹא־ נִשְׁאַר בָּהֶם עַד־ אֶחָד   Not *even* one of them remained.

  one *even* in them he remained not   Exod 14:28

- הֵן עַד־ יָרֵחַ וְלֹא יַאֲהִיל   Behold, *even* the moon is not bright.

  it is bright and not moon *even* behold   Job 25:5

- Another example is 2 Sam 17:22.

The preposition מִן [420]

315 **Separative מִן (from).**[421] Also called its **ablative use**, the preposition מִן can indicate a location or state from which something moves away.

- כִּי־ יִפֹּל הַנֹּפֵל מִמֶּנּוּ   if someone falls *from* it

  from it   the one falling   he will fall   if   Deut 22:8

- וַיַּעַל יְהוֹשֻׁעַ מִן־ הַגִּלְגָּל   Joshua went up *from* Gilgal.

  the Gilgal *from* Joshua he went up   Josh 10:7

- Another example is Deut 30:3.

316 **מִן for a starting time (from, after).**[422] The object of the preposition מִן can be the time when something begins.

---

[420] Cf. BHRG §39.14; GBHS §4.1.13; GKC §101a, 102b, 103i, m, 119v–z, 133a–e, 119ff; IBHS §11.2.11, 14.4b–d; JM §103d, h, 132d, 133e, 170i.

[421] Cf. BHRG §39.14.1; GBHS §4.1.13(a); GKC §119v, z; IBHS §11.2.11b; JM §133e. This is sometimes considered a subcategory of מִן for source (§322).

[422] Cf. BHRG §39.14.2; GBHS §4.1.13(b), 5.2.4; IBHS §11.2.11c; JM §133e.

- מִיּוֹם דַּעְתִּי אֶתְכֶם   *from* the day that I knew you

  you I knew *from* day   Deut 9:24

- וַיְהִי כְּמִשְׁלֹשׁ חֳדָשִׁים וַיֻּגַּד לִיהוּדָה

  to Judah it was told months about *after* three of (was)   Gen 38:24

             About three months *later*, it was told to Judah.

- Other examples include 1 Sam 18:9; Hos 6:2; Ps 73:20.

317   **Comparative מִן (…-er than).** As discussed in §76, the preposition מִן is used with an adjective to indicate comparison.

- מַה־מָּתוֹק מִדְּבַשׁ וּמֶה עַז מֵאֲרִי •

  than lion strong and what? *than* honey sweet what?   Judg 14:18

     What is sweet*er than* honey? What is strong*er than* a lion?

- טוֹב תִּתִּי אֹתָהּ לָךְ מִתִּתִּי אֹתָהּ לְאִישׁ אַחֵר •

  another to man her *than* I to give to you her I to give good   Gen 29:19

     It is bett*er* that I give her to you *than* that I give her to another man.

- Another example is Ezek 28:3.

318   **Absolute comparative מִן (too … for).** As discussed in §76, the object of the preposition מִן can be a standard of comparison, where something is judged to be excessive (e.g., 'too small,' 'too hard') for something else.

- הֲיִפָּלֵא מֵיהוָה דָּבָר •

  thing *too … for* YHWH it will be wonderful? Is anything *too* difficult *for* YHWH?

                                 Gen 18:14

  o   In Gen 18:14, the adjectival idea is expressed with the verb יִפָּלֵא 'it will be wonderful' rather than with an adjective.

- הָיָה רְכוּשָׁם רַב מִשֶּׁבֶת יַחְדָּו •

  together *too … for* to dwell great their possession was   Gen 36:7

       Their possessions were *too* great *for* them to dwell together.

- Other examples include Num 11:14; Deut 14:24; 1 Kgs 8:64.

319   **Causal מִן or מֵאֲשֶׁר (because, because of).**[423] The object of the preposition מִן can be the cause of something else. The object of מִן can be a noun, a pronoun, an infinitival phrase (§535), or a clause (§534).

- הָרִים רָעֲשׁוּ מִמֶּנּוּ •

  from him quake mountains   Mountains quake *because of* him.

                       Nah 1:5 (pronoun)

- וְלֹא־יָכֹל עוֹד לְהָשִׁיב אֶת־אַבְנֵר דָּבָר מִיִּרְאָתוֹ •

  because his to fear word Abner to return again he was able and not

     He was not able to answer Abner again *because* he was afraid. 2 Sam 3:11 (infinitive)

---

[423] Cf. BHRG §39.14.5; GBHS §4.1.13(d), 5.2.5(b); GKC §119z; IBHS §11.2.11d, 36.2.2b, 38.4a; JM §133e, 170i; Gaenssle 1915a, 158–9.

- מֵאֲשֶׁר יָקַרְתָּ בְּעֵינַי *because* you are precious in my eyes

  in my eyes   you are precious   *because*   Isa 43:4 (מֵאֲשֶׁר with clause)

- Other examples include Exod 2:23; Deut 7:7; 2 Sam 3:11.

320a מִן **for means (by, with).**[424] Also called the **instrumental use**, מִן can indicate the mechanism or means by which something happens. In the **material use**, מִן indicates the substance from which something is made.

- וְלֹא־ יִכָּרֵת כָּל־ בָּשָׂר עוֹד מִמֵּי הַמַּבּוּל

  of the flood *by* waters again flesh all of it will be cut off and not   Gen 9:11

  All flesh will not be cut off again *by* the waters of the flood.

- וְחִתַּתַּנִי בַחֲלֹמוֹת וּמֵחֶזְיֹנוֹת תְּבַעֲתַנִּי

  you will terrify me and *with* visions with dreams and you scare me   Job 7:14

  You scare me with dreams and terrify me *with* visions.

320b מִן **for agent (by).**[425] As with לְ (§280), the preposition מִן can indicate the agent who causes the action of a passive construction. This is rare (§159a).

- אִשָּׁה גְּרוּשָׁה מֵאִישָׁהּ a woman divorced *by* her husband

  by her husband   divorced   woman   Lev 21:7

- כָּלְתָה אֵלָיו הָרָעָה מֵאֵת הַמֶּלֶךְ

  the king *by* (+אֵת) the evil against him was determined   Esth 7:7

  Evil was determined against him *by* the king.

321 **Privative** מִן **(without).**[426] The object of the preposition מִן (a noun, an infinitive, or a clause) can be something that someone or something lacks.

- עָמְדוּ מִכֹּחַ נָסִים The fugitives stand *without* strength.

  ones fleeing *without* strength they stand   Jer 48:45 (noun)

- וַיִּמְאָסְךָ יְהוָה מִהְיוֹת מֶלֶךְ YHWH has rejected you *from* being king.

  king *from* to be YHWH rejected you   1 Sam 15:26 (infinitive)

- מִן־ יְקוּמוּן *without* them getting up

  they will get up *without*   Deut 33:11 (clause)

- Other examples include Lev 26:13 and 1 Sam 15:23.

322 מִן **for source (from, of).**[427] The object of the preposition מִן can be the thing or location from which something originates.

- מֵרְשָׁעִים יֵצֵא רֶשַׁע Wickedness comes *from* wicked people.

  wickedness comes *from* wicked people   1 Sam 24:14

---

[424] Cf. BHRG §39.14.6.a; IBHS §11.2.11d; JM §132d.
[425] Cf. BHRG §39.14.6.b; GBHS §4.1.13(d); IBHS §11.2.11d, 23.2.2f; JM §132d.
[426] Cf. BHRG §39.14.3; GBHS §4.1.13(g); GKC §119w–x; IBHS §11.2.11e.
[427] Cf. BHRG §39.14.1; GBHS §4.1.13(a); IBHS §11.2.11b; JM §133e.

- וַיִּשְׁפֹּט ... אֶת־יִשְׂרָאֵל אִבְצָן מִבֵּית לָחֶם   Ibzan *of* Bethlehem judged Israel.
  of Bethlehem   Ibzan   Israel   judged   Judg 12:8

- Other examples include Gen 2:7 and 1 Kgs 2:15.

23a   מִן **for relationship in space** (*idiomatic*).[428] The object of the preposition מִן can be a direction in space that is used to indicate a location in relation to something else. The translation must often be chosen idiomatically.

- וַיַּעְתֵּק מִשָּׁם הָהָרָה מִקֶּדֶם לְבֵית־אֵל
  to Bethel   (מִ) east   toward the mountain   from there   he moved on   Gen 12:8
          He moved on from there to the mountain *to* the east of Bethel.

- אֲשֶׁר בַּשָּׁמַיִם מִמַּעַל וַאֲשֶׁר בָּאָרֶץ מִתָּחַת
  (מִ) under   in the earth   and which   (מִ) above   in the heavens   which   Deut 5:8
       which are in the heavens above or which are in the earth underneath

- Other examples include Num 32:19 and Josh 8:13.

23b   מִן **for time (in, on).**[429] The object of the preposition מִן can be a time when something occurs or begins.

- וַיְהִי מִמָּחֳרָת וַתֹּאמֶר הַבְּכִירָה   *on* the following day, the firstborn said
  the firstborn   she said   *on* the next day   (was)   Gen 19:34

- עֶבֶד אָבִיךָ וַאֲנִי מֵאָז   I was the servant of your father *in* the past.
  in past   and I   your father   servant of   2 Sam 15:34

23c   מִן **for standpoint (in the sight of, before, from the standpoint of).**[430] The object of the preposition מִן can be the person from whose standpoint something is stated.

- וִהְיִיתֶם נְקִיִּם מֵיהוָה וּמִיִּשְׂרָאֵל
  and *before* Israel   *before* YHWH   free   you will be   Num 32:22
       You will be free *before* YHWH and *before* Israel.

- הַאֱנוֹשׁ מֵאֱלוֹהַּ יִצְדָּק אִם מֵעֹשֵׂהוּ יִטְהַר־גָּבֶר
  man   be pure   *before* his maker   or   be righteous   *before* God   human?   Job 4:17
       Can a human be righteous *before* God, or a man be pure *before* his maker?

- Other examples include Jer 51:5; Ps 18:22; Sir 3:18 (MS A), 10:7.

324   **Partitive מִן (some of, of).**[431] The object of the preposition מִן can be the whole from which a part is taken.

---

[428] Cf. BHRG §39.14.1; GBHS §4.1.13(i); IBHS §11.2.11b.
[429] Cf. BHRG §39.14.2; GBHS §4.1.13(b); IBHS §11.2.11c.
[430] Cf. IBHS §11.2.11d.
[431] Cf. BHRG §39.14.7; GBHS §4.1.13(f); IBHS §11.2.11e; JM §133e.

- וַיָּבֵא קַיִן מִפְּרִי הָאֲדָמָה   Cain brought *some of* the fruit of the ground.
  the ground *some of* fruit of Cain brought   Gen 4:3

- וְלוֹא נַכְרִית מֵהַבְּהֵמָה   We won't have to destroy *some of* the cattle.
  some of the cattle we will destroy not   1 Kgs 18:5

- Another example is Exod 16:27.

325 Emphatic מִן (even).[432] As with עַד (§314), the preposition מִן can draw attention to the fact that something extends as far as its object.

- וְעָשָׂה מֵאַחַת מֵהֵנָּה   He does *any* one of them.
  of them *even* one he will do   Lev 4:2

- אִם־יִפֹּל מִשַּׂעֲרַת בְּנֶךָ אָרְצָה
  to ground your son *even* a single hair of it will fall not   2 Sam 14:11
  Not *even* a single hair of your son shall fall to the ground.

- Another example is 1 Sam 14:45 (nearly identical to 2 Sam 14:11).

326 Explicative מִן (namely, *idiomatic*). The object of the preposition מִן can explain more precisely the meaning of a preceding substantive. This is also called the מִן **of explanation**.

- וַיִּקְחוּ לָהֶם נָשִׁים מִכֹּל אֲשֶׁר בָּחָרוּ
  they chose which *namely* all WIVES for themselves they took   Gen 6:2
  They took WIVES for themselves, any they chose.

  o In Gen 6:2, מִן introduces a clause that explains more precisely to whom the word נָשִׁים 'wives' refers.

- הִפְקִיד אִתּוֹ אֲנָשִׁים וְנָשִׁים וְטָף
  AND CHILDREN AND WOMEN   MEN   him he appointed   Jer 40:7
  וּמִדַּלַּת הָאָרֶץ מֵאֲשֶׁר לֹא־הָגְלוּ בָּבֶלָה
  to the Babylon they were exiled not *namely* whom the land and *namely* poor of
  He appointed him over THE MEN, WOMEN, AND CHILDREN,
  the poorest in the land, *the ones* who were not exiled to Babylon.

- Other examples include Gen 7:22, 9:10; Lev 11:32; Jer 44:28; 1 Chr 5:18.

327 Inclusive מִן (from … unto).[433] When מִן is followed by עַד (§313) or the directional suffix הָ and used with two extremes (e.g., young and old, sunrise and sunset) or prominent members, the construction can imply that everything in between is included. This figure of speech that implies the whole by listing the extremes or prominent members is called **merismus**.

---

[432] Cf. IBHS §11.2.11e.
[433] Cf. Honeyman 1952.

- מִנַּעַר   וְעַד־   זָקֵן   [everyone] *from* the young to the old
  old   and unto   *from* young   Gen 19:4 (with עַד־)

- מִכֹּל   חֹגֵר   חֲגֹרָה   וָמָעְלָה   all who could put on a belt and upwards
  and above   belt   gird oneself   *from* all   2 Kgs 3:21 (with מִ)

- Other examples include Exod 9:25 and 1 Sam 5:9.

The preposition עִם [434]

328 **עִם of accompaniment (with).** [435] The object of the preposition עִם can be someone or something that is accompanied by someone or something else. This is also called the **comitative** use of עִם.

- הוּא וְהָאֲנָשִׁים אֲשֶׁר־ עִמּוֹ   he and the men who were *with* him
  with him   who   and the men   he   Gen 24:54

- לֹא־ תֹאכַל הַנֶּפֶשׁ עִם־ הַבָּשָׂר   You will not eat the life *with* the flesh.
  the flesh   *with*   the life   you will eat   not   Deut 12:23

329 **Locative עִם (near).** [436] The preposition עִם can be used to indicate a location near or beside its object.

- וַיֵּשֶׁב יִצְחָק עִם־ בְּאֵר לַחַי רֹאִי   Isaac settled *near* Beer-lahai-roi.
  roi   lahai   beer   *near*   Isaac   settled   Gen 25:11

- הֵמָּה עִם־ בֵּית מִיכָה   They were *near* the house of Micah.
  of Micah   house   *near*   they   Judg 18:3

330 **עִם for possessor (has, in possession of).** The preposition עִם can indicate that its object possesses something. This is also called the **עִם of possession**.

- גַּם־ תֶּבֶן גַּם־ מִסְפּוֹא רַב עִמָּנוּ   We *have* plenty of both straw and fodder.
  with us   great   fodder   also   straw   also   Gen 24:25

- עִם אֲשֶׁר תִּמְצָא אֶת־אֱלֹהֶיךָ
  your gods   you find   whom   *with*   Gen 31:32

  whomever you find *in possession of* your gods

331 **עִם of advantage (for, for the sake of, on behalf of).** [437] The object of the preposition עִם can be one to whose advantage or benefit something is.

- וְאֵיטִיבָה עִמָּךְ   so that I may cause things to go well *for* you
  for you   and I will cause to go well   Gen 32:10

- וַעֲשֵׂה־ חֶסֶד עִם אֲדֹנִי אַבְרָהָם   Show loyalty *to* my master Abraham.
  Abraham   my lord   *for*   loyalty   do!   Gen 24:12

---

[434] Cf. BHRG §39.20; GBHS §4.1.17; GKC §101a, 103c; IBHS §11.2.14; JM §103i.
[435] Cf. BHRG §39.20.1(i); GBHS §4.1.17(a); IBHS §11.2.14.
[436] Cf. BHRG §39.20.3; GBHS §4.1.17(c); IBHS §11.2.14c.
[437] Cf. BHRG §39.20.2; GBHS §4.1.17(b).

- Another example is Gen 26:29.

332   עִם **of disadvantage (against, in spite of).**[438] The preposition עִם can indicate that something opposes its object, works to the disadvantage of its object, or occurs in spite of its object. This is also called the **adversative** use of עִם

- מִי־ יָקוּם לִי עִם־ מְרֵעִים   Who will stand up for me *against* evildoers?
  evildoers *against* for me will stand who?   Ps 94:16

- עִם־ זֶה לֶחֶם הַפֶּחָה לֹא בִקַּשְׁתִּי
  I demanded not the governor food of this *in spite of*   Neh 5:18
  In spite of this, I did not demand the governor's food allowance.

- Another example is Gen 26:29.

333   עִם **of coordination (as well as, and, along with).**[439] The object of the preposition עִם can be something that is in addition to something else. This is also called the **additive** or **comitative** use of עִם.

- עִם־ עָרֵיהֶם הֶחֱרִימָם יְהוֹשֻׁעַ
  Joshua devoted them to destruction their cities *as well as*   Josh 11:21
  Joshua devoted them to destruction, *along with* their cities.

334   עִם **of comparison (like, similar to).** The object of the preposition עִם can be something to which something else is compared.

- וְעִם־ אָדָם לֹא יְנֻגָּעוּ   They are not afflicted *like* mankind.
  they are afflicted not man and *like*   Ps 73:5

- חָלְפוּ עִם־ אֳנִיּוֹת אֵבֶה   They go by *like* papyrus boats.
  papyrus ships of *with* they go by   Job 9:26

- Another example is Ps 28:1.

335   **Reciprocal** עִם **(with).** The object of the preposition עִם can be a person with whom one performs a reciprocal activity – each acting on the other.

- וּפְלִשְׁתִּים נֶאֶסְפוּ לְהִלָּחֵם עִם־ יִשְׂרָאֵל
  Israel *with* to fight they gathered and Philistines   1 Sam 13:5
  The Philistines gathered to fight *with* Israel.

- חַלְּקוּ שְׁלַל־ אֹיְבֵיכֶם עִם־ אֲחֵיכֶם
  your brothers *with* your enemies plunder of divide!   Josh 22:8
  Divide the plunder of your enemies *with* your brothers.

- Other examples include Gen 30:8 and 26:28.

---

[438] Cf. BHRG §39.20.2; GBHS §4.1.17(b); IBHS §11.2.14b.
[439] Cf. BHRG §39.20.1(ii); GBHS §4.1.17(a).

336 עִם **of assistance (with the help of, with).**[440] The object of the preposition עִם can be a person by whose help something happens.

- עָשָׂה הַיּוֹם הַזֶּה עִם־ אֱלֹהִים He did it today *with the help of* God.
  the this   the day   he did   God   *with*   1 Sam 14:45

- וְעָשָׂה לְמִבְצְרֵי מָעֻזִּים עִם־ אֱלוֹהַּ נֵכָר
  foreignness god of *with* strongholds to fortresses of he will do   Dan 11:39

  He will take action against strong fortresses *with the help of* a foreign god.

337 עִם **of consciousness (in the mind of, in the eyes of, with).** The object of עִם can be a person from whose perspective something is evaluated.

- אִכָּבֵדָה עִמָּם *In* their *minds*, I shall be honoured.
  let me be honoured *in the minds of* them   2 Sam 6:22

- לֹא כֵן אָנֹכִי עִמָּדִי But I am not thus *in* my *own mind*.
  in the mind of me I thus not   Job 9:35

- Another example is Job 10:13.
- This use of עִם may have arisen from the expression עִם־לֵבָב.
  o וַיְהִי עִם־ לְבַב דָּוִד אָבִי It was *in* the heart of my father David
    my father David heart of *with* it was   1 Kgs 8:17
- Another example of עִם־לֵבָב is found in 1 Kgs 10:2.

The preposition אֵת / אֶת־ [441]

338 אֵת **of accompaniment (with).**[442] The object of the preposition אֵת can be a person or thing that goes along with something else.

- וְנָשְׂאוּ אִתָּךְ They will carry [it] *with* you.
  with you they will carry   Exod 18:22

339 **Locative אֵת (near, beside).**[443] The preposition אֵת can be used to indicate a location near its object.

- הַפְּסִילִים אֲשֶׁר אֶת־ הַגִּלְגָּל the idols which *were near* Gilgal
  the Gilgal *near* which the idols   Judg 3:19

- בְּעֶצְיוֹן־ גֶּבֶר אֲשֶׁר אֶת־ אֵלוֹת in Ezion-geber, which is *near* Eloth
  Eloth *near* which geber in Ezion   1 Kgs 9:26

340 אֵת **of possessor (have, in the possession of).**[444] The preposition אֵת can be used to indicate that its object owns or is in possession of something.

---

[440] Cf. GBHS §4.1.17(a); IBHS §11.2.14b.
[441] Cf. BHRG §39.5; GBHS §4.1.4; GKC §103b; IBHS §11.2.4; JM §103j; Althann 1991.
[442] Cf. BHRG §39.5.1(i); GBHS §4.1.4(a); IBHS §11.2.4.
[443] Cf. BHRG §39.5.1(ii); GBHS §4.1.4(d); IBHS §11.2.4.

- אֲנִי לְקַחְתִּיו   אִתִּי   הַכֶּסֶף   I *have* the silver; I took it.
  took it   I   *in the possession of* me   the silver   Judg 17:2

- אִתָּנוּ   מַה   What *do* we *have*?
  in the possession of us   what?   1 Sam 9:7

- Another example is Gen 27:15.

341 **אֵת of advantage (for).**[445] The object of the preposition אֵת can be a person
to whose advantage something is.

- כְּכֹל אֲשֶׁר עָשָׂה אִתְּכֶם בְּמִצְרָיִם   just as he did *for* you in Egypt
  in Egypt *for* you he did which like all   Deut 1:30

- עָשָׂה אִתְּכֶם וְאֶת־אֲבוֹתֵיכֶם   he did *for* you and *for* your fathers
  your fathers and *for* *for* you he did   1 Sam 12:7

- Another example is Deut 10:21.

342 **אֵת of disadvantage (against).**[446] The object of the preposition אֵת can be a
person to whose disadvantage something is. This is also referred to as the
adversative אֵת.

- אַתָּה עֹשֶׂה אִתִּי רָעָה   You are doing me wrong.
  evil *against* me doing you   Judg 11:27

343 **אֵת of coordination (as well as, along with, and).**[447] The preposition אֵת
may be used to indicate that its object is added to, included with, or
otherwise coordinated with something else.

- הָאָרֶץ   אֶת־   מַשְׁחִיתָם   וְהִנְנִי
  the earth *along with* destroying them and (behold) me   Gen 6:13
                                    I am about to destroy them *along with* the earth.

344 **Reciprocal אֵת (with).**[448] The object of the preposition אֵת can be a person
with whom one performs a reciprocal activity – each acting on the other.

- אֶתְכֶם לִפְנֵי יְהוָה   וְאִשָּׁפְטָה
  YHWH before *with* you so that I may go to court   1 Sam 12:7
                          so that I may go to court *with* you before YHWH

- שָׁלָל   יְחַלֵּק   עֲצוּמִים   אֶת־   He will divide booty *with* the strong.
  booty he will divide powerful ones *with*   Isa 53:12

---

[444] Cf. BHRG §39.5.1(iii); GBHS §4.1.4(b); IBHS §11.2.4.
[445] Cf. BHRG §39.5.2; GBHS §4.1.4(c); IBHS §11.2.4.
[446] Cf. BHRG §39.5.2; GBHS §4.1.4(c).
[447] Cf. GBHS §4.1.4(a); IBHS §11.2.4.
[448] Cf. GBHS §4.1.4(a).

345 אֵת **of assistance (with the help of, with).**[449] The object of the preposition אֵת can be a person or thing by whose help something happens.

- This is usually expressed with עִם (§336)

- קָנִיתִי אִישׁ אֶת־יְהוָה   I have acquired a man *with the help of* YHWH.
  YHWH *with* man I have acquired   Gen 4:1

- אֶת־מִי הִגַּדְתָּ מִלִּין   *With* whose *help* have you uttered words?
  words you uttered who? *with*   Job 26:4

- Another example is Judg 8:7.

346 אֵת **of partisanship (on the side of).**[450] The object of the preposition אֵת can be the one whose side someone takes. This is also called the אֵת **of assistance** and can be translated 'for,' 'on the side of,' or 'with.'

- מִי אִתִּי   Who *is on* my *side*?
  on the side of me who?   2 Kgs 9:32

347 אֵת **of consciousness (in the awareness of).** The object of the preposition אֵת can be a person who is aware of something.

- פְּשָׁעֵינוּ אִתָּנוּ וַעֲוֹנֹתֵינוּ יְדַעֲנוּם
  we know them our iniquities *in the awareness of* us our transgressions   Isa 59:12
       We *are aware of* our transgressions, and we know our iniquities.

- זְכַרְתַּנִי אִתְּךָ   Keep me in mind!
  in the awareness of you remember me   Gen 40:14

- Another example is Job 12:3.

The preposition תַּחַת [451]

348 **The preposition** תַּחַת **comes from the noun** תַּחַת **'what is underneath.'**[452]

- בִּרְכֹת תְּהוֹם רֹבֶצֶת תָּחַת
  what is underneath lying down of the deep blessings   Gen 49:25
       blessings of the deep that lies *beneath*

  o In Gen 49:25, תַּחַת is a noun that is used as an accusative of manner (§60).

- בָּאָרֶץ מִתָּחַת   in the earth *beneath*
  from *what is underneath* in the earth   Exod 20:4

349 **Locative** תַּחַת **(under, beneath, below, at the base of).**[453] The preposition תַּחַת can indicate a location under or at the bottom of its object.

---

[449] Cf. GBHS §4.1.4(a); IBHS §11.2.4.
[450] Cf. GBHS §4.1.4(a); IBHS §11.2.4.
[451] Cf. BHRG §39.21; GBHS §4.1.18; GKC §103o; IBHS §11.12.15; JM §103n.
[452] Cf. IBHS §11.12.15a.

- תַּחַת כָּל־הַשָּׁמָיִם   *under* the whole sky
  the heavens all of *under*   Gen 7:19

- וַיִּבֶן מִזְבֵּחַ תַּחַת הָהָר   He built an altar *at the base of* the mountain.
  the mountain *under* altar he built   Exod 24:4

350 תַּחַת **of authority (under the authority of)**.[454] The preposition תַּחַת can indicate that its object is in control of or has authority over someone or something. This is sometimes called the **metaphorical** use of תַּחַת, because something is 'under' its object, figuratively speaking.

- וְיִצְבְּרוּ בָר תַּחַת יַד־פַּרְעֹה
  Pharaoh hand of *under the authority of* grain let him pile up   Gen 41:35
  Let him pile up grain *under* Pharaoh's *authority*.

- וְאִם־לֹא שָׂטִית טֻמְאָה תַּחַת אִישֵׁךְ
  your husband *under authority of* uncleanness you strayed not and if   Num 5:19
  and if you have not strayed into uncleanness while *under* your husband's *authority*

- Another possible example is Isa 24:5.

351 תַּחַת **of identity of situation (in the place of, right where … was)**.[455] Also called תַּחַת of **static position**, the preposition תַּחַת may indicate a location where something is or happens, drawing attention to the fact that the location did not change at all.

- וְעָמַדְנוּ תַחְתֵּינוּ וְלֹא נַעֲלֶה אֲלֵיהֶם
  to them we will ascend and not *in the place of* us we will stand   1 Sam 14:9
  We will stay *right where* we *are* and not go up to them.

- וַיִּפֹּל־שָׁם וַיָּמָת תַּחְתָּיו   He fell there and died *right where* he *was*.
  on the spot of him he died there he fell   2 Sam 2:23

352 תַּחַת **of exchange (instead of, in place of)**.[456] The preposition תַּחַת may indicate that something is a substitute for its object. This is also referred to as the תַּחַת of **substitution**.

- וַיַּעֲלֵהוּ לְעֹלָה תַּחַת בְּנוֹ
  his son *in the place of* as burnt offering he offered it up   Gen 22:13
  He offered it up as a burnt offering *in place of* his son.

---

[453] Cf. BHRG §39.21.1(i); GBHS §4.1.18(a); IBHS §11.12.15b.
[454] Cf. BHRG §39.21.1(ii); GBHS §4.1.18(c); IBHS §11.12.15b.
[455] Cf. BHRG §39.21.1(iii); GBHS §4.1.18(b); IBHS §11.12.15b.
[456] Cf. BHRG §39.21.2; GBHS §4.1.18(d); IBHS §11.12.15b.

- וְנִשְׁאַרְתֶּם בִּמְתֵי מְעָט
  number   in men of   you will be left   Deut 28:62

  תַּחַת אֲשֶׁר הֱיִיתֶם כְּכוֹכְבֵי הַשָּׁמַיִם לָרֹב
  to greatness the heavens like stars of you were which *in the place of* (cont.)

  You will be left few in number
  in the place of having been as numerous as the stars of the sky.

- Other examples include Exod 21:23; 1 Kgs 11:43, 21:2.

353 תַּחַת **to introduce a causal clause (because, because of).**[457] The object of the preposition תַּחַת can be a causal clause (often beginning with אֲשֶׁר or כִּי), meaning that it indicates what causes the main clause (§534).

- תַּחַת אֲשֶׁר קִנֵּא לֵאלֹהָיו
  to his god he was jealous *because*
  because he was jealous for his God
  Num 25:13

- וְתַחַת כִּי אָהַב אֶת־אֲבֹתֶיךָ
  your fathers he loved *and because*
  and *because* he loved your fathers
  Deut 4:37

- Another example is 2 Kgs 22:17.

The preposition בְּעַד / בַּעַד [458]

354 **The preposition** בְּעַד **is the construct form of** בַּעַד, which can be either a noun or a preposition meaning 'behind.'

- עֵינַיִךְ יוֹנִים מִבַּעַד לְצַמָּתֵךְ
  (לְ) your veil from *behind* doves your eyes
  Your eyes are doves *behind* your veil.
  Song 4:1

  o In Song 4:1, בַּעַד may be a noun, meaning 'the place behind,' and be the object of the preposition מִן. Alternately, בַּעַד may be a preposition, combining with the preposition מִן to form a compound preposition.

- Other examples include Song 4:3 and 6:7.

355 **Locative** בַּעַד **(behind, through).**[459] Also called the **spatial** use, the preposition בַּעַד can indicate a location behind or through its object.

- וַיִּסְגְּרוּ בַּעֲדָם
  behind them they shut
  They shut [the door] *behind* them.
  Judg 9:51

- וַתּוֹרִדֵם בַּחֶבֶל בְּעַד הַחַלּוֹן
  the window *through* with the rope she caused them to go down
  She lowered them down with a rope *through* the window.
  Josh 2:15

- Another example is Judg 5:28.

---

[457] Cf. BHRG §40.9.I.3 note 55; IBHS §38.4a; JM §170g; Gaenssle 1915a, 150–2.
[458] Cf. BHRG §39.8; GBHS §4.1.7; IBHS §11.2.7; JM §103e.
[459] Cf. BHRG §39.8.1; GBHS §4.1.7(a); IBHS §11.2.7.

356 בְּעַד **of advantage (on behalf of, for, for the sake of).**[460] The object of the preposition בְּעַד can be a person or thing to whose advantage something is.

- וְאֶתְפַּלֵּל   בַּעַדְכֶם   אֶל־יְהוָה   I will pray to YHWH *on* your *behalf.*
  YHWH to *on behalf of* you I will pray   1 Sam 7:5

- אֲכַפְּרָה   בְּעַד   חַטַּאתְכֶם   Let me make atonement *for* your sin.
  your sin *for* let me make atonement   Exod 32:30

- Another example is 1 Sam 7:9.

The preposition אַחֲרֵי / אַחַר [461]

357 **The preposition** אַחֲרֵי / אַחַר may be the construct of the noun אַחַר.[462]

- וַיַּכֵּהוּ אַבְנֵר בְּאַחֲרֵי   הַחֲנִית   Abner struck him with *the butt of* the spear.
  the spear with *butt of* Abner struck him   2 Sam 2:23

358 **Locative** אַחַר **(behind, after, with).**[463] Also called the **spatial** use, the preposition אַחַר may indicate a location behind, after, or with its object.

- וַיֵּלֶךְ יוֹסֵף אַחַר   אֶחָיו   Joseph went *after* his brothers.
  his brothers *after* Joseph he went   Gen 37:17

- וַיִּקָּחֵנִי יְהוָה מֵאַחֲרֵי   הַצֹּאן   YHWH took me from being *with* the flock.
  the flock from *with* YHWH took me   Amos 7:15

- Other examples include Deut 11:28, 23:15; 1 Sam 14:13; 2 Kgs 13:2; Neh 3:16–31 (where אַחֲרָיו is parallel to עַל־יָדוֹ).

359 **Directional** אַחַר **(west of).**[464] The preposition אַחַר 'behind' may indicate a direction to the west of its object or on the west side of its object.

- Hebrew gives compass points relative to a person facing east, so that the right is south, behind is west, the left is north, and in front is east.

- וַיִּנְהַג אֶת־הַצֹּאן אַחַר   הַמִּדְבָּר
  the wilderness *west of* the flock he led   Exod 3:1
  He led the flock *to the west side* of the wilderness.

- אַחֲרֵי   קִרְיַת   יְעָרִים   *west of* Kiriath-jearim
  Jearim Kiriath *west of*   Judg 18:12

- Other examples include Deut 11:30; Josh 8:2; Ezek 41:15.

---

[460] Cf. BHRG §39.8.2; GBHS §4.1.7(b); IBHS §11.2.7.

[461] Cf. BHRG §39.2; GBHS §4.1.1; GKC §103o; IBHS §11.2.1; JM §103n.

[462] Cf. IBHS §9.6c, 11.1.1a; JM §20c, 103a.

[463] Cf. BHRG §39.2.1.a; GBHS §4.1.1(a); IBHS §11.2.1, 39.3.1g.

[464] Cf. BHRG §39.2.1.c; GBHS §4.1.1(a); IBHS §11.2.1.

360 **Temporal אַחַר (after).**[465] The preposition אַחַר may indicate a time after its object. The object may be a noun, an infinitive construct (§506), or a clause (§501; sometimes beginning with אֲשֶׁר).

- אַחַר הַדְּבָרִים הָאֵלֶּה
  after the things the these

  after these things
  Gen 15:1 (noun)

- אַחֲרֵי הִפָּרֶד־לוֹט מֵעִמּוֹ
  after to separate off Lot from with him

  after Lot separated from him
  Gen 13:14 (infinitive construct)

- וַיְהִי אַחַר דִּבֶּר יְהוָה
  after it happened spoke YHWH

  It happened *after* YHWH spoke.
  Job 42:7 (clause)

- Other examples include Gen 6:4, 9:28; Josh 9:16; 1 Sam 5:9; 1 Kgs 13:23.

361 **Adversative אַחַר (against, to the disadvantage of).**[466] The preposition אַחַר can indicate that something works to the disadvantage of its object.

- וּבִעַרְתִּי אַחֲרֶיךָ
  against you I will sweep away

  I will sweep you away.
  1 Kgs 21:21

- אַחֲרֶיךָ רֹאשׁ הֵנִיעָה
  she wagged head against you

  She wagged her head *at* you.
  2 Kgs 19:21

- Another example is 1 Kgs 14:10.

362 **אַחַר of the norm (in accordance with, after the manner of).**[467] The object of the preposition אַחַר can be a standard or a norm to which something is compared. This is also called the **metaphorical** use of אַחַר.

- הַהֹלְכִים ... אַחַר מַחְשְׁבֹתֵיהֶם walking *in accordance with* their own plans
  their plans in accordance with walking
  Isa 65:2

- הֹלְכִים אַחַר רוּחָם *walking in accordance with* their own spirit
  their spirit in accordance with walking
  Ezek 13:3

- Another possible example is 2 Chr 2:16.

The preposition יַעַן [468]

363a **The preposition יַעַן** may have been derived from the construct form of a noun.[469]

---

[465] Cf. BHRG §39.2.2; GBHS §4.1.1(b), 5.2.4; IBHS §11.2.1, 36.2.2b, 38.7a, 39.3.1h; JM §104b, 166k; Gaenssle 1915a, 152–3.

[466] Cf. IBHS §11.2.1.

[467] Cf. BHRG §39.2.1.b; GBHS §4.1.1(c); IBHS §11.2.1.

[468] Cf. GBHS §4.1.8; GKC §107q, 158b; IBHS §11.2.8, 38.4a.

[469] Cf. IBHS §38.4a; JM §170f note 2; JM93 §170f note 1. IBHS §38.4a states that יַעַן is derived from the root of the verb ענה 'to answer.'

363b **Causal יַעַן (because, because of).**[470] The word יַעַן always indicates the cause of something. It is used as a conjunction more often than it is used as a preposition. When it is used as a preposition, its object is usually an infinitive construct (§535), sometimes a clause (§534; sometimes beginning with אֲשֶׁר or כִּי), and rarely a substantive.

- יַעַן הִתְמַכֶּרְךָ לַעֲשׂוֹת הָרַע   *because* you sold yourself to do evil
  the evil   to do   you to sell yourself   *because*   1 Kgs 21:20 (infinitive construct)

- יַעַן לֹא־הֶאֱמַנְתֶּם בִּי   *because* you have not believed in me
  in me   you believed   not   *because*   Num 20:12 (clause)

- יַעַן כָּל־תּוֹעֲבֹתָיִךְ   *because of* all of your abominations
  your abominations   all of   *because of*   Ezek 5:9 (noun)

- Other examples include Gen 22:16 and Num 11:20.

The preposition לְמַעַן [471]

364 **The compound preposition** לְמַעַן consists of the preposition לְ prefixed to the noun מַעַן. In Biblical Hebrew, the noun מַעַן only occurs after לְ.[472]

- לְמַעַן may sometimes function as a conjunction.[473]

365 **לְמַעַן of advantage (for the sake of, for).** The object of the preposition לְמַעַן can be a person to whose advantage something is.

- וְלֹא־תִשָּׂא לַמָּקוֹם לְמַעַן חֲמִשִּׁים הַצַּדִּיקִם
  the righteous   fifty   *for the sake of* (לְ) the place   you will spare   and not   Gen 18:24
  Will you not spare the place *for the sake of* the fifty righteous?

- לְמַעַן שְׁמִי אַאֲרִיךְ אַפִּי
  my anger   I will delay   my name   *for the sake of*   Isa 48:9
  For the sake of my own name, I defer my anger.

- Other examples include Deut 30:6; 1 Kgs 11:13; Isa 37:35, 63:17.

366 **Causal לְמַעַן (on account of, because of).**[474] The preposition לְמַעַן may indicate that its object is the cause of something else.

- וַיִּתְעַבֵּר יְהוָה בִּי לְמַעַנְכֶם   YHWH was angry at me *because of* you.
  because of you   at me   YHWH   was angry   Deut 3:26

---

[470] Cf. BHRG §40.9.I.3 note 55; GBHS §4.1.8, 5.2.5; GKC §158b; IBHS §5.6d, 11.2.8, 36.2.2b, 38.4a, 39.3.4d; JM §170f; Gaennsle 1915a, 145–9.

[471] Cf. BHRG §39.12, 40.13; GBHS §4.1.11; GKC §119c.

[472] Cf. IBHS §11.3.1a.

[473] Cf. BHRG §40.13.

[474] Cf. GBHS §4.1.11(b); IBHS §5.6d.

- זֹאת לְמַעַן דָּוִד אֶת־זֶרַע וַאעַנֶּה
  this *on account of* David seed of I will afflict 1 Kgs 11:39

  I will afflict David's descendants *because of* this.

367 לְמַעַן **of purpose (in order to)**.[475] The preposition לְמַעַן may indicate that its object is the purpose for something else. Its object can be an infinitive construct (§197, §520) or a clause with an imperfect verb (§521, often beginning with אֲשֶׁר).

- הַבָּעַל אֶת־עֹבְדֵי הַאֲבִיד לְמַעַן *in order* to destroy the worshipers of Baal
  the Baal servants of to destroy *in order to* 2 Kgs 10:19 (infinitive construct)

- בַעֲבוּרֵךְ לִי יִיטַב־ לְמַעַן
  on account of you to me it will go well *in order that* Gen 12:3 (clause)

  in order that it go well with me on account of you

- Other examples include Gen 37:22; Num 17:5; 2 Sam 13:5.

368 לְמַעַן **for result (with the result that, thus ...-ing, therefore)**.[476] The object of the preposition לְמַעַן can be a **consequence** or **result**. When לְמַעַן is used this way, its object is usually an infinitive construct.

- הַכְעִיסֵנִי לְמַעַן אֲחֵרִים לֵאלֹהִים וַיְקַטְּרוּ
  to anger me *with the result that* other to gods they burned incense 2 Kgs 22:17

  They burned incense to other gods, *thus* provok*ing* me to anger.

- לְשַׁמָּה אֹתְךָ תִּתִּי לְמַעַן *Therefore* I will hand you over to destruction.
  to destruction you I to give *with the result that* Mic 6:16

The preposition לִפְנֵי [477]

369 **The preposition** לִפְנֵי is a compound consisting of the preposition לְ 'to' prefixed to the construct form of the plural noun פָּנִים 'front' or 'face.'[478]

370 **Locative** לִפְנֵי **(in front of, before)**.[479] The preposition לִפְנֵי can indicate a location in front of its object.

- יְהוָה לִפְנֵי עֹמֵד עוֹדֶנּוּ וְאַבְרָהָם
  YHWH *before* standing still him and Abraham Gen 18:22

  But Abraham was still standing *before* YHWH.

---

[475] Cf. BHRG §39.12.1, 40.13.1; GBHS §4.1.11(a), 5.2.3(a), (c); GKC §165b; IBHS §31.6.1c, 36.2.2b, 38.3b–c; JM §168d; Gaenssle 1915a, 157–8.

[476] Cf. BHRG §39.12.2, 40.13.2; GBHS §3.4.1(d), 5.2.3(b); IBHS §36.2.2b; JM §169g.

[477] Cf. BHRG §39.13; GBHS §4.1.12; GKC §119c; IBHS §11.3.1a.

[478] Cf. GKC §119c; IBHS §11.1.1a, 11.3.1a.

[479] Cf. BHRG §39.13.1; GBHS §4.1.12(a); IBHS §11.3.1a.

- בַּחֲלֹומִי וְהִנֵּה־ גֶּפֶן לְפָנָי
  before me   vine   and behold   in my dream   Gen 40:9

  In my dream, behold, there was a vine *in front of* me.

371 Temporal לִפְנֵי (before).[480] The preposition לִפְנֵי can indicate a point in time prior to its object. The object of לִפְנֵי can be an infinitive (§507).

- שְׁנָתַיִם לִפְנֵי הָרָעַשׁ
  the earthquake *before* two years   two years *before* the earthquake
                                                                                          Amos 1:1

- לִפְנֵי שַׁחֵת יְהוָה אֶת־סְדֹם וְאֶת־עֲמֹרָה
  and Gomorrah Sodom YHWH to destroy *before*   Gen 13:10 (infinitive)

  before YHWH destroyed Sodom and Gomorrah

372 Viewpoint לִפְנֵי (in the sight of, before).[481] The preposition לִפְנֵי can indicate that something is being described from the perspective of the object of the preposition. This is also called the **mental, perceptual,** or **referential** use of לִפְנֵי.

- אֹתְךָ רָאִיתִי צַדִּיק לְפָנָי   I have seen that you are righteous *before* me.
  in the sight of me righteous I saw you   Gen 7:1

- מֶה־ חַטָּאתִי לִפְנֵי אָבִיךָ   What is my sin *before* your father?
  your father *in the sight of* my sin what?   1 Sam 20:1

- Another example is 2 Kgs 5:1.

373 לִפְנֵי of comparison (like, as).[482] On rare occasions, לִפְנֵי is used to compare something to its object.

- אַל־ תִּתֵּן אֶת־אֲמָתְךָ לִפְנֵי בַּת־ בְּלִיָּעַל
  of worthless daughter *like* your female slave you will give not   1 Sam 1:16

  Do not regard your maidservant *as* a worthless woman.

- יְדַכְּאוּם לִפְנֵי־ עָשׁ   They crush them *like* a moth.
  moth *like* they crush them   Job 4:19

- Another possible example is Job 3:24.

The preposition מִפְנֵי [483]

374 The preposition מִפְנֵי is a compound consisting of the preposition מִן 'from' prefixed to the construct form of the noun פָּנִים 'front' or 'face.'[484]

---

[480] Cf. BHRG §39.13.2; GBHS §4.1.12(b), 5.2.4(b); IBHS §11.3.1a; JM §166k.
[481] Cf. GBHS §4.1.12(c); IBHS §11.3.1a.
[482] Cf. IBHS §11.3.1a.
[483] Cf. BHRG §39.15; GBHS §4.1.14; GKC §119c; IBHS §11.3.1a.
[484] Cf. GKC §119c; IBHS §11.1.1a, 11.3.1a.

375 **Locative** מִפְּנֵי **(from, from before).**[485] The preposition מִפְּנֵי can be used with a verb of motion to indicate that movement begins near or in front of the object of the preposition and moves away from there. This is also called the **ablative** use of מִפְּנֵי.

- וַיִּתְחַבֵּא הָאָדָם וְאִשְׁתּוֹ מִפְּנֵי יְהוָה אֱלֹהִים
  God YHWH *from before* and his wife the man he hid himself   Gen 3:8

  The man and his wife hid themselves *from* YHWH God.

- מִפְּנֵי שָׂרַי גְּבִרְתִּי אָנֹכִי בֹּרַחַת
  fleeing   I   my mistress   Sarai   *from before*   I am fleeing *from* Sarai, my mistress.
                                                                         Gen 16:8

- Another example is Exod 14:19.

376 **Causal** מִפְּנֵי **(because, because of).**[486] The preposition מִפְּנֵי can indicate that its object is the cause of something. The object of the preposition can be a noun, a pronoun, or a clause that begins with אֲשֶׁר (§534).

- מָלְאָה הָאָרֶץ חָמָס מִפְּנֵיהֶם
  from before them violence the earth is full   Gen 6:13

  The earth is full of violence *because of* them.

- וְאֶת־צַעֲקָתָם שָׁמַעְתִּי מִפְּנֵי נֹגְשָׂיו
  his taskmasters *because* I heard their cry and   Exod 3:7

  I have heard their cry *because of* their taskmasters.

- Another example is Exod 19:18

B   Adverbs [487]

377 **Hebrew has few words that are strictly adverbs.** Adverbial ideas are normally expressed in other ways, such as with a noun that is used in the accusative of manner (§60), with the preposition בְּ of a state or condition (§252), with the preposition לְ of manner (§274a), with the preposition עַל of a norm (290), or with verbal coordination (§223–6).

- Many adverbs are substantives with an adverbial ending, such as אָמְנָם 'really,' חִנָּם 'in vain,' רֵיקָם 'empty handedly,' יוֹמָם 'by day,' שִׁלְשׁוֹם 'previously,' and פִּתְאֹם 'suddenly.'

- A few adverbs of manner are discussed here (§378–93).

---

[485] Cf. BHRG §39.15.1; GBHS §4.1.14(a); IBHS §11.3.1a. GBHS §4.1.14(b) points out that with a verb that does not imply motion, מִפְּנֵי can indicate a location in front of its object.

[486] Cf. BHRG §39.15.2; GBHS §4.1.14(c); IBHS §11.3.1a; JM §170i; Gaenssle 1915a, 159.

[487] Cf. BHRG §41; GBHS §4.2; GKC §100; IBHS §4.6.2, 39.3.

- Negative adverbs are discussed with the negatives in §394–428.

The adverb גַּם [488]

378 גַּם **for addition (also, both … and also).**[489] גַּם can indicate that something is in addition to something else. גַּם(וְ) … גַּם means 'both … and also.'

- וַתִּתֵּן גַּם־לְאִישָׁהּ   She *also* gave [some] to her husband.
  to her husband *also* she gave   Gen 3:6

- בָּרֲכֵנִי גַם־אָנִי אָבִי   Bless me, me *also*, my father!
  my father I *also* bless me!   Gen 27:34

- גַּם־אֲנַחְנוּ גַּם אֲשֶׁר־נִמְצָא הַגָּבִיעַ בְּיָדוֹ
  in his hand the cup it was found which *also* we *both*   Gen 44:16
                  both we *and also* the one in whose hand the cup was found

- Other examples include Gen 24:19; 1 Sam 20:27; Ruth 2:21.

379 **Emphatic** גַּם **(even, just).**[490] The adverb גַּם can be used to assert that there is great significance to or certainty of the words that follow the גַּם. This is also called the **asseverative** use of גַּם.

- אִם־לֹא יַאֲמִינוּ גַּם לִשְׁנֵי הָאֹתוֹת הָאֵלֶּה
  the these the signs to two of *even* they will believe not if   Exod 4:9
                          if they will not believe *even* these two signs

- אָבִי רְאֵה גַּם רְאֵה אֶת־כְּנַף מְעִילְךָ בְּיָדִי
  in my hand your robe edge of look! *even* look! (my) father   1 Sam 24:12
                  Look, father! *Just* look at the edge of your robe in my hand!

- Other examples include Gen 46:4 and Num 22:33.

380 **Rhetorical** גַּם **(yes, even).**[491] The adverb גַּם can be used rhetorically.

- גַּם־בָּרוּךְ יִהְיֶה   *Yes*, and he will be blessed!
  he will be blessed *even*   Gen 27:33

- מַדּוּעַ רְשָׁעִים יִחְיוּ עָתְקוּ גַּם־גָּבְרוּ חָיִל
  power they increased *even* they grew old they will live wicked why? Job 21:7
                  Why do the wicked continue to live, grow old, *yes*, and increase in power?

---

[488] Cf. BHRG §41.4.5; GBHS §4.2.5; GKC §153, 154a note 1, 160b; IBHS §39.3.4d; Van der Merwe 1993, 35–7.

[489] Cf. BHRG §41.4.5.2; GBHS §4.2.5(a), 5.2.9; GKC §154a note 1; IBHS §39.3.4d; JM §177q.

[490] Cf. BHRG §41.4.5.2.c; GBHS §4.2.5(b), 5.2.9; GKC §154a note 1; IBHS §39.3.4d; JM §164g; Muraoka 1985, 143–6.

[491] Cf. BHRG §41.4.5.2; GBHS §5.2.9; GKC §153, 154a note 1; IBHS §39.3.4d; Muraoka 1985, 143–6.

- Other examples include Isa 13:3 and Jer 6:15.

381   **Correlative גַּם (on one's part).**[492] The adverb גַּם can be used to draw attention to the subject of a verb, sometimes in distinction to others.

- וְהֶבֶל הֵבִיא גַם־הוּא מִבְּכֹרוֹת צֹאנוֹ

  his flock   from firstborn of   he   *on part of*   brought   and Abel   Gen 4:4

  And Abel, *on his part*, he brought some of the firstborn of his flock.

- וְגַם אָנֹכִי הִשְׁאִלְתִּהוּ לַיהוָה   And *on my part*, I have lent him to YHWH.

  to YHWH   I lent him   I   and *on part of*   1 Sam 1:28

- Another possible example is 2 Sam 12:13.

382   **Concessive גַּם (although, even though).**[493] The adverb גַּם can introduce a concessive clause (§530), meaning that the clause that follows גַּם can describe something that does not prevent the main clause from being true or occurring, even though it would be expected to do so. When used concessively, גַּם is sometimes immediately followed by כִּי (§448, 530).

- בְּחָנוּנִי גַּם־רָאוּ פָעֳלִי   They tested me, *even though* they saw my work.

  my work   they saw   *although*   they tested me   Ps 95:9

- גַּם כִּי־תַרְבּוּ תְפִלָּה אֵינֶנִּי שֹׁמֵעַ

  hearing   there is not me   prayer   you will multiply   that   *even though*   Isa 1:15

  Even though you multiply prayers, I will not listen to you.

The adverb אַף [494]

383   The adverb אַף is rare in prose but common in poetry.

384   **אַף for addition (also, moreover).**[495] The adverb אַף can indicate that the word or clause that follows it is in addition to something else.

- יהוה מוֹרִישׁ וּמַעֲשִׁיר מַשְׁפִּיל אַף־מְרוֹמֵם

  exalting   *also*   humbling   and making rich   dispossessing   YHWH   1 Sam 2:7

  YHWH dispossesses and makes rich, he humbles, he *also* exalts.

- אַף־אֲנִי בַּחֲלוֹמִי   I *also* had a dream.

  in my dream   I   *also*   Gen 40:16

- Another example is Num 16:14

---

[492] Cf. BHRG §41.4.5.2; IBHS §39.3.4d. Be aware that IBHS §39.3.4d seems to define 'correlative' (at least for אַף) as 'lining up the situation of its clause with that of the previous clause.'

[493] Cf. GBHS §4.2.5(c), 5.2.12; GKC §160b; JM §171a, c.

[494] Cf. BHRG §41.4.3; GBHS §4.2.4; GKC §104c, 153, 154a note 1; IBHS §39.3.4d; Muraoka 1985, 141–3.

[495] Cf. BHRG §41.4.3.a; GBHS §4.2.4(a), 5.2.9; IBHS §39.3.4d.

385 Emphatic אַף (even, really).[496] The adverb אַף can assert the significance or unexpected nature of what follows. In a question, this indicates something contrary to expectation.

- אַף־עַל־זֶה פָּקַחְתָּ עֵינֶךָ   *Even* on such a one you have opened your eyes.
  your eyes you opened this on *also*   Job 14:3

- הַאַף שׂוֹנֵא מִשְׁפָּט יַחֲבוֹשׁ   Will one who hates justice *really* rule?
  he will rule justice hating *also*?   Job 34:17

- Other examples include Gen 18:13; Job 15:4, 40:8.

386 Rhetorical אַף (yes, even).[497] The adverb אַף can be used rhetorically.

- יִתְרוֹעֲעוּ אַף־יָשִׁירוּ   They shout for joy, *yes*, they sing!
  they sing *also* they shout for joy   Ps 65:14

- יָרִיעַ אַף־יַצְרִיחַ   He will shout; *yes*, he will raise a war cry.
  he will raise a war cry *yes* he will shout   Isa 42:13

- Other examples include Isa 40:24; Ps 16:6; Prov 23:28.

387 *A fortiori* אַף (how much more/less).[498] The combination אַף כִּי can introduce the second part of an *a fortiori* argument. Some authors refer to this as the **rhetorical** use (see note 497) or the **emphatic** use of אַף.

- הַשָּׁמַיִם לֹא יְכַלְכְּלוּךָ אַף כִּי־הַבַּיִת הַזֶּה
  the this the house *how much less* they can contain you not the heavens
                     The heavens cannot contain you; *how much less* this house! 1 Kgs 8:27

- וְאַף כִּי־אָמַר אֵלֶיךָ רְחַץ וּטְהָר
  and be clean! wash! to you he said that and *how much more*   2 Kgs 5:13
                     how much more when he says to you, 'Wash and be clean!'

- Other examples include 1 Sam 14:30, 23:3; 2 Sam 4:11; Job 9:14, 15:16; Prov 11:31.

The adverb אַךְ [499]

388 Restrictive אַךְ (only, however).[500] The adverb אַךְ can be used to indicate that the word or clause (§559) that follows it is an exception to or a

---

[496] Cf. BHRG §41.4.3.a; GBHS §4.2.4(a), 5.2.9; Muraoka 1985, 141–3.

[497] Cf. GBHS §4.2.4(b), 5.2.9; Muraoka 1985, 141–3. Be aware the GBHS §4.2.4(c) employs the term 'rhetorical' to refer to the use of אַף that this grammar refers to as 'a fortiori' (§387).

[498] Cf. BHRG §41.4.3.c; GBHS §4.2.4(c); IBHS §39.3.4d.

[499] Cf. BHRG §41.3.3, 41.4.2; GBHS §4.2.2; GKC §100i, 153; IBHS §39.3.5d.

[500] Cf. BHRG §41.4.2; GBHS §4.2.2(a), 5.2.7, 5.2.8; GKC §153; IBHS §39.3.5d; Snaith 1964; Muraoka 1985, 129–30.

limitation of another statement in the context. This is sometimes subdivided into the restrictive and **exceptive** uses of אַךְ.

- הַפָּעַם אַךְ־ וַאֲדַבְּרָה לַאדֹנִי יִחַר אַל־נָא

  the time *only* and let me speak (לְ) my lord may be angry   not   Gen 18:32

  May my lord not be angry, but let me speak *only* this once.

- תֹאכֵלוּ לֹא דָמוֹ בְנַפְשׁוֹ בָשָׂר אַךְ־

  you will eat not its blood in its life flesh *however*   Gen 9:4

  However, you must not eat flesh with its life, that is, its blood.

- Other examples include 1 Sam 18:8, 17; 1 Kgs 17:13; Jer 16:19.

389 **Asseverative אַךְ (surely).**[501] The adverb אַךְ can assert the certainty of something, meaning 'this is nothing other than.'

- טֹרָף טָרֹף אַךְ   He has *surely* been torn in pieces.

  he was torn in pieces to tear in pieces *surely*   Gen 44:28

- מְשִׁיחוֹ יְהוָה נֶגֶד אַךְ   *Surely* his anointed stands before YHWH.

  his anointed YHWH before *surely*   1 Sam 16:6

The adverb רַק [502]

390 **Restrictive רַק (only, however, except that, but).**[503] The adverb רַק can be used to indicate that the word or clause (§560) that follows is an exception to or a limitation of another statement in the context. This is sometimes subdivided into the restrictive and **exceptive** uses of רַק.

- מִמֶּךָ אֶגְדַּל הַכִּסֵּא רַק

  than you I will be great the throne *only*   Gen 41:40

  Only with regard to the throne will I be greater than you.

- וּמַקְטִיר מְזַבֵּחַ הוּא בַּבָּמוֹת רַק

  and burning incense sacrificing he in the high places *only*   1 Kgs 3:3

  except that he sacrificed and burned incense on the high places

- Other examples include Gen 24:8; Exod 10:17; Num 12:2 (אַךְ רַק).

391 **Asseverative רַק (surely, nothing but).**[504] The adverb רַק can assert the certainty of something, meaning 'this is nothing other than.'

---

[501] Cf. BHRG §41.3.3; GBHS §4.2.2(b), 5.3.3(d); IBHS §35.3.1f; JM §164a, g; Snaith 1964; Muraoka 1985, 129–30. Snaith argues that there is always a restrictive nuance, such as the statement being an exception, unexpected, or untrue.

[502] Cf. BHRG §41.3.10, 41.4.10; GBHS §4.2.15; GKC §153; IBHS §39.3.5c.

[503] Cf. BHRG §41.4.10; GBHS §4.2.15(a); GKC §153; IBHS §39.3.5c.

[504] Cf. BHRG §41.3.10; GBHS §4.2.15(b), 5.2.7, 5.2.8, 5.3.3(d); IBHS §164a, g; Muraoka 1985, 130–1.

- וְכָל־ יֵצֶר מַחְשְׁבֹת לִבּוֹ רַק רַע כָּל־ הַיּוֹם
  the day all of evil *nothing but* his heart thoughts of intent of and all of Gen 6:5
  And every intent of the thoughts of his heart was *nothing but* evil all day long.

- רַק־ שְׂנֵאתַנִי וְלֹא אֲהַבְתָּנִי   You *surely* hate me and do not love me.
  you love me and not you hate me *surely*   Judg 14:16

- Another example is Gen 26:29.

392 רַק **as exception to a negative (except, but only).**[505] The adverb רַק can be used after a negative (e.g., לֹא 'not') to give an exception. This is also called the **exceptive** or **limitative** use of רַק.

- This is like the restrictive use of רַק (§390), except that it follows a negative.

- לֹא נִשְׁאַר רַק שֵׁבֶט יְהוּדָה   None was left *except* the tribe of Judah.
  Judah tribe of *except* he was left not   2 Kgs 17:18

- אֵין בָּאָרוֹן רַק שְׁנֵי לֻחוֹת הָאֲבָנִים
  of the stones tablets two of *except* in the ark there is not   1 Kgs 8:9
  There was nothing in the ark *except* the two tablets of stone.

393 **Emphatic** רַק **in** רַק אִם **(if only).** The phrase רַק אִם occurs five times in the Hebrew Bible, each time at the beginning of the protasis (the 'if' part) of a real condition (§453). The combination רַק אִם emphasizes the certainty of the apodosis if the condition is met.

- רַק אִם־ שָׁמוֹעַ תִּשְׁמַע   if *only* you will listen
  you will listen to listen if *only*   Deut 15:5

- רַק אִם־ יִשְׁמְרוּ בָנֶיךָ אֶת־דַּרְכָּם
  their way your sons they will guard if *only*   1 Kgs 8:25
  if *only* your sons will take heed to their way

- The other three occurrences are 2 Kgs 21:8; 2 Chr 6:16, 33:8.

C Negatives [506]

394 **Double negatives make a strong negative.**[507]

- הַמִבְּלִי אֵין־ אֱלֹהִים בְּיִשְׂרָאֵל   Is it because there is *no* God *at all* in Israel?
  in Israel God *there is not* from *not*?   2 Kgs 1:3, 6, 16

- הַמִבְּלִי אֵין־ קְבָרִים   Was it because there were *no* graves?
  graves *lack of* *not*?   Exod 14:11

---

[505] Cf. BHRG §41.4.10; GBHS §4.2.15(a), 5.2.7, 5.2.8.
[506] Cf. BHRG §41.5; GKC §152; IBHS §39.3.3; JM §160; Walker 1896. Negatives are sometimes categorized under adverbs (e.g. GBHS §4.2; JM §102j).
[507] Cf. GKC §152y.

The negative לֹא [508]

395 **לֹא for objective denial of a fact (no, not).**[509] The negative לֹא can be used with a perfect or imperfect verb to deny that something is a fact.

- שָׁעָה   לֹא   מִנְחָתוֹ   וְאֶל־   קַיִן   וְאֶל־
  he looked with favour *not* his offering and to Cain and to   Gen 4:5

  But on Cain and his offering he did *not* look with favour.

- אֶת־הָאֲדָמָה   עוֹד   לְקַלֵּל   אֹסִף   לֹא־   *Never* again will I curse the ground.
  the ground again to curse I will add *not*   Gen 8:21

396 **לֹא for prohibition (must not, shall not).**[510] לֹא can indicate that the subject of an imperfect verb (§173b) is prohibited from doing the action (or being in the state) described by that verb.

- לֹא with the imperfect tends to indicate a permanent prohibition of a general nature, whereas אַל with the jussive (§402) more often indicates a prohibition that applies to a specific situation and that is not necessarily permanent.

- מִמֶּנּוּ   תֹאכַל   לֹא   You shall *not* eat from it.
  from it you will eat *not*   Gen 2:17

- תִּנְאָף   לֹא   You shall *not* commit adultery.
  you will commit adultery *not*   Exod 20:14

397 **לֹא to negate a gerundive infinitive (should not, is not to be).**[511] Things that should or must not be done can be indicated by לֹא followed by an infinitive construct (§196) with prefixed לְ (§278).

- לֹא   לָשֵׂאת   אֶת־אֲרוֹן   הָאֱלֹהִים   כִּי אִם־   הַלְוִיִּם
  the Levites if that the God ark of to carry *not*   1 Chr 15:2

  The ark of God is *not* to be carried except by the Levites.

- יְהוָה   בְּשֵׁם   לְהַזְכִּיר   לֹא   כִּי   הָס
  YHWH in name of to mention *not* because hush!   Amos 6:10

  Hush! For the name of YHWH is *not* to be mentioned.

- Other possible examples include Judg 1:19 and 1 Chr 5:1.

---

[508] Cf. BHRG §41.5.8; GBHS §4.2.11; GKC §100a, 107o, 109d; 150n, 152a–e, p, u, 159dd; JM §102j, 160a–e; Whitney 1988; Sivan and Schniedewind 1993; Brown 1987; Whitley 1985.

[509] Cf. BHRG §41.5.8(i); GBHS §4.2.11; GKC §152a–b, e; IBHS §38.3c, 39.3.3a; JM §160b. לֹא is also used to express negative purpose, as noted by JM §116j.

[510] Cf. BHRG §41.5.8(ii); GBHS §4.2.11, 5.3.5(a); GKC §107o; IBHS §31.5d, 34.2.1b; JM §113m.

[511] Cf. IBHS §36.2.1g.

398 **Elliptic לֹא ('No.').**[512] In conversation, when someone responds to someone else, the word לֹא can stand for an entire sentence (§594).

- וַיֹּאמְרוּ   לוֹ ... הַאֶפְרָתִי אַתָּה וַיֹּאמֶר לֹא
  no he said you Ephraimite? to him they said   Judg 12:5
  They would say to him … 'Are you an Ephraimite?' And he would say, '*No!*'

  o In Judg 12:5, לֹא stands for the sentence, 'No, I am not an Ephraimite.'

- וַיֹּאמֶר לֹא כִּי צָחָקְתְּ   He said, '*No*, but you did laugh.'
  you laughed that *no* he said   Gen 18:15

  o In Gen 18:15, לֹא stands for the sentence, 'What you just said is not true.'

399 **לֹא to negate a predicate that is not a verb (not).**[513] לֹא can negate a predicate that is a predicate adjective, a passive participle, a substantive, or a prepositional phrase.

- לֹא־טוֹב הֱיוֹת הָאָדָם לְבַדּוֹ   It is *not* good for the man to be alone.
  to his solitude the man to be good *not*   Gen 2:18 (predicate adjective with הָיָה)

- אֲשֶׁר לֹא כָתוּב בְּסֵפֶר הַתּוֹרָה   which is *not* written in the book of the law
  the law in book of written *not* which   Deut 28:61 (passive participle)

- לֹא אִישׁ דְּבָרִים אָנֹכִי   I am *not* a man of words.
  I words man of *not*   Exod 4:10 (substantive)

- לֹא בָאֵשׁ יְהוָה   YHWH was *not* in the fire.
  YHWH in the fire *not*   1 Kgs 19:12 (prepositional phrase)

- Other examples include Exod 18:17 (predicate adjective); 2 Sam 3:34 (passive participle); Num 23:19 (substantive); Job 18:14 (prepositional phrase).

400 **Privative לֹא (lacking, without, un-).**[514] The word לֹא can indicate a lack.

- The preposition בְּ (§252) can be prefixed to form the compound בְּלֹא 'without.'

- הוּא־בֵן לֹא חָכָם   He is an *un*wise son. (or 'a son *without* wisdom')
  wise *without* son he   Hos 13:13

- הוֹי בֹּנֶה בֵיתוֹ בְּלֹא־צֶדֶק
  righteousness in *without* his house building woe!   Jer 22:13
  Woe to the one who builds his house *without* righteousness.

- Other possible examples include Num 35:23; Jer 2:2; Job 8:11; Ps 36:5.

---

[512] Cf. BHRG §41.5.8(i); GBHS §5.3.6(d); GKC §150n, 152c, 159dd; IBHS §39.3.3a note 59; Zevit 1979.
[513] Predicate adjective: cf. BHRG §41.5.8(iii); GBHS §4.2.11, 5.3.5(b); JM §160b–c. Participle: cf. GKC §152d; IBHS §37.5f; JM §160c–d. Substantive: cf. BHRG §41.5.8(iii); GBHS §4.2.11; IBHS §18.1d note 2, 39.3.2a; JM §160c–d, k, oa. Prepositional phrase: cf. GBHS §4.2.11; JM §160c. See also Rechenmacher 2003.
[514] Cf. BHRG §41.5.8(iii); GKC §152u; JM §160o.

The negative אַל [515]

401 אַל **for a negative wish (not).**[516] The word אַל may be used with the jussive or cohortative verb to express a desire or prayer that something not be (§184b). This is like the use of the Greek word μή. This is also called the use of אַל to indicate a **negative volition**.

- אַל־אֶרְאֶה בְּמוֹת הַיָּלֶד   May I *not* see the boy's death!
  the lad in death of may I look *not*   Gen 21:16

402 **Jussive with** אַל **for prohibition (not).**[517] Also called the **Vetitive**, אַל 'not' is used with a jussive to give a negative command (§186). אַל with a second-person jussive is the negative of the imperative (§188).

- לֹא with the imperfect (§396) tends to indicate permanent prohibition of a general nature, whereas אַל with the jussive tends to indicate prohibition that applies to a specific situation and that is not necessarily permanent.

- אַל־תִּירָא אַבְרָם   Do *not* fear, Abram!
  Abram may you fear *not*   Gen 15:1

- וְאַל־תַּסְתֵּר פָּנֶיךָ מֵעַבְדֶּךָ
  from your servant your face may you hide and *not*   Ps 69:18

             Do *not* hide your face from your servant!

403 **Elliptic** אַל **(no).**[518] In conversation, when someone responds to someone else, the word אַל can stand for entire sentence (§595).

- וַיֹּאמֶר מֶלֶךְ יִשְׂרָאֵל אַל   The king of Israel said to him, '*No*.'
  no Israel king of to him he said   2 Kgs 3:13

  o In 2 Kgs 3:13, אַל stands for, 'No, I will not go to the prophets of my parents; instead, I am coming to you.'

- אַל בְּנֹתַי   '*No*, my daughters.'
  my daughters *no*   Ruth 1:13

  o In Ruth 1:13, אַל stands for, 'No, do not return with me to my people.'

404 אַל **for a negative obligation (not, should not).**[519] The word אַל can be used to indicate a negative obligation (i.e., ought not to). When it does so, אַל is followed by לְ of obligated person (§284).

---

[515] Cf. BHRG §41.5.3; GBHS §4.2.3; GKC §107p, 109c, 152f–h; JM §160f.

[516] Cf. BHRG §41.5.3(ii); GBHS §4.2.3(b); GKC §152f; IBHS §34.5.1a; JM §114c, i.

[517] Cf. BHRG §19.4.2(1), 19.4.4(i), 41.5.3(i); GBHS §3.3.1d, 4.2.3(a), 5.3.5(a); GKC §107p, 109c, e, 152f; IBHS §34.3, 34.2.1b note 6, 34.4a, 39.3.3a; JM §113m, 114g, i, 160f.

[518] Cf. BHRG §41.5.3(iii); GBHS §5.3.6(d); GKC §152g; IBHS §39.3.3a note 59.

- אַל לַמְלָכִים שְׁתוֹ־ יָיִן   It is *not* for kings to drink wine.
  wine   to drink   for kings   *not*   Prov 31:4

405 אַל **as a substantive (nothing).** אַל is used as a substantive once.

- וְיָשֵׂם לְאַל מִלָּתִי   and make my word *nothing*
  my word   to *nothing*   and he will put   Job 24:25

The negative אַיִן / אֵין [520]

406 אַיִן **as a substantive (nothing).**[521] The negative אַיִן can be a substantive,
meaning 'nothing.' This may have been its original meaning.

- כָּל־ הַגּוֹיִם כְּאַיִן נֶגְדּוֹ   All the nations are as *nothing* before him.
  before him   like *nothing*   the nations   all of   Isa 40:17

- הַנּוֹתֵן רוֹזְנִים לְאָיִן   The one who reduces rulers to *nothing*.
  to *nothing*   rulers   the one giving   Isa 40:23

- The word יֵשׁ is used similarly (§476).

407a אַיִן **in the construct state is** אֵין **(there is no).**[522] The negative אַיִן can be
used in the construct state (spelled אֵין), with the next word as a genitive
(§36–48). When used in this way, the negative אֵין denies the existence of
the thing represented by the following word, phrase, or clause.

- אֵין־ יוֹסֵף בַּבּוֹר   *There was no* Joseph in the pit.
  in the pit   Joseph   *there is no*   Gen 37:29

- אֵין־ חֵלֶק לַלְוִיִּם   *There is no* portion for the Levites.
  to the Levites   portion   *there is no*   Josh 18:7

- Another example is Gen 39:23.

407b **Negative** אֵין **(not).**[523] When the negative אֵין has a pronominal suffix and
is followed by a participle, the pronominal suffix can be the subject of the
participle, and אֵין can deny the action or state implied by the participle.

---

[519] Cf. GKC §152f.

[520] Cf. BHRG §41.5.2; GBHS §4.4.1; GKC §116q, 141k, 152i p; IBHS §39.3.3b; JM
§102j–k, 160g–j; Swiggers 1991; Muraoka 1985, 77–82, 102–11.

[521] Cf. GKC §141k; Swiggers 1991, 178. For a contrary view, see Muraoka 1985, 110;
JM §160g.

[522] Cf. BHRG §41.5.2(ii); GBHS §5.3.5(b); GKC §152i, l, o; IBHS §37.5f, 39.3.3b; JM
§154k, 160h; Swiggers 1991, 177. Rather than calling אֵין the construct form of אַיִן, JM
§160h calls it the 'contracted, light form,' similar to the relationship between שְׁנֵים and
שָׁנִים.

[523] Cf. BHRG §41.5.2(i); GBHS §4.4.1(c); GKC §116q, 141k, 152m; IBHS §39.3.3b; JM
§160g–i.

- אֵינֶנִּי נֹתֵן לָכֶם תֶּבֶן   I will *not* give you straw.
  straw to you giving *not* me   Exod 5:10

- אֵינֶנִּי עֹבֵר אֶת־הַיַּרְדֵּן   I will *not* pass over the Jordan.
  the Jordan passing over *not* me   Deut 4:22

- Another example is Deut 4:22.

408   **אֵין to deny the existence of a substantive (there is no).**[524]

- וְאָדָם אַיִן לַעֲבֹד אֶת־הָאֲדָמָה   There was *no* man to work the ground.
  the ground to serve *there is no* and man   Gen 2:5

- וְכֹחַ אַיִן לְלֵדָה   And *there is no* strength to give birth.
  to give birth *there is no* and strength   2 Kgs 19:3

409   **Elliptic אַיִן (there is no).**[525] The negative אַיִן can indicate the absence of something that is implied but not explicitly stated (§593).

- וַיַּעַבְרוּ בְאֶרֶץ־שַׁעֲלִים וְאַיִן
  and *there is no* of Shaalim in land they passed through   1 Sam 9:4

         They passed through the land of Shaalim, but *they were not there.*

  o   In 1 Sam 9:4, אַיִן stands for the clause 'the donkeys were not there.'

- הֲיֵשׁ יְהוָה בְּקִרְבֵּנוּ אִם־אָיִן   Is YHWH in our midst or *not?*
  there is no if in our midst YHWH there is?   Exod 17:7

10a   **אַיִן / אֵין with an infinitive construct to deny a possibility (it is impossible).**

- אֵין לַעֲמוֹד לְפָנֶיךָ   *It is impossible* to stand before you.
  before you to stand *there is not*   Ezra 9:15

- וְאֵין עִמְּךָ לְהִתְיַצֵּב   And *it is impossible* to resist you.
  to resist with you *and there is not*   2 Chr 20:6

10b   **אַיִן / אֵין with an infinitive construct to deny permission (it is not permitted).**[526]

- The preposition לְ may be prefixed to the infinitive construct.

- אֵין לָבוֹא אֶל־שַׁעַר הַמֶּלֶךְ בִּלְבוּשׁ שָׂק
  of sackcloth in garment the king gate of to to enter *it is not permitted*   Esth 4:2

       It is not permitted to enter the gate of the king clothed in sackcloth.

- וְאֵין לָנוּ אִישׁ לְהָמִית בְּיִשְׂרָאֵל   We *are not permitted* to kill a man in Israel.
  in Israel to kill man to us *and it is not permitted*   2 Sam 21:4

---

[524] Cf. BHRG §41.5.2(ii); GBHS §4.4.1(a), 5.3.4(b); GKC §152k; IBHS §37.5f, 39.3.3b; JM §154k, 160g; Swiggers 1991, 176.

[525] Cf. GBHS §5.3.6(d).

[526] Cf. IBHS §36.2.3f.

411   **Privative אֵין / אַיִן (without, lack of, un-).**[527] The word אֵין / אַיִן can indicate a lack of something.

- The preposition בְּ (§252) or לְ (§274a) can be prefixed to form בְּאֵין or לְאֵין.

- הוּא יָמוּת   בְּאֵין   מוּסָר   He will die for *lack of* instruction.

  he will die because of *lack of* instruction   Prov 5:23

- וַעֲצֵי   אֲרָזִים   לְאֵין   מִסְפָּר   and cedar timbers *without* number

  and timbers of cedars according to *lack of* number   1 Chr 22:4

The negative בַּל [528]

412   **The negative בַּל is mostly confined to poetry.**[529]

413   **בַּל for objective denial of a fact (no, not).**[530] The negative בַּל can be used with a perfect or imperfect verb to deny that something is a fact, just like לֹא (§395) and the Greek word οὐ.

- אָמַר   בְּלִבּוֹ   בַּל־   אֶמּוֹט   He said in his heart, 'I will *not* be shaken.'

  he said in his heart *not* I will be shaken   Ps 10:6

- בַּל־   יְדָעוּם   They have *not* known them.

  not they knew them   Ps 147:20

414a   **בַּל to negate a predicate adjective (not).**[531] This is like לֹא (§399).

- הַכֵּר־   פָּנִים   בְּמִשְׁפָּט   בַּל־   טוֹב   To show partiality in judgment is *not* good.

  to recognize faces in judgment *not* good   Prov 24:23

414b   **בַּל to negate a prepositional phrase (not).**[532] This is like לֹא (§399).

- וְלִבּוֹ   בַּל־   עִמָּךְ   But his heart is *not* with you.

  but his heart *not* with you   Prov 23:7

415   **בַּל for a negative wish (not).** The word בַּל may be used with the jussive or cohortative to express a desire that something not be (§184b). אַל is used in this way (§401), as is the Greek word μή.

- וּבַל־   אֶלְחַם   בְּמַנְעַמֵּיהֶם   Let me *not* eat of their delicacies!

  and *not* let me eat in their delicacies   Ps 141:4

416   **בַּל to negate an infinitive construct (not).** This occurs only once.

---

[527] Cf. BHRG §41.5.2(ii); JM §160o.

[528] Cf. BHRG §41.5.4; GKC §152t; JM §160m; Whitley 1972.

[529] Cf. GKC §152t; JM §160m.

[530] Cf. BHRG §41.5.4; GKC §152t; JM §160m.

[531] Cf. BHRG §41.5.4; GKC §152t; JM §160m.

[532] Cf. BHRG §41.5.4; GKC §152t; JM §160m.

- בַּל קְרֹב אֵלֶיךָ   It will *not* approach you.
  to you   to approach   *not*   Ps 32:9

The negative בְּלִי [533]

417   The negative בְּלִי occurs almost exclusively in poetry.[534]

418   **בְּלִי for objective denial of a fact (no, not).**[535] The negative בְּלִי can be used with a perfect or imperfect verb to deny that something is a fact, just like לֹא (§395), בַּל (§413), and the Greek word οὐ.

- בְּלִי הִגִּיד לוֹ כִּי בֹרֵחַ הוּא   He did *not* tell him that he was fleeing.
  he   fleeing   that   to him   he told   *not*   Gen 31:20

- אֹסֶף בְּלִי יָבוֹא   The harvest will *not* come.
  will come   *not*   harvest   Isa 32:10

- Other examples include Deut 28:55 and Isa 14:6.

419   **בְּלִי to negate a passive participle (not).**[536]

- בְּלִי נִשְׁמָע קוֹלָם   Their voices are *not* heard.
  their voice   being heard   *not*   Ps 19:3

- אֶפְרַיִם הָיָה עֻגָה בְּלִי הֲפוּכָה   Ephraim is a cake that is *not* turned.
  being turned   *not*   cake   was   Ephraim   Hos 7:8

420   **Privative בְּלִי (lacking, without, un-).**[537] The negative בְּלִי can indicate a lack of something, just like לֹא (§400) and אַיִן (§411). The preposition בְּ (§252) or לְ (§274a) can be prefixed to form בִּבְלִי or לִבְלִי.

- Examples include בְּלִי־מָיִם 'without water' (Job 8:11), בִּבְלִי־דַעַת 'without knowledge' or 'unwittingly' (Deut 4:42), and לִבְלִי־חֹק 'without limit' (Isa 5:14).

The negative לְבִלְתִּי / בִּלְתִּי [538]

421   **Privative בִּלְתִּי (lacking, without, un-).**[539] The negative בִּלְתִּי can indicate

---

[533] Cf. BHRG §41.5.5; GKC §152t; IBHS §36.2.1g; JM §160m.

[534] Cf. JM §160m.

[535] Cf. BHRG §41.5.5; GKC §152t; JM §160m.

[536] Cf. BHRG §41.5.5; GKC §152t; JM §160m. Previous editions of this textbook had the subcategory of בְּלִי modifying a predicate adjective, but the only example was problematic, so that subcategory has been removed.

[537] Cf. BHRG §41.5.5; GKC §152t; JM §160o.

[538] Cf. BHRG §41.4.6(i), 41.5.6; GKC §114s, 152t; IBHS §31.6.1c, 36.2.1g; JM §93q, 160l–m.

[539] Cf. BHRG §41.5.6; GKC §152t; JM §160m.

a lack of something. The negatives לֹא (§400), אֵין (§411), and בְּלִי (§419) are also used in this way.

- בְּעֶבְרָה מַכַּת בִּלְתִּי סָרָה   in fury, with *un*ceasing blows
  stopping *without* blow of in fury   Isa 14:6

- בִּלְתִּי טָהוֹר הוּא   He is *un*clean.
  he clean *without*   1 Sam 20:26

422   **Exceptive בִּלְתִּי (except, unless, only).**[540] Also called its **limitative** use, this use of בִּלְתִּי usually follows another negative word, and often is followed by אִם (pleonastic, §457). It can be followed by a clause (§557).

- אֵין בִּלְתֶּךָ   There is no one *except* you.
  except you there is not   1 Sam 2:2

- זֹאת בִּלְתִּי אִם־חֶרֶב גִּדְעוֹן   This is *none other than* the sword of Gideon.
  Gideon sword of *except* this   Judg 7:14 (with אִם)

- הֲיֵלְכוּ שְׁנַיִם יַחְדָּו בִּלְתִּי אִם־נוֹעָדוּ   they agreed *except* together two walk?   Amos 3:3 (with אִם and clause)
  Do two walk together *unless* they have agreed?

- Other examples include Gen 43:3; Exod 22:19; Amos 3:4.

423   **לְבִלְתִּי / בִּלְתִּי to negate an infinitive construct (not).**[541]

- צִוִּיתִיךָ לְבִלְתִּי אֲכָל־מִמֶּנּוּ   I commanded you *not* to eat from it.
  from it to eat *not* I commanded you   Gen 3:11

424   **לְבִלְתִּי to negate a purpose or result (so that not).**[542] When purpose or result is indicated by a clause (§524) or by an infinitive construct (§197), it can be negated by a preceding לְבִלְתִּי.

- לְבִלְתִּי תֶחֱטָאוּ   *so that* you will *not* sin
  so that you will sin *not*   Exod 20:20

- לְבִלְתִּי יִדַּח מִמֶּנּוּ נִדָּח   banished person from us so that he is cast out *not*   2 Sam 14:14
  so that the banished person is not cast out from us

---

[540] Cf. BHRG §41.4.6(i); GBHS §5.2.7; GKC §163c; IBHS §38.6b; JM §173a.

[541] Cf. BHRG §41.5.6(i)a; GBHS §5.3.5(c); GKC §114s, 152t; IBHS §36.2.1g, 39.3.3a; JM §124e, 160l.

[542] Cf. GBHS §5.2.3(c), 5.3.5(c); GKC §165b; IBHS §31.6.1c, 38.3c; JM §124e, 168c, 169d.

The negative אֶפֶס [543]

425 **The negative אֶפֶס** can be a substantive, meaning 'nothing.'[544] This may have been its original meaning.

- וְכָל־ שָׂרֶיהָ יִהְיוּ אָפֶס   And all of her princes will become *nothing*.
  nothing will be her princes and all of   Isa 34:12

- וּכְאֶפֶס אַנְשֵׁי מִלְחַמְתֶּךָ   כְּאַיִן יִהְיוּ
  your war men of and like *nothing*   like non-existence will be   Isa 41:12

  The men who war against you will be non-existent and like *nothing*.

426 **Privative אֶפֶס (lacking, without, un-, there is no).**[545] The negative אֶפֶס can indicate a lack of something, just like לֹא (§400), אַיִן (§411), בְּלִי (§420), and בִּלְתִּי (§421).

- The preposition בְּ (§252) can be prefixed to a privative אֶפֶס to form בְּאֶפֶס.

- עַד אֶפֶס מָקוֹם   until *there is no* room
  place *without* until   Isa 5:8

- וַיִּכְלוּ בְּאֶפֶס תִּקְוָה   They end *without* hope.
  hope in *lack of* they end   Job 7:6

- Other examples include 2 Sam 9:3; 2 Kgs 14:26; Prov 14:28.

427 **Restrictive אֶפֶס (only, however, yet, nevertheless).**[546] A restrictive clause can begin with אֶפֶס or אֶפֶס כִּי (§558).

- וְאֶפֶס אֶת־הַדָּבָר אֲשֶׁר־ אֲדַבֵּר אֵלֶיךָ
  to you I will speak which the word but *only*   Num 22:35

  But you will speak *only* the word which I tell you.

- אֶפֶס כִּי לֹא תִהְיֶה תִּפְאַרְתְּךָ   *Nevertheless*, the glory will not be yours.
  your glory it will be not *nevertheless*   Judg 4:9

The negative מָה

428 **מָה in a rhetorical question that implies 'not.'** See §128.

- מַה־ תָּעִירוּ וּמַה־ תְּעֹרְרוּ אֶת־הָאַהֲבָה
  the love you will awaken and *what?* you will arouse *what?*   Song 8:4

  Do *not* arouse or awaken love.   Or   What? Will you arouse or awaken love?

---

[543] Cf. BHRG §41.4.4; GKC §152s, 163c; JM §160n.

[544] Cf. BHRG §41.4.4(ii)b; GKC §152s. BHRG §41.4.4(ii)a points out that the noun אֶפֶס can also mean the 'ends' of the earth (1 Sam 2:10).

[545] Cf. GKC §152s; JM §160n.

[546] Cf. BHRG §41.4.4(i); GBHS §5.2.7, 5.2.8; GKC §163c; IBHS §39.3.5e; JM §173a.

- בְּרִית כָּרַתִּי לְעֵינָי וּמָה אֶתְבּוֹנֵן עַל־בְּתוּלָה

  virgin on I will gaze and *how?* with my eyes I cut covenant   Job 31:1

  I have made a covenant with my eyes that I will *not* gaze upon a virgin.

  OR   I have made a covenant with my eyes. How can I gaze upon a virgin?

D Conjunctions [547]

429 **Hebrew has few words that are strictly conjunctions.**[548] Often, a
meaning that might be expressed with a conjunction in English is
expressed with a preposition that has a clause for its object.

The conjunction וְ [549]

430a **Coordinative וְ (and, *untranslated*).**[550] The conjunction וְ can function to
coordinate two nouns, phrases, or clauses. This is also called the
conjunctive waw or the *waw copulativum*.

- In English, the conjunction 'and' is written only before the last item in a series,
  whereas in Hebrew, וְ is usually written before every item except the first.

- וַיִּקְרָא אֱלֹהִים לָאוֹר יוֹם וְלַחֹשֶׁךְ קָרָא לָיְלָה

  night called *and* (לְ) the darkness day (לְ) the light God called   Gen 1:5

  God called the light 'day,' *and* he called the darkness 'night.'

- בְּנֵי יֶפֶת גֹּמֶר וּמָגוֹג וּמָדַי ... וְתִירָס

  and Tiras   *and* Madai *and* Magog Gomer Jepheth sons of   Gen 10:2

  The sons of Jepheth are Gomer, Magog, Madai … *and* Tiras.

430b **וְ in hendiadys.** The conjunction וְ is sometimes used to join two
substantives in order to communicate one idea. See §72.

430c **וְ in verbal coordination.** The conjunction וְ sometimes joins two verbs
such that the second verb expresses the principal idea, and the first verb
functions as an adverb modifying the second verb. See §224.

---

[547] Cf. BHRG §40; GBHS §4.3; GKC §104; IBHS §38–9; JM §104, 176–7.

[548] Cf. JM §104a–b. What this grammar refers to as 'a preposition that has a clause for its
object' is referred as 'subordinating conjunctions compounded with אֲשֶׁר and כִּי' in JM
§104b.

[549] Cf. BHRG §31.1.1, 40.8; GBHS §4.3.3; GKC §104d–g, 120d–e, 134s, 143d, 154,
161a, 165a, 166a; IBHS §39.2.1–39.2.5; JM §104c–d, 115, 117–20, 176–7; Steiner 2000;
Gibson 1995.

[550] Cf. BHRG §40.8.1(i); GBHS §4.3.3(b); GKC §154; IBHS §39.2.1, 39.2.5; JM §177a,
o–p.

431 **ְו to join opposites (and).**[551]

- עֵץ הַדַּעַת טוֹב וָרָע   the tree of the knowledge of good *and* evil

  and evil   good   the knowledge of   tree of   Gen 2:17

- זֶרַע וְקָצִיר וְקֹר וָחֹם   seed time *and* harvest, cold *and* heat

  and heat   and cold   *and* harvest   seed   Gen 8:22

  o   The second ְו is coordinative ְו (§430a); it coordinates one pair and the next.

432 **Adversative ְו (but).**[552] The conjunction ְו can be used at the beginning of a clause that is in some way opposed to what precedes it (§552). When ְו is used in this way, it can often be translated 'but.'

- נִחַמְתִּי כִּי עֲשִׂיתִם וְנֹחַ מָצָא חֵן

  favour   he found   *but* Noah   I made them   that   I am sorry   Gen 6:7–8

  'I am sorry that I made them.' *But* Noah found favour.

- אִישׁ מָוֶת אַתָּה וּבַיּוֹם הַזֶּה לֹא אֲמִיתֶךָ

  I will kill you   not   the this   *but* in the day   you   death   man of   1 Kgs 2:26

  You deserve to die, *but* at this time I will not kill you.

433 **Alternative ְו (or).**[553] The conjunction ְו can be used to connect alternatives. When ְו is used in this way, it can often be translated 'or.'

- אַתָּה וּבִנְךָ־ וּבִתֶּךָ עַבְדְּךָ וַאֲמָתֶךָ

  or your female slave   your slave   *or* your daughter   *or* your son   you   Exod 20:10

  you *or* your son *or* your daughter, your male slave *or* your female slave

- וְגֹנֵב אִישׁ וּמְכָרוֹ וְנִמְצָא בְיָדוֹ

  in his hand   *or* he is found   and he sells him   man   and one stealing   Exod 21:16

  whoever kidnaps a man and sells him *or* he is found in his possession

- The conjunction ְו is not used, however, for alternatives between numbers.

  o   שְׁנַיִם שְׁלֹשָׁה סָרִיסִים   two *or* three eunuchs

    eunuchs   three   two   2 Kgs 9:32

---

[551] Cf. BHRG §40.8.1(i)c. In earlier editions of this textbook, this use of ְו was called **disjunctive**. This term has been dropped in this edition because several other grammars use the term 'disjunctive' to refer to what this textbook calls **adversative ְו** (§432).

[552] Cf. BHRG §40.8.1(iv); GBHS §4.3.3(a), 5.2.10; GKC §163a; IBHS §39.2.3b; JM §172a; Steiner 2000, 257–60. This is often referred to as (or as a subset of) the **disjunctive** use of ְו.

[553] Cf. BHRG §40.8.1(ii); GBHS §4.3.3(c), 5.2.14; IBHS §39.2.1b; JM §175a–b; Steiner 2000, 261–3. This use of ְו is sometimes included in the category of **disjunctive ְו** (referred to as adversative in this textbook, §432). Steiner argues that ְו never means 'or'; that this apparent use of ְו only occurs in negative and conditional clauses, and that the apparent meaning 'or' arises from ellipsis.

434 **Explicative** וְ **(namely, even, specifically).**[554] What follows the conjunction וְ is sometimes a clarification of something that preceded it. This is also called the *waw explicativum* or the **epexegetical waw**.

- וּמֵחֶלְבֵהֶן   צֹאנוֹ   מִבְּכֹרוֹת   הֵבִיא ... וְהֶבֶל
  specifically from their fat his flock from firstborn of brought and Abel   Gen 4:4
  But Abel brought ... some of the firstborn of his flock,
  specifically some of their fat portions.

- וּבַיַּלְקוּט   לוֹ   אֲשֶׁר־   הָרֹעִים   בִּכְלִי   אֹתָם   וַיָּשֶׂם
  and in the pouch to him which the shepherds in vessel of them he put   1 Sam 17:40
  He put them in his shepherd's vessel which he had, *specifically* in the pouch.

435 **Pleonastic** וְ (*untranslated*).[555] The conjunction וְ sometimes seems to be superfluous, perhaps used merely for stylistic reasons.

- וְשֹׁמֵמָה   תָּמָר   וַתֵּשֶׁב   Tamar sat desolate.
  (וְ) being desolate Tamar she sat   2 Sam 13:20

- עַבְדֶּךָ   וַאֲנִי   וְעַתָּה   מֵאָז   וַאֲנִי   אָבִיךָ   עֶבֶד
  your servant (וְ) I and now from then (וְ) I your father servant of   2 Sam 15:34
  I was the servant of your father in the past, and now I will be your servant.

436 וְ **of accompaniment (with, along with).**[556] The conjunction וְ can precede something that goes along with something else. This use is also called the *waw concomitantiae* or a **comitative construction**.

- This is also called the **circumstantial waw** because it introduces most circumstantial clauses (§494).

- יְקָרָה   וְאֶבֶן ... מַלְכָּם   עֲטֶרֶת־   אֶת־   וַיִּקַּח
  precious *with* stone their king crown of he took   2 Sam 12:30
  He took the crown of their king ... *and with it* was a precious stone.

- נַעֲרֹתֶיהָ   וְחָמֵשׁ   הַחֲמוֹר   עַל־   וַתִּרְכַּב
  her young women *along with* five the donkey on she rode   1 Sam 25:42
  She rode on her donkey, *accompanied by* her five female servants.

- Another example is 1 Sam 6:11.

437 **Comparative** וְ **(as).**[557] In poetry, the conjunction וְ can be used before something to which something else is compared. When וְ is used in this way, it can often be translated 'as' or 'like.'

---

[554] Cf. BHRG §40.8.2(vii); GBHS §4.3.3(d); GKC §154a note 1; IBHS §39.2.1b, 39.2.4; Baker 1980; Mastin 1984; Wilton 1994; Steiner 2000, 264–5.
[555] Cf. BHRG §40.8.3; Pope 1953; Wernberg-Møller 1958.
[556] Cf. BHRG §40.8.1(i); GBHS §4.3.3(e), 5.2.11; GKC §141e, 142d, 154a note 1.
[557] Cf. BHRG §40.8.2(vi); GKC §161a; IBHS §39.2.3b; JM §174h.

- הֲלֹא־אֹזֶן מִלִּין תִּבְחָן וְחֵךְ אֹכֶל יִטְעַם־לוֹ

  to him tastes food *as* palate tests words ear not?   Job 12:11

  Does not the ear test words *as* the palate tastes its food?

- כִּי־אָדָם לְעָמָל יוּלָּד וּבְנֵי־רֶשֶׁף יַגְבִּיהוּ עוּף

  to fly they will be high flame *as* sons of he is born to trouble man for   Job 5:7

  For man is born for trouble *as* sparks fly upward.

- Other examples include Job 16:21 and Prov 25:25.

438 Emphatic וְ (and especially).[558]

- שְׁלֹמֹה אָהַב נָשִׁים נָכְרִיּוֹת רַבּוֹת וְאֶת־בַּת־פַּרְעֹה

  Pharaoh daughter of *and* many foreign women loved Solomon   1 Kgs 11:1

  Solomon loved many foreign women, *and especially* the daughter of Pharaoh.

439 Sarcastic וְ (idiomatic).[559] Sometimes categorized as a type of **waw of emotion**, the conjunction וְ can be used at the beginning of a clause that is sarcastic.

- וְהִנֵּה יְהוָה עֹשֶׂה אֲרֻבּוֹת בַּשָּׁמַיִם הֲיִהְיֶה

  he will be? in the heavens windows making YHWH *and* behold   2 Kgs 7:19

  Even if YHWH were to make windows in the sky, could it happen?

- וּמִי אֲבִיהֶם   *And just* who is their father?

  their father *and* who?   1 Sam 10:12

- Other possible examples include Judg 14:16 and 2 Sam 18:11.

440 Resumptive וְ (then, *untranslated*).[560] Also called the **waw of resumption** or the **waw of linkage**, the conjunction וְ can begin a clause that resumes the train of thought from the clause that precedes it.

- It is also called the **waw of apodosis** or the **conditional waw** because it is often used in conditional sentences (§511) at the beginning of an apodosis to connect it logically to the protasis. The resumptive וְ is also used before result clauses (§525), and after temporal clauses (§496–510), causal clauses (§518–24), and long relative clauses that precede their main clauses (§536–40).

- בְּיוֹם אֲכָלְכֶם מִמֶּנּוּ וְנִפְקְחוּ עֵינֵיכֶם

  your eyes (וְ) will be opened from it your to eat in day   Gen 3:5

  In the day you eat from it, your eyes will be opened.

---

[558] Cf. GKC §154a note 1; IBHS §39.2.1b; JM §177n.

[559] Cf. JM §177m.

[560] Cf. BHRG §21.3.3; GBHS §4.3.3(f); GKC §143d; IBHS §32.2.1b, 38.2b; JM §167b, 176; Steiner 2000, 263–4.

- יַעַן מָאַסְתָּ אֶת־דְּבַר יְהוָה וַיִּמְאָסְךָ מִמֶּלֶךְ

  from king (ו) he rejected you YHWH word of you rejected because   1 Sam 15:23

  Because you have rejected the word of YHWH, he has rejected you from being king.

- Other examples include Gen 18:26 and 32:19.

441   **Adjunctive וְ (also).**[561] The conjunction וְ can be used before something that is in addition to something that precedes it.

- וְשַׁאֲלִי־ לוֹ אֶת־הַמְּלוּכָה   Ask for him the kingdom *also*!

  the kingdom to him *also* ask!   1 Kgs 2:22

442   **Distributive וְ (each, also, every).** See §101.

- זִקְנֵי־ עִיר וָעִיר   elders of *every* city

  (ו) city city elders of   Ezra 10:14

- לְשַׁעַר וָשָׁעַר   for *every* gate

  (ו) gate to gate   1 Chr 26:13

- Another example is Deut 32:7.

The conjunction אוֹ

443   **אוֹ for alternatives (or).**[562] Also called the **disjunctive אוֹ**, אוֹ can be placed before each alternative in a series (sometimes even before the first).

- אִם־ עֶבֶד יִגַּח הַשּׁוֹר אוֹ אָמָה

  female slave *or* the ox gores male slave if   Exod 21:32

                       if the ox gores a male slave *or* a female slave

- אוֹ־בֵן יִגָּח אוֹ־בַת יִגָּח   *whether* it gores a son *or* it gores a daughter

  he gores daughter *or* gores son *or*   Exod 21:31

The conjunction כִּי [563]

444   **Causal כִּי (because).**[564] כִּי can begin a causal clause (§533).

- כִּי עָשִׂיתָ זֹּאת   *because* you have done this

  this you did *because*   Gen 3:14

---

[561] Cf. BHRG §40.8.1(iii). JM §177m categorizes 1 Kgs 2:22 as a **waw of emotion**.

[562] Cf. BHRG §31.1.2, 31.1.3(ii), 40.3; GBHS §4.3.1, 5.2.14; GKC §104c, 150g, i, 159cc, 162; IBHS §39.2.6b; JM §148c note 3 (note 1 in JM93), 161e, 175a, d.

[563] Cf. BHRG §40.9, 41.3.9; GBHS §4.3.4; GKC §107u, 157a–b, 158b, 159aa–bb, ee, 160b, 163, 164d, 166b; Aejmelaeus 1986; Follingstad 2001; Meyer 2001; Muilenburg 1961.

[564] Cf. BHRG §40.9.I.3, 40.9.II.2; GBHS §4.3.4(a), 5.2.5; GKC §158b; IBHS §38.4a; JM §170d–da; Aejmelaeus 1986, 196–8, 201–7; Follingstad 2001, 9–10, 42–6, 238–41, 411; Claassen 1983; Van der Merwe 1993, 38–41.

● כִּי־ הִשְׁחִית כָּל־ בָּשָׂר אֶת־דַּרְכּוֹ *because* all flesh had corrupted its way.

  its way flesh all of corrupted *because*   Gen 6:12

● Another example is Gen 6:13.

445 Temporal כִּי (when).[565] כִּי can begin a temporal clause (§497).

● Temporal clauses with כִּי always have a verb.

● כִּי־ הֵחֵל הָאָדָם לָרֹב *when* mankind began to multiply

  to multiply the mankind began *when*   Gen 6:1

● כִּי יֹאמְרוּ פְּלִיטֵי אֶפְרַיִם אֶעֱבֹרָה

  let me pass over Ephraim fugitives of would say *when*   Judg 12:5

  when the fugitives of Ephraim would say, 'Let me pass over'

446 Conditional כִּי (if).[566] The conjunction כִּי can begin the protasis (the 'if'
part) of a real conditional sentence (§515).

● כִּי־ תִמְצָא אִישׁ לֹא תְבָרֲכֶנּוּ *If* you meet anyone, do not greet him.

  you will bless him not man you find *if*   2 Kgs 4:29

● וְכִי־ תֹאמְרוּן אֵלַי but *if* you will say to me

  to me you will say but *if*   2 Kgs 18:22

● Another example is 2 Sam 19:8.

● Ruth 1:12 may be the sole example of כִּי introducing the protasis of an unreal
  conditional sentence (§517) (unless it is concessive clause; see §448, 530).

○ כִּי אָמַרְתִּי יֶשׁ־ לִי תִקְוָה *if* I were to say that I have hope

  hope to me there is I said *if*   Ruth 1:12

447 Adversative כִּי (but, but rather, but instead).[567] After a negative word,
the conjunction כִּי (often followed by pleonastic אִם §457) can begin an
adversative clause (§555).

● לֹא־ תִקְרָא אֶת־שְׁמָהּ שָׂרָי כִּי שָׂרָה שְׁמָהּ

  her name Sarah *but instead* Sarai her name you will call not   Gen 17:15

  You will not call her name Sarai, *but* Sarah will be her name.

---

[565] Cf. BHRG §40.9.I.2; GBHS §4.3.4(e), 5.2.4(a)–(b); GKC §164d; IBHS §38.7a; JM
§166o; Aejmelaeus 1986, 196–7; Follingstad 2001, 10, 238–41, 267–8. GBHS §4.3.4(f)
points out that it can be difficult to decide whether כִּי is introducing a conditional clause
(§446) or a temporal clause (§445), particularly when a future situation is in view.

[566] Cf. BHRG §40.9.I.1; GBHS §4.3.4(f), 5.2.2(a)–(b); GKC §159aa–bb; IBHS §31.6.1b,
32.2.1b, 38.2d; JM §167c, f, i, q, s; Aejmelaeus 1986, 196–9, 207–8; Follingstad 2001,
10, 268–73.

[567] Cf. BHRG §40.9.II.3; GBHS §4.3.4(g), 5.2.10; GKC §163a–b; JM §172c; Aejmelaeus
1986, 200–1; Follingstad 2001, 12, 241–3, 252–7, 280–1.

- לֹא יַעֲקֹב יֵאָמֵר עוֹד שִׁמְךָ כִּי אִם־יִשְׂרָאֵל •
  Israel   if *but instead* your name still will be called Jacob not   Gen 32:29
  Your name will no longer be called Jacob, *but* Israel.

- Another example is 1 Kgs 21:15.

448 **Concessive כִּי (though, in spite of, even if).**[568] The conjunction כִּי can begin a concessive clause (§530).

- כִּי־ תַגְבִּיהַ כַּנֶּשֶׁר קִנֶּךָ מִשָּׁם אוֹרִידְךָ •
  I will bring you down from there your nest like the eagle you make high *though*
  Though you make your nest high like the eagle, I will bring you down from there.
  Jer 49:16

- כִּי־ יִפֹּל לֹא־ יוּטָל •   *Though* he falls, he will not be thrown.
  he will be thrown not he will fall *though*   Ps 37:24

- Another example is Ezek 2:6.

449 **Asseverative כִּי (certainly, indeed, truly).**[569] Also called the כִּי of **affirmation**, the conjunction כִּי (sometimes with pleonastic אִם §457) can be used to assert the certainty of what follows it (such as an **oath**).

- חֵי פַרְעֹה כִּי מְרַגְּלִים אַתֶּם •   By the life of Pharaoh, you are *indeed* spies.
  you spies *indeed* Pharaoh life of   Gen 42:16

- כִּי־ עַתָּה שַׁבְנוּ זֶה פַעֲמָיִם •   *Surely* by now we would have returned twice.
  two times this we returned now *surely*   Gen 43:10

- Other examples include 1 Sam 14:44; 2 Kgs 5:20; Job 5:2.

450 **Result כִּי (with the result that).**[570] The conjunction כִּי can begin a result clause (§527). Most examples seem to be in rhetorical questions.

- מַה־ מָּצְאוּ אֲבוֹתֵיכֶם בִּי עָוֶל כִּי רָחֲקוּ מֵעָלָי •
  from on me went far *that* injustice in me your fathers found what?   Jer 2:5
  What injustice did your fathers find in me *with the result that* they went far from me?

---

[568] Cf. GBHS §4.3.4(h), 5.2.12; GKC §160b; JM §171a–c; Aejmelaeus 1986, 198–9, 205–7; Follingstad 2001, 11, 238–41, 273–7.

[569] Cf. BHRG §40.9.II.5, 41.3.9(i); GBHS §4.3.4(i), 5.3.2; GKC §159ee; IBHS §40.2.2b; JM §164b–c, 165a, e, g, i, 167s; Muraoka 1985, 158–64; Gordis 1943, 176–8; Follingstad 2001, 11–12, 49–51, 241–3, 277–9; Claassen 1983, 29–46.

[570] Cf. BHRG §40.9.II.4; GBHS §4.3.4(d), 5.2.3(b); GKC §107u, 166b; IBHS §18.2g, 38.3b; JM §169e; Aejmelaeus 1986, 201–2; Follingstad 2001, 14, 282–8; Selms 1971–2; Selms 1978.

- הֲכַף זֶבַח ... עַתָּה בְּיָדְךָ כִּי־ נִתֵּן לִצְבָאֲךָ לָחֶם
  bread to your army we will give *that* in your hand now Zebah hand? Judg 8:6

  Are the hands of Zebah … now in your hand

  with the result that we should give bread to your army?

- Other examples include Job 38:20 and 2 Kgs 18:34.

51a **Nominalizing כִּי (that).**[571] The conjunction כִּי can begin a substantival clause (§483), just like the Greek conjunction ὅτι. Such a clause can be the subject of another clause (§484) or the direct object of a verb (§490). This is also called the **perceptual use** of כִּי when used with a verb of perception or cognition.

- וַיַּרְא אֱלֹהִים כִּי־ טוֹב
  good *that* God saw

  God saw *that* it was good.

  Gen 1:10

- עַתָּה יָדַעְתִּי כִּי־ יְרֵא אֱלֹהִים אַתָּה
  you God afraid of *that* I know now

  Now I know *that* you fear God.

  Gen 22:12

51b **כִּי in a question (is it (not) the case that?).**[572] After the interrogative particle הֲ, the conjunction כִּי can begin a substantival clause that is the subject of a interrogative sentence. This can be considered a subcategory of the **recitative use** of כִּי (§452).

- הֲכִי יֵשׁ־ עוֹד אֲשֶׁר נוֹתַר לְבֵית שָׁאוּל
  Saul to house of is left who still there is *that*?   2 Sam 9:1

  Is it the case that there is still someone left of Saul's house?

- הֲלוֹא כִּי אָנֹכִי צִוִּיתִי אֶתְכֶם   *Is it* not *the case that* I have commanded you?
  you I commanded I *that* not?   2 Sam 13:28

- Other examples include 1 Sam 10:1 and Job 6:22.

452 **Recitative כִּי (quotation marks).**[573] Also called the כִּי *recitativum*, the conjunction כִּי can introduce direct speech, just like the Greek word ὅτι.

- וַיֹּאמֶר חֲזָהאֵל כִּי מָה עַבְדְּךָ   Hazael said, 'What is your servant?'
  your servant what (*quote*) Hazael said   2 Kgs 8:13

- וַיְדַבֵּר אֵלֶיהָ כִּי־ אֲדַבֵּר אֶל־ נָבוֹת   He said to her, 'I spoke to Naboth.'
  Naboth to I spoke (*quote*) to her he spoke   1 Kgs 21:6

- Another example is Exod 3:12.

---

[571] Cf. BHRG §40.9.II.1; GBHS §4.3.4(j)–(k), 5.2.1(a), (c); GKC §157a–b; IBHS §38.8; JM §157a, c–ca; Aejmelaeus 1986, 199–200; Follingstad 2001, 13–14, 445–55, *passim*.
[572] Cf. GBHS §4.3.4(l), (n).
[573] Cf. GBHS §4.3.4(l), 5.2.1(c); GKC §157b; JM §157c; Aejmelaeus 1986, 208; Goldenberg 1991, 84–7; Follingstad 2001, 13–14, 47–9, *passim*.

The conjunction אִם [574]

453   **Conditional אִם (if).**[575] The conjunction אִם can begin the protasis (the 'if' part) of a real conditional sentence (§515).

- אִם־אֶמְצָא בִסְדֹם חֲמִשִּׁים צַדִּיקִם   *if* I find fifty righteous people in Sodom
  righteous   fifty   in Sodom   I find   *if*   Gen 18:26
- This is quite common in laws such as Lev 14:21, וְאִם־דַּל 'but if he is poor ...'
- Jer 37:10 and Ps 50:12 may be the sole examples of אִם introducing the protasis of an unreal conditional sentence (§517) (unless they are concessive, §454, 529).

  ○ אִם־אֶרְעַב לֹא־אֹמַר לָךְ   *If* I were hungry, I would not tell you.
    to you   I would tell   not   I were hungry   *if*   Ps 50:12

454   **Concessive אִם (though, in spite of, even if).**[576] The conjunction אִם can begin a concessive clause (§529).

- אִם־יַעֲמֹד מֹשֶׁה וּשְׁמוּאֵל לְפָנַי
  before me   and Samuel   Moses   standing   *though*   Jer 15:1
                                              though Moses and Samuel were to stand before me
- Multiple examples occur in Amos 9:2–4; for example וְאִם־יֵחָבְאוּ 'even if they hide.'

455   **Alternative אִם (or).**[577] אִם can connect alternatives (§544) in questions.

- הֲלָנוּ אַתָּה אִם־לְצָרֵינוּ   Are you for us *or* for our foes?
  to our foes   *or*   you   for us?   Josh 5:13
- Another example is 2 Sam 24:13.

456   **אִם in oaths and exclamations (if, not).**[578] After an oath formula (explicit or implied) or an exclamation, אִם is used to begin the protasis of a conditional sentence ('if ...'). But as an oath, the protasis is functioning as a declaration. When the protasis that begins with אִם is understood as a declaration, one must reverse its positive or negative sense, meaning that a negative protasis (אִם לֹא) is a positive declaration, and a positive protasis (אִם) is a negative declaration. Because of this reversal, this use of אִם is sometimes called the **privative אִם**.

---

[574] Cf. BHRG §31.3(iii), 40.5, 41.3.6; GBHS §4.3.2; GKC §149, 150c, f–i, 151e, 159l–v, dd, 160a; Elwolde 1990.

[575] Cf. BHRG §19.4.1, 40.5.1, 40.9.I.1; GBHS §4.3.2(a), 5.2.2(a); GKC §159l–v, dd; IBHS §31.6.1b, 32.2.1b, 38.2d; JM §165a, c, f–j, 167c, f–h, p–q; Elwolde 1990, 222.

[576] Cf. BHRG §40.5.2; GBHS §4.3.2(b), 5.2.12; GKC §160a; JM §171a, d.

[577] Cf. BHRG §40.5.3; GBHS §4.3.2(c), 5.3.1(b); GKC §150g–i; IBHS §18.1c, 40.3b; JM §161e–f, 175c.

[578] Cf. BHRG §40.5.4, 41.3.6(i); GBHS §4.3.2(e)–(f), 5.3.2; GKC §149; IBHS §40.2.2a–c; JM §165a, c–d, f–k; Elwolde 1990; Sanders 2004; Lehmann 1969.

- כֹּה־ יַעֲשֶׂה אֱלֹהִים לְאֹיְבֵי דָוִד וְכֹה יֹסִיף

  he will add and thus David to enemies of God he will do thus   1 Sam 25:22

  אִם־ אַשְׁאִיר מִכָּל־ אֲשֶׁר־ לוֹ עַד־ הַבֹּקֶר

  the morning until to him which from all of I will leave over if   (cont.)

  Thus may God do to the enemies of David and more

  if I leave over until morning some who belong to him.

  OR   … I will *not* leave over until morning some who belong to him.

- חֵי־ נַפְשְׁךָ הַמֶּלֶךְ אִם־יָדַעְתִּי

  I know *if* the king your soul life of   1 Sam 17:55

  By your life, O king, *if* I know. OR By your life, O king, I do *not* know.

- אִם־לֹא אֶת־דְּמֵי נָבוֹת וְאֶת־דְּמֵי בָנָיו רָאִיתִי

  I saw his sons and bloods of Naboth bloods of not if   2 Kgs 9:26

  If I did not see the blood of Naboth and the blood of his sons.

  OR *As surely as* I saw the blood of Naboth and the blood of his sons.

- Other examples include 2 Sam 11:11; 2 Kgs 3:14; Job 1:11.

457 Pleonastic אִם (*untranslated*).[579] The conjunction אִם is sometimes superfluous, used merely for stylistic reasons after certain particles.

- Pleonastic אִם may be used after an adversative כִּי (§447), asseverative כִּי (§449), exceptive בִּלְתִּי (§422), עַד, and עַד אֲשֶׁר. When אִם is used after עַד 'until,' it might introduce an element of doubt, so it may not be completely superfluous.

- עַד אִם־ כִּלּוּ אֵת כָּל־ הַקָּצִיר   until they have finished the entire harvest

  the harvest all of they finished   until   Ruth 2:21

- עַד אֲשֶׁר אִם־ הֲבִיאֹנֻם   until we have brought them

  we brought them which until   Num 32:17

- Other examples include Gen 24:19 and 28:15.

458 Optative אִם (if only, Oh that!).[580] On rare occasions, a desire is expressed with אִם (§550) instead of לוּ (§460, 548). This is also called the **desiderative** use of אִם.

- אִם־ בָּרֵךְ תְּבָרֲכֵנִי   *Oh that* you would bless me!

  you would bless me to bless *oh that!*   1 Chr 4:10

- אִם־ תַּחְשׂוֹךְ   *If only* you would restrain them!

  you will restrain *if only*   Prov 24:11

---

[579] Cf. JM §164c.
[580] Cf. GBHS §5.3.3(a); GKC §151e; IBHS §40.2.2d; JM §163c; Elwolde 1990.

The conjunction (לוּ / לוּלֵי / לוּלֵא) [581]

459a **Unreal conditional** לֻא / לוּ **(if).**[582] The conjunction לוּ (also spelled לֻא, and occasionally mis-vocalized as לֹא) can be used to begin the protasis (the 'if' part) of an unreal conditional sentence (§516a).

- If the verb after לוּ is perfect, the condition is usually in the past time.
- If the verb after לוּ is a participle, the condition is usually in the present time.
- If the verb after לוּ is imperfect, the condition is usually in the future time.
- If the protasis is negative, לוּלֵא or לוּלֵי is used (§459b).

- עֹלָה   מִיָּדֵנוּ   לָקַח   לֹא־   לַהֲמִיתֵנוּ   יְהוָה   חָפֵץ   לוּ   (perfect)
  burnt offering   from our hands   took   not   to kill us   YHWH   desired   *if*   Judg 13:23
  If YHWH desired to kill us, he would not have accepted a burnt offering from us.

- כֶּסֶף   אֶלֶף   כַּפַּי   עַל־   שֹׁקֵל   אָנֹכִי   וְלוּ   (participle)
  silver   thousand of   my hands   on   weighing out   I   and *if*   2 Sam 18:12 qere
  and *if* I were weighing out in my hands a thousand silver pieces

- בָּאָרֶץ   אַעֲבִיר   רָעָה   חַיָּה   לוּ־   (imperfect)
  in the land   I would cause to pass through   evil   beasts   *if*   Ezek 14:15
  if I were to cause wild animals to pass through the land

459b **Negative unreal conditional** לוּלֵי / לוּלֵא **(if not).**[583] The conjunction לוּלֵי (also spelled לוּלֵא) can be used to begin the protasis (the 'if' part) of a negative unreal conditional sentence (§516b).

- חִידָתִי   מְצָאתֶם   לֹא   בְּעֶגְלָתִי   חֲרַשְׁתֶּם   לוּלֵא
  my riddle   you found   not   in my heifer   you ploughed   *if not*   Judg 14:18
  If you had *not* ploughed with my heifer, you would not have discovered my riddle.

- אֵלֶיךָ   אַבִּיט   אִם־   נֹשֵׂא   אֲנִי   ... יְהוֹשָׁפָט   פְּנֵי   לוּלֵי
  to you   I will look   if   lifting up   I   Jehoshaphat   face of   *if not*   2 Kgs 3:14
  If I did *not* respect Jehoshaphat … I would not look at you.

460 **Optative** לוּ **(if only, O that!).**[584] A desire can be expressed with לוּ (§548). This is also called the **desiderative** use of לוּ.

- If the verb after לוּ is perfect, the desire is usually in the past time.
- If the verb after לוּ is imperfect or jussive, the desire is usually in the future time.

---

[581] Cf. BHRG §40.10, 40.11; GKC §27w, 151e, 159l–m, x–z.

[582] Cf. BHRG §19.2.1(iii), 40.10; GBHS §5.2.2(b); GKC §159l–m, x–z; IBHS §31.6.1b, 38.2e; JM §167f, k.

[583] Cf. BHRG §40.11; GBHS §5.2.2(b); GKC §159l–m, x–z; IBHS §38.2e; JM §29h, 167f, k.

[584] Cf. BHRG §40.10; GBHS §5.3.3(a); GKC §151e; IBHS §38.2e, 40.2.2d; JM §163c.

- לוּ־ מַתְנוּ בְּאֶרֶץ מִצְרַיִם

  Egypt   in land of   we died   *if only*

  If only we had died in the land of Egypt!
  Num 14:2 (perfect)

- לוּ יִשְׁמָעֵאל יִחְיֶה לְפָנֶיךָ

  before you   would live   Ishmael   *if only*

  If only Ishmael might live before you!
  Gen 17:18 (imperfect)

- לוּ יְהִי כִדְבָרֶךָ

  like your word   may it be   *if only*

  May it be as you have said!
  Gen 30:34 (jussive)

The conjunction פֶּן

461   **פֶּן for negative purpose (lest, or else, beware lest, in order not).**[585] The conjunction פֶּן can begin a negative purpose clause (§524).

- לֹא תֹאכְלוּ מִמֶּנּוּ וְלֹא תִגְּעוּ בּוֹ פֶּן־ תְּמֻתוּן

  you will die   *lest*   (בְּ) it   you will touch   and not   from it   you will eat   not   Gen 3:3

  You shall not eat from it and you shall not touch it, *lest* you die.

- פֶּן־ יַסִּית אֶתְכֶם חִזְקִיָּהוּ

  Hezekiah   you   would mislead   *lest*

  Beware lest Hezekiah mislead you.
  Isa 36:18

- Other examples include Gen 24:6, 32:12; Deut 29:17.

E   Relative Particles [586]

The relative particle אֲשֶׁר [587]

462   **אֲשֶׁר introduces a clause**. Relative clauses (§463a–b) are most common after אֲשֶׁר, but other clause types occur (§464–9).[588] אֲשֶׁר may have been derived from a noun meaning 'place' (cf. Akkadian *ašru*).[589]

463a   **Relative אֲשֶׁר (who, which, that)**.[590] The particle אֲשֶׁר can begin a relative clause, particularly in prose (§538).

---

[585] Cf. BHRG §40.14; GBHS §4.3.5, 5.2.3(c); GKC §107q, 152w; IBHS §31.6.1c, 38.3c, 39.3.3a; JM §168g–h.

[586] Cf. BHRG §36.3, 40.6; GBHS §5.2.13; GKC §36, 138, 155; IBHS §19; JM §38, 145, 158; Holmstedt 2002.

[587] Cf. BHRG §36.3.1, 40.6; GBHS §5.2.13; GKC §36, 104b, 129h, 138, 155, 157c, 158a, 159cc, 164d, 165b, 166b; IBHS §19.2b, 19.3; JM §38, 145, 158e–u; Kraetzschmar 1890; Gaenssle 1914; Gaenssle 1915a; Gaenssle 1915b; Holmstedt 2006; Holmstedt forthcoming-a; Holmstedt forthcoming-b; Huehnergard 2006.

[588] Some scholars argue that many putative examples of other uses of אֲשֶׁר (§465–8) are actually relative (§463) or nominalizing (§464); see Holmstedt 2001; Gottstein 1949.

[589] Cf. GKC §36, 138a note 1; JM §38 note 2; Gaenssle 1915b; Schwarzchild 1990; Huehnergard 2006, 107–10, 121.

- אֲנִי יוֹסֵף אֲחִיכֶם אֲשֶׁר־מְכַרְתֶּם אֹתִי מִצְרָיְמָה

  toward Egypt ME you sold *whom* your brother Joseph I   Gen 45:4

  I am Joseph your brother, *whom* you sold into Egypt.

  - The relative clause אֲשֶׁר־מְכַרְתֶּם אֹתִי מִצְרָיְמָה 'whom you sold into Egypt'
    describes its antecedent, אֲחִיכֶם 'your brother.' The resumptive pronominal
    suffix יֹ on the definite direct object marker אֵת (forming אֹתִי) refers to the
    antecedent, indicating its role in the relative clause (i.e., the direct object of the
    verb מְכַרְתֶּם 'you sold'). The resumptive pronoun is not translated into English.

- הַמָּקוֹם אֲשֶׁר אַתָּה עוֹמֵד עָלָיו   the place on *which* you are standing

  on IT standing you *which* the place   Exod 3:5

- Other examples include Num 10:29 and Deut 11:10.

463b **Independent relative אֲשֶׁר (who, he who, what, etc.).**[591] The particle אֲשֶׁר
can begin an 'independent relative clause' (the term is an oxymoron),
meaning that the clause is descriptive like a relative clause, but the word
that it is describing (the **antecedent** or **head**) is omitted in the main
clause. Such clauses are also called **headless relative clauses** or **null head
relative clauses**. In English translation, the antecedent is often added
(e.g., 'he who …').

- What distinguishes this from a nominalizing אֲשֶׁר (§464) is that an independent
  relative clause describes something (its omitted antecedent) that has a role within the
  relative clause (where a resumptive pronoun or adverb could be put).[592]

- יָדַעְתִּי אֵת אֲשֶׁר־תְּבָרֵךְ מְבֹרָךְ   I know that *he whom* you bless is blessed.

  blessed you bless *he whom*   I know   Num 22:6

  - The אֲשֶׁר clause describes something (its antecedent) that has a grammatical
    role within the אֲשֶׁר clause (the object of its verb: 'you bless him'), so it is a
    relative clause (§463a–b) rather than a substantival clause (§464). The
    antecedent is omitted in the main clause (for example, there is no word הָאִישׁ
    'the man' after אֵת), so the relative clause is independent (in contrast with a
    normal relative clause, §463a).

- וַיֹּאמֶר כָּלֵב אֲשֶׁר־יַכֶּה אֶת־קִרְיַת־סֵפֶר

  Kiriath-sepher smites *he who* Caleb he said   Judg 1:12

  Caleb said, '*He who* smites Kiriath-sepher …'

---

[590] Cf. BHRG §36.3.1, 40.6.1; GBHS §5.2.13; GKC §138a–d, 155; IBHS §19.3a–b; JM
§38, 130e–fa, 145a, 158e–k; Holmstedt 2001, 2–4; Holmstedt 2002, 17–38, 54–125.
[591] Cf. BHRG §36.3.1(i); GBHS §5.2.1(a), (c); GKC §139e–f, 155; IBHS §19.3c; JM
§145a, 157a, c–ca, f, 158l–m; Holmstedt 2001, 4; Holmstedt 2002, 71–9.
[592] Holmstedt 2001, 5. For an explanation of the distinctions between §463a, §463b, and
§464, see Holmstedt 2001, 2–5; Holmstedt 2002, 65–79, 294–5.

    o   The אֲשֶׁר clause describes something that has a grammatical role within the אֲשֶׁר clause (the subject of its verb: 'he who smites'), so this is a relative clause.

464 **Nominalizing אֲשֶׁר (that).**[593] The particle אֲשֶׁר can introduce a **substantival clause** (§483), just as the conjunction כִּי (§451a) can. This is sometimes referred to as the use of אֲשֶׁר as a **complementizer**.

- וַיַּרְא שָׁאוּל אֲשֶׁר־הוּא מַשְׂכִּיל מְאֹד   Saul saw *that* he was very successful.
very successful he *that* Saul saw   1 Sam 18:15

    o   The אֲשֶׁר clause does not describe something that has a grammatical role within the אֲשֶׁר clause (i.e., there is no place to put a resumptive element), so it cannot be an independent relative clause (§463b). Instead it is a nominalizing אֲשֶׁר.

- אַל־תִּשְׁכַּח אֵת אֲשֶׁר־הִקְצַפְתָּ אֶת־יְהוָה
YHWH you angered *that* you forget not   Deut 9:7
            Do not forget *that* you angered YHWH.

465 **Result אֲשֶׁר (with the result that).**[594] On rare occasions, אֲשֶׁר begins a result clause (§527).

- אֲשֶׁר לֹא־יֹאמְרוּ זֹאת אִיזָבֶל
Jezebel this they can say not *with the result that*   2 Kgs 9:37
            with the result that they cannot say, 'This is Jezebel'
- אֲשֶׁר לֹא־הָיָה כָמוֹךָ אִישׁ   *with the result that* there is no one like you
man like you is not *with the result that*   1 Kgs 3:13
- Another example is Gen 13:16.

466 **Purpose אֲשֶׁר (in order that).**[595] On at least three occasions, אֲשֶׁר begins a purpose clause (§523).

- אֲשֶׁר לֹא־תִגָּלֶה עֶרְוָתְךָ עָלָיו
on it your nakedness will be uncovered not *in order that*   Exod 20:26
            in order that your nakedness not be uncovered on it
- אֲשֶׁר יִיטַב לָךְ   *in order that* it go well with you
to your advantage it will go well *in order that*   Deut 4:40
- Another example is Josh 3:7.

---

[593] Cf. BHRG §40.6.2; GKC §157c; IBHS §27.3b, 38.8; JM §157a, c–ca, 158l–m; Gaenssle 1914, 37–44; Holmstedt 2001, 5; Holmstedt 2002, 294–5; Rooker 1990, 111–12.
[594] Cf. BHRG §40.6.3; GBHS §5.2.3(b)–(c); GKC §166b; IBHS §38.3b–c; JM §169f; Gaenssle 1915a, 107–9.
[595] Cf. BHRG §40.6.4; GBHS §5.2.3(a), (c); GKC §165b; IBHS §31.6.1c, 38.3b–c; JM §168f; Gaenssle 1915a, 104–6.

467 **Recitative אֲשֶׁר (quotation marks).**[596] On rare occasions, the particle אֲשֶׁר is used to introduce direct speech, like כִּי (§452) and the Greek ὅτι.

- וַיֹּאמֶר שָׁאוּל אֶל־שְׁמוּאֵל אֲשֶׁר שָׁמַעְתִּי בְּקוֹל יְהוָה

  of YHWH   in voice   I heard (*quote*) Samuel to Saul   said   1 Sam 15:20

  Saul said to Samuel, 'I have obeyed the voice of YHWH.'

- וַיֹּאמֶר אֲשֶׁר־נָס הָעָם

  the people   fled (*quote*) he said   He said, 'The people fled.'

                                                        2 Sam 1:4

468 **Causal אֲשֶׁר (because).**[597] אֲשֶׁר can introduce a causal clause. See §533.

- וַיָּמָת בֶּן־הָאִשָּׁה הַזֹּאת לָיְלָה אֲשֶׁר שָׁכְבָה עָלָיו

  on him she lay *because* night the this the woman son of died   1 Kgs 3:19

  The son of this woman died during the night *because* she lay on him.

- אֲשֶׁר חָמַל הָעָם עַל־מֵיטַב הַצֹּאן

  the flock best of (to the advantage of) the people spared *because*   1 Sam 15:15

  because the people spared the best of the flock

- Other examples include Gen 34:13 and Josh 4:23.

469 **Conditional אֲשֶׁר (if).**[598] Very rarely, the relative particle אֲשֶׁר begins the protasis of a real conditional sentence (§515), just as כִּי (§446) does.

- אֶת־הַבְּרָכָה אֲשֶׁר תִּשְׁמְעוּ אֶל־מִצְוֹת יְהוָה

  YHWH commandments of to you listen *if* the blessing   Deut 11:27

  the blessing – *if* you listen to the commandments of YHWH

  o The conditional אֲשֶׁר in Deut 11:27 is parallel to a conditional אִם in verse 28.

- וַאֲשֶׁר לֹא צָדָה

  he lay in wait not but *if*   but *if* he did not lie in wait

                                                          Exod 21:13

- אֵת אֲשֶׁר יֶחֱטָא אִישׁ לְרֵעֵהוּ

  to his neighbour man sins *if*   *if* a man sins against his neighbour

                                                          1 Kgs 8:31

  o The fact that the conditional אֲשֶׁר clause in 1 Kgs 8:31 occurs after אֵת suggests that causal אֲשֶׁר clauses should be understood as substantival clauses in the accusative case. 2 Chr 6:22 is identical to 1 Kgs 8:31, except that it has אִם instead of אֵת אֲשֶׁר, thus confirming the conditional sense of אֲשֶׁר 1 Kgs 8:31.

- Josh 4:21 may be another example, unless its אֲשֶׁר clause is temporal. See the discussion of this ambiguity in §515.

---

[596] Cf. BHRG §40.6.8; GKC §157c; Gaenssle 1915a, 126–7.

[597] Cf. BHRG §40.6.5; GBHS §5.2.5; GKC §158a; IBHS §38.4a; JM §170e; Gaenssle 1915a, 97–104.

[598] Cf. BHRG §40.6.7; GBHS §5.2.2(a); GKC §159cc; IBHS §38.2d; JM §167j; Gaenssle 1915a, 109–16.

The relative particle ◌ֶשׁ / ◌ַשׁ [599]

470 **The origin of** ◌ֶשׁ/ ◌ַשׁ **is disputed.**[600] It is a relative particle without gender or number (§129b). Its uses parallel those of אֲשֶׁר (§462–9). Most of its occurrences are in Ecclesiastes, Song of Songs, and Psalms.

471 **Relative** ◌ַשׁ / ◌ֶשׁ **(who, which, that).**[601] The particle ◌ַשׁ / ◌ֶשׁ can begin a relative clause (§537).

- לָרֹב   הַיָּם   שְׂפַת־   שֶׁעַל־   כַּחוֹל   מִסְפָּר   אֵין •

  to greatness   the sea lip of *which* on like the sand number there is no   Judg 7:12

  without number, like the sand *which* is on the seashore as to greatness

- לְשִׁנֵּיהֶם   טֶרֶף   נְתָנָנוּ   שֶׁלֹּא   יְהוָה   בָּרוּךְ •

  to their teeth prey gave us *who* not YHWH blessed   Ps 124:6

  Blessed be YHWH *who* has not given us as prey for their teeth.

- Other examples include Ps 144:15 and Eccl 1:9.

472 **Nominalizing** ◌ַשׁ / ◌ֶשׁ **(that).**[602] The relative particle ◌ַשׁ / ◌ֶשׁ can begin a substantival clause (§483), just as אֲשֶׁר can (§464).

- When ◌ַשׁ / ◌ֶשׁ follows a preposition, it is considered to be nominalizing.

- עִמִּי   מְדַבֵּר   שָׁאַתָּה   אוֹת   לִי   וְעָשִׂיתָ •

  with me speaking *that* you sign to me (you) give   Judg 6:17

  Give to me a sign *that* it is you who are speaking with me.

- לַחָכְמָה   יִתְרוֹן   שֶׁיֵּשׁ   אָנִי   וְרָאִיתִי • And I saw *that* there is profit in wisdom.

  to wisdom profit *that* there is I   saw   Eccl 2:13

- Other examples include Judg 5:7 (after עַד); Eccl 2:14, 2:16 (after בְּ), 9:12 (after כְּ), 10:3 (after כְּ).

473 **Result** ◌ַשׁ / ◌ֶשׁ **(with the result that, so that).** ◌ַשׁ / ◌ֶשׁ can begin a result clause (§527).

- הִשְׁבַּעְתָּנוּ   שֶׁכָּכָה   מִדּוֹד   דּוֹדֵךְ   מַה־ •

  you adjure us *with the result that* thus than beloved your beloved how?   Song 5:9

  How is your beloved better than another beloved, *that* you adjure us thus?

---

[599] Cf. BHRG §36.3.2; GBHS §5.2.13; GKC §36, 155; IBHS §19.2, 19.4; JM §38, 104a, 145b; Gaenssle 1915b, 5–15; Kraetzschmar 1890, 296–302; Holmstedt 2002, 80–2.

[600] Cf. Huehnergard 2006; Holmstedt forthcoming-b.

[601] Cf. BHRG §36.3.2; GBHS §5.2.13; GKC §36, 155; IBHS §19.4a–b; JM §38, 104a, 145b.

[602] Cf. IBHS §19.4b.

- מֵאֵלֶּה   טוֹבִים   הָיוּ   הָרִאשֹׁנִים   שֶׁהַיָּמִים   הָיָה   מֶה

than these   better   were   the first   *with the result that* the days   was   how?   Eccl 7:10

How has it happened *that* the earlier days were better than these?

474 Causal ⊙שׁ / ⊙שֶׁ (because). שׁ⊙ / שֶׁ⊙ can introduce a causal clause (§533).

- אַחֲרַי   שֶׁיִּהְיֶה   לָאָדָם   שֶׁאַנִּיחֶנּוּ

after me   who will be   to the man   *because* I must leave it   Eccl 2:18

because I must leave it to the man who will come after me

- הַשָּׁמֶשׁ   שֶׁשֱּׁזָפַתְנִי

the sun   *because* it tanned me   *because* the sun has tanned me   Song 1:6

F   The Accusative Particle אֵת / אֶת־ [603]

475a **The particle אֵת (also spelled אֶת־)** is rare in poetry but normal in prose.[604] In almost all of its occurrences it precedes a determined substantive. Thus, although it occurs with מִי 'who?' it does not occur with מָה 'what?' because מָה is indefinite. The particle אֵת is generally not translated. It is referred to as the **accusative particle**, the **definite direct-object marker**, or the ***nota accusativi***.

475b **אֵת before a definite direct object.**[605] In prose, the particle אֵת routinely precedes a direct object (§50) that is definite.

- בָּרָא אֱלֹהִים אֵת הַשָּׁמַיִם וְאֵת הָאָרֶץ   God created *the heavens* and *the earth.*

the earth   and   the heavens   God   created   Gen 1:1

- וַיְבָרֶךְ   אֹתָם   אֱלֹהִים   God blessed *them.*

God   *them*   he blessed   Gen 1:22

475c **אֵת before an indefinite direct object.**[606] On very rare occasions, אֵת is used before what appears to be a direct object (§50) that is indefinite.

- וַיַּעַשׂ אֶת־בֵּית   בָּמוֹת   He built *high-place temples.*

high places   house of   he made   1 Kgs 12:31

- הָרְגוּ אֶת־אִישׁ־צַדִּיק   בְּבֵיתוֹ   They killed *a righteous man* in his house.

in his house   righteous   man   they killed   2 Sam 4:11

---

[603] Cf. BHRG §33.1; GKC §117a–m; IBHS §10.1a–b, 10.3; JM §103k, 125e–j; Elwolde 1994; MacDonald 1964; Walker 1955; Saydon 1964; Davies 1991; Andersen and Forbes 1983; Wilson 1890a; Wilson 1890b; Hoftijzer 1965.

[604] Cf. GKC §117a–b; JM §103k.

[605] Cf. BHRG §33.1; GKC §117a, c, e; IBHS §10.2.1c, 10.3.1a; JM §125e–ib; JM93 §125e–ia; Elwolde 1994, 171–4; Saydon 1964, 192–5.

[606] Cf. GKC §117d; IBHS §10.3.1b; JM §125h; Elwolde 1994, 175–7, 180.

75d אֵת **before an accusative of specification.**[607] אֵת often occurs before an accusative of specification (§57a) that is definite.

- חָלָה אֶת־רַגְלָיו   He was diseased *in his feet.*
  his feet   he was sick   1 Kgs 15:23

- עָשִׂיתָה אִתִּי טוֹבָה
  good   to my advantage   you did   1 Sam 24:19

  אֵת אֲשֶׁר סִגְּרַנִי יְהוָה בְּיָדְךָ וְלֹא הֲרַגְתָּנִי
  you killed me   *and not*   *in your hand*   *YHWH*   *delivered me*   *that*   (cont.)

  You did me good *in that when YHWH delivered me into your hand, you did not kill me.*

75e אֵת **before an emphatic accusative of specification.** See §58.

- וַיַּרְא אֱלֹהִים אֶת־הָאוֹר כִּי־ טוֹב   God saw that *the light* was good.
  good   that   *the light*   God   saw   Gen 1:4

75f אֵת **before a determinative accusative.** See §59.

- וַיֻּגַּד לְרִבְקָה אֶת־דִּבְרֵי עֵשָׂו   *Esau's words* were told to Rebekah.
  Esau   words of   to Rebekah   was told   Gen 27:42

  o דִּבְרֵי 'words' is a determinative accusative because it is preceded by the accusative particle אֶת־; it is the 'subject' of the preceding verb וַיֻּגַּד 'it was told.' The accusative and verb do not exhibit concord – the determinative accusative is plural whereas the verb is singular.

- הֲלֹא־ הֻגַּד לַאדֹנִי אֵת אֲשֶׁר־עָשִׂיתִי   Has not *what I did* been told to my lord?
  I did   *what*   to my lord   was told   not?   1 Kgs 18:13

75g אֵת **before a temporal accusative.**[608] See §56a–b.

- מַצּוֹת יֵאָכֵל אֵת שִׁבְעַת הַיָּמִים
  the days   seven of   will be eaten   unleavened bread   Exod 13:7

  Unleavened bread will be eaten *during the seven days.*

75h אֵת **before an accusative of material.**[609] See §53.

- וַתִּמָּלֵא הָאָרֶץ אֶת־הַמָּיִם   The land was filled *with the water.*
  the water   the land   was filled   2 Kgs 3:20

---

[607] Cf. IBHS §10.3.1c; JM §125j, 126g; Elwolde 1994, 177; Saydon 1964, 205.
[608] Cf. IBHS §10.3.1c; JM §126i; Elwolde 1994, 175.
[609] Cf. IBHS §10.3.1c; Saydon 1964, 194–5.

G The Existential Particle יֵשׁ [610]

476   **יֵשׁ as a noun (wealth).**[611] יֵשׁ is occasionally used as a noun meaning 'property' or 'wealth.' This may have been its original use.

- יֵשׁ   אֹהֲבַי   לְהַנְחִיל   to cause the ones who love me to inherit *wealth*
  wealth   ones loving me   to cause to inherit   Prov 8:21

- וָיֵשׁ   נַחֲלָה   עַל מַחְלֹקֶת   on the division of inheritance and *wealth*
  and *wealth*   inheritance   division of   on   Sir 42:3 (MS M)

- Another example is Sir 25:21.

477   **יֵשׁ of existence (there is).**[612] The particle יֵשׁ commonly indicates the existence of the substantive or substantival clause that follows it. When יֵשׁ is used in this way, it can often be translated 'there is' or 'there are.'

- נָבִיא   יֵשׁ   כִּי   וְיֵדַע   He will know that *there is* a prophet.
  prophet   *there is*   that   he will know   2 Kgs 5:8

- צַדִּיקִם   חֲמִשִּׁים   יֵשׁ   אוּלַי   Perhaps *there are* fifty righteous.
  righteous   fifty   *there are*   perhaps   Gen 18:24

- Other examples include Num 9:20–1.

478   **יֵשׁ for possession (has).**[613] When followed by the preposition לְ of possession (§270), the particle יֵשׁ often means that the object of the preposition לְ possesses something. The concept of possession is rather broad in both English and Hebrew; if a person is the one 'possessed' (e.g., 'my husband'), 'possession' often refers to a relationship rather than to literally owning the person.

- זָקֵן   אָב   לָנוּ   יֵשׁ־   We *have* an old father.
  old   father   belonging to us   *there is*   Gen 44:20

- לְיִשְׂרָאֵל   אֱלֹהִים   יֵשׁ   כִּי   ... וְיֵדְעוּ
  belonging to Israel   God   *there is*   that   they will know   1 Sam 17:46
  They will know … that Israel *has* a God.

- Another example is 2 Kgs 4:2.

479   **יֵשׁ before the pronominal subject of a participle** (*untranslated*).[614] Also called its **predicate** use, the particle יֵשׁ occasionally takes a pronominal

---

[610] Cf. BHRG §42.3; GBHS §4.4.2; GKC §100o, p, 116q, 141k, 152i, 159dd; JM §102k, 154k–l; Muraoka 1985, 77–82, 99–101, 110–11.

[611] Cf. GKC §141k.

[612] Cf. BHRG §42.3(i); GBHS §4.4.2(a), 5.3.4(b); GKC §152i; JM §154k.

[613] Cf. GBHS §4.4.2(b).

[614] Cf. GBHS §4.4.2(c); GKC §116q; IBHS §37.6a; JM §154l.

suffix that is the subject of a participle. This use is particularly frequent after אִם when the construction expresses an intention.

- לָדַעַת הֲיִשְׁכֶם אֹהֲבִים אֶת־יְהוָה   to know if you love YHWH
  YHWH   loving   (יֵשׁ) you?   to know   Deut 13:4

- אִם־יֶשְׁךָ־ נָּא מַצְלִיחַ דַּרְכִּי   if you will make my journey successful
  my road   making successful   (יֵשׁ) you if   Gen 24:42

- Another example is Gen 43:4.

480   **יֵשׁ for obligation** (*untranslated*).[615] A gerundive infinitive construct (§196, meaning 'ought to') can be preceded by יֵשׁ.

- הֲיֵשׁ לְדַבֶּר־ לָךְ אֶל־הַמֶּלֶךְ   *Ought one* to speak for you to the king?
  the king to for you ought to speak   (יֵשׁ)?   2 Kgs 4:13

- Another possible example is 2 Chr 25:9.

481   **Elliptic יֵשׁ (there is).**[616] In conversation, when someone responds to someone else, the word יֵשׁ can stand for an entire sentence that is elided (§598).

- וַיֹּאמְרוּ לָהֶן הֲיֵשׁ בָּזֶה הָרֹאֶה
  the seer in this there is? to them they said   1 Sam 9:11–12

  יֵשׁ וַתַּעֲנֶינָה אוֹתָם וַתֹּאמַרְנָה
  there is and they said them they answered   (cont.)

       They said to them, 'Is there the seer in this place?' They answered, '*There is.*'

- יֵשׁ וַיֹּאמֶר אֵלָיו הֲיֵשׁ אֶת־לְבָבְךָ יָשָׁר ... וַיֹּאמֶר יְהוֹנָדָב
  there is Jehonadab he said upright your heart there is? to him he said

       He said to him, 'Is your heart upright?' ... Jehonadab said, '*It is.*' 2 Kgs 10:15

---

[615] Cf. IBHS §36.2.3f.
[616] Cf. BHRG §42.3(ii).

4 Syntax of Clauses [617]

- **A clause** is a set of words with a subject, a predicate, and any words that modify them. The subject or predicate can be implied rather than stated, and the modifiers can be absent.
- **An asyndetic clause** lacks an introductory word (such as וְ 'and,' אֲשֶׁר 'which,' or כִּי 'that') to connect it to the clause before it.

482 Parataxis.[618]

- In English it is common to use words such as 'while' and 'because' to specify the logical relationship between clauses. For example, in the English sentence, 'I eat while I study,' there are two clauses: 'I eat' and 'while I study.' The word 'while' indicates that the second clause specifies the time when the first clause occurs. The second clause is logically subordinate to the first clause. The use of markers such as 'while' to indicate the subordination of clauses is termed **hypotaxis**.
- In Hebrew, however, subordinate clauses are usually not marked explicitly with words such as 'while.' Instead, most clauses begin with the conjunction וְ. The use of a coordinating conjunction (such as וְ) to begin a clause that is logically subordinate is termed **parataxis**. The relationship between paratactic clauses must usually be deduced from the context rather than from the presence of a word such as 'while.'

A Substantival Clauses [619]

483 A substantival clause is a clause that functions as a noun within a larger sentence; the larger sentence would have the same meaning if the noun

---

[617] Cf. BHRG §12; GKC §140–67; IBHS §8.1–8.4, 38–40; JM §153–77; Meek 1945; Kroeze 2003.

[618] Cf. GKC §154; IBHS §39.2.1c; JM §177a; Thorion 1985; Gibson 1995. Word order, however, can be very helpful in detecting subordination; see Niccacci 1994a, 127–8. Talstra 1997b argues that there is less parataxis in Hebrew than commonly supposed.

[619] Cf. GBHS §5.2.1; IBHS §38.8; JM §157; Grossberg 1980.

clause were replaced with a noun or a pronoun. For example, in the sentence 'Baruch wrote what Jeremiah said,' the clause 'what Jeremiah said' functions as a noun, as can be checked by replacing it with a pronoun such as 'it' (yielding 'Baruch wrote it'). Substantival clauses are also called **noun clauses** or **constituent noun clauses**.[620]

- In Hebrew, the first word of a substantival clause is often אֲשֶׁר 'which' (§464) or כִּי 'that' (§451a). Occasionally substantival clauses begin with the article (הַ֯ 'the') (§91). Substantival clauses that have an accusative function in the larger sentence are sometimes introduced by the accusative particle אֵת (§475a–h). Many substantival clauses are **asyndetic**, meaning that they begin with none of these words.

- Substantival clauses are classified based on their function in the larger sentence as nominative, genitive, or accusative.

Nominative substantival clauses [621]

484   **Subject clause.**[622] A clause can function as the subject of another clause.

- וּלְשָׁאוּל   הֻגַּד   כִּי־   נִמְלַט   דָּוִד   מִקְּעִילָה
  from Keilah   David   escaped   that   was told   and to Saul   1 Sam 23:13

           That David had escaped from Keilah was told to Saul.

- A similar example is 1 Sam 27:4.

485   **Clause in apposition to a nominative substantive.**[623] A clause can be in apposition (§65–71) to a nominative (§32–5).

- וְהִנֵּה   אֱמֶת   נָכוֹן   הַדָּבָר   נֶעֶשְׂתָה   הַתּוֹעֵבָה
  THE ABOMINATION   WAS DONE   *the report*   certain   truth   and if   Deut 13:15, 17:4

       and if *the report* THAT THE ABOMINATION HAPPENED is true and certain

486   **Predicate nominative clause.**[624] See §33a.

- וְזֶה   אֲשֶׁר   תַּעֲשֶׂה   אֹתָהּ   And this is *how you will make it.*
  it   you will make   how   and this   Gen 6:15

---

[620] Cf. IBHS §38.8a. The terms 'noun-clause' (GKC §140) and 'nominal clause' (GBHS §5.1.1; JM §154) are often used to refer to what this book calls a 'verbless clause.'

[621] Cf. GBHS §5.2.1(a); IBHS §38.8b; JM §157a.

[622] Cf. GBHS §5.2.1(a); IBHS §38.8b; JM §157a. As stated in prior editions of this textbook, it is often possible to understand a clause that follows the discourse marker וַיְהִי as a nominative substantival clause that is the subject of the verb וַיְהִי 'and (it) happened that.'

[623] Cf. GKC §131a; IBHS §12.1–12.2, 38.8b; JM §131a, 157a; Thorion 1985.

[624] Cf. GBHS §5.2.1(a); IBHS §38.8b; JM §157a.

- וְזֶה אֲשֶׁר תַּעֲשֶׂה עַל־הַמִּזְבֵּחַ   This is *what you will offer on the altar.*
  the altar   on   you will offer   what   and this   Exod 29:38

487   Subject clause in an interrogative sentence.[625]

- הֲכִי יֵשׁ־עוֹד אֲשֶׁר נוֹתָר לְבֵית שָׁאוּל
  Saul   to house of   is left   who   still   there is   that?   2 Sam 9:1
  Is it the case that there is still *someone left of Saul's house?*

- אַף כִּי־אָמַר אֱלֹהִים לֹא תֹאכְלוּ מִכֹּל עֵץ הַגָּן
  the garden   tree of   from all   you will eat   not   God   said   that   really?   Gen 3:1
  Is it really the case *that God has said, 'You will not eat from any tree of the garden'?*

488   Subject clause with an adjectival predicate.[626] A clause can serve as the subject of a sentence with an adjective as the predicate (§75).

- טוֹב אֲשֶׁר לֹא־תִדֹּר מִשֶּׁתִּדּוֹר וְלֹא תְשַׁלֵּם
  pay   and not   than that you vow   you vow   not   that   BETTER   Eccl 5:4
  That you not vow IS BETTER than that you should vow and not pay.

- טוֹב אֲשֶׁר תֶּאֱחֹז בָּזֶה
  this   you grasp   that   GOOD   *That you grasp this is* GOOD.   Eccl 7:18

Genitive substantival clauses

489   A genitive substantival clause is a clause that immediately follows a preposition or a word in the construct state (§36). It can begin with אֲשֶׁר or כִּי, or it can be asyndetic (i.e., without any introductory particle).[627]

- מְקוֹם אֲשֶׁר־אֲסִירֵי הַמֶּלֶךְ אֲסוּרִים
  imprisoned   the king   prisoners of   WHERE   place of   Gen 39:20 (אֲשֶׁר)
  the place WHERE *the king's prisoners were imprisoned*

- תְּחִלַּת דִּבֶּר־יְהוָה בְּהוֹשֵׁעַ
  through Hosea   YHWH   spoke   beginning of   Hos 1:2
  the beginning of *YHWH speaking through Hosea*

- Other examples include Gen 40:3 (אֲשֶׁר), 31:20; Lev 7:35, 13:46 (אֲשֶׁר); Num 9:18 (אֲשֶׁר); Josh 23:1 (אֲשֶׁר); Judg 3:12 (כִּי); 1 Sam 25:15; 2 Kgs 8:6; Amos 2:8; Job 16:17.

Accusative substantival clauses

490   Direct object clause.[628] Also called an **object clause**, an **objective**

---

[625] Cf. GBHS §5.2.1(a); JM §157a.
[626] Cf. GBHS §5.2.1(a).
[627] Cf. GBHS §5.2.1(b); IBHS §38.8c; JM §129p–q.
[628] Cf. GBHS §5.2.1(c); GKC §157; IBHS §38.8d; JM §157b-d.

clause, or an *oratio obliqua*, a direct object clause is the direct object of a verb (§50). Most begin with כִּי, but some begin with אֲשֶׁר or are asyndetic.

- וַיַּרְא יְהוָה כִּי רַבָּה רָעַת הָאָדָם

  the man   evil of   great   that   YHWH   saw   Gen 6:5

  YHWH saw *that mankind's evil was great.*

- וַיַּרְא שָׁאוּל אֲשֶׁר־הוּא מַשְׂכִּיל מְאֹד   Saul saw *that he was very successful.*

  very   successful   he   that   Saul   saw   1 Sam 18:15

- Other examples include Deut 16:12; Judg 9:48; 1 Sam 24:11; 2 Kgs 8:5, 8:12.

491 **Adverbial clause of manner (by …-ing).**[629] A clause can function like an adverbial accusative of manner (§60). Such clauses are usually asyndetic (i.e., with no introductory particle), although they occasionally begin with וְ. The subject or a prepositional phrase usually precedes the verb (§576).

- וַיָּבֹא אֲלֵיהֶם יְהוֹשֻׁעַ פִּתְאֹם כָּל־הַלַּיְלָה עָלָה

  went up   the night   all of   suddenly   Joshua   to them   came   Josh 10:9

  Joshua came upon them suddenly *by marching up all night.*

- וַיַּעֲשׂוּ … אֶת־הָרַע … וַיַּעַבְדוּ אֶת־הַבְּעָלִים

  the Baals   they served   the evil   they did   Judg 2:11

  They did … evil … *by serving the Baals.*

  o This adverbial clause is unusual because the verb is first and it begins with וְ.

- An adverbial clause is negated with לֹא if it portrays something as a fact, whereas it is negated with אַל if it expresses a command, desire, etc.

- וַיַּעֲשֶׂה הָרַע … לֹא סָר   He did evil … *by not turning away.*

  he turned   not   the evil   he did   2 Kgs 13:11 (לֹא for a fact)

- חֲזַק … אַל־תָּסוּר מִמֶּנּוּ   Be strong … *by not turning away from it.*

  from it   you will turn   not   be strong!   Josh 1:7 (אַל for a command)

- Other examples include Deut 9:16 (verb first) and Judg 2:12.

492 **Accusative of specification clause.** A clause can function as an accusative of specification (also called an **accusative of limitation**, §57a). Such clauses begin with אֲשֶׁר or אֶת אֲשֶׁר.

- וַיִּקְרָא … שֵׁם הַמָּקוֹם … אֲשֶׁר יֵאָמֵר הַיּוֹם

  the day   he will say   as   the place   name of   he called   Gen 22:14

  He called … the name of the place … *as it is said today.*

493 **Determinative accusative clause.** See §59.

- הֲלֹא־הֻגַּד לַאדֹנִי אֵת אֲשֶׁר־עָשִׂיתִי   Has not *what I did* been told to my lord?

  I did   what   to my lord   was told   not?   1 Kgs 18:13

---

[629] Cf. IBHS §38.8d; JM §177g; Meek 1929.

- וַיֻּגַּד   לְדָוִד אֶת אֲשֶׁר־ עָשְׂתָה   *What she did* was told to David.
  she did   what   to David   was told   2 Sam 21:11

B Circumstantial Clauses [630]

- **A circumstantial clause** describes the manner, circumstances, or conditions under which the main clause occurs. For example, in the sentence 'I slept *while the sun was shining*' the circumstantial clause 'while the sun was shining' indicates the conditions under which 'I slept' occurred. Such clauses can often be translated beginning with 'while,' 'with,' 'inasmuch as,' 'since,' 'seeing that,' or 'now that.'
- It can be difficult to decide if a clause is circumstantial (§494–5), temporal (§496–510), or causal (§533–5). The difference is a matter of emphasis. In the example 'I slept *while the sun was shining*,' if the time is emphasized, then the 'while' clause is temporal, whereas if the weather is emphasized, then the 'while' clause is circumstantial.
- Circumstantial clauses usually begin with וְ (וַ of accompaniment, §436), then the subject, then the predicate (§582).

494   **A concomitant circumstantial clause**[631] occurs at the same time as the main clause. Its predicate may be a participle (§219), a predicate adjective (§75), a prepositional phrase, or a copulative demonstrative (§115).

- בָּאֵשׁ   בֹּעֵר   וְהָהָר   *while the mountain* WAS BURNING *with fire*
  with (the) fire   BURNING   and the mountain   Deut 5:23 (participle)

- וְהָרָעָב   חָזָק   בְּשֹׁמְרוֹן   *while the famine* WAS SEVERE *in Samaria*
  in Samaria   SEVERE   and the famine   1 Kgs 18:2 (predicate adjective)

- וְהָאִישׁ   נֹשֵׂא   הַצִּנָּה   לְפָנָיו   *with his shield bearer* BEFORE HIM
  BEFORE HIM *the shield   carrying   and the man*   1 Sam 17:41 (prepositional phrase)

- פֶּסַח   הוּא   לַיהוָה   *since* IT IS *YHWH's Passover*
  to YHWH   (IT)   Passover   Exod 12:11 (anaphoric demonstrative pronoun)

  o   This circumstantial clause is unusual because it does not begin with וְ.

- Other examples include Gen 11:4; Exod 22:9 (no וְ); 2 Kgs 8:7.

495a   **An antecedent circumstantial clause**[632] explains circumstances that precede the main clause. Its predicate is a perfect verb.

---

[630] Cf. GBHS §5.2.11; GKC §156; JM §159; Driver 1892, 211; Gibson 1995.
[631] Cf. GBHS §5.2.11; GKC §141e, 142d–e, 156; JM §159; Steiner 2000.
[632] Cf. GBHS §5.2.11.

- אַל־ תְּאַחֲרוּ אֹתִי וַיהוָה הִצְלִיחַ דַּרְכִּי

my way MADE SUCCESSFUL *and YHWH* me (you) delay not   Gen 24:56

Do not delay me, *now that YHWH* HAS MADE *my trip* SUCCESSFUL.

- וַאֲבִימֶלֶךְ לֹא קָרַב אֵלֶיהָ וַיֹּאמַר

he said *to her* APPROACHED *not and Abimelech*   Gen 20:4

Now Abimelech HAD *not* APPROACHED *her*, and he said …

- Other possible examples include Gen 1:2, 26:27; 2 Kgs 3:22.

495b **A subsequent circumstantial clause**[633] explains circumstances that occur after the main clause. Its predicate is an imperfect verb.

- הַמְכַסֶּה אֲנִי מֵאַבְרָהָם אֲשֶׁר אֲנִי עֹשֶׂה

doing I what from Abraham I hiding?   Gen 18:17–18

וְאַבְרָהָם הָיוֹ יִהְיֶה לְגוֹי גָּדוֹל וְעָצוּם

and mighty great (to) *nation* WILL BECOME (to be) *and Abraham*   (cont.)

Shall I hide from Abraham what I am about to do,

since Abraham WILL *certainly* BECOME *a great and mighty nation*?

C   Temporal Clauses [634]

- A **temporal clause** indicates the time when another clause occurs.

496 **Temporal clause beginning with an imperfect waw consecutive (when).**[635] Such temporal clauses are often used in past time narratives.

- A clause beginning with an imperfect waw consecutive (§178) can have a variety of functions. Only the context indicates when such a clause is temporal.

- וַתֹּאמֶר לְהַשְׁקֹתוֹ וַתְּכַל

and she said *to give him a drink* SHE FINISHED   Gen 24:19

WHEN SHE FINISHED *giving him a drink*, she said …

497 **Temporal clause beginning with כִּי (when).** See §445.

- וַיִּשְׁקֵף הַיָּמִים שָׁם לוֹ־ אָרְכוּ כִּי וַיְהִי

he looked down *the days* there *to him were long* WHEN (it was)   Gen 26:8

WHEN *he had been there a long time*, he looked down.

498 **Temporal clause beginning with a preposition.**[636] §499–502 describe how a variety of prepositions are used to form temporal clauses.

---

[633] Cf. GBHS §5.2.11.

[634] Cf. GBHS §5.2.4; GKC §164; IBHS §38.7; JM §166; Van der Merwe 1996; Van der Merwe 1997.

[635] Cf. GBHS §5.2.4b; GKC §111d, 164b; JM §166a–i, 167f–g.

499 **Temporal clause beginning with בְּ (when). See §241.**

- A temporal clause never begins with בַּאֲשֶׁר (contrast §500b).

- חַי ... בְּעוֹדֶנּוּ נָתַן אַבְרָהָם מַתָּנֹת Abraham gave gifts WHILE *he was still alive.*
  alive WHEN *he still* gifts Abraham gave   Gen 25:6

- מָנַעְתִּי מִכֶּם אֶת־הַגֶּשֶׁם בְּעוֹד שְׁלֹשָׁה חֳדָשִׁים לַקָּצִיר
  to the harvest months three WHEN *still* the rain from you I withheld Amos 4:7
  I withheld the rain from you WHEN *there were still three months to the harvest.*

500a **A temporal clause that begins with כְּ / כְּמוֹ (as soon as)** indicates the precise time when something happens (§262a).

- כְּמוֹ הַשַּׁחַר עָלָה וַיָּאִיצוּ הַמַּלְאָכִים בְּלוֹט
  (בְּ) Lot the angels they urged *rose the dawn* AS SOON AS   Gen 19:15
  AS SOON AS *dawn broke*, the angels urged Lot.

500b **A temporal clause that begins with כַּאֲשֶׁר** means 'when' (§262b).

- וַיְהִי כַּאֲשֶׁר כִּלּוּ ... וַיִּקַּח הָאִישׁ נֶזֶם זָהָב
  gold ring of the man took *they finished* WHEN (it was)   Gen 24:22
  WHEN *they finished* … the man took a gold ring.

501 **A temporal clause that begins with אַחַר / אַחֲרֵי (after)** indicates something that occurs before the main clause (§360). The preposition אַחֲרֵי can be followed by אֲשֶׁר, but there is no change in meaning.

- אַחֲרֵי הֵסַבּוּ אֹתוֹ וַתְּהִי יַד־יְהוָה בָּעִיר
  against the city YHWH hand of was *it they brought around* AFTER   1 Sam 5:9
  AFTER *they brought it around*, YHWH's hand was against the city.

- אַחֲרֵי אֲשֶׁר־כָּרְתוּ לָהֶם בְּרִית וַיִּשְׁמְעוּ
  they heard *covenant with them they cut* AFTER   Josh 9:16
  AFTER *they made a covenant with them*, they heard …

502 **A temporal clause that begins with עַד (until)** indicates the time when the main clause ends (§311). The preposition עַד can be followed by אֲשֶׁר or כִּי with no change in meaning.

- וְלֹא־הֶאֱמַנְתִּי לַדְּבָרִים עַד אֲשֶׁר־בָּאתִי
  I came UNTIL (לְ) the words I believed not   1 Kgs 10:7
  But I did not believe the report UNTIL *I came.*

---

[636] Because such a clause is the object of a preposition, it is also a genitive substantival clause (§489). Some grammarians regard such a structure as a prepositional phrase rather than a clause that begins with a preposition.

- וַיִּצְבֹּר יוֹסֵף בָּר... עַד כִּי־ חָדַל לִסְפֹּר •

  to count he stopped UNTIL grain Joseph He piled up   Gen 41:49

  Joseph piled up grain … UNTIL *he stopped counting*.

- Another possible example is 1 Kgs 17:17.

503 **Temporal infinitival phrase beginning with a preposition.** If the object of a preposition contains an infinitive but not a finite verb, it can be considered to be a phrase (§504–8) rather than a clause (§496–502).

504 **Temporal phrase with בְּ + infinitive (when).** See §241.

- בִּהְיוֹתָם בַּשָּׂדֶה וַיָּקָם קַיִן •

  WHEN *they* WERE *in the field*, Cain rose up.

  Cain rose up *in the field* WHEN *they* TO BE   Gen 4:8

- וְיוֹסֵף בֶּן־ שְׁלֹשִׁים שָׁנָה בְּעָמְדוֹ לִפְנֵי פַרְעֹה •

  Pharaoh *before* WHEN *he* TO STAND year of thirty son and Joseph   Gen 41:46

  And Joseph was thirty years old WHEN *he* STOOD *before Pharaoh*.

505 **Temporal phrase with כְּ + infinitive (as soon as).** See §262a.

- כְּבוֹא אַבְרָם מִצְרַיְמָה וַיִּרְאוּ הַמִּצְרִים •

  the Egyptians saw *toward Egypt* *Abram* AS SOON AS TO COME   Gen 12:14

  AS SOON AS *Abram* CAME *into Egypt*, the Egyptians saw …

- כְּהוֹצִיאָם אֹתָם הַחוּצָה וַיֹּאמֶר •

  he said *toward the outside* *them* AS SOON AS TO BRING *them* OUT   Gen 19:17

  AS SOON AS *they* BROUGHT *them* OUT, he said …

506 **Temporal phrase with אַחֲרֵי + infinitive (after).** See §360 and §501.

- וַיֵּצֵא מֶלֶךְ־ סְדֹם ... אַחֲרֵי שׁוּבוֹ •

  his TO RETURN AFTER Sodom king of went out   Gen 14:17

  The king of Sodom went out … AFTER *he* RETURNED …

- וַיָּשָׁב יוֹסֵף מִצְרַיְמָה ... אַחֲרֵי קָבְרוֹ אֶת־אָבִיו •

  his father *his* TO BURY AFTER *toward Egypt* Joseph returned   Gen 40:14

  Joseph returned to Egypt … AFTER *he* BURIED *his father*.

507 **Temporal phrase with לִפְנֵי + infinitive (before).** See §371.

- כִּי אִם־ לִפְנֵי־ בוֹא הַשֶּׁמֶשׁ אֶטְעַם •

  I (will) eat *the sun* TO ENTER BEFORE if   if I eat BEFORE *the sun* SETS

                                              2 Sam 3:35

- הַשֶּׁמֶשׁ יֵהָפֵךְ לְחֹשֶׁךְ ... לִפְנֵי בּוֹא יוֹם יְהוָה •

  of YHWH *day* TO COME BEFORE to darkness will turn the sun   Joel 3:4

  The sun will turn to darkness … BEFORE *the day of YHWH* COMES.

508 **Temporal phrase with עַד + infinitive (until).** See §311 and §502.

- וְיָשַׁבְתָּ עִמּוֹ ... עַד־ שׁוּב אַף־ אָחִיךָ •

  your brother *anger of* TO RETURN UNTIL with him (you will) stay   Gen 27:43–44

  Stay with him … UNTIL *your brother's anger* SUBSIDES.

- לֹא אוּכַל לַעֲשׂוֹת דָּבָר עַד־ בֹּאֲךָ שָׁמָּה
  toward there you TO ENTER UNTIL thing to do I am able not   Gen 19:22

  I am not able to do anything UNTIL you ENTER there.

509   **Temporal clause beginning with טֶרֶם / בְּטֶרֶם (before).**[637] A temporal clause with an imperfect verb can begin with טֶרֶם or בְּטֶרֶם. The event of the main clause happens before the event of the temporal clause. If the event of the main clause is past time, the event of the temporal clause is usually also past time. If the event of the main clause is future time, the event of the temporal clause is necessarily also future time, since it occurs after the main clause. The imperfect tense is used because the action is viewed from the standpoint of its being incomplete (§167).

- וָאֹכַל מִכֹּל בְּטֶרֶם תָּבוֹא
  you entered BEFORE from all I ate   I ate from all of it BEFORE you entered.
                                               Gen 27:33 (past time)

- וְאֶרְאֶנּוּ בְּטֶרֶם אָמוּת
  I will die BEFORE and I will see him   I will see him BEFORE I die.
                                               Gen 45:28 (future time)

- Other examples include Gen 19:4, 24:45, 27:4; Exod 1:19; Ps 39:14; Ezek 16:57.

510   **Temporal clause or phrase beginning with מִדֵּי (as often as).** A temporal clause with an imperfect verb or a temporal phrase with an infinitive construct can begin with מִדֵּי. The word מִדֵּי is a compound of the preposition מִן 'from' and the construct form of the noun דַּי 'sufficiency.'

- מִדֵּי אֲדַבֵּר אֶזְעָק
  I cry out I speak AS OFTEN AS   AS OFTEN AS I speak, I cry out.
                                            Jer 20:8 (imperfect)

- מִדֵּי־ בֹא הַמֶּלֶךְ בֵּית יְהוָה
  YHWH house of the king to enter AS OFTEN AS   1 Kgs 14:28 (infinitive)

  AS OFTEN AS the king entered the house of YHWH

D Conditional Sentences (if-then) [638]

- A **conditional sentence** is an 'if-then' statement. For example, 'If it rains, then I will get wet.'
- The **protasis** (also called the **condition** or a **conditional clause**) is the 'if' part of a conditional sentence (e.g., 'If it rains').
- The **apodosis** is the 'then' part of a conditional sentence (e.g., 'then I will become wet').

---

[637] Cf. BHRG §41.2.2; GBHS §5.2.4(b); GKC §152r, 164c; IBHS §38.7a; JM §104b, 160n.

[638] Cf. GBHS §5.2.2; GKC §159; IBHS §38.2; JM §167; Driver 1892, 174–94; Gordis 1930.

Apodosis ('then')

511 **The apodosis of a conditional clause** usually begins with a resumptive וְ (§440), but can also begin with אָז or כִּי אָז,[639] or without a conjunction.[640]

- אִם־הַשְּׂמֹאל   וְאֵימִנָה   If [you choose] the left, THEN *I will go right.*

  THEN *I will go right*   the left   if   Gen 13:9 (וְ)

- אִם־ תְּבַקְשֶׁנָּה ... אָז   תָּבִין   יִרְאַת יְהוָה

  YHWH   *fear of*   *you will understand*   THEN   *you seek her*   if   Prov 2:4–5 (אָז)

  If you seek her ... THEN *you will understand the fear of YHWH.*

- לוּ אַבְשָׁלוֹם   חַי ... כִּי־אָז   יָשָׁר   בְּעֵינֶיךָ

  in your eyes   *right*   THEN   *living*   Absalom   if   2 Sam 19:7 (כִּי אָז)

  If Absalom were alive ... THEN *it would be right in your eyes.*

- כִּי־ תִמְצָא אִישׁ   לֹא   תְבָרְכֶנּוּ   If you meet anyone, *do not greet him.*

  bless him   not   anyone   you meet   if   2 Kgs 4:29 (no conjunction)

Protasis ('if') – real condition

- A **real condition** is a protasis that is presented as one that has been or could be fulfilled,[641] such as 'If I finish the assignment tonight ...'
- Sections §512–15 discuss different ways to write a protasis in Hebrew that presents a real condition.

512 **Real condition beginning with וְ.**[642] The protasis of a real condition can begin with the conjunction וְ 'and' prefixed to the verb of the protasis. Such a protasis is sometimes called a **virtual conditional**, or the clauses are said to be **juxtaposed**.

- וְעָזַב אֶת־אָבִיו   וָמֵת   IF *he leaves his father*, he will die.

  then he will die   *his father*   IF he leaves   Gen 44:22

- וְרָאִיתִי מָה   וְהִגַּדְתִּי   לָךְ   IF *I see anything*, I will tell you.

  to you   then I will tell   *anything*   IF I see   1 Sam 19:3

513 **Real condition that is a circumstantial clause.** The protasis of a real condition can be written as a circumstantial clause (§494–5b), that is, with the subject preceding the verb, and perhaps introduced with וְ.

---

[639] Cf. BHRG §40.4.1; GBHS §4.2.1(c).

[640] Cf. JM §167a; Rooker 1990, 120–1.

[641] We say 'presented as' because it is possible for a speaker to be mistaken or to lie. The distinction between real and unreal conditions is not an issue of their actual reality, but of how the speaker talks about them.

[642] Cf. BHRG §21.3.4(ii); JM §167b.

- הַדָּבָר הֲיִהְיֶה אֲרֻבּוֹת בַּשָּׁמַיִם עֹשֶׂה יְהוָה הִנֵּה
  the thing   will happen?   *in the sky   windows   making   YHWH   (behold)*   2 Kgs 7:2

  Even if YHWH makes windows in the sky, could the thing happen?

  o This is a real condition because the speaker is saying, 'Even if YHWH did a miracle (and for the sake of argument, let's assume that he does), then what you describe still could not happen.' The protasis is written as a circumstantial clause because the subject precedes the verb, although the expected וְ is absent.

- אֲלֵהֶם אֹמַר מָה ... בָא אָנֹכִי הִנֵּה   *If I come* … then what will I say to them?
  to them   I will say   what?   *come   I   (behold)*   Exod 3:13

514 Real condition beginning with the particle הֵן.[643] This is disputed.

- This may be related to the use of הֵן for 'if' in Biblical Aramaic (e.g., Ezra 4:13).

- רָשָׁע כִּי־ אַף יְשֻׁלָּם בָּאָרֶץ צַדִּיק הֵן
  wicked   all the more   *will be repaid   in the earth   righteous*   IF   Prov 11:31

  IF *the righteous is repaid on earth*, how much more so the wicked!

- אֵלֶיהָ הֲיָשׁוּב ... אֶת־אִשְׁתּוֹ אִישׁ יְשַׁלַּח הֵן
  to her   he will return?   *his wife   man   sends away*   IF   Jer 3:1

  IF *a man divorces his wife* … will he return to her?

515 Real condition with the particle אִם, כִּי, or אֲשֶׁר. The protasis of a real condition can begin with the particle אִם (§453), the particle כִּי (§446), or the particle אֲשֶׁר (very rare, §469).

- The time of the condition depends on the conjugation (aspect) of its verb. A perfect verb in the protasis typically indicates past time. An imperfect verb can indicate future time or iterative action in the past, present, or future. A participle typically indicates present time or imminent future time.

- תַעֲבֹר אַל־נָא בְּעֵינֶיךָ חֵן מָצָאתִי אִם־נָא
  you pass by   not   *in your eyes   favour   I have found*   IF   Gen 18:3

  IF *I have found favour in your eyes*, do not pass by.

- אִישֵׁךְ תַּחַת שָׂטִית כִּי
  your husband   under authority of   *you have gone astray*   IF   Num 5:20

  IF *you have gone astray while under your husband's authority*

- יִסָּעוּ וְלֹא הֶעָנָן יֵעָלֶה לֹא וְאִם־
  they would set out   then not   *the cloud   was taken up   not   but* IF   Exod 40:37

  But IF *the cloud was not taken up*, then they would not set out.

---

[643] Cf. BHRG §44.2; GBHS §5.2.2(a); IBHS §38.2d; JM §1671; Garr 2004, 336–9. BHRG §44.2 states: 'Although it is claimed that הֵן indicates a conditional clause, the conditional function may be ascribed to the context rather than to הֵן itself.'

- וְאִם לֹא תֵיטִיב •
  you do well　not　but IF

  but IF *you do not do well*
  Gen 4:7

- אֲשֶׁר תִּשְׁמְעוּ אֶל־מִצְוֹת יְהוָה •
  of YHWH　commands　(to) you obey　IF

  IF *you obey YHWH's commands*
  Deut 11:17

- אִם־יִהְיֶה אֱלֹהִים עִמָּדִי •
  with me　God　will be　IF

  IF *God will be with me*
  Gen 28:20

- אִם־לֹקֵחַ יַעֲקֹב אִשָּׁה •
  woman　Jacob　going to marry　IF

  IF *Jacob is going to marry a woman*
  Gen 27:46

- When a clause begins with כִּי or אֲשֶׁר and the reference is to a future time, it may be difficult to decide if the clause is conditional (§446, 469) or temporal (§445).[644]

  - אֲשֶׁר יִשְׁאָלוּן בְּנֵיכֶם מָחָר אֶת־אֲבוֹתָם
    their fathers　in the future　your sons　will ask　IF
    Josh 4:21

    IF / WHEN *in the future your sons ask their fathers*

Protasis ('if') – unreal condition

- An **unreal condition** (also called a **condition contrary to fact**) is a protasis that is presented as one that has not and could not be fulfilled,[645] such as 'If I were you ...'

516a **An unreal condition can begin with the particle** לוּ / לֹא / לוּא. See §459a. לֹא is occasionally misvocalized as לֹא. Most unreal conditions are in the past time, using a perfect verb to describe something as not having happened. An unreal condition is rarely in the present or future; when it is, it uses a participle to describe something as not going to happen.

- לוּ הַחֲיִתֶם אוֹתָם לֹא הָרַגְתִּי אֶתְכֶם •
  you　I killed　not　*them　you let live*　IF
  Judg 8:19

  IF *you had let them live*, then I would not kill you.

- לוּ אַבְשָׁלוֹם חַי ... כִּי־אָז יָשָׁר בְּעֵינֶיךָ •
  in your eyes　right　then　*alive　Absalom*　IF
  2 Sam 19:6

  IF *Absalom were alive* ... then you would be pleased.

- Other examples include Judg 13:23 and 2 Sam 18:12 (qere).

516b **A negative unreal condition begins with** לוּלֵי / לוּלֵא (**if not**). See §459b.

---

[644] Cf. GBHS §4.3.4f.

[645] We use the terminology 'presented as' because it is possible for a speaker to lie or to be mistaken. What is relevant for a condition being unreal is not the unreality of the event, but that the speaker refers to it as being unreal.

- לוּלֵא הִתְמַהְמָהְנוּ כִּי־ עַתָּה שַׁבְנוּ
  we returned now surely *we delayed* IF NOT   Gen 43:10

  IF *we had* NOT *delayed*, we surely could have returned by now.

- לוּלֵי פְּנֵי יְהוֹשָׁפָט ... אֲנִי נֹשֵׂא   if *I did* NOT *respect Jehoshaphat*
  respecting I Jehoshaphat (face of) IF NOT   2 Kgs 3:14

516c **Unreal condition with אִלּוּ.** The word אִלּוּ is used twice in the Hebrew
Bible, both times to introduce the protasis of an unreal condition.

- וְאִלּוּ חָיָה אֶלֶף שָׁנִים פַּעֲמַיִם   if *he lived a thousand years twice over*
  twice years thousand of he lived (but) IF   Eccl 6:6

- וְאִלּוּ לַעֲבָדִים וְלִשְׁפָחוֹת נִמְכַּרְנוּ
  we were sold and as female slaves as male slaves (but) IF   Esth 7:4

  IF *we had only been sold as male and female slaves*

517 **Unreal condition with כִּי or אִם.** On rare occasions, the protasis of an
unreal condition begins with כִּי (§446) or אִם (§453).

- כִּי אָמַרְתִּי יֶשׁ־ לִי תִקְוָה   if *I said that I had hope*
  hope to me there is I said IF   Ruth 1:12

- אִם־ אֶרְעַב לֹא־ אֹמַר לָךְ   if *I were hungry*, I would not tell you.
  to you I will say not *I will be hungry* IF   Ps 50:12

E Purpose Clauses (in order that) [646]

- A **purpose clause** explains why the action of another clause happens,
  in the sense of a goal, purpose, or motivation.[647] A purpose clause
  answers the questions What motivates the person to do it? What are
  they trying to accomplish? What is their goal? Purpose clauses can
  often be translated beginning with 'in order that,' 'that,' or 'so that.'

- Purpose clauses are also called **telic clauses**, **final clauses**, or
  conclusion clauses. The term **telic clauses** is sometimes used to refer
  to both purpose clauses (§518–24) and result clauses (§525–7).

- If purpose is expressed with an infinitive construct instead of a finite
  verb, the text contains a purpose phrase instead of a purpose clause.
  Purpose phrases can often be translated beginning with 'in order to.'

---

[646] Cf. GBHS §5.2.3(a), (c); GKC §165; IBHS §38.3; JM §168; Mitchell 1915; Sutcliffe
1954.
[647] Causal clauses (§533–5) also explain why another clause happens, but they answer a
different question. Instead of addressing the issue of goal, purpose, or motivation, causal
clauses address the issue of cause and effect.

- §518–24 describe different ways of writing a purpose clause or phrase in Hebrew.

518   **Purpose clause with וְ and the jussive or cohortative**. See §181a, 187.

- וְהָבִיאָה   לִּי   וְאֹכֵלָה   Bring it to me IN ORDER THAT *I may eat.*
  AND *I shall eat*   to me   and bring!   Gen 27:4 (cohortative)

- וְיֵרָא   אֲלֵיכֶם   כְּבוֹד   יְהוָה   IN ORDER THAT *YHWH's glory appear to you*
  YHWH   glory of   to you   AND *may appear*   Lev 9:6 (jussive)

519   **Purpose clause with וְ and the imperative**. See §181a, 189.

- וּבָמָה   אֲכַפֵּר   וּבָרְכוּ   אֶת־נַחֲלַת   יְהוָה
  YHWH   inheritance of   AND *bless!*   I will atone   and in what?   2 Sam 21:3
  And how can I atone IN ORDER THAT *you bless YHWH's inheritance?*

- פְּנוּ־אֵלַי   וְהִוָּשְׁעוּ   Turn to me IN ORDER THAT *you be saved!*
  AND *be saved!*   to me   turn!   Isa 45:22

520   **Purpose with לְ or לְמַעַן and an infinitive construct**. Purpose can be expressed with an infinitive construct (§197) that is preceded by the preposition לְ 'to' (§277) or the preposition לְמַעַן (§367).

- וַיַּעֲלֶה   אַחְאָב   לֶאֱכֹל   וְלִשְׁתּוֹת   Ahab went up IN ORDER *to eat* and *to drink.*
  and TO *drink*   TO *eat*   Ahab   he went up   1 Kgs 18:42

- הַצִּיל   אֹתוֹ   לְמַעַן   IN ORDER *to rescue him*
  him   *to rescue*   IN ORDER THAT   Gen 37:22

521   **Purpose clause with לְמַעַן and the imperfect**. A purpose clause can begin with לְמַעַן followed by an imperfect verb (§175, 367). The particle אֲשֶׁר sometimes follows לְמַעַן in such a construction.

- נִשְׁמָע   לְמַעַן אֲשֶׁר   יִיטַב־   לָנוּ
  to us   *it will go well*   IN ORDER THAT   we will obey   Jer 42:6
  We will obey IN ORDER THAT *it go well with us.*

- אִמְרִי־נָא   אֲחֹתִי   אָתְּ   לְמַעַן   יִיטַב־   לִי
  with me   *it will go well*   IN ORDER THAT   you   my sister   say!   Gen 12:13
  Say that you are my sister IN ORDER THAT *it go well with me.*

522a   **Purpose clause with בַּעֲבוּר and the imperfect**.[648] A purpose clause can begin with בַּעֲבוּר followed by an imperfect verb (§175). The particle אֲשֶׁר sometimes follows בַּעֲבוּר in such a construction.

- וְהָבִיאָה   לִּי ... בַּעֲבוּר   תְּבָרֶכְךָ   נַפְשִׁי
  my soul   *may bless you*   IN ORDER THAT   to me   and bring!   Gen 27:4
  Bring it to me ... IN ORDER THAT *my soul may bless you.*

---

[648] Cf. BHRG §40.7; GBHS §5.2.3(a); GKC §165b; Gaenssle 1915a, 158.

- לְעֵדָה   לִי   תִּהְיֶה־   בַּעֲבוּר •

  as witness   for me   it will be   IN ORDER THAT

  IN ORDER THAT *it be a witness for me*

  Gen 21:30

- Another example is Gen 27:10.

522b **Purpose with בַּעֲבוּר / לְבַעֲבוּר and an infinitive construct**. See §197.

- אֶת־כֹּחִי   הַרְאֹתְךָ   בַּעֲבוּר   הֶעֱמַדְתִּיךָ •

  my power   to make you see   IN ORDER TO   *I made you stand*

  Exod 9:16

  I caused you to stand, IN ORDER *to make you see my power*.

- אֶת־הָעִיר   חֲקוֹר   בַּעֲבוּר •

  the city   to spy out   IN ORDER TO

  IN ORDER *to spy out the city*

  2 Sam 10:3

- לְבַעֲבוּר is used three times: Exod 20:20; 2 Sam 14:20, 17:14.

523 **Purpose clause with אֲשֶׁר**. Very rarely, a purpose clause can begin with אֲשֶׁר (§466) followed by an imperfect verb (§175).

- לְךָ   יִיטַב   אֲשֶׁר   ... אֶת־חֻקָּיו   וְשָׁמַרְתָּ •

  to you   it will go well   IN ORDER THAT   *his statutes   you will keep*

  Deut 4:40

  You will keep his statutes … IN ORDER THAT *it go well with you*.

- יֵדְעוּן   אֲשֶׁר   גַּדֶּלְךָ ...   אָחֵל •

  they will know   IN ORDER THAT   *to make you great   I will begin*

  Josh 3:7

  I will begin to make you great … IN ORDER THAT *they know*

524 **Negative purpose (in order that not)**. A negative purpose (that is, a purpose to prevent something) is often expressed with לְבִלְתִּי (§424) followed by an imperfect verb (§175) or an infinitive construct (§197). לְמַעַן אֲשֶׁר לֹא or לְמַעַן לֹא (§367, 521) is sometimes used instead of לְבִלְתִּי.

- תֶּחֱטָאוּ   לְבִלְתִּי ...   הָאֱלֹהִים   בָּא •

  you will sin   IN ORDER THAT NOT   *God   came*

  Exod 20:20

  God has come … IN ORDER THAT *you* NOT *sin*.

- מֹצְאוֹ   כָּל־   אֹתוֹ   הַכּוֹת־   לְבִלְתִּי •

  finding him   any of   him   to strike   IN ORDER THAT NOT

  Gen 4:15

  IN ORDER THAT *anyone who found him* NOT *strike him*

- יִתְעוּ   לֹא־   לְמַעַן •

  they will stray   NOT   IN ORDER THAT

  IN ORDER THAT *they* NOT *stray*

  Ezek 14:11

- Other examples include Num 17:5; 2 Sam 14:14; 2 Kgs 23:10.

F   Result Clauses (with the result that) [649]

- A result clause (also called a **consecutive clause**) states the outcome, effect, or consequence of something. It can often be translated as 'with

---

[649] Cf. GBHS §5.2.3(b)–(c); GKC §166; IBHS §38.3; JM §169.

the result that,' 'that,' 'thus,' 'thereby,' or 'so that.'

- The categories 'result clause' and 'purpose clause' overlap when the result is intended.
- §525–7 explain different ways that result clauses are written.

525 **Result clause with the waw consecutive or simple waw.** A result clause can begin with an imperfect waw consecutive verb (§178), a perfect waw consecutive verb (§179), an imperfect with a simple waw (§180), or a jussive, cohortative, or imperative with a simple waw (§181a).

- וַיָּמֹת   בָּאֲבָנִים   וַיִּסְקְלֻהוּ
  WITH THE RESULT THAT *he died* with the stones they stoned him   1 Kgs 21:13

  They stoned him with stones WITH THE RESULT THAT *he died*.

526 **Result with לְ or לְמַעַן and an infinitive construct.** A result can be expressed with the preposition לְ followed by an infinitive construct (§279). On rare occasions, לְמַעַן (§368) is used instead of לְ.

- אֶת־מִקְדָּשִׁי   טַמֵּא   לְמַעַן   לַמֹּלֶךְ   נָתַן   מִזַּרְעוֹ Lev 20:3
  my sanctuary to defile WITH THE RESULT THAT to Molech he gave from his seed

  He gave some of his offspring to Molech, THEREBY *defiling my sanctuary*.

527 **Result clause with כִּי, אֲשֶׁר, or שֶׁ◌.** A result clause can begin with כִּי (§450), אֲשֶׁר (rare, §465), or שֶׁ◌ (§473).

- עָלָיו   תַלִּינוּ   כִּי   הוּא   מַה־   וְאַהֲרֹן
  at him you grumble WITH THE RESULT THAT he what? but Aaron Num 16:11 (qere)

  But as for Aaron, what is he WITH THE RESULT THAT *you grumble at him*?

- לְפָנֶיךָ   הָיָה   לֹא־   כָּמוֹךָ   אֲשֶׁר
  before you he was not like you WITH THE RESULT THAT   1 Kgs 3:12

  WITH THE RESULT THAT *no one like you has existed before you*

- Another example is Gen 20:10.

G Concessive Clauses (although) [650]

- A concessive clause indicates something that might be expected to cause (or prevent) something but in fact does not. Something happens (or does not happen) even though the concessive clause happens. A concessive clause can often be translated beginning with 'although,' 'even though,' or 'in spite of the fact that.'
- §528–32 discuss different ways that concessive clauses are written.

---

[650] Cf. GBHS §5.2.12; GKC §160; JM §171.

528 Concessive circumstantial clause.[651] A concessive clause can be written as a circumstantial clause (§494–5b), with the subject before the verb and often with the conjunction וְ prefixed to the subject.

- הוֹאַלְתִּי לְדַבֵּר אֶל־אֲדֹנָי וְאָנֹכִי עָפָר וָאֵפֶר

  and ashes dust ALTHOUGH *I* lord to to speak I began   Gen 18:27

  I have ventured to speak to the Lord, ALTHOUGH *I am dust and ashes.*

- אֵיךְ תֹּאמַר אֲהַבְתִּיךְ וְלִבְּךָ אֵין אִתִּי

  with me is not ALTHOUGH *your heart* I love you you can say how?   Judg 16:15

  How can you say, 'I love you,' ALTHOUGH *your heart is not with me?*

529 Concessive clause with אִם. See §454.

- אִם־ צָדַקְתִּי לֹא אֶעֱנֶה

  I can answer not *I am in the right* ALTHOUGH

  ALTHOUGH *I am in the right*, I cannot answer.   Job 9:15

- אִם־ קָטֹן אַתָּה בְּעֵינֶיךָ רֹאשׁ שִׁבְטֵי יִשְׂרָאֵל אָתָּה

  you Israel tribes of head of in your eyes you small ALTHOUGH   1 Sam 15:17

  ALTHOUGH *you were small in your eyes*, you became head of the tribes of Israel.

- There are several examples in Amos 9:2–4.

530 Concessive clause with גַּם, כִּי, or גַּם כִּי. A concessive clause can begin with גַּם (§382), כִּי (§448), or גַּם כִּי (§382).

- גַּם כִּי־ אֵלֵךְ בְּגֵיא צַלְמָוֶת

  darkness in valley of I walk EVEN THOUGH

  EVEN THOUGH *I walk in a very dark valley*   Ps 23:4

- כִּי־ תַעֲלֶה בָבֶל הַשָּׁמַיִם

  the heavens Babylon she should ascend ALTHOUGH   Jer 51:53

  ALTHOUGH *Babylon should climb into the skies*

- בְּחָנוּנִי גַּם־ רָאוּ פָעֳלִי

  my work they saw ALTHOUGH they tested me   They tested me, ALTHOUGH *they saw my work.*   Ps 95:9

- Other examples include Jer 36:25 and Ps 129:2.

531 Concessive clause with עַל. See §288b.

- עַל עַפְעַפַּי צַלְמָוֶת עַל לֹא חָמָס בְּכַפָּי

  in my hands violence no ALTHOUGH darkness my eyelids on   Job 16:16–17

  Darkness is on my eyelids, ALTHOUGH *there is no violence in my hands.*

- עַל לֹא־ חָמָס עָשָׂה

  he did violence not ALTHOUGH   ALTHOUGH *he did no violence*   Isa 53:9

  ○ This might be causal instead of concessive ('because he did no violence').

---

[651] Cf. GKC §141e, 142d, 156f; JM §171f.

532 **Concessive with כְּ and an infinitive construct**. See §258.

- כְּדַבְּרָה אֶל־יוֹסֵף יוֹם יוֹם וְלֹא־שָׁמַע אֵלֶיהָ   Gen 39:10

  to her   he listened but not *day day Joseph to* ALTHOUGH *she to speak*

                ALTHOUGH *she spoke to Joseph day after day*, he did not listen to her.

H Causal Clauses (because) [652]

- A causal clause explains why something happens in terms of cause and effect. Causal clauses can often be translated beginning with 'because,' 'since,' or 'for.'
- §533–5 describe different ways that causal clauses are written.

533 **A causal clause** can begin with כִּי (§444), אֲשֶׁר (§468), or שׁ◌ (§474).

- קֵץ כָּל־בָּשָׂר בָּא לְפָנַי כִּי־מָלְאָה הָאָרֶץ חָמָס   Gen 6:13

  violence the earth is full BECAUSE before me came flesh all of end of

      I have decided to put an end to every creature, BECAUSE *the earth is full of violence.*

- הֱבִיאוּם אֲשֶׁר חָמַל הָעָם   1 Sam 15:15

  the people spared BECAUSE they brought them

            They brought them BECAUSE *the people spared …*

- שֶׁרֹּאשִׁי נִמְלָא־טָל   BECAUSE *my head is drenched with dew*

  dew is filled BECAUSE *my head*   Song 5:2

- Other examples include 2 Sam 2:5 (אֲשֶׁר) and Eccl 2:18 (שׁ◌).

534 **A causal clause** can begin with יַעַן (אֲשֶׁר/כִּי) (§363b), with עַל (אֲשֶׁר/כִּי) (§291), with בְּ or בַּאֲשֶׁר (§247), with כַּאֲשֶׁר (§260), with מִן or מֵאֲשֶׁר (§319), with עֵקֶב,[653] with תַּחַת (אֲשֶׁר/כִּי) (§353), or with מִפְּנֵי (אֲשֶׁר) (§376).

- יַעַן כִּי גָבְהוּ בְּנוֹת צִיּוֹן   BECAUSE *the women of Zion are proud*

  Zion daughters of are proud BECAUSE   Isa 3:16

- פַּלְגֵי־מַיִם יָרְדוּ עֵינָי עַל לֹא־שָׁמְרוּ תוֹרָתֶךָ   Ps 119:136

  your law they keep not BECAUSE my eyes run down water streams of

      Streams of water run down my eyes BECAUSE *they do not keep your law.*

- בַּאֲשֶׁר יְהוָה אִתּוֹ   BECAUSE *YHWH was with him*

  with him YHWH BECAUSE   Gen 39:23

- כַּאֲשֶׁר לֹא־שָׁמַעְתָּ   BECAUSE *you did not obey*

  you obeyed not BECAUSE   1 Sam 28:18

---

[652] Cf. GBHS §5.2.5; GKC §158; IBHS §38.4; JM §170.

[653] Cf. BHRG §40.9.1.3 note 55; GBHS §5.2.5a; GKC §158b; IBHS §38.4a; JM §104b, 170g; Gaenssle 1915a, 149–50.

- בְּעֵינַי   יָקַרְתָּ   מֵאֲשֶׁר •

  in my eyes you are precious BECAUSE

  BECAUSE *you are precious in my eyes*

  Isa 43:4

- עִמּוֹ   אַחֶרֶת רוּחַ הָיְתָה   עֵקֶב •

  with him different spirit was BECAUSE

  BECAUSE *a different spirit was with him*

  Num 14:24

- דָעַת   שָׂנְאוּ   כִּי־תַחַת •

  knowledge they hated BECAUSE

  BECAUSE *they hated knowledge*

  Prov 1:29

- קִטַּרְתֶּם   אֲשֶׁר מִפְּנֵי •

  you burned sacrifices BECAUSE

  BECAUSE *you have burned sacrifices*

  Jer 44:23

- Other examples include Gen 22:16 and Num 20:12 (יַעַן), Judg 3:12 and 2 Sam 3:30 (עַל), Gen 39:9 (בַּאֲשֶׁר), Num 27:14 and 2 Kgs 17:26 (כַּאֲשֶׁר), Gen 22:18 and 2 Sam 12:10 (עֵקֶב), Num 25:13 and 2 Kgs 22:17 (תַּחַת), and Exod 19:18 (מִפְּנֵי).

535   A cause can be expressed with an infinitive construct that is preceded by יַעַן (§363b), by עַל (§291), by בְּ (§247), or by מִן (§319).

- הָרַע   לַעֲשׂוֹת   הִתְמַכֶּרְךָ   יַעַן •

  the evil to do your to sell yourself BECAUSE

  BECAUSE *you sold yourself to do evil*

  1 Kgs 21:20

- צַדִּיק   בַּכֶּסֶף   מִכְרָם   עַל־ •

  righteous for the silver their to sell BECAUSE

  BECAUSE *they sell the righteous for silver*

  Amos 2:6

- יְהוָה   אֶת־מִצְוֺת   בַּעֲזׇבְכֶם •

  of YHWH commandments BECAUSE your to abandon

  1 Kgs 18:18

  BECAUSE *you abandoned the commandments of YHWH*

- אֹתוֹ   מִיִּרְאָתוֹ •

  him BECAUSE his to fear

  BECAUSE *of his fear of him*

  2 Sam 3:11

- Other examples include 2 Kgs 19:28 and Isa 37:29 (יַעַן), Amos 1:9 (עַל), Exod 33:16 (בְּ, possible), and Deut 7:7 (מִן).

I   Relative Clauses (that, which, who) [654]

- A relative clause describes its **antecedent** (a noun or other substantive that precedes it – usually immediately). For example, in 'I read the book *that I bought*,' the words 'that I bought' constitute a relative clause that describes its antecedent 'book.' Relative clauses can usually be translated beginning with 'that,' 'which,' 'who,' or 'whom.'
- In Hebrew, a relative clause often has a resumptive element that indicates the role of the antecedent within the relative clause, such as the word 'it' in 'I read the book *that I bought it*.' The resumptive element is usually not translated into English.

---

[654] Cf. GBHS §5.2.13; GKC §138, 155; IBHS §19; JM §38, 145, 158; Gottstein 1949; Holmstedt 2001; Holmstedt 2002; Thorion 1985.

- §536–40 describe different ways of writing a relative clause.

536 **Relative clause with זֶה / זוֹ / זוּ.** See §129a.

- טָבְעוּ גוֹיִם ... בְּרֶשֶׁת זוּ טָמָנוּ
  they hid THAT in net nations sank

  The nations sank … in a net THAT *they hid.*
  Ps 9:16

- עַם־ זוּ יָצַרְתִּי לִי
  for me I formed WHOM people

  a people WHOM *I formed for myself*
  Isa 43:21

- Another example is Job 19:19.

537 **Relative clause with שֶׁ.** See §470–1 (also §129b).

- הָאַרְגָּמָן שֶׁעַל מַלְכֵי מִדְיָן
  Midian kings of THAT *on* the purple

  the purple robes THAT *were on the kings of Midian*
  Judg 8:26

- כָּל־ הֶעָמָל שֶׁעָמַלְתִּי תַּחַת הַשָּׁמֶשׁ
  the sun under THAT *I laboured* the labour all of

  all of the labour THAT *I laboured under the sun*
  Eccl 2:20

- Other examples include Judg 7:12; 2 Kgs 6:11; Eccl 1:9.

538 **Relative clause with אֲשֶׁר.** In prose, most relative clauses begin with אֲשֶׁר (§129c, 462–3b). אֲשֶׁר is rare, however, in poetry.

- הַמָּקוֹם אֲשֶׁר אַתָּה עוֹמֵד עָלָיו אַדְמַת־ קֹדֶשׁ הוּא
  it holiness ground of *on it standing you* THAT the place

  The place on WHICH *you are standing* is holy ground.
  Exod 3:5

539a **Relative clause with a participle.**[655] A relative clause can begin with a participle (§218). Such a participle usually has the article (§90).

- וְאֶל־ מֶלֶךְ יְהוּדָה הַשֹּׁלֵחַ אֶתְכֶם
  you THE SENDING of Judah king but to

  but to the king of Judah WHO SENT *you*
  2 Kgs 22:18 (with article)

- רוּחַ סְעָרָה בָּאָה מִן הַצָּפוֹן
  the north from COMING gale wind of

  a storm wind THAT WAS COMING *from the north*
  Ezek 1:4 (without article)

539b **Relative clause with the article on a finite verb.** A relative clause can begin with an article on a finite verb (§91). Most occurrences seem to be with perfect verbs in Chronicles and Ezra.

- אֱלֹהֵי יִשְׂרָאֵל הַנִּרְאָה אֵלָיו
  to him THE HE APPEARED of Israel God

  the God of Israel WHO HAD APPEARED *to him*
  1 Kgs 11:9

- אֲנָשִׁים הַהֹשִׁיבוּ נָשִׁים נָכְרִיּוֹת
  foreign women THE THEY CAUSED TO DWELL men

  men WHO HAD MARRIED *foreign women*
  Ezra 10:17

---

[655] Prior editions of this textbook implied that the article on the participle was acting as a relative particle. The example from Ezek 1:4 is from BHRG §36.3.4 and IBHS §19.7a.

540 **Relative clause with no marker.**[656] A relative clause can begin without any marker; that is, the relative clause is simply juxtaposed to another clause. Also called a **virtual relative**, a **paratactic relative**, an **unmarked relative**, a **bare relative**, or an **asyndetic relative**, this is common in poetry.

- In asyndetic relative clauses, the resumptive pronoun (if there is one) is almost always in the third person, even if the antecedent is first or second person.

- בּוֹ   חָסָיוּ   צוּר   the rock *in which they sought refuge*
  in it   *they sought refuge*   rock   Deut 32:37

- בָהּ   יֵלְכוּ   אֶת־הַדֶּרֶךְ   the path *in which they should walk*
  in it   *they should walk*   the path   Exod 18:20

- Other examples include Gen 15:13 (prose); Deut 32:17; Isa 40:20; Jer 13:20; Ps 18:44; Job 3:3.

J   Interrogative Clauses [657]

- An **interrogative clause** asks a question. §541–5 describe different ways of writing different types of interrogative clauses in Hebrew.

541 **Direct question with the interrogative particle הֲ (?).**[658] Direct questions often begin with the interrogative particle הֲ.

- הַזֶּה   הָאִישׁ   עִם־   הֲתֵלְכִי   *Will you go with this man?*
  the this   *the man*   *with*   *you will go?*   Gen 24:58

- הֲתַחַת אֱלֹהִים אָנִי   *Am I in God's place?*
  I   *God*   *place of?*   Gen 50:19

542 **Direct question without any marker (?).**[659] A direct question may have nothing other than the context to indicate that it is a question. Thus, in principle nearly any statement in Hebrew could be a question. In spoken Hebrew, such questions may have been marked by intonation.

- בֹּאֶךָ   שָׁלֹם   וַיֹּאמֶר   He said, '*Do you come in peace?*'
  your to come   *peace*   *he said*   1 Sam 16:4

---

[656] Cf. GKC §155e–m; IBHS §19.6; JM §158a–db; Joosten 1993; Holmstedt 2002, 107–14.

[657] Cf. BHRG §43; GBHS §5.3.1; GKC §100i–n, 107t, 150, 151a–b; IBHS §18, 31.4f, 40.3; JM §37, 102i, 144, 154g, 155l, 161; Gordis 1933. In this textbook see also §119–28, 573g, 574b, and 581 for further explanation and references.

[658] Cf. BHRG §43.2.1; GBHS §5.3.1(a); GKC §150b–h; IBHS §18.1c, 40.3b; JM §161a.

[659] Cf. BHRG §43.2.2; GBHS §5.3.1; GKC §150a–b; IBHS §40.3b; JM §161a; Sperber 1943, 226–7.

- וַאֲנִי אָבוֹא אֶל־בֵּיתִי
  my house   to   will go   but I

  Shall I go to my house?
  2 Sam 11:11

- Another example is 1 Sam 11:12.

543 Indirect question with הֲ or אִם (whether).[660] Indirect questions often begin with the interrogative particle הֲ or the conjunction אִם. Such questions can often be translated with 'whether' or 'if.'

- לָדַעַת הֲיִשְׁכֶם אֹהֲבִים אֶת־יְהוָה
  YHWH   loving   WHETHER you   to know

  to find out WHETHER *you love YHWH*
  Deut 13:4

- לְכוּ דִרְשׁוּ ... אִם־אֶחְיֶה מֵחֳלִי זֶה
  this   from illness   I will live   WHETHER   seek!   go!

  Go, inquire … WHETHER *I will recover from this illness.*
  2 Kgs 1:2

544 Disjunctive question with הֲ ... אִם / וְאִם / הֲ / אוֹ (whether ... or).[661] A disjunctive question asks about two (or more) possibilities. The different possibilities may be negating (e.g., this or not this) or contrasting (e.g., strong or weak, wise or foolish). Disjunctive questions generally begin with הֲ before the first possibility. The second possibility is preceded by אִם or וְאִם (§455), by הֲ (less common), or by אוֹ (§443, rare).

- הַכֶּר־נָא הַכְּתֹנֶת בִּנְךָ הִוא אִם־לֹא
  not   OR   it   your son   WHETHER   tunic of   examine!

  Examine it to see WHETHER *it is your son's tunic* OR *not.*
  Gen 37:32

- הֶחָזָק הוּא הֲרָפֶה
  OR weak   it   WHETHER strong

  WHETHER *it is strong* OR *weak*
  Num 13:18

- Other examples include Judg 18:19; Job 22:3; Eccl 2:19.

545 Question with an interrogative pronoun or adverb. An interrogative clause can begin with an interrogative pronoun or an interrogative adverb, such as מִי 'who?' (§120, 123), מָה 'what?' 'how?' or 'why?' (§124, 126, 128), אֵי 'where?' אָן 'where?' or אֵיךְ 'how?'

K Desire Clauses [662]

- A **desire clause** expresses a desire or a wish. Desire clauses are also called **desiderative clauses**, **wish clauses**, **volitive clauses**, or **optative clauses**. Depending on the shade of meaning, they can often be translated with 'let,' 'may,' 'if only,' or 'would that.'

---

[660] Cf. BHRG §43.2.1(ii)c; GBHS §4.3.2(g), 5.3.1(d); GKC §150i; JM §161f.
[661] Cf. BHRG §43.2.1(ii)b; GBHS §5.3.1(b); IBHS §40.3b; JM §161e.
[662] Cf. BHRG §45.3; GBHS §5.3.3; GKC §151; IBHS §40.2.2d; JM §163.

- §546–51 discuss different ways of writing desire clauses in Hebrew.

546 **Desire clause with the jussive or cohortative (let).** A jussive or cohortative verb can express a desire (§184a–b). This is often translated with 'let' or 'may,' although such a translation may be mistakenly understood as a request for permission.

- אָשִׂ֫ימָה עָלַי מֶ֫לֶךְ   LET ME SET *a king over myself!*
  king over me LET ME SET   Deut 17:14 (cohortative)

- יָקֵם יְהוָה אֶת־דְּבָרוֹ   MAY *YHWH* ESTABLISH *his word!*
  his word YHWH LET ESTABLISH   1 Sam 1:23 (jussive)

547 **Desire clause with מִי־יִתֵּן (if only, oh that, would that).**[663]

- מִי יִתֵּן בִּשְׁאוֹל תַּצְפִּנֵ֫נִי   WOULD THAT *you would hide me in Sheol!*
  you will hide me in Sheol WILL GIVE WHO?   Job 14:13

- וּמִי יִתֵּן כָּל־עַם יְהוָה נְבִיאִים   *and* WHO? WILL GIVE *all of people of YHWH prophets*
  prophets YHWH people of all of WILL GIVE *and* WHO?   Num 11:29
  WOULD THAT *all of YHWH's people were prophets!*

- מִי יַשְׁקֵ֫נִי מַ֫יִם   IF ONLY *someone would give me a drink of water!*
  water will give me a drink WHO?   2 Sam 23:15 (יִתֵּן omitted)

- Other examples include Exod 16:3; Deut 5:29, 28:67; 2 Sam 15:4, 19:1; Job 6:8, 23:3.

548 **Desire clause with לוּ (if only).** A desire clause can begin with לוּ (§460) followed by the imperfect, the perfect, the jussive, the cohortative, or an existential clause (§567–9b). Such clauses often, but not always, indicate a desire for something that did not or could not happen.

- לוּ שָׁקוֹל יִשָּׁקֵל כַּעְשִׂי   IF ONLY *my grief could be weighed out!*
  my anger will be weighed to weigh IF ONLY   Job 6:2 (imperfect)

- וְלוּ הוֹאַ֫לְנוּ וַנֵּ֫שֶׁב בְּעֵ֫בֶר הַיַּרְדֵּן   IF ONLY
  the Jordan beyond and dwelt we were willing IF ONLY   Josh 7:7 (perfect)
  IF ONLY *we had been willing to dwell beyond the Jordan!*

- לוּ יֶשׁ־חֶ֫רֶב בְּיָדִי   IF ONLY *there were a sword in my hand!*
  in my hand sword there were IF ONLY   Num 22:29 (existential clause)

- Other examples include Gen 17:18; Num 14:2.

---

[663] Cf. BHRG §43.3.1(iv), 45.3(ii); GBHS §5.3.3(b); GKC §151a–d; IBHS §40.2.2d; JM §163d.

549 **Desire clause with אַחֲלֵי / אַחֲלַי (if only).**[664]

- אַחֲלֵי אֲדֹנִי לִפְנֵי הַנָּבִיא   IF ONLY *my master were with the prophet!*
  the prophet   before   my master   IF ONLY!   2 Kgs 5:3

- אַחֲלַי יִכֹּנוּ דְּרָכָי   IF ONLY *my ways would be established!*
  my ways   would be established   IF ONLY!   Ps 119:5

550 **Desire clause with אִם (if only).** See §458. This is rare.

- אִם־תִּקְטֹל אֱלוֹהַּ רָשָׁע   IF ONLY *you would kill the wicked, O God!*
  wicked   God   you would kill   IF ONLY   Ps 139:19

551 **Verbless desire clause (may it be!).**[665] A desire may be expressed by means of a verbless clause. The predicate may be a noun, a participle, or a prepositional phrase. The word order in such clauses is discussed in §580.

- עֵד הַגַּל הַזֶּה   MAY *this heap* BE A WITNESS!
  the this   the heap   WITNESS   Gen 31:52 (noun)

- בָּרוּךְ בְּנִי לַיהוָה   MAY *my son* BE BLESSED *by YHWH!*
  by YHWH   my son   BLESSED   Judg 17:2 (participle)

- חַג לַיהוָה מָחָר   LET YHWH HAVE *a festival tomorrow!*
  tomorrow   TO YHWH   festival   Exod 32:5 (prepositional phrase)

L   Adversative Clauses (but) [666]

- An **adversative clause** opposes another statement. It may state what is true instead of another clause, or state something that invalidates another clause. It can usually be translated beginning with 'but.'
- Adversative clauses are sometimes classified with restrictive clauses (§558–60).
- The clause that is opposed is often negated with a word such as לֹא and usually precedes the adversative clause.

552 **Adversative clause with וְ.** See §432.

- וְלֹא־יִקָּרֵא עוֹד אֶת־שִׁמְךָ אַבְרָם וְהָיָה שִׁמְךָ אַבְרָהָם
  Abraham   your name BUT *will be* Abram your name still will be called not
  Your name will no longer be called Abram, BUT *your name will be Abraham.* Gen 17:5

- לֹא שָׁאַלְתָּ נֶפֶשׁ אֹיְבֶיךָ וְשָׁאַלְתָּ לְּךָ הָבִין
  to understand   for you BUT *you asked* your enemies life of you asked not 1 Kgs 3:11
  You did not ask for the life of your enemies, BUT *you asked for yourself understanding.*

---

[664] Cf. BHRG §45.3(i); GKC §151e; JM §163c.
[665] Cf. GBHS §5.3.3(c); GKC §116r note, 141f; JM §163b.
[666] Cf. GBHS §4.5.2(c.6), 5.2.10; GKC §163a–b; IBHS §39.3.5d–e; JM §123i, 172.

553 Adversative clause with וְאוּלָם / אוּלָם.[667]

- וְאוּלָם   בַּעֲבוּר   זֹאת   הֶעֱמַדְתִּיךָ

  I caused you to stand   this   on account of   BUT   Exod 9:16

  BUT *for this reason I caused you to stand*

- כֹּל   אֲשֶׁר   לָאִישׁ   אוּלָם   שְׁלַח־נָא   יָדְךָ

  your hand   stretch out   BUT   his life   for   he will give   to man   which   all

  All which a man has he will give for his life, BUT *stretch out your hand …* Job 2:4–5

- Other examples include Judg 18:29; Micah 3:8; Job 1:11.

554 Adversative clause with אֲבָל.[668] Adversative clauses can begin with אֲבָל. This seems to occur only in late texts; in earlier texts, אֲבָל seems to be used only asseveratively ('truly'), emphasizing the certainty of something.

- אֲבָל   אֲרוֹן   הָאֱלֹהִים   הֶעֱלָה   דָוִיד   מִקִּרְיַת   יְעָרִים

  Jearim   from Kiriath   David   brought up   the God   ark of   BUT   2 Chr 1:4

  BUT *David had brought up the ark of God from Kiriath-jearim.*

555 Adversative clause with כִּי or כִּי אִם after a negative. After a negative, a clause that begins with כִּי can be adversative (§447). When used in this way, כִּי is often followed by a pleonastic אִם (§457).

- לֹא־   נָבִיא   אָנֹכִי … כִּי־   בוֹקֵר   אָנֹכִי   I am not a prophet … BUT *I am a herdsman.*

  I herdsman   BUT   I   prophet   not   Amos 7:14

- וַיֹּאמְרוּ   לֹא   כִּי אִם־   מֶלֶךְ   יִהְיֶה   עָלֵינוּ

  over us   will be   king   BUT   no!   they said   1 Sam 8:19

  They said, 'No! BUT *a king will be over us!'*

- Other examples include Gen 17:15; Deut 7:5; Ps 1:2.

M Exceptive Clauses (unless, except that) [669]

- An **exceptive clause** (also called a **limitative clause**) gives an exception to the truth of another clause.
- Some exceptive clauses state something that would invalidate another clause (e.g., 'I will fail the test *unless I study more*').
- Other exceptive clauses limit the truth or applicability of another clause (e.g., 'I can't eat today, *except that I can have breakfast*').

---

[667] Cf. GBHS §5.2.10; IBHS §39.3.5e; JM §172b.

[668] Cf. BHRG §40.2.1; GBHS §5.2.10; IBHS §39.3.5e.

[669] Cf. GBHS §5.2.7; GKC §163c–d; IBHS §38.6; JM §173a–b; Zewi 1998. Some authors group exceptive clauses with adversative clauses and/or restrictive clauses, or divide the three categories differently.

556 **Exceptive clause with כִּי אִם.**[670] An exceptive clause can begin with כִּי אִם in a rhetorical question or after a negative word such as לֹא.

- לֹא   אֲשַׁלֵּחֲךָ   כִּי אִם־   בֵּרַכְתָּנִי
  you blessed me UNLESS I will let you go not   Gen 32:27

  I will not let you go UNLESS *you have blessed me.*

- לֹא־   יֹאכַל   מִן־   הַקֳּדָשִׁים   כִּי אִם־   רָחַץ
  he washed UNLESS the holy things from he will eat not   Lev 22:7

  He will not eat from the holy things UNLESS *he has washed.*

- Another possible example is Amos 3:7 (but it may be privative).

557 **Exceptive clause with בִּלְתִּי.** An exceptive clause can begin with בִּלְתִּי (§422). A pleonastic אִם (§457) often follows בִּלְתִּי.

- הֲיִתֵּן   כְּפִיר   קוֹלוֹ   מִמְּעֹנָתוֹ   בִּלְתִּי אִם־   לָכָד
  he captured IF NOT from his den his voice young lion will he give? Amos 3:4

  Does a young lion growl from his den UNLESS *he has captured something?*

- לֹא־   תִרְאוּ   פָנַי   בִּלְתִּי   אֲחִיכֶם   אִתְּכֶם
  with you your brother NOT my face you will see not   Gen 43:3

  You will not see my face UNLESS *your brother is with you.*

- Other examples include Num 11:6 and Isa 10:4.

N   Restrictive Clauses (nevertheless, but) [671]

- A **restrictive clause** states something that is true despite the fact that the information stated in another clause is true; it limits the application or implications of another clause. For example, in the sentence, 'I am tired, *but I will nevertheless keep on studying,*' the words 'but I will nevertheless keep on studying' are a restrictive clause.

- A restrictive clause can often be translated beginning with 'nevertheless,' 'yet,' 'on the other hand,' 'however,' or 'but.'

558 **Restrictive clause with אֶפֶס כִּי.** See §427.

- אֶפֶס כִּי־   עַז   הָעָם   הַיֹּשֵׁב   בָּאָרֶץ
  in the land the dwelling the people strong NEVERTHELESS   Num 13:28

  [The land flows with milk and honey. (Num 13:27)]

  NEVERTHELESS, *the people who dwell in the land are strong.*

---

[670] Cf. GBHS §4.3.4(m), 5.2.7; GKC §163c–d; IBHS §38.6; JM §173b; Aejmelaeus 1986, 201.

[671] Cf. GBHS §5.2.7–5.2.8; GKC §153; IBHS §39.3.5; JM §173a–b.

- אֶפֶס כִּי לֹא הַשְׁמֵיד אַשְׁמִיד אֶת־בֵּית יַעֲקֹב

  Jacob house of I will destroy to destroy not NEVERTHELESS   Amos 9:8

  NEVERTHELESS, *I will not totally destroy the house of Jacob.*

- Another example is 2 Sam 12:14.

559 Restrictive clause with אַךְ. See §388.

- עֲשִׂי כִדְבָרֵךְ אַךְ עֲשִׂי־ לִי מִשָּׁם עֻגָה

  bread cake from there for me make! NEVERTHELESS *like your word do!* 1 Kgs 17:13

  Do as you said; BUT *[first] make a bread cake from it for me.*

- Other possible examples include Gen 9:4 and 1 Sam 18:17.

560 Restrictive clause with רַק. See §390.

- רַק לָאֲנָשִׁים הָאֵל אַל־ תַּעֲשׂוּ דָבָר

  thing do not the these to the men BUT   Gen 19:8

  [*Do whatever you like to my daughters. Gen 19:7*]

  BUT *do not do anything to these men.*

- Other possible examples include Deut 12:15 and 1 Kgs 3:3.

O Equational Clauses (is) [672]

- Some equational clauses (**identifying clauses**) assert that the subject and the predicate refer to the same thing (e.g., 'She is my mother').
- Other equational clauses (**classifying clauses**) assert that the thing referred to by the subject is described by the predicate (e.g., 'She is tall') or is a member of the class described by the predicate (e.g., 'She is a mother').
- Equational clauses are typically translated with a form of the verb 'to be' in English.

561 Equational clauses in present time (from the standpoint of the writer or speaker) usually lack a finite verb, in which case they are **verbless clauses** (sometimes called **nominal clauses**).[673] Equational clauses in past or future time usually use a form of the verb הָיָה.[674] Sections 562–6 describe different ways of writing the predicate of an equational clause.

---

[672] Cf. GBHS §5.1.1; IBHS §8.4; JM §154.
[673] Cf. BHRG §12.4.3; GBHS §5.1.1; Andersen 1970; Hoftijzer 1973.
[674] Cf. BHRG §44.4.3; JM §154m–na; JM93 §154m–n; Sinclair 1999.

562 **Equational clause with a substantive for a predicate.**[675]

- אֵלֶּה שְׁמוֹת בְּנֵי־עֵשָׂו

  ESAU   SONS OF   NAMES OF   *these*

  These ARE THE NAMES OF THE SONS OF ESAU.

  Gen 36:10

- A substantive in predicate apposition (§67) is often used instead of a predicate adjective (§563).

  ○ הֲשָׁלוֹם בֹּאֶךָ

  your to come   PEACE?

  Is *your coming* PEACEABLE?

  1 Kgs 2:13

  ○ אֱמֶת הָיָה הַדָּבָר אֲשֶׁר שָׁמַעְתִּי

  I heard   *that*   *the word*   WAS   TRUTH

  The report that I heard WAS TRUE.

  1 Kgs 10:6

- A negative equational clause typically uses לֹא before a substantival predicate.

  ○ לֹא־נָבִיא אָנֹכִי

  I   PROPHET   NOT

  I AM NOT A PROPHET.

  Amos 7:14

- Other examples include Gen 4:2 (past time with וַיְהִי), Gen 13:8; Deut 13:15 (predicate apposition §67); Deut 17:15 (negated with לֹא); 2 Kgs 4:23 (negated with לֹא, the subject is unexpressed).

563 **Equational clause with predicate adjective.** See §75.

- רָעַתְכֶם רַבָּה

  GREAT   *your wickedness*

  Your wickedness IS GREAT.

  1 Sam 12:17

- A negative equational clause typically uses לֹא before a predicate adjective.

  ○ לֹא־טוֹב הַדָּבָר

  the thing   GOOD   NOT

  The thing IS NOT GOOD.

  Exod 18:17

- Other examples include Gen 6:5, 29:17, 38:7.

564 **Equational clause with the preposition בְּ of identity.** The preposition בְּ of identity (§249, also called the *beth essentiae* or the **beth of essence**) can precede the substantival predicate of an equational clause (§562).

- אֱלֹהֵי אָבִי בְּעֶזְרִי

  WAS *my help*   *my father*   God of

  The God of my father WAS *my help*.

  Exod 18:4

- קוֹל־יְהוָה בַּכֹּחַ

  IS *the strength*   YHWH   voice of

  The voice of YHWH IS *strong*.

  Ps 29:4

565 **Equational clause with a prepositional phrase as the predicate.**[676] A prepositional phrase can be the predicate of an equational clause.

- This is disputed; some scholars would not classify such clauses as equational.

- רִבְקָה לְפָנֶיךָ

  IS BEFORE YOU   *Rebekah*

  Rebekah IS BEFORE YOU.

  Gen 24:51

---

[675] Cf. BHRG §34.3; GBHS §5.1.1(a); GKC §141b; IBHS §4.5c, 8.3c; JM §154d.
[676] Cf. BHRG §32.2.1; GBHS §5.1.1(d); GKC §141b; IBHS §4.5c; JM §154d.

- וּדְבַר־ אַבְנֵר הָיָה עִם־ זִקְנֵי יִשְׂרָאֵל
  ISRAEL ELDERS OF WITH IT WAS *Abner and word of*   2 Sam 3:17
  The discussion of Abner WAS WITH THE ELDERS OF ISRAEL.

- A negative equational clause typically uses לֹא before a prepositional predicate.

  ○ יְהוָה בָרַעַשׁ לֹא   *YHWH* WAS NOT IN THE EARTHQUAKE.
    YHWH IN THE QUAKING NOT   1 Kgs 19:11

566 **Equational clause with an adverb as the predicate.**[677] An adverb can be
the predicate of an equational clause.

- This is disputed; some scholars would not classify such clauses as equational.

- זֶבַח הַיָּמִים שָׁם   *The yearly sacrifice* IS THERE.
  THERE *the days sacrifice of*   1 Sam 20:6

P   Existential Clauses (there is) [678]

- An existential clause asserts, questions, or denies that something
  exists. It can often be translated 'there was,' 'there is.'

567 **Existential clause with הָיָה.**[679] To express existence in past or future time
(from the standpoint of the writer or speaker), a form of the verb הָיָה is
typically used. Such clauses are negated with לֹא.

- אִישׁ הָיָה בְאֶרֶץ־ עוּץ   *There* WAS *a man in the land of Uz.*
  Uz *in land of* WAS *man*   Job 1:1

- לֹא־ הָיָה שָׁם לֶחֶם   *There* WAS NO *bread there.*
  bread there WAS NOT   1 Sam 21:7

568 **Existential clause with יֵשׁ.** See §477. The time is often (but not always)
present from the standpoint of the speaker or writer.

- הַזֶּה בַּמָּקוֹם יְהוָה יֵשׁ אָכֵן   *Truly YHWH* IS *in this place.*
  the this in the place YHWH THERE IS *truly*   Gen 28:16

569a **Negative existential clause with אַיִן / אֵין.** The thing whose existence is
denied can be followed by אַיִן in apposition or be preceded by its construct
אֵין (§407a–408). The time is usually present.

- אֵין נָבוֹן וְחָכָם כָּמוֹךָ   *like you and wise understanding* THERE IS NOT
  like you and wise understanding THERE IS NOT   Gen 41:39
  THERE IS NO ONE *as understanding and wise as you.*

---

[677] Cf. GKC §141b; IBHS §4.5c; JM §154d.
[678] Cf. BHRG §42; GBHS §5.3.4.
[679] Cf. GBHS §5.3.4(a); JM §154m–na; JM93 §m–n; Zewi 1999.

- וְכֹחַ   אַיִן   לְלֵדָה   *And* THERE IS NO *strength to give birth.*

  to give birth   THERE IS NOT   *and strength*   2 Kgs 19:3

- Judg 21:25 contains an example of אַיִן used in the past time.

- In 1 Sam 21:9 and Ps 135:17, אַיִן is followed by a redundant יֵשׁ.

569b **Negative existential clause with אֶפֶס (there is not).** See §426. The thing whose existence is denied follows אֶפֶס, as a genitive or in apposition.

- עָזוּב   וְאֶפֶס   עָצוּר   וְאֶפֶס   THERE WAS NEITHER *bound* NOR *free.*

  free   *and* THERE WAS NOT   *bound*   THERE WAS NOT   2 Kgs 14:26

- שָׁאוּל   לְבֵית   אִישׁ   עוֹד   הַאֶפֶס

  Saul   *to house of*   *man*   *still*   THERE IS NOT?   2 Sam 9:3

  IS THERE NO *longer a man belonging to Saul's house?*

Q   Word Order [680]

570 **Word order is an important feature of Hebrew syntax.** Its importance may have increased when Hebrew nouns lost their case endings (§31). Word order is a topic of intense research at present; what follows is a traditional analysis of the topic.

Word order in verbal clauses [681]

571 **A verbal clause** has a finite verb (perfect, imperfect, perfect waw consecutive, imperfect waw consecutive, preterite, imperative, jussive, or cohortative).[682]

572a **The normal order for verbal clauses** is verb + subject + direct object + adverb or prepositional phrase.[683]

---

[680] Cf. BHRG §46–47; GBHS §5.1.2(b); GKC §141l–n, 142f–g; IBHS §8.4, 9.1c; Regt 1991; DeCaen 1999; Muraoka 1985, 6–46; Niccacci 1999; Mirsky 1977; Bandstra 1992; Goldfajn 1998; Shimasaki 2002; Holmstedt 2003; Van der Merwe and Talstra 2002–3.

[681] Cf. BHRG §46.1; GBHS §5.1.2(b); GKC §142f–g; JM §155k–t; Jongeling 1991; Van der Merwe 1991; Van der Merwe 1994, 29–34; Van der Merwe 1999a; Van der Merwe 1999b; Muraoka 1985, 28–37; Niccacci 1990; Niccacci 1994a; Niccacci 1996; Shimasaki 2002, 22–9; Gentry 1998, 31–9; Revell 1989b; Lode 1984; Lode 1989; Holmstedt 2005a; Holmstedt 2005b; Moshavi 2006.

[682] Cf. GKC §140b; JM §153. Be aware that some scholars define a verbal clause as a clause that starts with a verb.

[683] Cf. BHRG §46.1.1, 46.1.3(iii)a; GBHS §5.1.2(b.1); GKC §142f; IBHS §8.3b; JM §155k; Jongeling 1991; Shimasaki 2002, 84–133.

- וַיָּבֵא יוֹסֵף אֶת־דִּבָּתָם רָעָה אֶל־ אֲבִיהֶם

  their father to bad their report Joseph brought   Gen 37:2

  Joseph brought a bad report about them to their father.

  o The verb (וַיָּבֵא 'he brought') is first. The subject (יוֹסֵף 'Joseph') follows the verb. A direct object (אֶת־דִּבָּתָם) and its modifier (רָעָה) follow the subject. The clause ends with a prepositional phrase (אֶל־אֲבִיהֶם). This order is typical.

572b **An expression of time usually comes first, before the verb.**[684] An expression of time usually precedes the verb.

- בָּעֵת הַהִיא אָמַר יְהוָה   *at that time*, YHWH said …

  YHWH said *the that* *in the time*   Josh 5:2

- בַּיָּמִים הָהֵם חָלָה חִזְקִיָּהוּ   *In those days*, Hezekiah became sick.

  Hezekiah became sick *the those* *in the days*   2 Kgs 20:1

572c **A word that negates the verb usually precedes the verb.**[685] If the verb is negated, the word that negates it usually comes right before the verb.

- לֹא הִמְטִיר יְהוָה אֱלֹהִים   YHWH God had *not* caused rain.

  God YHWH caused rain *not*   Gen 2:5

572d **The direct object may precede the subject.**[686] A direct object usually follows the subject in a verbal clause (§572a), but sometimes it precedes the subject (thus directly following the verb). Having a direct object precede the subject is more common when the direct object is a pronoun.

- וְלֹא־ נָשָׂא אֹתָם הָאָרֶץ לָשֶׁבֶת יַחְדָּו

  together to dwell THE LAND *them* carried and not   Gen 13:6

  THE LAND was not able to support *them* dwelling together.

- וַיַּחְנְכוּ אֶת־בֵּית יְהוָה הַמֶּלֶךְ וְכָל־ בְּנֵי יִשְׂרָאֵל

  ISRAEL SONS OF AND ALL OF THE KING *YHWH* *house of* dedicated   1 Kgs 8:63

  THE KING AND ALL OF THE ISRAELITES dedicated *the house of YHWH*.

572e **A preposition with a pronominal suffix may precede the subject.**[687] A prepositional phrase usually comes at the end of a verbal clause (§572a). If a preposition has a pronominal suffix, however, the prepositional phrase may come before the subject (and thus right after the verb).

- וַיֹּאמֶר לָהֶם יוֹסֵף   JOSEPH said *to them*

  JOSEPH *to them* said   Gen 44:15

---

[684] Cf. BHRG §46.1.2(i)(4); GBHS §5.1.2(b.1); GKC §142g.

[685] Cf. BHRG §46.1.2(i)(2), 46.1.3(i)b.

[686] Cf. BHRG §46.1.3(ii)a; GKC §142f; Muraoka 1985, 38–41.

[687] Cf. BHRG §46.1.3(ii)a; JM §155t.

573a **The subject may precede the verb to focus attention on the subject.**[688]

- הַנָּחָשׁ הִשִּׁיאַנִי — *The snake* deceived me.
  the snake deceived me — Gen 3:13

- אֱלֹהִים יִרְאֶה־לּוֹ הַשֶּׂה לְעֹלָה
  God will provide for himself the lamb to burnt offering — Gen 22:8
  God will provide for himself the lamb for the burnt offering.

573b **The subject may precede the verb to contrast the subject.**[689]

- אַבְרָם יָשַׁב בְּאֶרֶץ־כְּנָעַן
  Abram dwelt in land of Canaan — Gen 13:12

  וְלוֹט יָשַׁב בְּעָרֵי הַכִּכָּר
  and *Lot* dwelt in cities of the circle — (cont.)
  Abram dwelt in the land of Canaan, but *Lot* dwelt in the cities of the plain.

- וַיַּעַל הָאִישׁ אֶלְקָנָה ... וְחַנָּה לֹא עָלָתָה
  went up the man Elkanah *Hannah* but not went up — 1 Sam 1:21–2
  The man Elkanah went up ... but *Hannah* did not go up.

- Other examples include Gen 4:2 and 37:11.

573c **The subject may precede the verb when the subject has changed.**[690]

- וּמַלְכִּי־צֶדֶק מֶלֶךְ שָׁלֵם הוֹצִיא לֶחֶם
  and *Melchizedek* king of *Salem* brought out bread — Gen 14:18
  And *Melchizedek, the king of Salem*, brought out bread.

  o The preceding subject (in Gen 14:17) is the king of Sodom.

- וְרִבְקָה אָמְרָה אֶל־יַעֲקֹב בְּנָהּ
  and *Rebekah* said to Jacob her son — *Rebekah* said to her son Jacob
  Gen 27:6

  o The immediately preceding subject (in Gen 27:5) is Esau.

573d **The subject may precede the verb to express anterior time.**[691] In past time narrative, to indicate something even earlier in the past, the subject may precede the verb (a perfect verb; see §162.3).

- וְנֹחַ מָצָא חֵן בְּעֵינֵי יְהוָה — But *Noah* had found favour in YHWH's eyes.
  but *Noah* found favour in eyes of YHWH — Gen 6:8

---

[688] Cf. BHRG §47.2(i); GBHS §5.1.2(b.2); JM §155nb; Shimasaki 2002, 134–84.
[689] Cf. BHRG §47.2(ii)e; JM §155nb; Shimasaki 2002, 134–84.
[690] Cf. BHRG §47.2(ii); GBHS §5.1.2(b.2); Shimasaki 2002, 134–84.
[691] Cf. BHRG §47.2(iii); Zevit 1999. The **anterior construction**, according to Zevit (1999, 15), is a clause in a narrative context that begins with waw, then the subject, then a perfect verb, and that is preceded by a clause that indicates past time with a perfect verb or an imperfect waw consecutive verb.

- וְיַעֲקֹב תָּקַע אֶת־אָהֳלוֹ   *Jacob* had pitched his tent.
  his tent pitched *Jacob*   Gen 31:25

573e   **The subject may precede the verb to indicate simultaneous actions.** See §235 and §237.

- הוּא בָא עַד־לֶחִי וּפְלִשְׁתִּים הֵרִיעוּ לִקְרָאתוֹ
  to meet him shouted and *Philistines* Lehi unto entered *he*   Judg 15:14
  As *he* entered Lehi, *the Philistines* came shouting to meet him.

573f   **A long subject may precede the verb as a nominative absolute.** See §35.

- אִישׁ הָאֱלֹהִים אֲשֶׁר שָׁלַחְתָּ יָבוֹא־נָא
  may he come *you sent* *whom* *the God* *man of*   Judg 13:8
  The man of God whom you sent – may he come.

- הָאִשָּׁה אֲשֶׁר נָתַתָּה עִמָּדִי הִוא נָתְנָה־לִּי
  to me gave she *with me* *you gave* *whom* *the woman*   Gen 3:12
  the woman whom you gave to be with me – she gave me

573g   **An interrogative pronoun precedes the verb.**[692] See §119–23.

- מִי יַעֲלֶה־לָּנוּ   *Who* will go up for us?
  for us will go up *who?*   Judg 1:1

573h   **A subject may precede the verb in poetry for reason of style.**[693]

574a   **The direct object may precede the verb to focus attention on it.**[694]

- סֵפֶר הַתּוֹרָה מָצָאתִי בְּבֵית יְהוָה
  YHWH in house of I found *the law* *book of*   2 Kgs 22:8
  I found *the book of the law* in the house of YHWH.

    o   To communicate the emphasis in English, this could be translated as 'The book of the law is what I found in the house of YHWH.'

- אֶת־קֹלְךָ שָׁמַעְתִּי בַּגָּן   I heard *your sound* in the garden.
  in the garden I heard *your sound*   Gen 3:10

- Two other examples are found in 1 Sam 8:7.

574b   **An interrogative pronoun direct object precedes the verb.**[695] See §119–28.

---

[692] Cf. BHRG §46.1.2(ii)a; GBHS §5.1.2(b.2).
[693] Cf. BHRG §46.1.2(i)(6); GBHS §5.1.2(b.2); JM §155nd.
[694] Cf. GBHS §5.1.2(b.2); GKC §142f; JM §155o; Muraoka 1985, 38–41; Shimasaki 2002, 134–84.
[695] Cf. BHRG §46.1.2(ii)a; GBHS §5.1.2(b.2).

- מָה־ אֶעֱשֶׂה לָאֵלֶּה •

  to these   I can do   what?

  What can I do to these?

  Gen 31:43

- וְאֶת־מִי עָשַׁקְתִּי •

  I wronged   and whom?

  Whom have I wronged?

  1 Sam 12:3

574c A long direct object may precede the verb.[696]

- אֵת־אֲשֶׁר יֹאמַר יְהוָה אֵלַי אֹתוֹ אֲדַבֵּר •

  I will speak   it   to me   YHWH   will say   whatever

  1 Kgs 22:14

  Whatever YHWH says to me – that I will speak.

- אֶת־כָּל־ הָאָרֶץ אֲשֶׁר־אַתָּה רֹאֶה לְךָ אֶתְּנֶנָּה •

  I will give it   to you   seeing   you   that   the land   all of

  Gen 13:15

  I will give to you *all of the land that you see.*

- Other examples include 1 Kgs 15:13 and 2 Kgs 23:19.

575a A prepositional phrase may precede the verb to put it in focus.[697]

- בְּזֵעַת אַפֶּיךָ תֹּאכַל לֶחֶם •   *By the sweat of your face* you will eat food.

  food   you will eat   your face   by sweat of

  Gen 3:19

- בַּיַּבָּשָׁה עָבַר יִשְׂרָאֵל אֶת־הַיַּרְדֵּן •

  the Jordan   Israel   passed over   on the dry ground

  Josh 4:22

  On dry ground Israel passed over the Jordan.

- Another example is Gen 2:17.

575b A prepositional phrase may precede the verb for contrast.

- וַיִּקְרָא אֱלֹהִים לָאוֹר יוֹם וְלַחֹשֶׁךְ קָרָא לָיְלָה •

  night   called   and [לְ] the darkness   day   [לְ] the light   God   called

  Gen 1:5

  God called the light 'day,' and *the darkness* he called 'night.'

- וַיִּשַׁע יְהוָה אֶל־הֶבֶל וְאֶל־ מִנְחָתוֹ •

  his offering   and to   Abel   to   YHWH   looked with favour

  Gen 4:4–5

  וְאֶל־ קַיִן וְאֶל־ מִנְחָתוֹ לֹא שָׁעָה

  he looked with favour   not   his offering   and to   Cain   but to

  (cont.)

  YHWH looked with favour on Abel and his offering,

  but *on Cain and on his offering* YHWH did not look with favour.

575c A long object of a preposition may precede the verb. If the object of a preposition is long, it may be placed at the front of the sentence in an absolute construction (similar to a nominative absolute §35).

---

[696] Cf. JM §156c.

[697] Cf. JM §155p; Shimasaki 2002, 134–84.

- הַמִּטָּה אֲשֶׁר־עָלִיתָ שָּׁם לֹא־תֵרֵד מִמֶּנָּה

  from it YOU WILL GO DOWN not *there* *you went up* *which* *the bed*   2 Kgs 1:4

  The bed on which you went up – YOU WILL not COME DOWN from it.

  o   'The bed which you went up there' would be the object of the preposition מִן,
      but because it is so long, it was put before the verb תֵּרֵד. The resumptive 3fs
      pronominal suffix הָ ◌ 'it' (in מִמֶּנָּה) indicates its role in the sentence.

576   Inverted word order in an adverbial clause of manner. An adverbial
clause of manner (§491) usually has inverted word order, meaning that the
verb is not the first word in the clause; usually the subject or a
prepositional phrase precedes the verb.

- אִישׁ לְפִי־אָכְלוֹ לָקָטוּ   *by everyone gathering according to his eating*
  they gathered *his to eat* *per* *person*   Exod 16:18

- וַיָּבֹא אֲלֵיהֶם יְהוֹשֻׁעַ פִּתְאֹם כָּל־הַלַּיְלָה עָלָה
  went up *the night* *all of* suddenly *Joshua* to them *came*   Josh 10:9

  Joshua came upon them suddenly *by marching all night.*

Word order in verbless clauses [698]

- A verbless clause (also called a **nominal clause**) lacks a finite verb.[699]
  Verbless clauses are typically equational clauses (§561).

577   Verbless clauses fall into two major categories.[700]

- Some verbless clauses *identify the subject*, asserting that the subject is
  the predicate. The subject and predicate are usually definite.

- Other verbless clauses *describe or classify the subject*, asserting that
  the subject is described by the predicate or is a member of the class
  denoted by the predicate. The predicate is usually indefinite.

- These two types of verbless clauses can usually be distinguished on
  the basis of word order, as described in §578–9.

---

[698] Cf. BHRG §46.2; GBHS §5.1.1; GKC §141l–n; IBHS §8.4; JM §154f–j; Muraoka
1991; Muraoka 1985, 6–28; Andersen 1970; Buth 1999; Revell 1999.

[699] Cf. GKC §140a; JM §153, 154a. Verbless clauses are sometimes called **noun clauses**,
but be aware that the term **noun clauses** is also used to refer to substantival clauses
(§483–93). Also, be aware that the term **nominal clause** is used by some scholars to refer
to a clause that does not *begin* with a verb – even if the clause has a verb; for an
explanation, see Niccacci 1999, 243.

[700] Cf. IBHS §8.4a; JM §154ea.

578   **Subject first in verbless clauses that identify the subject.**[701]

- אָנֹכִי אֱלֹהֵי אָבִיךָ   *I* am the God of your father.
  your father   God of   *I*   Exod 3:6

- זֶה הַדָּבָר   *This* is the thing.
  the thing *this*   2 Kgs 11:5

- When a demonstrative pronoun is used anaphorically as a copulative verb (§115) the typical word order is subject – copulative demonstrative – predicate.

  - יְהוָה הוּא נַחֲלָתוֹ   *YHWH* is his inheritance.
    his inheritance (he) *YHWH*   Deut 18:2

579   **Predicate first in verbless clauses that classify or describe the subject.**[702]

- נְקִיִּם אֲנַחְנוּ מִשְּׁבֻעָתֵךְ הַזֶּה   We *are free* from this oath of yours.
  the this from your oath we *free*   Josh 2:17

- לֹא אָדָם הוּא   He *is not a human being.*
  he *human* not   1 Sam 15:29

- אָחִי הוּא   He *is a brother of mine.*
  he *my brother*   Gen 20:5

  - This is unusual because the predicate is definite. The word order indicates that the clause classifies the subject rather than identifying it.

- When a demonstrative pronoun is used anaphorically as a copulative verb (§115) the typical word order is subject – predicate – copulative demonstrative.

  - הָאֲנָשִׁים הָאֵלֶּה שְׁלֵמִים הֵם אִתָּנוּ   These men *are peaceable* with us.
    with us *they* *peaceable* the these the men   Gen 34:21

- Other examples include Gen 4:13, 12:10, 13:8.

580   **Word order in verbless desire clauses.** The predicate usually comes first in prose if it is a noun or participle. It may come last if it is in poetry. It usually comes last if it is a prepositional phrase. See the examples in §551.

581   **Interrogative words normally come first in a clause.**[703] An interrogative word, such as אֵי 'where?' מִי 'who?' or מָה 'what?' is normally located at the beginning of a clause. Examples include אֵי הֶבֶל אָחִיךָ 'Where is Abel your brother?' (Gen 4:9), מִי־הָאִישׁ הַלָּזֶה 'Who is this man?' (Gen 24:65), and מַה־שְּׁמוֹ 'What is his name?' (Exod 3:13).

---

[701] Cf. BHRG §46.2.1; GBHS §5.1.1; GKC §141l; IBHS §8.4a, 8.4.1; Shimasaki 2002, 134–84.

[702] Cf. BHRG §46.2.2, 47.3; GBHS §5.1.1; GKC §141l–m; IBHS §8.4a, 8.4.2; Shimasaki 2002, 84–133.

[703] Cf. BHRG §46.1.2(ii)a; GBHS §5.1.2(b.2); GKC §141l.

582 **Subject precedes predicate in circumstantial clauses**. See §494–5b.

R Ellipsis [704]

- When a word, phrase, or clause is omitted where it is expected to occur and is understood from the context, the word, phrase, or clause is said to be **elided**, **omitted**, **gapped**, or to have undergone **ellipsis**.
- §583–98 describe circumstances in which ellipsis is common.

583 **Omission of a substantive in a comparison.**[705] A substantive that is common to both sides of a comparison is often written only once.

- כָּאַיָּלוֹת   רַגְלַי   מְשַׁוֶּה   He makes my *feet* like [*the feet of*] the does.
  like the does   my *feet*   making like   Ps 18:34 = 2 Sam 22:34 (qere)

- קַרְנִי   כִּרְאֵים   וַתָּרֶם
  my *horn*   like wild oxen   you exalted   Ps 92:11
        You have exalted my *horn* like [*the horns of*] wild oxen.

584 **Omission of a predicate adjective in a comparison.** In a comparison, a predicate adjective is sometimes omitted.

- חָלֶד   יָקוּם   וּמִצָּהֳרַיִם   And your life will rise [*greater*] than noonday.
  life   will rise   and than noon   Job 11:17

- וּמִשֹּׁמְרוֹן   מִירוּשָׁלַ͏ִם   וּפְסִילֵיהֶם
  and than Samaria   than Jerusalem   and their idols   Isa 10:10
        And their idols [*were greater*] than [those of] Jerusalem and Samaria.

585 **Omission of a pronoun.** Pronouns are frequently omitted when they are clear from the context, as described in §586–8.

586 **Omission of a pronoun that is the subject of an infinitive.**[706] The subject of an infinitive construct can be expressed with a pronominal suffix on the infinitive (§109), but it is often omitted.

- אֶת־הֶעָרִים   בַּהֲפֹךְ   when [he] *overthrew* the cities
  the cities   when *to overturn*   Gen 19:29

- הַזֶּה   אֶת־הַדָּבָר   כִּשְׁמֹעַ   וַיְהִי   when [he] *heard* this message
  the this   the word   when *to hear*   (and it was)   1 Kgs 20:12

587 **Omission of a pronoun that is the subject of a participle.**[707] A pronoun that is the subject of a participle is often omitted.

---

[704] Cf. GBHS §5.3.6.
[705] Cf. GBHS §5.3.6(a).
[706] Cf. GBHS §5.3.6(b).
[707] Cf. GBHS §5.3.6(b).

- וְהִנֵּה עֹמֵד עַל־הַגְּמַלִּים   And behold, [he] *was standing* beside the camels.
  the camels   near   *standing*   and behold   Gen 24:30

- וּלְבֵנִים אֹמְרִים לָנוּ עֲשׂוּ   And [they] *are saying* to us, 'Make bricks!'
  make!   to us   *saying*   and bricks   Exod 5:16

- Other examples include Gen 32:7, 37:15; Josh 8:6; Amos 7:1.

588   Omission of a pronoun that is the direct object of a verb.[708] A pronoun that is the direct object of a verb can be omitted.

- וַיָּבֵא אֶל־הָאָדָם   *He brought* [them] to the man.
  the man   to   *he brought*   Gen 2:19

- וַתָּשֶׂם אֶל־הַמִּטָּה   *She put* [it] on the bed.
  the bed   to   *she put*   1 Sam 19:13

- Other examples include Gen 18:7; 1 Sam 17:35; 2 Kgs 4:5.

589   Omission of the expected direct object of a verb.[709] Some verbs have a specific direct object that is expected to occur with the verb. For example, in the context of a covenant, the verb כָּרַת 'to cut' is expected to have the direct object בְּרִית 'covenant' (e.g., Gen 21:32). Often, however, the direct object בְּרִית 'covenant' is omitted, although it is understood from the context (e.g., 1 Sam 20:16 and 2 Chr 7:18).

- Other direct objects that are often omitted after certain verbs include קוֹל 'voice' after the verb נָשָׂא 'to lift up' (meaning 'to cry out': Isa 3:7, 42:2), לֵב 'heart' after the verb שִׂים 'to put' (meaning 'to pay attention': Job 4:20; Isa 41:20), גּוֹרָל 'lot' after הִפִּיל 'to cause to fall' (meaning 'to cast lots': 1 Sam 14:42; Job 6:27), and דָּבָר 'a word' after הֵשִׁיב 'to return' (meaning 'to reply': Job 13:22).

590   Omission of a word after a numeral.[710] After a number, certain words may be omitted when they are clear from the context. For example, the word שֶׁקֶל 'shekel' is omitted after a number in 2 Sam 18:12 and Num 7:68, and יוֹם 'day' is omitted in 2 Kgs 25:1. Units of measure can also be omitted, such as אֵפָה 'ephah' and סְאָה 'seah' in Ruth 3:15, 17.

591   Omission of a verb that is clear from the context.[711] If a verb is clear from the context, it may be omitted. If the omitted verb occurs in a parallel line of poetry, the one occurrence of the verb is sometimes said to perform **double duty**. This often occurs with the particle פֶּן 'lest' (§461).

---

[708] Cf. GBHS §5.3.6(b).
[709] Cf. BHRG §33.1 note 42. In prior editions, this was referred to as **brachylogy**.
[710] Cf. GBHS §5.3.6(c).
[711] Cf. IBHS §11.4.3d; Andersen 1994, 113–14.

- אָבִי יִסַּר אֶתְכֶם בַּשּׁוֹטִים וַאֲנִי בָּעְקְרַבִּים

  with the scorpions but I with the whips you *disciplined* my father   2 Chr 10:11, 14

  My father *disciplined* you with whips, but I [*will discipline* you] with scorpions.

- Another example is Josh 24:15.

592 **Omissions frequently occur with negatives**. Words are often omitted after a negative word, as described in §593–5.

593 **Omission with the negative אַיִן / אֵין**.[712] In a clause that contains the negative word אַיִן / אֵין 'there is not,' other words are often omitted (§409).

- הָבָה־ לִי בָנִים וְאִם־ אַיִן מֵתָה אָנֹכִי

  I   dying *there is not* and if children to me give!   Gen 30:1

  Give me children, or else, if [I do] *not* [get them], I will die!

594 **Omission with the negative לֹא**.[713] In a clause that contains the negative word לֹא 'not,' other words are often omitted (§398).

- וַיֹּאמֶר לֹא כִּי צָחָקְתְּ   He said, '*No*, but you did laugh.'

  you laughed but *no* he said   Gen 18:15

  o   In Gen 18:15, many words are omitted after the word לֹא 'not,' because the statement לֹא means something like, 'No, what you just said is not true.'

595 **Omission with the negative אַל**.[714] In a clause that contains the negative word אַל 'not,' other words are often omitted (§403).

- אַל בְּנֹתַי   '*No*, my daughters [, do not return with me to my people].'

  my daughters *no*   Ruth 1:13

- Other examples include 2 Sam 1:21 and Isa 62:6.

596 **Omission of the oath formula**.[715] A typical oath is found in 2 Sam 3:9, which states, 'Thus may God do to Abner and more if ...' Sometimes an oath begins with 'if' (אִם) but the 'thus may ...' part is omitted.

- וַיִּשָּׁבַע לֵאמֹר אִם־יִרְאֶה אִישׁ בָּאֲנָשִׁים הָאֵלֶּה ... אֵת הָאָרֶץ

  the land   the these among the men man will see if to say he swore

  He swore, saying, '[Thus may God do to me and more]

  if any of these men see ... the land.' Deut 1:34–35

- עֵדָה הַמַּצֵּבָה אִם־אָנִי לֹא־ אֶעֱבֹר אֵלֶיךָ

  to you will pass over not I if the pillar witness   Gen 31:52

  May the pillar be a witness *if I do not pass over to you*.

---

[712] Cf. GBHS §5.3.6(d).

[713] Cf. GBHS §5.3.6(d); Zevit 1979.

[714] Cf. GBHS §5.3.6(d).

[715] Cf. JM §165h.

- Another example is Job 1:11.

597 **Omission of the conclusion of a statement.**[716] Sometimes the conclusion of a statement, such as the apodosis of a conditional sentence, is omitted. This 'breaking off' of a sentence is sometimes called **aposiopesis**.

- אִם־ תִּשָּׂא חַטָּאתָם וְאִם־ אַיִן מְחֵנִי נָא מִסִּפְרְךָ
  from your book wipe me there is not and if their sin you will lift if Exod 32:32
  If you will forgive their sin, [then do so,] but if not, then wipe me out of your book!

- Other possible examples include Gen 50:15 and 2 Chr 2:2.

598 **Omission of every word except one.**[717] Occasionally a single word may constitute an **elliptical utterance**. This occurs with negatives, such as אַיִן (§409), לֹא (§398), and אַל (§403), but it also occurs with other words.

- וַיֹּאמֶר עֵד   He said, '[YHWH is] *a witness.*'
  witness he said   1 Sam 12:5

- וַתֹּאמֶר שָׁלוֹם   She said, '[All is] *well.*'
  peace she said   2 Kgs 4:23, 26

- Another example is 2 Kgs 3:23.

---

[716] Cf. GKC §167a; JM §167r.
[717] Cf. GKC §152c.

References

Aejmelaeus, A. 1986. Function and interpretation of כִּי in biblical Hebrew. *JBL* 105:193–209.

Allegro, J. 1955. Uses of the Semitic demonstrative element *z* in Hebrew. *VT* 5:309–12.

Althann, R. 1981. *mwl* 'circumcise' with the *lamedh* of agency. *Bib* 62:239–40.

– 1991. Does 'et ('aet-) sometimes signify >from< in the Hebrew Bible? *ZAW* 103:121–4.

Andersen, F.I. 1970. *The Hebrew verbless clause in the Pentateuch*. Nashville: Abingdon.

– 1974. *The sentence in biblical Hebrew*. The Hague: Mouton.

– 1994. Salience, implicature, ambiguity, and redundancy in clause-clause relationships in biblical Hebrew. In *Biblical Hebrew and discourse linguistics*, ed. R.D. Bergen, 99–116. Winona Lake, IN: Eisenbrauns.

Andersen, F.I., and A.D. Forbes. 1983. 'Prose particle' counts of the Hebrew Bible. In *The word of the Lord shall go forth*, ed. C.L. Meyers and M. O'Connor, 165–83. Winona Lake, IN: Eisenbrauns.

Andersen, T.D. 2000. The evolution of the Hebrew verbal system. *ZAH* 13:1–66.

Arnold, B.T., and J.H. Choi. 2003. *A guide to biblical Hebrew syntax*. New York: Cambridge University Press.

Avishur, Y. 1971–2. Pairs of synonymous words in the construct state (and in appositional hendiadys) in biblical Hebrew. *Semitics* 2:17–81.

Baden, J.S. Forthcoming. The wəyiqtol and the volitive sequence. *VT*.

Baker, D.W. 1980. Further examples of the waw explicativum. *VT* 30:129–36.

Bandstra, B.L. 1992. Word order and emphasis in biblical Hebrew narrative. In *Linguistics and biblical Hebrew*, ed. W.R. Bodine, 109–23. Winona Lake, IN: Eisenbrauns.

Barr, J. 1969. Review of *Hebrew syntax: An outline*, by R.J. Williams. *BSOAS* 32:599–601.

– 1978. Some notes on *ben* 'between' in classical Hebrew. *JSS* 23:1–22.

– 1982. Hebrew עַד, especially at Job 1.18 and Neh. VII.3. *JSS* 27:177–88.

– 1989. 'Determination' and the definite article in biblical Hebrew. *JSS* 34:307–35.

Ben-Asher, M. 1978. The gender of nouns in biblical Hebrew. *Semitics* 6:1–14.

Berry, G.R. 1904. Waw consecutive with the perfect in Hebrew. *JBL* 22:60–9.

Blake, F.R. 1903. The so-called intransitive verbal forms in Hebrew. *JAOS* 24:145–204

– 1915. The expression of indefinite pronominal ideas in hebrew. *JAOS* 34:115–228.

– 1944. The Hebrew waw conversive. *JBL* 63:271–95.

– 1951. *A resurvey of Hebrew tenses*. Rome: Pontificium Institutum Biblicum.

Blau, J. 1971. Marginalia semitica I. *IOS* 1:15–24.

Blommerde, A.C.M. 1974. The broken construct chain, further examples. *Bib* 55:549–52.

Brin, G. 1992. The superlative in the Hebrew Bible: Additional cases. *VT* 42:115–18.

Brown, M.L. 1987. 'Is it not?' or 'Indeed!': *HL* in Northwest Semitic. *Maarav* 4:201–19.

Brown, F., S.R. Driver, and C.A. Briggs. 1907. *A Hebrew and English lexicon of the Old Testament*. Oxford: Clarendon. Repr., Peabody, MA: Hendrickson, 2005.

Buth, R. 1994. Methodological collision between source criticism and discourse analysis: The problem of 'unmarked temporal overlay' and the pluperfect/nonsequential *wayyiqtol*. In *Biblical Hebrew and discourse linguistics*, ed. R.D. Bergen, 138–54. Winona Lake, IN: Eisenbrauns.

– 1999. Word order in the verbless clause: A generative-functional approach. In *The verbless clause in biblical Hebrew: Linguistic approaches*, ed. C.L. Miller, 79–108. Winona Lake, IN: Eisenbrauns.

Claassen, W.T. 1972. The declarative-estimative Hiphʻil. *JNSL* 2:5–16

– 1983. Speaker-oriented functions of kî in biblical Hebrew. *JNSL* 11:29–46.

Collins, C.J. 1995. The *wayyiqtol* as 'pluperfect': When and why. *TynBul* 46:117–140.

Cook, J.A. 2004. The semantics of verbal pragmatics: clarifying the roles of *Yayyiqtol* and *Weqatal* in biblical Hebrew prose. *JSS* 49:247–73.

Dahood, M. 1956. Enclitic mem and emphatic lamed in Psalm 85. *Bib* 37:338–40.

– 1966. Vocative lamedh in the psalter. *VT* 16:299–311.

– 1971. Causal *beth* and the root NKR in Nahum 3,4. *Bib* 52:395–6.

– 1975a. Emphatic *lamedh* in Jer 14:21 and Ezek 34:29. *CBQ* 37:341–2.

– 1975b. The emphatic double negative *mʾyn* in Jer 10:6–7. *CBQ* 37:458–9.

– 1981. Vocative lamedh in Exodus 2,14 und Merismus in 34,21. *Bib* 62:413–15.

Davies, G.I. 1991. The use and non-use of the particle ʾet in Hebrew inscriptions. In *Studies in Hebrew and Aramaic syntax*, ed. K. Jongeling et al., 14–26. Leiden: Brill.

DeCaen, V. 1999. A unified analysis of verbal and verbless clauses within government-binding theory. In *The verbless clause in biblical Hebrew: Linguistic approaches*, ed. C.L. Miller, 109–31. Winona Lake, IN: Eisenbrauns.

Denio, F.B. 1885. Grammatical questions. *Hebraica* 1:244–6.

– 1900. The relations expressed by the genitive in Hebrew. *JBL* 19:107–13.

Driver, S.R. 1892. *A treatise on the use of the tenses in Hebrew and some other syntactical questions*. 3rd ed. London: Oxford University Press. Repr. Grand Rapids, MI: Eerdmans, 1998.

Dyk, J., and E. Talstra. 1999. Paradigmatic and syntagmatic features in identifying subject and predicate in nominal clauses. In *The verbless clause in biblical Hebrew: Linguistic approaches*, ed. C.L. Miller, 133–85. Winona Lake, IN: Eisenbrauns.

Ehrensvärd, M. 1999. An unusual use of the article in biblical and post-biblical Hebrew. In *Sirach, scrolls, and sages*, ed. T. Muraoka and J.F. Elwolde, 68–76. Leiden: Brill.

Elwolde, J. 1990. Non-biblical supplements to classical Hebrew ʾim. *VT* 40:221–3.

– 1994. The use of ʾēt in non-biblical Hebrew texts. *VT* 44:170–82.

Ember, A. 1905. The pluralis intensivus in Hebrew. *AJSL* 21:195–231.

Eskhult, M. 1998. The verb *sbb* as a marker of inception in biblical Hebrew. *OrSu* 47:21–6.

– 2000. Hebrew infinitival paranomasia. *OrSu* 39:27–32.

Fassberg, S.E. 1999. The lengthened imperative קָטְלָה in biblical Hebrew. *HS* 40:7–13.

– 2001. The movement from *Qal* to *Piʻel* in Hebrew and the disappearance of the *Qal* internal passive. *HS* 42:243–55.

– 2006. Sequences of positive commands in biblical Hebrew: לֵךְ אֱמֹר , לֵךְ וְאָמַרְתָּ , הָלֹךְ וְאָמַרְתָּ. In *Biblical Hebrew in its Northwest Semitic setting*, ed. S.E. Fassberg and A.Hurvitz, 51–64. Winona Lake, IN: Eisenbrauns.

Fokkelman, J.P. 1991. Iterative forms of the classical Hebrew verb: Exploring the triangle of style, syntax, and text grammar. In *Studies in Hebrew and Aramaic syntax*, ed. K. Jongeling et al., 38–55. Leiden: Brill.

Follingstad, C.M. 2001. Deictic viewpoint in biblical Hebrew text: Paradigmatic analysis of the particle כִּי (kî). Dallas: SIL International.

Freedman, D.N. 1972. The broken construct chain. *Bib* 53:534–6. Reprinted in *Pottery, poetry, and prophesy: Studies in early Hebrew poetry*, 339–41. Winona Lake, IN: Eisenbrauns, 1980.

Frendo, A. 1981. The 'Broken construct chain' in Qoh 10,10b. *Bib* 62:544–5.

Gaenssle, C. 1914. The Hebrew particle אֲשֶׁר: Part I. *AJSL* 31:5–15.

– 1915a. The Hebrew particle אֲשֶׁר: Part II. *AJSL* 31:93–159.

– 1915b. *The Hebrew particle אֲשֶׁר*. Chicago: University of Chicago Press.

Garr, W.R. 2004. הֵן. *RB* 111:321–44.

Gentry, P.J. 1998. The system of the verb in classical biblical Hebrew. *HS* 39:7–39.

Gesenius, W., and E. Kautzsch. 1910. *Gesenius' Hebrew grammar*. Translated by A.E. Cowley. 2nd English ed. New York: Oxford University Press. Repr., Mineola, NY: Dover, 2006.

Gianto, A. 1996. Variations in biblical Hebrew. *Bib* 77:494–508.

Gibson, J.C.L. 1995. Coordination by *vav* in biblical Hebrew. In *Words remembered, texts renewed*, ed. J. Davies, G. Harvey, and W.G.E. Watson, 272–9. Sheffield: Sheffield Academic.

Ginsberg, H.L. 1929. Studies on the biblical Hebrew verb. *AJSL* 46:53–8.

Glinert, L.H. 1982. The preposition in biblical and modern Hebrew: Towards a redefinition. *HS* 23:115–25.

Goetze, A. 1942. The so-called intensive of the Semitic languages. *JAOS* 62:1–8.

Goldenberg, G. 1971. Tautological infinitive. *IOS* 1:36–85.

– 1991. On direct speech and the Hebrew Bible. In *Studies in Hebrew and Aramaic syntax*, ed. K. Jongeling et al., 79–96. Leiden: Brill.

Goldfajn, T. 1998. *Word order and time in biblical Hebrew narrative*. Oxford: Clarendon.

Gordis, R. 1930. Note on general conditional sentences in Hebrew. *JBL* 49:200–3. Reprinted in *The word and the book: Studies in biblical language and literature*, 214–17. New York: Ktav, 1976.

– 1933. A rhetorical use of interrogative sentences in biblical Hebrew. *AJSL* 49:212–17. Reprinted in *The word and the book: Studies in biblical language and literature*, 152–157. New York: Ktav, 1976.

– 1943. The asseverative kaph in Hebrew and Ugaritic. *JAOS* 63:176–8. Reprinted in *The word and the book: Studies in biblical language and literature*, 211–13. New York: Ktav, 1976.

Gordon, C.H. 1981. 'In' of predication or equivalence. *JBL* 100:612–13.

Gosling, F.A. 1998. An interesting use of the waw consecutive. *ZAW* 110:403–10.

Gottstein, M.H. 1949. Afterthought and the syntax of relative clauses in biblical Hebrew. *JBL* 68:35–47.

Greenstein, E.L. 1988. On the prefixed preterite in biblical Hebrew. *HS* 29:7–17.

Gropp, D.M. 1991. The function of the finite verb in classical biblical Hebrew. *HAR* 13:45–62.

Grossberg, D. 1979–80. Nominalization in biblical Hebrew. *HS* 20–1:29–33.

– 1980. Noun/verb parallelism: Syntactic or asyntactic. *JBL* 99:481–8.

Hillers, D.R. 1967. Delocutive verbs in biblical Hebrew. *JBL* 86:320–4.

Hoftijzer, J. 1965. Remarks concerning the use of the particle '*t* in classical Hebrew. *OtSt* 14:1–99.

– 1973. Review: The nominal clause reconsidered. *VT* 23:446–510.

– 1981. *A search for method: A study in the syntactic use of the h-locale in classical Hebrew.* Leiden: Brill.

Holmstedt, R.D. 2001. Headlessness and extraposition: Another look at the syntax of אשר. *JNSL* 27:1–16.

– 2002. The relative clause in biblical Hebrew: A linguistic analysis. PhD diss., The University of Wisconsin – Madison. http://individual.utoronto.ca/holmstedt/PDF.html.

– 2003. Adjusting our focus. Review of *Focus structure in biblical Hebrew*, by K. Shimasaki. *HS* 44:203–15.

– 2005a. Word order in the book of Proverbs. In *Seeking out the wisdom of the ancients*, ed. K.G. Friebel, D.R. Magary, and R.L. Troxel, 135–54. Winona Lake, IN: Eisenbrauns.

– 2005b. Topic and focus in biblical Hebrew if it is an SV Language. Paper presented at the annual meeting of the SBL, Philadelphia, 20 November 2005. http://individual. utoronto.ca/holmstedt/PDF.html.

– 2006. The story of ancient Hebrew 'ăšer. *Ancient Near Eastern Studies* 43:9–28.

– Forthcoming-a. *The relative clause in ancient Hebrew.* Winona Lake, IN: Eisenbrauns.

– Forthcoming-b. The etymologies of Hebrew '*šer* and *šeC*-. *JNES*.

Honeyman, A.M. 1952. *Merismus* in biblical Hebrew. *JBL* 71:11–18.

Hospers, J.H. 1991. Some remarks about the so-called imperative use of the infinitive absolute (infinitivus pro imperativo) in classical Hebrew. In *Studies in Hebrew and Aramaic syntax*, ed. K. Jongeling et al., 97–102. Leiden: Brill.

Huehnergard, J. 1983. Asseverative *la* and hypothetical *lu/law* in Semitic. *JAOS* 103:569–93.

– 2000. *A grammar of Akkadian.* Winona Lake, IN: Eisenbrauns.

– 2006. On the etymology of the Hebrew relative šɛ-. In *Biblical Hebrew in its Northwest Semitic setting*, ed. S. Fassberg and A. Hurvitz, 103–25. Winona Lake, IN: Eisenbrauns.

Huesman, J. 1956a. Finite uses of the infinitive absolute. *Bib* 37:271–95.

– 1956b. The infinitive absolute and the waw + perfect problem. *Bib* 37:410–34.

Hughes, J.A. 1970. Another look at the Hebrew tenses. *JNES* 29:12–24.

Hughes, J. 1982. Additional note. *JSS* 27:189–92.

Jongeling, K. 1991. On the VSO character of Hebrew. In *Studies in Hebrew and Aramaic syntax*, ed. K. Jongeling et al., 102–11. Leiden: Brill.

Joosten, J. 1991. The syntax of habərākāh 'ahat hī' ləkā 'ābī (Gen. 27:38aα). JSS 36:207–21.

– 1993. The syntax of relative clauses with a first or second person antecedent in biblical Hebrew. *JNSL* 52:275–80.

– 1997. The indicative system of the biblical Hebrew verb and its literary exploitation. In *Narrative syntax and the Hebrew Bible*, ed. E. van Wolde, 51–71. Leiden: Brill.

– 1998. The functions of the Semitic D stem: Biblical Hebrew materials for a comparative-historical approach. *Or* 67:202–30.

– 1999a. The long form of the prefix conjugation referring to the past in biblical Hebrew prose. *HS* 40:15–26.

– 1999b. The lengthened imperative with accusative suffix in biblical Hebrew. *ZAW* 111:423–6.

– 2002. Do finite verbal forms in biblical Hebrew express aspect? *JANES* 29:49–70.

– 2006. The disappearance of iterative weqatal in the biblical Hebrew verbal system. In *Biblical Hebrew in its Northwest Semitic setting*, ed. S.E. Fassberg and A. Hurvitz, 135–47. Winona Lake, IN: Eisenbrauns.

Joüon, P., and T. Muraoka. 1993. *A grammar of biblical Hebrew*. 2 vols. Subsidia biblica 14/1–2. Rome: Editrice Pontificio Istituto Biblico.

Joüon, P., and T. Muraoka. 2006. *A grammar of biblical Hebrew*, revised edition. Subsidia biblica 27. Rome: Editrice Pontificio Istituto Biblico.

Junger, J. 1989. Aspect and cohesion in biblical Hebrew narratives. *Semitics* 10:71–129.

Khan, G. 2006. Some aspects of the copula in North West Semitic. In *Biblical Hebrew in its Northwest Semitic setting*, ed. S.E. Fassberg and A. Hurvitz, 155–76. Winona Lake, IN: Eisenbrauns.

Kelly, F.T. 1920. The imperfect with simple waw in Hebrew. *JBL* 39:1–23.

Kelso, J.A. 1903. Is the divine name ever equivalent to the superlative? *AJSL* 19:152–8.

Klein, G.L. 1990. The 'prophetic perfect.' *JNSL* 16:45–60.

Koehler, L., and W. Baumgartner. 1994–9. *The Hebrew and Aramaic lexicon of the Old Testament*. Tr. and ed. M.E.J. Richardson. 4 vols. Leiden: Brill.

Kraetzschmar, R. 1890. The origin of the notae relationis in Hebrew. *Hebraica* 6:296–302.

Kroeze, J.H. 1997a. Semantic relations in construct phrases of biblical Hebrew: A functional approach. *ZAH* 10:27–41.

– 1997b. Alternatives for the accusative in biblical Hebrew. In *Studien zur hebräischen Grammatik*, ed. A. Wagner, 11–25. Göttingen: Vandenhoeck & Ruprecht.

– 2001. Alternatives for the nominative in biblical Hebrew. *JSS* 46:33–50.

– 2002. The Hof'al in biblical Hebrew: Simple passives, single passives and double passives – and reflexives? *JNSL* 28:39–55.

– 2003. The semantic functions of embedded constructions in biblical Hebrew. *JNSL* 29:107–20.

Lambdin, T.O. 1971. *Introduction to biblical Hebrew*. New York: Scribner's.

Landes, G.M. 2001. *Building your biblical Hebrew vocabulary*. Atlanta: Society of Biblical Literature.

Lehmann, M.R. 1969. Biblical oaths. *ZAW* 81:74–92.

Lode, L. 1984. Postverbal word order in biblical Hebrew: Structure and function (Part 1). *Semitics* 9:113–64.

– 1989. Postverbal word order in biblical Hebrew: Structure and function (Part 2). *Semitics* 10:24–39.

Longacre, R.E. 1992. Discourse perspective on the Hebrew verb: Affirmation and restatement. In *Linguistics and biblical Hebrew*, ed. W.R. Bodine, 177–189. Winona Lake, IN: Eisenbrauns.

– 1994. *Weqatal* forms in biblical Hebrew prose: A discourse-modular approach. In *Biblical Hebrew and discourse linguistics*, ed. R.D. Bergen, 50–98. Winona Lake, IN: Eisenbrauns.

Lowery, K.E. 1999. Relative definiteness and the verbless clause. In *The verbless clause in biblical Hebrew: Linguistic approaches*, ed. C.L. Miller, 251–72. Winona Lake, IN: Eisenbrauns.

MacDonald, J. 1964. The particle 't in classical Hebrew: Some new data on its use with the nominative. *VT* 14:264–75.

Manross, L.N. 1954. Bêth essentiae. *JBL* 73:238–9.

Mastin, B.A. 1984. Waw explicativum in 2 Kings VIII 9. *VT* 34:353–5.

McFall, L. 1982. *The enigma of the Hebrew verbal system: Solutions from Ewald to the present day*. Sheffield: Almond.

Meek, T.J. 1929. The co-ordinate adverbial clause in Hebrew. *JAOS* 49:156–9.

– 1940. The Hebrew accusative of time and place. *JAOS* 60:224–8.

– 1945. The syntax of the sentence in Hebrew. *JBL* 64:1–13.

Meyer, E.E. 2001. The particle כִּי, a mere conjunction or something more? *JNSL* 27:39–62.

Miller, C.H. 1970. The infinitive construct in the lawbooks of the Old Testament: A statistical study. *CBQ* 32:222–6.

Miller, C.L. 1994. Introducing direct discourse in biblical Hebrew narrative. In *Biblical Hebrew and discourse linguistics*, ed. R.D. Bergen, 199–241. Winona Lake, IN: Eisenbrauns.

Mirsky, A. 1977. Stylistic device for conclusion in Hebrew. *Semitics* 5:9–23.

Mitchell, H.G. 1888. The preposition אֶל. *JSBLE* 8:43–120.

– 1915. Final constructions of biblical Hebrew. *JBL* 34:83–161.

Moomo, D.O. 2005. The imperfective meaning of *weqatal* in biblical Hebrew. *JNSL* 31:89–106.

Moshavi, A. 2006. The discourse functions of object/adverbial-fronting in biblical Hebrew. In *Biblical Hebrew in its Northwest Semitic setting*, ed. S.E. Fassberg and A. Hurvitz, 231–45. Winona Lake, IN: Eisenbrauns.

Muilenburg, J. 1961. The linguistic and rhetorical usages of the particle כִּי in the Old Testament. *HUCA* 32:135–60.

Muraoka, T. 1978. On the so-called *dativus ethicus* in Hebrew. *JTS* 29:495–8.

– 1985. *Emphatic words and structures in biblical Hebrew*. Leiden: Brill.

– 1991. The biblical Hebrew nominal clause with a prepositional phrase. In *Studies in Hebrew and Aramaic syntax*, ed. K. Jongeling et al., 143–51. Leiden: Brill.

– 1997. The alleged final function of the biblical Hebrew syntagm <*waw* + a volitive form>. In *Narrative syntax and the Hebrew Bible*, ed. E. van Wolde, 229–41. Leiden: Brill.

– 1999. The tripartite nominal clause revisited. In *The verbless clause in biblical Hebrew: Linguistic approaches*, ed. C.L. Miller, 187–213. Winona Lake, IN: Eisenbrauns.

Muraoka, T., and M. Rogland. 1998. The waw consecutive in old Aramaic? A rejoinder to Victor Sasson. *VT* 48:99–104.

Naudé, J.A. 1990. A syntactic analysis of dislocations in biblical Hebrew. *JNSL* 16:115–30.

– 1999. Syntactic aspects of co-ordinate subjects with independent personal pronouns. *JNSL* 25:75–99.

Niccacci, A. 1990. *The syntax of the verb in classical Hebrew prose*. Tr. W.G.E. Watson. Sheffield: Sheffield Academic.

– 1994a. On the Hebrew verbal system. In *Biblical Hebrew and discourse linguistics*, ed. R.D. Bergen, 117–37. Winona Lake, IN: Eisenbrauns.

– 1994b. Analysis of biblical narrative. In *Biblical Hebrew and discourse linguistics*, ed. R.D. Bergen, 175–98. Winona Lake, IN: Eisenbrauns.

– 1996. Finite verb in the second position of the sentence: Coherence of the Hebrew verbal system. *ZAW* 108:434–40.

– 1997. Basic facts and theory of the biblical Hebrew verb system in prose. In *Narrative syntax and the Hebrew Bible*, ed. E. van Wolde, 167–202. Leiden: Brill.

– 1999. Types and functions of the nominal sentence. In *The verbless clause in biblical Hebrew: Linguistic approaches*, ed. C.L. Miller, 215–48. Winona Lake, IN: Eisenbrauns.

– 2006. The biblical Hebrew verbal system in poetry. In *Biblical Hebrew in its Northwest Semitic setting*, ed. S.E. Fassberg and A. Hurvitz, 247–68. Winona Lake, IN: Eisenbrauns.

Noss, P. 1995. The Hebrew post-verbal *lamed* preposition plus pronoun. *BT* 46:326–35.

Pardee, D. 1979. Review of *Hebrew syntax: An outline*, by R.J. Williams. *JNES* 38:148.

Plank, F. 2005. Delocutive verbs, crosslinguistically. *Linguistic Typology* 9:459–91.

Pope, M. 1953. 'Pleonastic' wāw before nouns in Ugaritic and Hebrew. *JAOS* 73:95–8.

Qimron, E. 1986–7. Consecutive and conjunctive imperfect: The form of the imperfect with waw in biblical Hebrew. *JQR*, n.s., 77:149–61.

Rabinowitz, I. 1984. 'az followed by imperfect verb form in preterite contexts: A redactional device in biblical Hebrew. *VT* 34:53–62.

Rainey, A.F. 1986. The ancient Hebrew prefix conjugation in the light of Amarnah Canaanite. *HS* 27:4–19.

Rechenmacher, H. 2003. לֹא and אַיִן in nominal clauses. *JNSL* 29:67–85.

Regt, L.J. de. 1991. Word order in different clause types in Deuteronomy 1–30. In *Studies in Hebrew and Aramaic syntax*, ed. K. Jongeling et al., 152–72. Leiden: Brill.

Reider, J. 1940. Substantival 'al in biblical Hebrew. *JQR*, n.s., 30:263–70.

Rendsburg, G. 1982. Dual personal pronouns and dual verbs in Hebrew. *JQR*, n.s., 73:38–58.

Revell, E.J. 1984. Stress and the *waw* 'consecutive' in biblical Hebrew. *JAOS* 104:437–44.

– 1985. The conditioning of stress position in *waw* consecutive perfect forms in biblical Hebrew. *HAR* 9:277–300.

– 1988. First person imperfect forms with waw consecutive. *VT* 38:419–26.

– 1989a. The system of the verb in standard biblical prose. *HUCA* 60:1–37.

– 1989b. The conditioning of word order in verbless clauses in biblical Hebrew. *JSS* 34:1–24.

– 1991. First person imperfect forms with waw consecutive: Addenda. *VT* 41:127–8.

– 1999. Thematic continuity and the conditioning of word order in verbless clauses. In *The verbless clause in biblical Hebrew: Linguistic approaches*, ed. C.L. Miller, 297–319. Winona Lake, IN: Eisenbrauns.

– 2002. Logic of concord with collectives in biblical Narrative. *Maarav* 9:61–91.

Riekert, S.J.P.K. 1979. The struct patterns of the paranomastic and co-ordinated infinitives absolute in Genesis. *JNSL* 7:69–83.

Rogland, M. 2003. *Alleged non-past uses of* qatal *in classical Hebrew*. Assen: Van Gorcum.

Rooker, M.F. 1990. *Biblical Hebrew in transition: The language of the Book of Ezekiel*. Sheffield: Sheffield Academic.

Rosén, H.B. 1984–6. On some nominal morphological categories in biblical Hebrew. *OrSu* 33–35:355–65.

Rubinstein, A. 1952. A finite verb continued by an infinitive absolute in biblical Hebrew. *VT* 2:362–7.

– 1963. The anomalous perfect with *waw*–conjunctive in biblical Hebrew. *Bib* 44:62–9.

Sanders, P. 2004. So may God do to me! *Bib* 85:91–8.

Sasson, V. 1997. Some observations on the use and original purpose of the *waw* consecutive in old Aramaic and biblical Hebrew. *VT* 47:111–27.

Saydon, P.P. 1954. The inceptive imperfect in Hebrew and the verb הֵחֵל «to begin». *Bib* 35:43–50.

– 1964. Meaning and uses of the particle 't. *VT* 14:192–210.

Schwarzchild, R. 1990. The syntax of אשר in biblical Hebrew with special reference to Qoheleth. *HS* 31:7–39.

Selms, A. van. 1971–2. Motivated interrogative sentences in biblical Hebrew. *Semitics* 2:143–9.

– 1978. Motivated interrogative sentences in the Book of Job. *Semitics* 6:28–35.

Sheehan, J.F.X. 1975. Conversive waw and accentual shift. *Bib* 51:545–8.

Shereshevsky, E. 1967. The use of prepositions and conjunctions in Rashi's commentary. *JQR*, n.s., 57:200–11.

Shimasaki, K. 2002. *Focus Structure in biblical Hebrew: A study of word order and information structure*. Bethesda, MD: CDL.

Shulman, A. 2001. Imperative and second person indicative forms in biblical Hebrew prose. *HS* 42:271–87.

Siebsma, P.A. 1991. *The function of the Niph'al in biblical Hebrew in relationship to Other passive-reflexive verbal stems and to the Pu'al and Hoph'al in particular*. Maastricht: Van Gorcum.

Sinclair, C. 1999. Are nominal clauses a distinct clausal type? In *The verbless clause in biblical Hebrew: Linguistic approaches*, ed. C.L. Miller, 51–75. Winona Lake, IN: Eisenbrauns.

Sivan, D., and W. Schniedewind. 1993. Letting your 'yes' be 'no' in ancient Israel: A study of the asseverative לא and הֲלֹא. *JSS* 38:209–26.

Slonim, M.G. 1941. The deliberate substitution of the masculine for the feminine pronominal suffixes in the Hebrew Bible. *JQR*, n.s., 32:139–58.

– 1944. Masculine predicates with feminine subjects in the Hebrew Bible. *JBL* 63:297–302.

Smith, J.M.P. 1929. The use of divine names as superlatives. *AJSL* 45:212–13.

Smith, M.S. 1991. *The origins and development of the* waw-*consecutive*. Atlanta: Scholars Press.

– 1999. Grammatically speaking: The participle as a main verb of clauses (predicative participle) in direct discourse and narrative in pre-Mishnaic Hebrew. In *Sirach, scrolls, and sages*, ed. T. Muraoka and J.F. Elwolde, 278–332. Leiden: Brill.

Snaith, N.H. 1964. The meaning of the Hebrew 'kh. *VT* 14:221–5.

Speiser, E.A. 1955. The durative Hithpa'el: A *tan*-form. *JAOS* 75:118–21.

Sperber, A. 1943. Hebrew grammar: A new approach. *JBL* 62:261–262, 137–242.

Steiner, R.C. 2000. Does the biblical Hebrew conjunction -ו have many meanings, one meaning, or no meaning at all? *JBL* 119:249–67.

Sutcliffe, E.F. 1954. Effect as purpose: A study in Hebrew thought patterns. *Bib* 35:320–7.

– 1955. A note on 'al, le, and from. *VT* 5:436–9.

Swiggers, P. 1991. Nominal sentence negation in biblical Hebrew: The grammatical status of אין. In *Studies in Hebrew and Aramaic syntax*, ed. K. Jongeling et al., 173–9. Leiden: Brill.

Talstra, E. 1997a. Tense, mood, aspect and clause connections in biblical Hebrew: A textual approach. *JNSL* 23:81–103.

– 1997b. A hierarchy of clauses in biblical Hebrew narrative. In *Narrative syntax and the Hebrew Bible*, ed. E. van Wolde, 85–118. Leiden: Brill.

Thomas, D.W. 1953. A consideration of some unusual ways of expressing the superlative in Hebrew. *VT* 3:209–24.

– 1968. Some further remarks on unusual ways of expressing the superlative in Hebrew. *VT* 18:120–4.

Thorion, Y. 1985. Fundamental and derivative constructions: Subordinate and independent clauses in the Old Testament. In *Mélanges bibliques et orientaux en l'honneur de M. Mathias Delcor*, ed. K. Bergerhof, M. Dietrich, and O. Loretz, 409–16. Neukirchen-Vluyn: Neukirchener Verlag.

Tigay, J.H. 1999. Some more delocutives in Hebrew. In *Ki baruch hu*, ed. R. Chazan, W.W. Hallo, and L.H. Schiffman, 409–12. Winona Lake, IN: Eisenbrauns.

Van der Merwe, C.H.J. 1991. The function of word order in old Hebrew – With special reference to cases where a syntagmeme precedes a verb in Joshua. *JNSL* 17:129–44.

– 1993. Old Hebrew particles and the interpretation of Old Testament texts. *JSOT* 60:27–44.

– 1994. Discourse linguistics and biblical Hebrew grammar. In *Biblical Hebrew and discourse linguistics*, ed. R.D. Bergen, 13–49. Winona Lake, IN: Eisenbrauns.

– 1996. Reconsidering biblical Hebrew temporal expressions. *ZAH* 9:42–62.

– 1997. 'Reference time' in some biblical temporal constructions. *Bib* 78:503–24.

– 1999a. Explaining fronting in biblical Hebrew. *JNSL* 25:173–86.

– 1999b. Toward a better understanding of biblical Hebrew word order. *JNSL* 25:277–300.

Van der Merwe, C.H.J., J.A. Naudé, and J.H. Kroeze. 2002. *A biblical Hebrew reference grammar*. Sheffield: Sheffield Academic.

Van der Merwe, C.H.J., and E. Talstra. 2002–3. Biblical Hebrew word order: The interface of information structure and formal features. *ZAH* 15–16:68–107.

Van der Westhuizen, J.P. 1978. Hendiadys in biblical hymns of praise. *Semitics* 6:50–7.

Verheij, A.J.C. 1989. The genitive construction with two *nomina recta*. *ZAH* 2:210–12.

Walker, D.A. 1896. The Semitic negative with special reference to the negative in Hebrew. *AJSL* 12:230–67.

Walker, N. 1955. Concerning the function of 'eth. *VT* 5:314–15.

– 1957. Do plural nouns of majesty exist in Hebrew? *VT* 7:208.

Waltke, B.K., and M. O'Connor. 1990. *An introduction to biblical Hebrew syntax*. Winona Lake, IN: Eisenbrauns.

Washburn, D.L. 1994. Chomsky's separation of syntax and semantics. *HS* 35:27–46.

Watts, J.D.W. 1962. Infinitive absolute as imperative and the interpretation of Exodus 20:8. *ZAW* 74:141–5.

Weingreen, J. 1954. The construct-genitive relation in Hebrew syntax. *VT* 4:50–9.

– 1983. The Pi'el in Hebrew: A suggested new concept. *Henoch* 5:21–9.

Weitzman, S. 1996. The shifting syntax of numerals in biblical Hebrew: A reassessment. *JNES* 55:175–85.

Wernberg-Møller, P. 1958. 'Pleonastic' *waw* in classical Hebrew. *JSS* 3:321–6.

– 1959. Observations on the Hebrew participle. *ZAW* 71:54–67.

– 1988. The old accusative case ending in biblical Hebrew: Observations on הַמָּוְתָה in Ps. 116:15. *JSS* 33:155–64.

Whitley, C.F. 1972. The positive force of the Hebrew particle כֹּל. *ZAW* 84:213–19.

– 1985. Some remarks on *lû* and *lo*. *ZAW* 87:202–4.

Whitney, G.E. 1988. 'Lō' as 'not yet' in the Hebrew Bible. *HS* 29:43–8.

Williams, J.G. 1964. A critical note on the Aramaic indefinite plural of the verb. *JBL* 83:180–2.

Wilson, A.M. 1890a. The particle אֵת in Hebrew, I. *Hebraica* 6:139–50.

– 1890b. The particle אֵת in Hebrew, II. *Hebraica* 6:212–24.

Wilton, P. 1994. More cases of *waw explicativum*. *VT* 44:125–8.

Wolde, E. van. 1997. Linguistic motivation and biblical exegesis. In *Narrative syntax and the Hebrew Bible*, ed. E. van Wolde, 21–50. Leiden: Brill.

Young, I. 1999. *'Am* construed as singular and plural in Hebrew biblical texts: Diachronic and textual perspectives. *ZAH* 12:48–82.

– 2001. *'Edah* and *qahal* as collective nouns in Hebrew biblical texts. *ZAH* 14:68–78.

Zehnder, M. 2004. Variation in grammatical gender in biblical Hebrew: A study on the variable gender agreements of דֶּרֶךְ 'way.' *JSS* 49:21–45.

Zevit, Z. 1979. Expressing denial in biblical Hebrew and Mishnaic Hebrew, and in Amos. *VT* 29:505–9.

– 1988. Talking funny in biblical Henglish and solving a problem of the yaqtul past tense. *HS* 29:25–33.

– 1998. *The anterior construction in classical Hebrew*. Atlanta: Scholars Press.

Zewi, T. 1997. Subjects preceded by the preposition *'et* in biblical Hebrew. In *Studien zur hebräischen Grammatik*, ed. A. Wagner, 171–83. Göttingen: Vandenhoeck & Ruprecht.

– 1998. The syntactical status of exceptive phrases in biblical Hebrew. *Bib* 79:544–8.

– 1999. Time in nominal sentences in the Semitic languages. *JSS* 44:195–214.

– 2000. Is there a tripartite nominal sentence in biblical Hebrew? *JNSL* 26:51–63.

Index of Passages

Scripture references are according to the Hebrew text, not the English. References are to section numbers.

1:1 - ‍‍מ - Partative

1:4 - ‍‍ב - upon the house

5:4 - ‍‍ודרש - subordinate, final/result clause

5:5 - waw - opens an adversative, contrasts v.4

5:12 - ki causal discontinuous oracle

5:14 ‍‍ויהי - jussive w/ resultative waw, prayer or benediction AC 3.3.1

5:15 - Hith ptc substantival

5:19 - disjunctive waws, consecutive?

5:22 - ki Asseverative, oracle, protasis

5:24 - impf not JUSS; ‍‍1 resultative → from context

5:25 - ‍‍ה - exclamatory JM161b or Polar Question WO 40.3b

5:26 - waw, conversive or protasis G112x, rr

5:27 - conversive waw

8:1

8:2 : seeing,

8:5 : result waws w/ coh. ‍‍ב, JM116c; WO 34.5.2a-b

    ל - purpose clause - to make small

    ‍‍וא - conj. waw/ purpose?

8:7 : ‍‍ב - by the pride of Jacob, essence ‍‍ב, sarcasm

8:10 : ל - product (both)

8:11 ל- DN WO 39.3.5d #18, restrictive/ adv specification AC 4.3. kg)

8:12 waw - resultative, logically sequential

    ל - purpose?

9:1 - waw-result, 3rd waw is sequential/resultative

9:2 - conssesive clauses DN

Index of Subjects

References are to section numbers unless otherwise stated.
The subject is sometimes addressed in a footnote.

Index of Hebrew Words

All references are to section numbers.

The main discussion of a word is in **bold print**.

The article, the directional suffix, the interrogative particle, and pronouns are in the subject index.